M000196800

Escape Routes

Control and Subversion
in the Twenty-first Century

DIMITRIS PAPADOPOULOS,
NIAMH STEPHENSON
and VASSILIS TSIANOS

Pluto Press

LONDON • ANN ARBOR, MI

First published 2008 by Pluto Press
345 Archway Road, London N6 5AA
and 839 Greene Street, Ann Arbor, MI 48106

www.plutobooks.com

British Library Cataloguing in Publication Data
A catalogue record for this book is available from the British Library

ISBN   978 0 7453 2779 2   Hardback
ISBN   978 0 7453 2778 5   Paperback

Library of Congress Cataloging in Publication Data applied for

This book is printed on paper suitable for recycling and made from fully managed and
sustained forest sources. Logging, pulping and manufacturing processes are expected
to conform to the environmental standards of the country of origin.

10   9   8   7   6   5   4   3   2   1

Designed and produced for Pluto Press by
Chase Publishing Services Ltd, Fortescue, Sidmouth, EX10 9QG, England
Typeset from disk by Stanford DTP Services, Northampton
Printed and bound in the European Union by
CPI Antony Rowe, Chippenham and Eastbourne

Escape Routes

Joy is the ultimate proof.

Oswald de Andrade

All the acts of the drama of world history were
performed before a chorus of the laughing people.

Mikhail Bakhtin

Contents

Acknowledgements

If there is something imperceptible in this book it is the connections, relations and cooperation with people who have sustained our living and thinking over the years we have spent working on this project. We are grateful to our parents, our families and all the people who have in so many various, precious and irreplaceable ways accompanied us throughout the process of this book. We deeply thank all of you: Rutvica Andrijasevic, Thomas Atzert, Jill Bennett, Lone Bertelsen, Huw Beynon, Barbara Biglia, Hywel Bishop, Deborah Black, Finn Bowring, Bruce Braun, Steven Brown, Jayne Bye, Cathryn Carson, James Clifford, John Cromby, Nick Dines, Rosalyn Diprose, Emma Dowling, Amanda Ehrenstein, Peter Fairbrother, Akis Gavriilidis, Irina Giles, Ros Gill, Angel Gordo-Lopez, Ghassan Hage, Frigga Haug, Nanna Heidenreich, Berenice Hernadez, Gail Hershatter, Martin Hildebrand-Nilshon, Arnd Hofmeister, Wendy Hollway, Jan Simon Hutta, Frank John, Vassilis Karavezyris, Chung-Woon Kim, Susan Kippax, Hermann Korte, Giorgos Koutsoubas, Astrid Kusser, Brigitta Kuster, Olga Lafazani, Joanna Latimer, Ramona Lenz, Isabell Lorey, Alessio Lunghi, Brent Mackie, Elisabetta Magnani, Marta Malo, Athanasios Marvakis, Angela Melitopoulos, Sandro Mezzadra, Catherine Mills, Yann Moulier Boutang, Jost Müller, Tobias Mulot, Anna Munster, Andrew Murphie, Toni Negri, Brett Neilson, Paul O'Beirne, Sven Opitz, Mary Orgel, José Pérez de Lama/Osfa, Ute Osterkamp, Natascha Panagiotidis, Dimitris Parsanoglou, Ilektra Petrakou, Marianne Pieper, Maria Puig de la Bellacasa, Kane Race, Gerald Raunig, Enrica Rigo, Regina Röhmhild, Klaus Ronneberger, Marsha Rosengarten, Cécile Schenck, Ernst Schraube, Thomas Seibert, Kostas Sfyris, Sanjay Sharma, Peter Spielmann, Hank Stam, Steven Stanley, Paul Stenner, Giorgos Tsiakalos, kylie valentine, Marion von Osten, Valerie Walkerdine, Wibke Widuch, Debi Withers, Anthony Zwi.

We are immensely thankful to our Pluto editor, David Castle, whose encouraging and steady support made this book possible, and to Ioannis Savvidis, whose views on things have not only resulted in the cover, but also contributed to many ideas in this book. Special thanks go also to Aida Ibrahim for her invaluable help in preparing the images and to Douglas Henderson for his editorial work on our texts over the past years. The reviews of the four anonymous readers of the book helped us greatly as we reworked the original manuscript. When we later learnt the names of three of these reviewers – Graeme Chesters, Chris Connery and Ian Welsh – we realised that this was no coincidence, as their work had already shaped our thinking a lot. Finally we are indebted to Sabine Hess, Serhat Karakayali and Efthimia Panagiotidis for all these years of close cooperation – some of the chapters in this book not only are the result of common work and activism, but were researched in close collaboration; in particular Chapter 10 with Sabine, Chapter 4 with Serhat and Chapters 10 and 11 with Efthimia.

We have greatly benefited from participating in or being supported by the following organisations: the Association for Cultural Studies; Assoziation A Berlin; the Alexander von Humboldt Foundation; the annual meetings of the Society for the Social Studies of Science; the Australian National Centre for HIV Social Research; b_books Berlin; the Federal Cultural Foundation of Germany (Kulturstiftung des Bundes); the New Mobilities conference at the Centre for Contemporary Art and Politics in the College of Fine Arts, University of New South Wales; the Center for Cultural Studies at the University of California, Santa Cruz; Cologne Kunstverein; the Crossroads Conferences for Cultural Studies; the Department of Psychology and Education at the Free University of Berlin; the German Research Foundation (DFG); the Institute for European Ethnology and Cultural Anthropology at the University of Frankfurt; the Institute for Sociology at Hamburg University; the International Society for Theoretical Psychology; LaborK3000; the Office for History of Science and Technology at the University of California, Berkeley; Project Transit Migration; the School of Public Health and Community Medicine at the University of New South Wales; the School of Social Sciences at Cardiff University.

Most of the ideas in this book originate in our involvement in the EuroMayDay activist network, the Frassanito network, the HIV and gay communities in Sydney, the Kanak Attak group, the MigMap collective, the no borders activist group, the PRECLAB network and the Webring/Mapping Precarity collective. Were this book to have a future life we would like to see it in these contexts.

Duke University Press, Palgrave Macmillan, Sage Publications and Verlag Turia + Kant have granted permission to use material from papers they have published. An earlier version of Section I was published in 'How to Do Sovereignty Without People? The Subjectless

Condition of Postliberal Power' in *Boundary 2: International Journal of Literature and Culture*. Chapter 9 contains ideas which were initially published in 'Breaking Alignments Between "the Personal" and "the Individual" or What Can Psychology Do for Feminist Politics Now' in *Feminism and Psychology*. The second part of Chapter 12 was adapted from 'The Autonomy of Migration: The Animals of Undocumented Mobility', in A. Hickey-Moody and P. Malins (eds), *Deleuzian Encounters: Studies in Contemporary Social Issues* and it is reproduced with the permission of Palgrave Macmillan. Parts of earlier versions of Chapters 14 and 15 appeared in 'Prekarität: eine wilde Reise ins Herz des verkörperten Kapitalismus, oder: Wer hat Angst vor der immateriellen Arbeit?' in G. Raunig and U. Wuggenig (eds), *Kritik der Kreativität*. Wien: Verlag Turia + Kant.

List of Figures

Prologue

This book is about social transformation; it proposes a processual vision of change. We want to move away from thinking about change as primarily effected through events. To focus on the role of events is to foreground particular moments when a set of material, social and imaginary ruptures come together and produce a break in the flow of history – a new truth. Much of the twentieth century's political thinking casts revolt and revolution as the most central events in creating social change. But the (left's) fixation on events cannot nurture the productive energy required to challenge the formation of contemporary modes of control in Global North Atlantic societies. An event is never in the present; it can only be designated as an event in retrospect or anticipated as a future possibility. To pin our hopes on events is a nominalist move which draws on the masculinist luxury of having the power both to name things and to wait about for salvation. Because events are never in the present, if we highlight their role in social change we do so at the expense of considering the potence of the present that is made of people's everyday practices: the practices employed to navigate daily life and to sustain relations, the practices which are at the heart of social transformation long before we are able to name it as such. This book is about such fugitive occurrences rather than the epiphany of events. Social transformation, we argue, is not about cultivating faith in the change to come, it is about honing our senses so that we can perceive the processes which create change in ordinary life. Social transformation is not about reason and belief, it is about perception and hope. It is not about the production of subjects, but about the making of life. It is not about subjectivity, it is about experience.

In the following pages, we look for social change in seemingly insignificant occurrences of life: refusing to subscribe to a clichéd account of one's life story; sustaining the capacity to work in insecure and highly precarious conditions by developing informal social networks on which one can rely; or living as an illegal migrant below the radar of surveillance. These everyday experiences are commonly neglected in accounts of social and political transformation. This might be partly because they neither refer to a grand narrative of social change nor are they identifiable elements of broader, unified social movements. However, this book presents the argument that such imperceptible moments of social life are the starting point of contemporary forces of change.

But what makes some everyday occurrences transformative and many others not? Transformative processes change the conditions of social existence by paving the way for new transformations (rather than by creating fixed identifiable things or identities). We can trace social change in experiences that point towards an exit from a given organisation of social life without ever intending to create an event. This is why we talk about ways of escaping. The thesis of the book is that people escape: only *after* control tries to recapture escape routes can we speak of 'escape from'. Prior to its regulation, escape is primarily imperceptible. We argue that these moments where people subvert their existing situations without naming their practice (or having it named) as subversion are the most crucial for understanding social transformation. These imperceptible moments trigger social transformation, trigger shifts which would have appeared impossible if described from the perspective of the existing situation. You can never really know exactly when people will engage in acts of escape. The art of escape appears magical, but it is the mundane, hard and sometimes painful everyday practices that enable people to craft situations that seem unimaginable when viewed through the lens of the constraints of the present. The account we give of social transformation does not entail cultivating faith in the event to come, rather it involves cultivating faith in the elasticity and magic of the present. Another world is here.

Escape routes are transformative because they confront control with something which cannot be ignored. A system of power must try to control and reappropriate acts of escape. Thus, the measure of escape is not whether it avoids capture; virtually all trajectories of escape will, at some point, be redirected towards control. We are trained to think that the end product of political struggle is all about a transformative end point, a revolt, a strike, a successfully built up organisation, a revolution. However, this perspective neglects the most important question of all: How does social transformation begin? Addressing this question demands that we cultivate the sensibility to perceive moments when things do not yet have a name.

There is nothing heroic about escape. It usually begins with an initial refusal to subscribe to some aspects of the social order that seem to be inescapable and indispensable for governing the practicalities of life. In other words, the very first moment of subversion is the detachment from what may seem essential for holding a situation together and for making sense of that situation. Escape is a mode of social change that is simultaneously elusive and forceful enough to challenge the present configuration of control.

What is the contemporary configuration of control? Section I addresses this question. Historically, sovereignty has transformed itself in response to the continual emergence of new modes of evading control. We start by considering how *national sovereignty* (Chapter 1) culminated in the attempt to bind the 'people as One' to the nation state with promises of rights and representation, i.e. the promise of the double-R axiom, as we call it. The impossibility of such an all-inclusive nation state (plainly evident today) started to become clearer in the 1960s and 1970s, when excluded social groups contested the inclusiveness of so-called 'universal' modes of political representation. During this same period there was a shift from national towards transnational modes of control. Together these changes triggered a crisis at the heart of national sovereignty. In response, *transnational governance* (Chapter 2) emerged as a distinct form of sovereignty.

Transnational governance is marked by its attempt to create a global horizontal space of control; others call this project globalisation, neo-imperialism, or empire. Of course this is no level playing field and the creation of a global unified, horizontal geo-space is, in itself, a means of domination. Nevertheless, there is something different in this mode of domination: the winners and losers of globalisation cannot be conceived as nation states. Nor is it the case that nation states in their entirety participate in the processes of globalisation. Rather, particular segments of different nation states, certain institutions, social groups, local or transnational companies and cultural and technoscientific bodies align together in the attempt to dominate global transnational space. In Chapter 3 we discuss the formation and function of these *postliberal aggregates*. Postliberal aggregates represent a distinct form of sovereignty which arises as a contemporary response to the limits of the double-R axiom in national and transnational governance. Their *raison d'être* is to build powerful, vertical composites lying beyond the liberal axiomatic of the double-R principle. The rest of the book investigates where we can locate sites for intervention and subversion in these postliberal conditions.

Power functions by rendering individuals the actors of subjecti-fication and/or by rendering populations the objects of biopolitical control. This is a common explanation of the productivity of power; however in Section II we argue that this understanding of power does not help us to grasp or intervene in some fundamentally important aspects of power. From this vantage point, social transformation always appears as the effect of people's *response* to their regulation. Instead we argue that people are often moving, creating, connecting, escaping the immediate moments and given conditions of their lives, and that it is only *after* the imposition of control that some of these actions come to be seen as responses to regulation. Escape comes first! People's efforts to escape can force the reorganisation of control itself; regimes of control must respond to the new situations created by escape.

We cannot understand escape as a decontextualised, overarching form of social transformation; it is always historically and culturally situated. In fact there is never escape as such, there are multiple ways of escaping: escape routes. In Chapter 4, 'Vagabonds', we consider how people's mobility in the late Middle Ages forced the transformation of feudal power and the adoption of a new, early capitalist, system of control. Capture, in this instance, saw the vagabonds' mobility translated into the subjectivity of the wage worker. Chapter 5, 'Outside Representation', traces the contours of escape across different struggles in the post-Second World War period (e.g. feminist and workers struggles). In each case, escape is a betrayal of existing forms of representation, forms of representation that regulate everyday life through the co-option and domesticisation of people's struggles. With Jacques Rancière, we understand representational politics as policing. Possibilities for breaking this closure lie in what we call *imperceptible politics* (Chapter 6). Politics (as opposed to policing) arises when those who remain unrepresented and whose capacities remain imperceptible emerge within the normalising organisation of the social realm. Imperceptible politics does not refer to something which is invisible, but to social forces which are outside of existing regulation and outside policing. Imperceptible politics is first and foremost a question of deploying a new perceptual strategy; the senses are honed less to reflection and more to diffraction – perception now involves tracing disturbance and intrusion instead of mirroring existing conditions. Here we can say that the process and 'method' of researching this book has involved cultivating this same perceptual strategy. Together, we have subjected our material to this perceptual experimentation: films, autobiographies, interviews, our own experiences of political activism, ethnographic accounts, historiography, legislation, maps and existing attempts to make sense of and/or find ways out of the terrain in which we tread. An attunement to diffraction underpins the interpretations and analyses of existing and possible routes of escape in the following pages. And it is the diffractive quality of imperceptible politics that allows us to see political struggles which strive to evacuate the terrain of a given regime of control. These struggles are overlooked when viewed through a lens attuned to practices of and claims for representation. Rather than giving an exhaustive account of imperceptible politics, in Part II of the book we investigate a contemporary itinerary of escape through three important fields in which we can find departures from the given regime of control – the fields of life, mobility and labour.

Our discussion of escape in the field of life begins with considering transformations in the regime of life control, the *life/culture system* (Chapter 7). The early twentieth century saw the first pervasive attempt to employ the concept of life as a powerful tool for initiating social and political change. At this time, ideas about the uncontrollability of life were celebrated for both their cultural and their political potence. Formed around a masculinist and violent ideology, the life/culture system of control was finally appropriated by the fascist project. After the Second World War, life's uncontrollability figured as a threat to be suppressed, in part, with the patriarchal welfare state's promises of democratic tranquillity. But statist control was resisted with increasing intensity (e.g. the events of 1968, the proliferation of different sexualities, new biomedical discourses of the body). The erosion of a sense of security brings a renewed interest in life, and risk and its pervasive government are called forth. As risk goes transnational, a new network of life control comes to the fore. The *formation of emergent life* (Chapter 8) envisages life as inherently amenable to recombinant formation on a genetic or cyber-carnal/robotic level. This vision of life's potential has been celebrated because it breaks with traditional dichotomies which have framed understandings of life, such as nature/culture or sex/gender. Despite this break, the formation of emergent life is central to the ascendance of postliberal sovereignty. The regime's alignment with postliberal power occurs as its vision is mobilised and embedded not only in high-tech laboratories but in the everyday, when it becomes ordinary.

Possibilities for subverting this regime of life control lie in mobilising new modes of experience. The formation of emergent life is interrupted, diffracted, undone on the immediate level of the everyday. In Chapter 9, 'Everyday Excess and Continuous Experience', we examine how attempts to work with 'the politics of experience' can be easily reinserted into the control and regulation of the private sphere. However, in this chapter we develop an alternative account of experience. The escape from postliberal attempts to canalise and order life occurs in the continuous refusal to reflect on or represent oneself as a set of congealed, solidified experiences produced through political projects, in entering into a process of unbecoming in order to repoliticise, not oneself, but the present. As experience unfolds on the level of the everyday it creates processes of escape, what we call continuous experience, which escape the policing practices of subjectivity. With A. N. Whitehead, we argue that this form of experience does not belong to a person, it is dispersed in the multifarious connections between people, animals, things and occasions. Continuous experience is the ultimate ingredient of any escape route. In this sense, escape in not a human privilege or a human capacity; rather it is the matter of social transformation and social transformation is a process which is shared by people, animals and things.

The regime of mobility control – the second field of our contemporary itinerary of escape – plays a key role in the political constitution of postliberal conditions. Chapter 10, 'Liminal Porocratic Institutions', explores the formation of the contemporary regime of migration control through the lens of migration policies in Europe. The different institutions partaking in the regulation of European migration are all evolving, merging and disseminating throughout transnational European space. These institutions contribute to the development of specific postliberal aggregates in European space, liminal porocratic institutions. Their liminality stems from the fact that they are in constant transition, continually adjusting to the European Union's rapidly changing borders. Liminal porocratic institutions are beyond open democratic control. Their main function is to regulate mobility flows and to govern the porosity of borders (hence *poro*cratic). Now, instead of controlling populations or individuals at geographic borders the focus is on creating various levees far beyond, on, *and* inside the borders in order to manage migratory flows.

In Chapter 11, 'Excessive Movements in Aegean Transit', we trace the main techniques of postliberal migration control at work in one of the most permeable and heavily policed lines of border crossing in Europe, the Aegean sea. We consider how migration evades its regulation, creates new conditions for mobility and movement and challenges the liminal porocratic institutions' regime of mobility control. For instance, when we examine how migrants incorporate camps into their overall tactics of movement, we can see that the disciplinary and biopolitical functions of the camps only evolve by following the escaping and moving masses. In Chapter 12 we draw on a theoretical approach, the *autonomy of migration*, to jettison the ubiquitous notions of the migrant as either a useful worker or as a victim. Instead of conceiving of migrational movements as derivatives of social, cultural and economic structures, the autonomy-of-migration lens reveals migration to be a constituent creative force which fuels social, cultural and economic transformations. Migration can be understood as a force which evades the policing practices of subjectivity.

Finally, in turning to the third field in our itinerary of escape routes, the regime of labour control, we explore the conditions for value creation in contemporary, embodied capitalism. Drawing on our analysis of the formation of emergent life in Section III, we argue that the production of value in postliberal capitalism is based on the recombination of matter: humans, animals, artefacts and things. The recombination of matter includes also the recombination of the worker's body (Chapter 13, 'Precarious Life and Labour'). The postliberal regime of labour control does not try to dominate by training the body; it tries to fracture it, to reorder its material, affective, social potentials in unexpected ways, to harness the body's own capacities for creative recombination. Notably, as workers' bodies are recombined, only *some* parts of a worker's body, capacities and potentials are dissected and exploited. This form of exploitation is precarity.

Sociological accounts of precarity point to its connection with the post-Fordist rise of insecure labour conditions, or they cast precarity as another instance of broader transformations in labour (such as the feminisation of work, de-industrialisation, immaterial labour). But these kinds of sociological descriptions tend to misrecognise precarity as the emergence of a unified category of workers (i.e. as an actor like 'the working class', for example). They gloss over the very different ways in which precarity is lived. Neither do they grasp how people's embodied experiences of precarity expand far beyond the immediate conditions of labour and colonise one's whole life time-space. How, then, can we recognise and understand the politics of precarious workers if invoking a new unified category of workers does not suffice? What routes does escape take here? Chapter 14, 'Normalising the Excess of Precarity', considers the limited relevance of three forms of political organisation which have proved effective in the history of labour and social movements: the political party, the trade union and micropolitics. None of these forms of organisation impels the conflicts of precarity to the point of destabilising embodied capitalism. Traditional party and trade union politics is both anchored in and seeks to augment normalising rationalities and practices of employment. It fails to address the inequalities emerging with the new regime of labour control (e.g. it does not extend to representing illegalised workers). Social movements which operate on the newer terrain of micropolitics seem to be equally ineffective at addressing precarity. Micropolitics contests prevalent representational practices by claiming new forms of extended belonging or citizenship. Micro-political calls for the inclusion of social actors have been important responses to the embodied experience of precarity. Nevertheless, they reterritorialise precarious workers' subjectivities in the matrix of a new postliberal statism.

However, the embodied experience of precarity can and does escape reterritorialisation. Embodied capitalism necessitates the creation of sociability (think of the sociability required to find the next contract or to deflect questions about one's work visa). Sociability produces value that cannot be completely commodified and appropriated by embodied capitalism. Much of this sociability generated in precarious conditions is inappropriate to the current regime of labour regulation and cannot be represented within it. *Inappropriate/d sociability*, as we call it in Chapter 15, is the excess generated by workers' experience of precarity; it simultaneously operates within the heart of embodied capitalism and it exists in a vacuum of control. This is the movement of escape; inappropriate/d sociability is the means through which precarious workers do imperceptible politics.

In this book we introduce escape not because we are looking for either a principle behind people's actions or the hidden principle of historical change. Rather, focusing on escape allows us to imagine, see and interrogate those ordinary moments when people's actions put processes in motion, processes which are effective in confronting the social order with a force of change that cannot be avoided, silenced, neglected, erased. In retrospect, such moments can be explained in many different theoretical ways: as resistance, revolt, refusal, revolution, as an event. Rather than draw on these concepts inherited from twentieth-century political theory and practice, attuning ourselves to escape allows us to work with transformation that is more pertinent to process than to event, to skilfullness than to anticipation, to togetherness than to sublimation, to imagination than to logic, to joy than to seriousness.

Joy is crucial to this book. The joy of escape defies seriousness and this, as we try to show, is the most crucial condition for revealing truth. Paraphrasing Bakhtin's (1984, p. 285) reading of Rabelais' concept of truth, we could say that behind the sanctimonious seriousness of many exalted and official concepts of social transformation of the traditional left (and beyond) we find barking instead of acting and laughing. Rather than succumbing to barking out the fidelity to the coming event or to the new truth we prefer to enjoy the ways in which truth erupts out of the present. The emergence of 'a truth inwardly free, gay and materialistic' is made possible by the kind of laughter and hilarity that pervades the atmosphere of the carnival banquet (Bakhtin 1984, p. 285; see also pp. 94ff.). And it is the collective joy of eating and drinking in a 'banquet for all the world' (Bakhtin 1984, p. 278) which opens the possibility to partake in the world instead of being devoured by it. The laughter and joy of those who partake in the world defies seriousness, disperses fear, liberates the word and the body and reveals a truth escaping the injustices of the present. This laughter is the prime mover of escape. Escape is joyful. This is not an intellectual argument we are advancing in order to resist the ubiquitous melancholy and mourning of the left. Rather we are pointing to an embodied political practice which contests a dominant understanding of social change as the result of a response to suffering. Casting action as the force of pain is a terribly Eurocentric view. It demands that we become, or worse wheel in, a victim whose capacity to act is reduced to a mere response to pain. With Oswald de Andrade we prefer to talk about the pleasure of anthropophagy (Andrade, 1990, p. 51). Joyfully devouring the sacred enemy in order to create a new body and new conditions for seeing and acting in the world, anthropophagy triggers processes of transformation which simultaneously act at the heart of and escape the practices underpinning modernity and postmodernity in Global North Atlantic societies. Joy marks the routes of social transformation. Joy is the ultimate proof.

PART I

THE POLITICAL CONSTITUTION OF THE PRESENT

Section I
SOVEREIGNTY AND
CONTROL RECONSIDERED

1   NATIONAL SOVEREIGNTY

Spaces of the Nation

Giovanni Battista Piranesi's *Carceri d'Invenzione* (*Imaginary Prisons*), a series of capriccios issued around 1750, present fantastic imaginary interiors, visionary dungeons. Piranesi, who in most of his other works delivered a romanticised version of Roman architecture, created here an image of social space characteristic of the emerging modern form of political sovereignty.

Piranesi's capriccio 'The Drawbridge' can be read as a metaphor of a highly structured political space, filled with mysterious scaffolding and different interconnected hierarchical levels (Figure 1). Each level is clearly distinct from the others; some of them are under surveillance from the internal tower. There are chasms between the levels, but also controlled possibilities for mobility. It seems that the main purpose of this structure is to make individuals and their bodies identifiable and manageable in space. The human body becomes domesticated, disciplined, productive, and individuals become subjects. This is the logic of representation which constitutes the political scene of modernity and with it a collective subject, the people, whose members are distributed in an ordered way within a certain space, occupy specific positions, perform certain activities and have rights. But space is never abstract, it is always delineated and limited: space in modernity is territory.

Formalising the Relation Between National Territory and People: the Double-R Axiom

The core principle of post-medieval modern polity is national sovereignty, which is the ideal correspondence between people and territory. Modern political theory employs distinct ideologies, models and practices in the attempt to grasp how the relation between people

3

1.   Giovanni Battista Piranesi, *Carceri d'Invenzione*, plate VII: The Drawbridge, c. 1750 (new edition, 1761), etching, 54.5 × 41.5 cm, Staatsgalerie, Graphische Sammlung, Stuttgart. © Rheinisches Bildarchiv, Köln. Printed with permission.

and territory can be configured to engender a viable form of spatio-temporal coherence and integrity of the nation (Hobsbawm, 1990; Bhabha, 1990; Benedict Anderson, 1991; Balibar and Wallerstein, 1991). One main tradition, for example, highlights the role of territory and refers back to the Schmittian (1997) concept of sovereignty according to which sovereign law is the rationalisation of *Landnahme*, the appropriation of land – for critical evaluations of Schmitt's concept of sovereignty see Balibar (2004b) and Balakrishnan (2000). A second major model highlights the role of the people and refers back to Hobbes (1994). Here sovereignty is the outcome of an agreement between the people and the sovereign. In the tradition of Rousseau (1997), sovereignty can be understood as the ideal identification of the people's will with the national constitution – Habermas (2001) attempted a continuation of this latter line of thought in the debates on world citizenship. Common to all these vastly differing accounts is the notion of national sovereignty as an attempt to systematise and describe the relation between people and territory.

The correspondence between people and territory is instituted in two sequential moves. Firstly on the level of representation, people are separated and classified into social groups, that is, classes or social strata. Secondly, the nation state assigns rights of participation to each of the represented groups. National sovereignty is sustained by the existence of a national social compromise – a stable but changing balance of institutional power between the represented social groups, which is developed as a means of regulating the distribution of rights amongst these groups (Laclau and Mouffe, 1985; Poulantzas, 1978). Initially, the city state – and later the nation state – consisted of wealthy, property owners only (Sennett, 1994). Citizenship was available to those people who already recognised each other as participating in forging state institutions (Koschorke, 2007). The majority of the inhabitants of the territory of the state were excluded. But, in the process of the expansion and consolidation of the nation state, exclusion is not the primary concern; rather what solidifies the centrality of the state in modern sovereignty is a form of differential inclusion of certain social groups through granting rights (social, civil and political). Rights become a means of expanding the category of citizenship (citizenship is here understood as belonging to a nation state, where the belonging is both legitimate through law and codified through culture); but this move is always partial and in this sense citizenship is always imperfect (Gunsteren, 1998; Sassen, 2004). For instance, the working class can be deemed eligible for social rights such as protection from unemployment and can be granted rights such as access to education for their children on the basis that they are involved in wealth production. But as social rights are extended to some they are held beyond the reach of others – on the basis, for example, of their sex, age, mode of employment, country of birth, or length of stay in the territory of the nation state. Because the move is always partial, its outcome, the national social compromise, is continually open to being contested and transformed. Thus, the national social compromise is the legitimate order of institutional power which is achieved in each particular historical moment of each particular society as a pragmatic equilibrium between those who are represented and have rights. In other words, the national social compromise is a balance between rights and representation of 'the people' in a certain territory.

We call this balance between rights and representation the *double-R axiom*. It is only through the continuous interplay between rights and representation that the unity of people and territory is maintained. The double-R axiom is the insurmountable precondition of national sovereignty. In modern national sovereignty, constitutionalism (as in an established set of formalised rights in sovereign law) has always been the predominant mode of political government. Rights have dominated over issues of representation and have absorbed more attention than questions such as how different social groups are represented in the social and cultural imaginary and in everyday public life. The reason for this is that representation was mainly organised throughout the emergence of national interests according to the positioning of social groups in the national territory in relation to the production process. Representation in national sovereignty is mainly an affair of economically defined social classes (consider for example the absence of women, queer, cultural or generational identities). But despite this predominance of rights, representation was always a key element in the process of emergence of national sovereignty. However, as we discuss in the next chapter, the problem of representation has only recently attained an equal role as the problem of rights in the organisation of polity in Global North Atlantic nation states.

Escaping the Limits of Global North Atlantic National Sovereignty

The double-R axiom is central to national sovereignty, not only because it organises political life inside the national space, but also because of its unavailability to certain social groups in the realm of the nation state and, of course, outside of it. The double-R axiom not only binds people and territory but also designates the nation state's relation to other states and their people. It simultaneously defines the matrix of positive rights and representation within the national territory, and the non-existence of rights and symbolic presence *beyond* the nation's borders. Hence, the double-R axiom constantly refers to its exact opposite: to the absence of rights and representation. The monopolisation of state power has a double function, as Elias describes it. On the one hand state power reconciles social antagonisms inside the borders of the nation, on the other hand it creates a belligerent and hostile competition with other states beyond its borders (Elias, 1981).

The double-R axiom retains its power not only when it is active and functional in the domain of a certain territory but also when it is absent – this is its potency. Much contemporary political theory devotes considerable interest to the state of exception – that is the suspension of the double-R axiom and the withdrawal of the state from (or its inability to impose) any legal restraints which govern the execution of its power. For different reasons the state of exception is often cast as the crucial moment of modern national sovereignty (Schmitt, 1963; Agamben, 2005; Mills, 2008). However, overemphasising the role of the state of exception in the consolidation of power in the modern Global North Atlantic nation state creates a false picture. For example, Agamben's pathetic fixation on bare life (1998) and the camp (2001), both conditions beyond the protection of polity and the public, pervades some understandings of modern political sovereignty. But explaining the genesis of modern sovereignty as simply naked violence over life is a reductionist move (Bojadzijev, Karakayali and Tsianos, 2004). Agamben acknowledges that neither rights nor representation can exist without each other and that both the absence and presence of the double-R axiom are necessary in order to maintain national sovereignty (Agamben, 2005; Mills, 2008). Yet, because he explains modern polity by prioritising the role of those who are connected to sovereignty through their exclusion, he fails to understand the agency of the excluded; he cannot grasp their involvement in immanent processes of social change. That is, the excluded are cast as another characteristic of modern sovereignty; they may pose a logical or political problem about the extension and limits of sovereignty, but – from this perspective – they do not figure as a possible constituent force which can trigger transformations on the part of sovereignty.

To say that national sovereignty is incomplete is not to say that it can improve and become potentially all-inclusive, rather it means that national sovereignty is unequal and incomplete by design. It is exactly this ultimate incompleteness of national sovereignty that creates the possibility for social change and for its potential overcoming. This book attempts to trace the formation and transformation of modes of being which exist in the spaces where sovereignty pervades without holding a totalising grasp. It traces the emergence of many immanent, imperceptible and violent acts of subversion, silent retreats, forceful refusals and unexpected insurgencies which question current forms of sovereignty, reveal its incompleteness and escape its control.

These imperceptible actions have never ceased to exist; in fact they have always accompanied the emergence of sovereignty, designating its limits and foiling the repressive machinations of modern political constitution. Modern social and political history is full of people's attempts to refuse and to subvert modern polity. Remember these incidents: 26 March 1871, Belleville, Menilmontant (and the massacre of 30,000 citizens of Paris); the Declaration of the Rights of Woman (rights which were not granted; instead women's bodies were sexualised and neutralised: *Liberty Guiding the People/Liberty on the Barricades*); the Haitian revolution (whose representatives on being sent to the French revolution were simply executed); the Räterepublik (and the Freikorps); and more ...

From Imperceptible Subjectivities to Subjects of Power

The precise task facing modern political sovereignty is to respond to such acts of refusal and subversion. The uncontrollable, singular potentialities of bodies which escape its order become the matter necessary for the creation of the 'big Leviathan', that is the modern nation state. Modern political sovereignty digests and incorporates imperceptible subjectivities, actions, potentialities into the grand corpus of modern polity. Imperceptible subjectivities have to be subsumed under the guidance of polity. The thing is that all these escaping subjectivities cannot be simply eradicated, they must be appropriated. For control to function, anything that looks like questioning sovereign power must be translated and mediated. We consider this to be the core moment of modern polity: insurgency and subversion are repressed only if they cannot be incorporated. Modern power is cynical and indifferent to morality: it is not concerned with ideological exclusion and ethical purity but with instrumental inclusion.

Crucially, national sovereignty is *not* primarily organised around the oppression of singular potentialities. Its main objective is not the suppression of those social groups which attempt to escape. Rather, modern national sovereignty attempts to *absorb* unruly potentialities by including them in its social reproduction. Imperceptible subjectivities are marked by their intimate relation to potentialities which escape fixed forms of regulation and control (Grosz, 1993; Gatens, 1996). Modern national sovereignty does not refuse to harness these potentialities. Rather, it transforms them by domesticating, adjusting, educating, tormenting, disciplining and training imperceptible bodies – by breaking the immanent relation between bodies and potentialities. In Chapter 4 we give a fuller account of the centuries of attempts to immobilise and capture the bodies of vagabonds and how these attempts culminate, in the nineteenth century, in the effort, not to contain, but to utilise their mobility and harness bodily potentials into a capitalist system of production and accumulation.

In other words, modern national sovereignty operates by mediating the relation between subjectivity and its potentials with a series of 'body techniques' (Mauss, 1978) which incorporate the body into the given mechanics of polity. This is a long and painful process, a process which very much resembles the meticulous transformation of the body's habits, so powerfully described by Elias (1994). National sovereignty works with the reflexive subject. Escaping, mobbing, refusing, revolting, subverting individuals are transformed into the main ingredient of modern polity: subjects of power.

2.   Albrecht Dürer, *Der Zeichner des weiblichen Models* (*Draughtsman Drawing a Recumbent Woman*) 1525, woodcut, 8 × 22 cm, Albertina Museum, Vienna. © Albertina, Wien. Printed with permission.

Consider Albrecht Dürer's famous painting *Draughtsman Drawing a Recumbent Woman* (Figure 2). The painting invokes surveillance and method, domination and order, the invasive gaze and the scopic regime of controlling space. But these are widely discussed topics (Alpers, 1982; Nead, 1992; Haraway, 1997). What is particularly important for us is the relation between the subject of study and the device which makes study possible: the grid. It is through this grid that the (male) artist's vision of control can dominate and order the object of study.

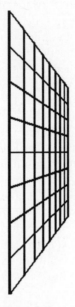

3.   Perspectival Grid. Courtesy of the authors.

This upright grid of wires is the major actor in this woodcut: it splits the picture into two, transforming the artist into a male subject, and the object of the drawing into a sexualised female subject (Figure 3). The grid transforms imperceptible bodies and subjectivities into subjects; it classifies subjects into groups, groups into a territory. *Before* the grid is placed between the two subjects, these subjects do not exist at all. The grid is the metonymy for the order of modern sovereignty. It produces social classes, institutional positions, social actors, it directs them to the pervasive regime of productivity and, finally, it establishes hierarchical relations between them. The hierarchical organisation of gender relations and the organisation of space along the terms of masculinised and homophobic imaginaries is an outcome of the very existence of subjects of power. The stand-alone, self sufficient, reflexive subject, with the capacity to carry out intentional acts – this is the valorised individual actor of modern national sovereignty. The subject is the extreme opposite of the imperceptible body. By becoming a subject, imperceptible subjectivity is made amenable to discipline, to work and to production, to being trained and tormented. The imperceptible body is simultaneously the building material of modern political sovereignty and the most elusive and absent element of modern polity.

Unregulated Struggles

There is nothing new about this observation about the centrality of the subject for the constitution of national sovereignty and about the subject's role in the taming of imperceptible subjectivities. The debate between the two *maitres penseurs* of the crisis of the social state, Michel Foucault and Nikos Poulantzas, as well as of their common teacher Luis Althusser (1971), has completely exposed the centrality of the subject for understanding power. Foucault interrupts the classic dualism between individual freedom and repressive sovereign power, linking together discipline and freedom, sovereignty and the body. Discipline is the 'art of the human body', discipline attempts to make the body productive; and in becoming productive the body becomes docile. Co-option and training, subjugation and usefulness are inseparable for the operation of modern political rationalities of government (Foucault, 1991). Moreover, these microphysics of power effect how pervasive social antagonisms between different groups are transformed into technologies of the body. Social antagonisms are rarely played out as violent struggles, they are increasingly managed through disciplining the body. For Foucault, in his later lectures (2004a, 2004b), there is no external relation between the modern state and the subject, government is what connects practices of the subject and practices of domination (see also Foucault, 1987, 1990). The modern state is understood as an individualising and, simultaneously, a totalising form of power. Foucault's genealogy of the modern state is concurrently a genealogy of the subject itself (Lemke, 1997).

Nevertheless this extraordinary attempt to link the subject with power seems to neglect one important aspect of the modern state, what Elias calls its capacity to pacify society (Elias, 1981). The modern state is more than a paramount form of government. It is not exhausted in technologies of the self and technologies of government. Rather, it deals in and relies on social antagonisms. Social antagonisms are productive; they create their own conditions for balancing and pacifying social conflicts. These conflicts are fought, resolved and contested against and out of these processes. For example, the welfare state arises in response to competing claims from different social actors (e.g. workers wanting protection from unemployment, people wanting access to healthcare, employers demanding flexibilisation and fragmentation of labour agreements while trade unions are demanding comprehensive collective labour agreements, councils trying to ameliorate social inequalities and striving to instate socially mixed urban planning while specific social groups are striving for segmentation) – the balance it delivers acts to pacify social conflicts (even if temporarily). Following but also criticising Foucault, Poulantzas (1978) highlights how the modern state evolves as a permanent but unstable balance of compromises between different social groups and classes. This view retains Foucault's insight about the interconnectedness of the subject and state power, and builds on it by seeking to understand how the development of political sovereignty and social and subjective existence can often follow disparate paths. This is distinct from both the classic Marxist approach which sees state power and society as a binary (Kautsky, 1915; Lenin, 1917) and Foucauldian proclamations about a fusion between state power and society (N. Rose, 1999; Dean, 1999). Poulantzas reads the state as a partly autonomous condensation of the energies of social conflicts. State power is the unstable but, at the same time, reliable space for the articulation and resolution of social conflicts. State power is thus a platform which guarantees social cohesion and simultaneously leaves open space for transformation. Although the modern state creates the ground for the articulation of a commonality of conflicting social groups, this ground is open to change.

The importance of Poulantzas' move is that it breaks the vicious and eternal Foucauldian circularity between power and resistance. Social struggles are now tightly connected to the function of the state power but they also evolve along relatively autonomous trajectories. In Section II we discuss this autonomous transformation in more detail. And the second part of the book elucidates contemporary processes of subversion through imperceptible politics in the realms of life (Section III), mobility (IV) and labour (V).

The nation state does not have the *resolution* of social conflicts as its ultimate aim. Rather it attempts to regulate and ultimately control conflicts by developing multiple ways to include subaltern social groups and classes. These complex inclusion practices create various social actors, or subjects of power, who participate in preserving and reorganising the national social compromise (think of trade unions, for instance, or pressure groups formed around various aspects of welfare and environment). Compromise, condensation of social conflicts, inclusion, production of subjects – this is the pathway which stabilises sovereignty in the realm of the Global North Atlantic nation state. But such responses to social struggles leave open spaces, excesses to processes of subject production and inclusion. Strategies of subversion emerge in these spaces and push the state to transform itself *beyond* the coordinates of the existing social compromise. It is common to cast these moments when the state is forced into a process of change as the *effects* of control, and thus to read them as complicit with control. However, throughout this book we argue that the refusal and subversion of imperceptible subjectivities trigger social transformation first, and any transformation of the state follows this social change. Imperceptible struggles come first. The primacy of subversion. Adieu Foucault! Adieu melancholic Keynesianism! Adieu anxious liberalism! Ha!

That the struggles come first does not mean that these are always addressed towards the state. We are tired of the Marxist and post-Marxian readings of social conflict as solely organised around the state and its institutions (e.g. Callinicos, 1994; Jessop, 1990; Laclau and Mouffe, 1985). Understanding the modern state as a 'material condensation' of relations of power and of the multiple energies of social conflicts (Poulantzas, 1978) prevents the typical reduction of state power to the material scaffolding which supports the domination of a sole class. This goes far beyond the simplistic 'Marxist' reading of state power as an instrument in the hands of a single social actor. State power is neither an instrument in the hands of the dominant class nor a superstructure hovering over society or over subaltern groups and strata. Thus when we say that the struggles come first and that subversion and escape are pivotal to social transformation we mean that this form of politics is not primarily addressing state power. Rather the opposite is the case; subversion, imperceptible politics is performed by social actors who negotiate their embeddedness in state power under the signature of 'escape', not under the imperative of inclusion. The imperceptible politics of escape eschews the Marxist obsession with the state as well as the Foucauldian paranoia about control pervading the whole of society.

Imperceptible Politics and the Pressure to Escape National Sovereignty

Understanding control and subversion in terms of interconnected but also relative autonomous formations of state and imperceptible, transformative modes of social existence enables us to identify distinct modes of escape from national sovereignty. Casting national sovereignty as primarily a space for compromise inside the borders of a certain nation constitutes a break with the panoptical fixation on tracking the extension of total control. It is then possible to investigate all these imperceptible spaces in which practices of escape are being formulated and performed. We can interrogate forms of social and political excess which surpass (or slip between) the given mechanics of control, pressuring the declining nation state into transformation.

Writing two decades after Poulantzas and Foucault faced the crisis of the nation state, Balibar (1993) examines its ongoing erosion. For Balibar, the nation state is a historical potentiality which emerged out of social struggles calling for its redefinition. At the very core of the welfare state is the attempt to reconcile social conflicts by implementing a continually more inclusive form of biopolitical regulation in the realms of education, family, health, social rights and in the space of private life (Balibar and Wallerstein, 1991). This resulted in new practices of inclusion for various, primarily under-represented, social groups and it solidified the citizenship–nation–sovereignty triptych. But now the very same triptych seems to be under attack from the vocal demands for further expansion of the nation state's compromising structure. New social conflicts and new emerging social actors challenge the given structures of inclusion and create new situations which cannot be conceived within the existing framework of citizenship (Lowe, 1996; Isin, 2002). Consider shifts in migration, new forms of gender and queer politics, the increasing diversifica-tion of work beyond full time employment, new forms of cultural politics, new forms of biotechnological regulation of health and the human body (all of these examples will be discussed in the second part of this book). And this is the exact moment when the Global North Atlantic post-war social compromise underpinning national sovereignty seems to be unable to extend to these demands.

Drawing on Poulantzas we can see this as the moment where subaltern social groups put so much pressure on the modern state that the state cannot respond by expanding its inclusion practices; instead a fundamental transformation of the state's own structure is initiated. In place of granting more rights, such pressures have triggered a new configuration of social regulation and a new regime of control, described in the next chapter. The calls of the social movements of the 1970s and 1980s for a radical expansion of citizenship and rights were articulated within the realm of the state. Consider how civil rights movements concentrated their efforts on demands for recognition and inclusion within the state and the granting of rights by the state (Laclau, 1996). But they pointed in a direction which would radically surpass the oppressive national social compromise which existed at that time. Unable to negotiate these calls for expansion within its own terms, national sovereignty went transnational and implemented new forms of neoliberal social regulation. We call this new regime of control *transnational governance*. In the next chapter we will examine how transnational modes of sovereignty arose in response to the pressures of all these imperceptible and escaping subjectivities calling for an exit from the patriarchal dominance of the nation state.

2   TRANSNATIONAL GOVERNANCE

The Garden of Exile and Emigration

The Jewish Museum in Berlin, on the borders of Mitte and Kreuzberg, was finished in 1998. In its rear courtyard, the *Garden of Exile and Emigration*, stand 49 rectangular concrete columns, each over six feet tall. Each column contains earth in which willow oaks grow (Figure 4). The oaks come together at the top of the pillars, unreachable. The distance between the columns is quite narrow, the ground inclined, walking between the columns you feel the urge to look up. There you see the sky through the leaves and branches of the willow oaks, a feeling of calmness immediately descends upon you, and yet there is something unapproachable and strange about this garden.

The space of the *Garden of Exile* is open, nothing of the subterranean darkness of Piranesi's capriccios. The garden seems to be the opposite of Piranesi's hermetic order with no exit and no entrance, regulated by fear, with chains, racks, wheels and dreadful engines. Instead we have an evolving and virtual order, with many different groups and actors. The different columns seem to represent trajectories or rather flows evolving independently from each other. When you are in this space you never have an overview of the whole garden at once; each different column can be encountered as a relatively coherent entity. At the same time these flows break, there are edges, blocked views. And yet the columns exist as a whole and come together in the form of a thousand multiple connections. They have their individual story and still they are part of the same network of existence. They evoke a political order that seems to present a shift away from national sovereignty.

The notion of neoliberalism has been deployed by critical social theory in order to conceptualise socio-political transformations after

4. *The Garden of Exile and Emigration* in the Jewish Museum of Berlin, architect Daniel Libeskind, 1998. Courtesy of the authors.

the Second World War (e.g. Harvey, 2005; Tickell and Peck, 2003). The concept has been developed in the attempt to address: (a) the emergence of new modes of global sovereignty on the geopolitical plane (Jessop, 2001); (b) the consolidation and expansion of post-Fordist employment relations on the plane of production in Global North Atlantic societies (Lipietz, 1992; Marazzï, 1998); (c) the dismantling of social welfare systems and the development of biopolitics on the social plane (Swaan, 1994); (d) the dissemination of postmodern life on the cultural plane (Bauman, 1993; Jameson, 1991); and (e) the rapid development of high tech, biotech and neuroscience on the plane of knowledge (Castells, 1996). Neoliberalism delineates a passage which has undermined modern national sovereignty since the Second World War, leading to the contemporary formation of sovereignty, *postliberal sovereignty* as we call it (see page 25). This passage, we use the term transnational governance to describe it, is our most recent past. We have to historicise neoliberalism to escape its seemingly inescapable presence.

Together, neoliberalism and the biopolitical turn have weakened both modern national sovereignty and the Fordist regime of production. On the one hand, global capital practised its own exodus from national regulation. On the other hand, the migratory mobility of workers intensified long-standing pressure on national borders. Neoliberalism introduced the virtual order of global markets and irrevocably undermined nation states' monopoly on power. At the same time, the biopolitical, deregulated, fluid governance of the population arrived at the heart of the established Fordist regime of immobility. The 1980s and the 1990s saw the emergence of transnational global sovereignty and the post-Fordist reorganisation of production in Global North Atlantic societies. These transformations have resulted in a deep crisis of the national social compromise, as discussed in the previous chapter, and a move to a new form of social regulation.

Representation: the Second R of the Double-R Axiom

Modern national sovereignty's major concern was the assignment of rights in order to sustain the national compromise between competing social classes and strata of society. Representation was a minor concern, always present and active but still minor (i.e. representation was principally conceived as the ways in which different social classes are interpellated by state apparatuses and are codified in the cultural imaginary). In the double-R axiom of national sovereignty rights were more central than representation. But neoliberalism changed this: the dismantling of social welfare systems and the rapidly rising levels of mobility on the part of post-Fordist labour led to an increasing diversification of social strata and classes. And this diversification brought with it the politics of difference. In other words, the cultural politics of neoliberalism has been postmodernism: the fight for representation. Cultural studies, feminism, postcolonial studies, queer politics have all participated in and critiqued this fight for representation (Hall and Jefferson, 1976; Clifford, 1986; Sedgwick, 1990; Spivak, 1999; Warner, 1999b; Butler, Laclau and Žižek, 2000; Mouffe, 2000).

But what is this fight for representation, where does it come from? First of all, it stems from the dissolution of social class as the central actor in society. The different levels in Piranesi's etching seem to represent interconnected but contained social classes. This is not the case for the columns in Libeskind's *Garden of Exile*. Rather, the 49 columns appear as different social groups on a small scale, more akin to emerging subjectivities than to hierarchically organised classes. The political order of transnational sovereignty is an order with *multiple* players working to foster alliances between themselves and to establish new relations of power. And it is precisely this form of relationality which triggers the imperative for representation. Representation enters the realm of politics as the attempt to give voice and operative agency to social groups who have been excluded in the national social compromise's distribution of rights. After the Second World War, social actors focused more on matters of representation than on rights. This is the moment when hitherto imperceptible subjectivities emerge on the political scene and threaten to disrupt national sovereign power, which functions through a centralised allocation of rights. We can trace the singular trajectories of these subjectivities in civil rights movements, in the events of '68, in feminist movements, anti-work movements and new forms of cooperation, in the 1960s cultural rebellions and fights against colonialism. By the 1960s, the wild anomaly of the escaping and refusing mobs once again spreads through society and disseminates into the world (Connery, 2005). This is the moment when imperceptible politics coalesces as an escape from national sovereignty.

The Intimacy of Power

New social subjectivities and new social actors now emerge as a productive force, an immanent force which the modern nation state can no longer negate; national sovereignty is challenged. But this challenge, in turn, triggers its own response. Neoliberalism is not primarily the answer to the quest for a new mode of economic regulation (Aglietta, 1979). Nor does it primarily address demands for a new relation between culture and production (Jameson, 1991) or between market and society (Barry, Osborne and Rose, 1996; Donzelot, 1984). Neoliberalism is the answer to the wild insurgency and escape which emerges after the Second World War. Transnational neoliberal sovereignty only emerges in response to the necessity to tame the reappearance of imperceptible and escaping subjectivities in the post-Second World War period. It attempts to reabsorb the potentials of actors made evident in the 1960s and 1970s. This capture transforms what national sovereignty neglects, now the wild anomaly of the new social subjectivities is channelled into those of docile, productive actors in globalised, transnational neoliberal networks of power. There are neither historical laws nor inherent necessities of other kinds determining the emergence of transnational neoliberal sovereignty; there is only the necessity to tame the imperceptible and escaping subjectivities of the post-Second World War period.

The forms of domestication imposed on these subjectivities by modern sovereignty become constraining and even obsolete.

Transnational sovereignty functions without starting from a transcendent viewpoint, that is without being able to adopt a perspective from which society can be seen as a whole and without managing to impose a centralised form of regulation on the different social actors involved. Luhmann's (1995) vision of 'non-society' is the most brilliant and apt description of the workings and intricate relationalities dwelling in the social worlds emerging in transnational sovereignty. Instead of disrupting and negating the intimate affection between these new escaping subjectivities and their potentials, transnational sovereignty understands this intimate relation as the immanent, driving force of social life. Transnational sovereignty accepts and does not try to suppress the challenge of insurgent and escaping actors which emerged in the post-war period. Rather than negating the potentials of these subjectivities and imposing a transcendent relation between subjectivity and power, transnational sovereignty turns the intrinsic affection between subjectivity and its potentials into its core functioning principle. In the moment at which the intimacy of subjectivity and its potentials is installed at the heart of sovereignty, sovereignty itself becomes intimate. And of course, what emerges is an intimate form of power.

We have here a new form of working with the body's potentialities. Modern sovereignty negates disruptive trajectories and the body's remaining potentials are absorbed into the grand corpus of society (the nation and the big Leviathan). Modern national sovereignty installs a hierarchical, transcendent relation between body and polity. In contrast, transnational sovereignty generalises the intrinsic relation between body, potential and power into the paramount principle according to which society functions. The body's potentials are redoubled and incorporated – not as the object of power – but as the very means through which transnational sovereignty operates. Singularity, potentiality are affirmed as necessary for participation in this flexible regime of control. Transnational sovereignty is decentralised and contagious. The redoubling of the body's potentials in transnational sovereignty means that the body itself takes on its own control. Control is not constructed as a transcendent relation between power and the body but is internalised in the very existence of the body itself (Deleuze, 1992).

Transnational sovereignty no longer attempts to regulate the connections between the triptych of people, nation and state territory, rather it abandons the notion that there must be one persistent and prevalent mode of ordering this triptych. In place of any primary organising principle, now organisation arises out of subjectivities as autopoeitic systems and out of the relationality of self-activating bodies (Luhmann, 1985). The self-activating body appears in different guises – the self-organising agent, the robot, the cyborg, the embodied mind, embodied feelings (Varela, Thompson and Rosch, 1991; Haraway, 1991b; Brooks, 2002; Clark, 1997; Damasio, 1999; De Landa, 2002).

Consider Guy Debord's psycho-geographical maps of Paris, made at the end of the 1950s, maps which attempt to disrupt existing representations and convey different visions of subjective existence in space (Figure 5). They are not entirely new images of urban space, his psycho-geographic maps are modified versions of ordinary maps. The fight for representation comes from within modernity and turns it upside down. Cartographic order and categorisation was and still is the canon. What changes is the method.

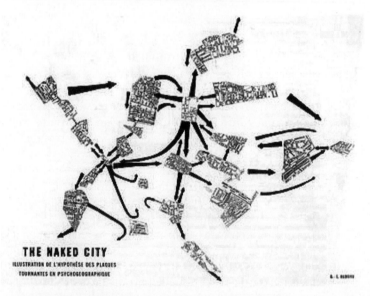

THE NAKED CITY
ILLUSTRATION DE L'HYPOTHÈSE DES PLAQUES
TOURNANTES EN PSYCHOGÉOGRAPHIQUE

5.   Guy Debord with Asger Jorn, *The Naked City: A Psychogeographic Map of Paris*, 1957, collage. © Alice Debord. Printed with permission.

Conventional maps convey a certain abstract and geometric truth about the social environment through use of the grid (as discussed in the previous chapter). Debord's maps simultaneously deconstruct conventional cartography (both literally and figuratively) and preserve the logic of a graphic expression of spatial order; psycho-geography tries to convey a subjective, existential or autopoeitic optic. The maps show an experience of space as fragmented, discontinuous, undecided, interconnected, relational: as networks (for different conceptualisations and understandings of the notion of a network see Barabási, 2002; Castells, 1996; Latour, 1987; Taylor, 2001; Wittel, 2001). The imagination of neoliberalism and of transnational sovereignty is dominated by one banal picture: nodes and lines, no beginning or end. You can constantly withdraw or add new nodes. Some of them are more powerful than others and manage a certain region of the network (Figure 6).

The logic of the network not only implies a specific way of ordering and making society, but it also reorganises the very concept of subject. As discussed in the previous chapter, modern national sovereignty domesticates people, transforming actors into subjects of power. In contrast, people do not become subjects in transnational sovereignty. Rather they become self-responsible agents in perpetual adaptation to others.

I think we have gone through a period when too many children and people have been given to understand 'I have a problem, it is the Government's job to cope with it!' or ... 'I am homeless, the Government must house me!' and so they are casting their problems on society, and who is society? There is no such thing as society! There are individual men and women and there are families and no government can do anything except through people, and people look to themselves first.

This is not a quote from Nikolas Rose; it is Margaret Thatcher in 1987 (Thatcher, 1987).

In order to function, neoliberalism and biopolitics rely on advanced technologies of the self. Governmentality theory attempts to grasp how postmodern and neoliberal conditions of existence work upon the individual's sense of the self and of conduct (Burchell, Gordon and Miller, 1991; Foucault, 2004a; N. Rose, 1996b; Papadopoulos, 2003). This is commonly conceived as the process of subjectification: that is, the production of subjectivities in the network of power. Nodes in transnational sovereign networks are regulated through relating to themselves as self-governing subjects and through their investment in constantly attending to and working on their relations with others. There is nothing liberating or fascinating in this (as some might believe). These forms of subjectification can only affirm the neoliberal structure of power. The wild anomaly of the 1960s and

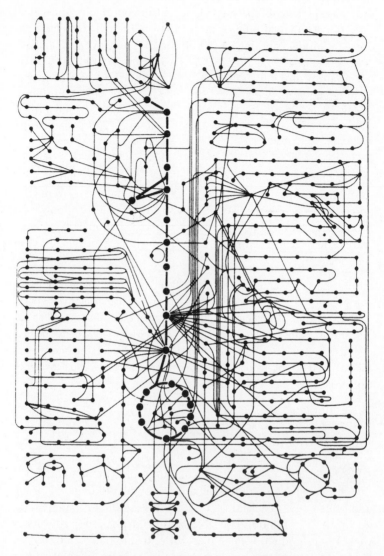

6.   Stuart Kauffman, *Cellular Traffic*. Reprinted from Stuart Kauffman, *At Home in the Universe: The Search for the Laws of Self-organization and Complexity*, New York: Oxford University Press, 1995. © Stuart Kauffman 1995. Used with permission of Oxford University Press, Inc.

1970s was, in the 1980s and 1990s, once again transformed into a subjugated form of life.

The Limits of Transnational Sovereignty

In the post-war period, the potentials of escaping subjectivities become the means, the material of the new transnational sovereignty, that is they become open to corruption. In modern sovereignty the national social compromise was based on the concept of rights. The crisis of modern sovereignty, which we described earlier, mobilises the most intimate functioning of these escaping social actors: their existence becomes globalised and their productivity in cooperatively organised transnational networks of subjectivity becomes indispensable (Atzert and Müller, 2004; Papadopoulos, 2002). But transnational sovereignty fails to integrate all these evolving spaces and capacities into a new system of transnational rights. The double-R axiom *still* fails to perform its function of ordering society: neither representation nor rights are powerful enough to accommodate or to address the life of the majority of people in transnational conditions. We said in the previous chapter that the order of the double-R axiom in the era of national sovereignty was incapable of achieving an effective national social compromise in the face of pressure from the social movements of the 1960s and 1970s. This lead to the transformation from national sovereignty to transnational governance. But now, again, a limit has been reached. And it is now, at this moment at which we find ourselves writing this book: transnational governance cannot cope with the social and political forces that are challenging its existence. At the moment we are writing this book we encounter a double movement questioning transnational sovereignty. On the one hand there is a new articulation of radical politics emerging in Global North Atlantic societies, the politics of *Escape* which we will describe in the last three sections of this book. On the other hand, and at the same time, there is an ongoing transformation of the current transnational sovereign regimes of control into a new system of postliberal control (we describe this transformation in the next chapter).

Now the double-R axiom – both in the form of a national social compromise and in its more recent form of transnational governance which emphasises representation over rights – is insufficient to tackle today's social exclusions and inequalities. And in the odd case where the double-R axiom seems to be still active today, it becomes the privilege of a few. Only those few social actors who manage to make of themselves proper subjects of representation and rights can play the game of the double-R axiom and shape society. The double-R axiom ceases to be a *commune bonum*, a property of the whole society and of everyone. Only some can use it. Only some can have it. The rest dwell in a non-space, beyond rights and beyond representation. Consider how IMF 'debt relief' programmes have left many people of the South in poorer health, or consider the proliferation of camps, Guantanamo, gated communities, banned sexualities, queer subjectivities, new post-identitarian forms of experience, *banlieues*, the prison-industrial complex, *favelas*, townships, informal settlements, detention centres, illegal migrants, undocumented workers, precarious labourers.

In transnational sovereignty the potentials of escaping subjectivities get absorbed into the process of subjectification. By becoming autopoeitic, self-governed agents these subjectivities are not so much dominated by state apparatuses of modern national sovereignty; rather, they incorporate the state into themselves. The unsettled subjectivities of the 1980s and 1990s come to confine themselves. Walking in Daniel Libeskind's *Garden of Exile and Emigration* unveils this ambivalence of the newly co-opted social actors as a banal everyday perception (Figure 7).

7.   *The Garden of Exile and Emigration* in the Jewish Museum of Berlin (detail), architect Daniel Libeskind, 1998. Courtesy of the authors.

As you navigate the uneven terrain of the narrow spaces between the columns, your gaze tries to escape the coldness of the concrete and the confining strict geometrical order of the columns' edges. The feeling is one of incarceration in the inescapable logic of these columns which support the machine of transnational sovereignty. Certainly you are not prevented from walking, moving, looking around, getting out of the garden, but ... But while you are there, you definitely know that there is something – willow oaks, sky – which is simply there but is never within reach. Something which is there, but never accessible, because of the already finished, already occurring materiality around you. That which has been accomplished, that mode of post-war transnational sovereignty which has already reabsorbed the unsettled and insurgent subjectivities of the previous decades.

3   POSTLIBERAL AGGREGATES

Postliberal Sovereignty: Network and Grid

The BMW plant in Leipzig Germany started production on 1 May 2005. In the medium term, the plant will produce up to 650 vehicles per day and has the capacity to manage the planned growth in sales of up to 1.4 million vehicles per year. According to the architect, Zaha Hadid, the building enables innovative working-time models and operating times of 60 to 140 hours per week, and because of this the plant can react quickly to specific changes in the market (Figure 8).

The BMW plant is a strange building. You don't really know if it is modern or postmodern, Fordist or post-Fordist; it is a mixture of Piranesi's multi-level scaled structure and the breathing porosity of Libeskind's construction. It is simultaneously a network and a grid. Despite the similarities to both Piranesi's and Libeskind's visions, the BMW plant does not represent a totality, as in Piranesi's hermetic environment, nor does it reproduce the transversal design of Libeskind's garden. The BMW plant is a highly contingent and closed structure, inherently fluid and simultaneously inherently stratified.

From the worker on the production line to the managers, all share the same space; they seem to belong to the same group of people. In fact, social stratification in the form of classes or subjectivities is

8.   Central Building, BMW Plant, Leipzig, architect Zaha Hadid, 2005. © BMW AG, photograph: Martin Klindtworth. Used with permission.

reversed here and reincorporated into a virtual but effective matrix of a new commonality, into a vertical aggregate. And this vertical aggregate attains its strength precisely by placing all actors on a common horizontal corridor of action. The BMW plant is an interactive order, neither open nor closed, but open as soon as it incorporates the actors necessary for its functioning, and closed as soon as it can protect and sustain its functionality. The plant is not maintained by its exclusivity nor by an internally generated authenticity, but rather by a fluid belonging of different independent trajectories to an effective system of production. It is an aggressive structure, opposing everything that sets limits to its own internal interests or tries to infuse it with impurity. The BMW plant reacts aggressively to the fear of viruses, it is aseptic, clean, pragmatic: Western oblivion at the highest level; immunity is its major concern.

We use this image as the paradigmatic figure for the emergence of a new mode of political power, postliberal sovereignty, which breeds in the core of the dominant transnational sovereignty. Postliberal sovereignty is neither a substitute, nor an alternative, nor the next stage of transnational sovereignty. Transnationalism is an integral component of postliberal sovereignty. The concept of postliberal sovereignty allows us to recognise the formation of emerging hegemonic projects which make up the space of transnationalism in the beginning of the twenty-first century (Greven and Pauly, 2000). The commonality between transnationalism and postliberal sovereignty is that both deal with the aporias of constitutionalism, that is, they both attempt to solve, on a global level, the national crisis of the double-R axiom. The difference between them is that transnationalism is inherently apolitical; it pretends to solve the problem on a simply horizontal level, while postliberal sovereignty inserts hegemonic political claims into the global horizontal space.

Transnational sovereignty presents a solution for the problem of rights and representation by adding dynamism to the borders of national sovereignty. Historically borders were lines of demarcation between national sovereignties. Transnationalism implodes these demarcation lines and reinterpellates, on a global scale, the participating actors of national sovereignty in many different ways (Brenner, 2004). Transnational sovereignty merges national spaces and their actors with other international players into a unified horizontal plane by asserting arbitrariness in the way borders are established (Castells, 1997). Borders are no longer by definition the limits between national sovereignties; rather – as discussed in Section IV – they are erected wherever there is a need to solve and to organise social space and political governance (Larner and Walters, 2004; Rigo, 2005). Consider, for example, the emergence of the new virtual European borders in North Africa – borders erected to control the flow of migration into Europe by maintaining aspiring migrants in externalised camps or internal borders erected in the heart of metropolises of Global North Atlantic countries. Making and remaking borders in a contingent way was the strategy transnationalism deployed to solve the crisis of the double-R axiom.

Postliberalism appropriates this solution – and in this sense postliberalism is also the heir to the crisis of sovereignty and relies on the same organisational substratum as transnationalism. But postliberalism attempts to initiate a strategic rearrangement of the transnationalist horizontal and networked organisation of space: in the midst of an even plane of global action it establishes vertical aggregates of power. The break occurs when postliberalism leaves nationalist imperialist geopolitics behind irrevocably. Instead it uses the global transnational space to install dominant hegemonic alliances which cannot be simply reduced to the imperialist geopolitics of entire nation states. Rather these new postliberal aggregates reconnect different *segments* of nation states and different social actors who have emerged in the phase of transnational governance into new condensations of power. Although postliberal sovereignty feeds on the horizontal transnational order of power, it introduces a new hegemonic strategy with a project of global corporativism. Postliberalism involves the verticalisation of horizontal transnational geopolitics. Transnationalism is the legal algorithm of post-Fordist, neoliberal globalisation. And in this sense, transnationalism is hegemonic on a global scale. What postliberal sovereignty does now is to hegemonise hegemony, that is, to insert and realise conflict in the hegemonic project of transnational neoliberalism. In the years from 1970 to 2000, we used to think of the neoliberal globalisation which transnational governance made possible as a more or less unified project of domination on a planetary scale (Held, 1995; Urbinati, 2003). However, the concept of postliberal sovereignty is an attempt to contest this position and to trace the internal conflicts and ambivalences of this project.

The globalisation of transnational neoliberalism can no longer be characterised as a bloc of global power; this notion does not help us to understand or to gain any purchase on the political constitution of the present. Although it is the hegemonic form of geopolitics today, the globalisation of transnational neoliberalism is not unified. Rather it contains conflicting alliances of diverse interests which try to dominate the process of transnational neoliberal globalisation. In this sense, postliberal vertical aggregates attempt to appropriate the space which was created by transnational governance and in so doing they conflict with other vertical aggregates attempting to do the same. The concept of postliberal sovereignty gives us the possibility to move beyond a simplistic understanding of globalisation as a matter of dominant neoliberal forces being opposed by the rest of the world. Rather global domination is itself a diverse and conflicted process. The conflict emerges through the formation of vertical aggregates which try to seize more power with the global unfurling of transnational neoliberalism.

The Making of Vertical Aggregates

The figure of the BMW plant in Leipzig illustrates this verticalisation of horizontal relations and terrains. The social is not only constituted out of horizontal layers of different actors, whether these be social classes, interest groups, or social subjectivities. The social consists of vertical aggregates containing and intermingling segments of social classes, groups or subjectivities into large formations which coalesce along an imagined commonality. These social bodies condense economic, technoscientific, political and cultural power and control decision-making processes. They are unlike the social structures we have known up to this moment. There are no clearcut social institutions, social classes or associations of civil society interacting in the making of polity. There are no people (*Volk*) in the BMW plant (Figure 9). We rather observe the emergence of legitimate players consisting of many different bits of all these various actors and which together constitute social bodies vertically traversing society and its institutions.

9.   Central Building, BMW Plant, Leipzig (detail), architect Zaha Hadid, 2005. © BMW AG, photograph: Martin Klindtworth. Used with permission.

There is nothing left over from the base–superstructure formation of political power. There is nothing left over from the politics of difference and subjectification. Neither ideology, nor discourse. The politics of difference of the 1980s and 1990s intervenes in the given conditions of representation, renegotiating and rearticulating them under the imperative that resistance is possible. Cultural politics, post-feminist positions, queer mainstreaming, radical democratic approaches – all have revealed that the given systems of representa-tion generate the effacement of certain differences (the migrant, the queer, the subaltern, the excluded) and they have introduced a new subversive strategy of visibility. But these times are over. The crisis of multiculturalism, the difficulties of aligning queer politics with other social movements, the occupation of postfeminist positions by neo-essentialist understandings of what women are, the obsession of radical democratic approaches with the question of formal rights, all these mark a phase of stagnation of subversive politics and its absorption into the vortex of neoliberal thinking. The politics of difference fails to grasp how actors participating in vertical aggregates are detached from their original indexes. These actors do not refer to themselves as members of collective interest formations (social class, ethnicity, gender, etc.). Their self-understanding and their agency are not derived from what they are but from their position in particular vertical aggregates. For instance, in Chapter 8 we discuss the vertical alignment of the transnational pharmaceutical company, Baxter, and the Indonesian Ministry of Health. Because this alignment arose in response to the seeming acceptance of unequal access to vaccines for pandemic influenza on the part of those most deeply involved in coordinating global preparedness for a pandemic, there has been considerable sympathy for Indonesia's move from countries of the South. However, Indonesia does not represent the collective interests of these countries in their alliance with Baxter; in fact the alliance excludes them, and potentially poses a risk to the health of those living in countries which cannot pay for vaccines.

Vertical aggregates are by no means solidified, unchangeable, closed systems. They are rather interactional entities, neither open nor closed. They are open to the extent that they can assimilate the actors necessary for their functioning and the retention of their power, and closed as much as is necessary to protect their existence. In the previous chapter we identified the network as the functional principle of transnational sovereignty. The figure of a network promises unlimited potential for connectedness. But the promise of the vertical aggregate lies more in its becoming and holding together a series of different actors, akin to the pluripotence of stem cells which might develop into a valued body part or into a cancerous growth (Waldby and Mitchell, 2006). Stem cells entail the possibility of transforming into almost any other cell, but engage in this transformation by creating 'colonies' made of different kinds of cells, colonies which close their porous boundaries, and by creating a tight division between their becoming and all that is excluded by it (Figure 10).

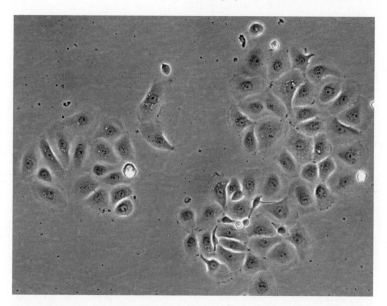

10.   Nick Di Girolamo, phase contrast micrograph of stem cell colonies isolated from human corneas by enzymatic digestion (×200 final magnification), 2008. Reproduced with the permission of Dr Nick Di Girolamo, School of Medical Sciences, University of New South Wales, Sydney.

The cultures of assemblages of stem cells serve as a paradigmatic figure of how artificial postliberal aggregates arise to be able to respond to the ad hoc needs of a certain situation. If the network was the emblematic image of the political organisation around the turn of the new millennium, cultures of stem cell lines now become the image of political organisation as we move towards postliberalism.

Postliberal aggregates carry neither the modern fetish of wholeness, nor the postmodern obsession with partiality. It is not so much that the state disappears or that transnational processes and institutions take control. We know that states play much harder now than at many other times in history. And we also know that patriotisms, fundamentalisms, new nationalisms play a crucial role in the make-up of current geopolitics. The difference is that the state ceases to act as representing itself, it splits itself, and certain parts of the state participate in broader social aggregates. It participates by articulating interests, wills and political views and by linking with many different, selected segments of social classes, social groups, associations of civil society (such as trade unions, customers organisations, pressure groups), local business companies, transnational companies, non-governmental organisations, international governments, transnational organisations. These aggregates use the cultural politics of patriotism, nationalism and fundamentalism in an arbitrary way, not because these politics refer to a nationalist ideology, but because they help to maintain the coherence of the aggregate. The main objective of postliberal sovereignty is to articulate, in a positive way, a not-yet-represented commonality of the actors participating in a postliberal aggregate.

The emergence of vertical aggregates of this kind constitutes a renewed form of corporativism, a form which attempts to get rid of totalitarian ideas and of any commitment to a liberal democratic organisation. Here we do not mean corporativism as the domination of local or multinational companies and economic trusts in decision making. Rather, we use it in the Gramscian sense, to denote a form of social organisation which attempts to resolve the crisis of state power and its inability to govern effectively by developing new modes of regulating social institutions (Gramsci, 1991; Sternhell, Sznajder and Asheri, 1994). Such neo-corporate social regulation cuts across established social interests vertically aligning *segments* of distinct class, interest and social groups with each other.

This mode of organisation can be illustrated by comparing how neoliberal and postliberal modes of social regulation function. Neoliberalism responded to the nation state's inability to deliver on its promises of rights and representation through the centralising powers of the state, by introducing the need for actors to demonstrate responsibility before they could make claims on the double-R axiom (Bayertz, 1995). The neoliberal imperative to demonstrate responsibility works to break the coherence of distinct social groups or class: individuals' attempts to claim rights are dissociated from their belonging to segments of a particular group or class. Neoliberalism can be understood as a doctrine of governance that opposes protectionism, interventionism and central economic planning in the modern state, and rehabilitates the individual as the historic subject of the modern era, combating conservative preference for traditional collectives or socialist humanist visions (Wallerstein, 1995). Milton Friedman summarised it as early as 1962, saying that 'a liberal is fundamentally fearful of concentrated power' (Friedman, 1962).

In contrast, postliberalism takes distance from this doctrine. In postliberal conditions neither the centralised government of the state nor the individualising principle of neoliberalism are seen as effective ways to organise polity. The principal figure of postliberalism is neither state nor individual; rather, it is new aggregates of power which articulate and incorporate particular segments of the state together with certain individuals or segments of social groups. Isaiah Berlin's (1958) two concepts of liberty are turned upside down and finally neutralised in postliberal conditions with the emergence of a new concept of political organisation which neither wants to minimise state intervention nor to maximise individual self-determination. This is the reason why we call the current condition *post*liberal. It moves beyond the liberal principle of the individual and beyond any form of political organisation which finally sees state institutions as the guarantors of individual freedom. Hence, in the scheme of postliberal power we have neither state supremacy and omnipotence (as in national sovereignty) nor self-governed actors (as in transnational sovereignty). How have we come to this? How has postliberalism evolved out of these two forms of political order?

As the constitutionalist structure of modern national sovereignty retreats, the practices of neoliberal governments create the conditions for the emergence of transnational governance. In transnational neoliberal conditions, connecting and realigning particular segments of social groups on a horizontal plane on the basis of common global normative principles becomes the predominant mode of governance (Commission of the European Communities, 2001; Rosenau and Czempiel, 1992; Castells, 1997). In transnational sovereignty, governance signifies the erosion of the boundaries which delineate individual self-governed actors as well as the limits of constitutional-ism. Governance is post-constitutionalist, that is, in a scene populated by many different self-governing actors, governance is the way to achieve a common mode of functioning. In other words, global action and the coordination of multiple self-governed actors is not made possible by common observation or by following some predefined or abstract principles imposed by a central authority. (Such organi-sational processes pertain to government in conditions of national sovereignty.) Rather, in transnational sovereignty, governance involves regulating the search for and allocation of normative principles and this occurs in the absence of any predefined authority which holds on to some foundational principles. These normative principles are developed ad hoc through intensive processes of negotiation between participating self-governing actors. It is through the process of governance that self-governing actors are able to co-exist and operate effectively in conditions of transnational sovereignty. Thus, we can now sketch two modi of polity: first, national sovereignty, which operates through the process: state – foundational principles – government; second, transnational sovereignty, which operates through the process: self-governing actors in relation to state and non-state institutions – ad hoc normative principles – governance.

  With the emergence of postliberal sovereignty there is no longer either a centralised statist apparatus or a fluid network of negotiation and regulation. In other words, neither government nor governance. The project of postliberal sovereignty attacks the search for ad hoc normative principles. For example, zones of exception in which human rights are deactivated or are only partially extended are sanctioned or created without prior negotiation; wars (Afghanistan, Iraq) are fought despite the fact that they are not grounded in a set of normative principles which legitimise them (here, the second Gulf War is an emblematic event of a postliberal vertical aggregate of power). Such attacks serve to install hegemonic claims into the geopolitics of governance. In fact vertical aggregates bypass governance. They interrupt the process of governance and instead they impose a series of actions whose sole legitimisation is the simple fact that vertical aggregates have the power to do them. Consider, for instance, how the 'coalition of the willing', refusing the UN, split transnational space (incorporating some actors, such as Halliburton and Blackwater) and split nations (with military forces being sent to Iraq despite the strong opposition of the majority of people they are supposed to represent). Not only does postliberalism interrupt the horizontality of power by installing vertical aggregates at the horizontal level, as we described earlier. It also renounces the liberal foundational principles of polity and strives to install a set of eclectic principles whose only aim is to solidify the internal coherence and alliances of the vertical aggregate.

  Of course this leads to paradoxical political configurations which, if we were operating in conditions of national or transnational sovereignty, would result in non-government: consider for example the mix of economic liberalism and neo-conservatism in the United States, or the new white supremacist politics of Howard's Australia, the blend of democracy and Western fundamentalism in European societies, etc. Vertical aggregates close down the horizontal, 'open' social spaces occupied by self-governing actors involved in transnational governance, and consolidate new hegemonic modalities of power which come to colonise these spaces. Post-liberalism employs a strategic selectivity as it works on the level of horizontal geopolitics installing dominance in the, by definition, unstable and decentralised global space of geopolitical operations. At the beginning of the twenty-first century and after more than 30 years of neoliberal transnational sovereignty, postliberalism changes the political constitution of the present. This shift occurs in tandem with a second, the radical reorganisation of global social actors and of the way they enter into and sustain global postliberal vertical alliances. We want to show this in two examples, one from Europe and one from the United States.

Postliberal Sovereignty and the Question of People in Europe

The 2005 debates about the European constitution reflected some of the main features of the crisis of constitutionalism. These debates make apparent the need for a post-constitutional solution to the tension between national sovereignty, on the one hand, and transnational governance of the European space as a whole, on the other. To a certain extent both the failure of the 2005 referenda for the European constitution (which were supposed to establish for the first time a post-constitutional Europe) in France and in the Netherlands, and the resulting Euro-scepticism, address an issue which has been circulating in the dispute about the future of Europe for many years, namely if there is a state in Europe (Balibar, 2004b). A peculiar alliance of left and right *souverainistes* celebrates this failure, seeing in it the reappearance of the European people of different nations on the political scene. They proclaim that this reappearance answers two questions. Firstly, it addresses the absence of representation of European people in the constitutional initiatives, and, secondly, it responds to the neoliberal support of this constitution. But the invention of 'European people' is just another European myth. We argue that the reason for the failure of the referenda is not the result of the inherent weakness of post-constitutionalism to revitalise the double-R axiom, as *souverainistes* assert. There are no people (*Volk*) in Europe, and it is good that it is so. And there are no people because Europe can be neither a state nor a confederation of states (Beck and Grande, 2004; Nicolaïdis and Howse, 2001).

Modern national sovereignty is finished in Europe and transnational sovereignty cannot yet solve the problem of a common European vision. It is true that transnational sovereignty and governance created the ground for a common European space. And here we know that this transnational space is by definition a hegemonic project (Chakrabarty, 2000; Mezzadra, 2005). But this horizontal governmental space of European unification has not answered the question of a unified hegemonic European bloc on a global scale – the territory of the debate is left confused. So, even people who supported the 'No' to the constitution cannot hide their peculiar form of Eurocentric euphoria that actively calls for a new planetary hegemonic role for Europe:

To put it bluntly, do we want to live in a world in which the only choice is between the American civilisation and the emerging Chinese authoritarian–capitalist one? If the answer is no then the only alternative is Europe. The third world cannot generate a strong enough resistance to the ideology of the American dream. In the present world constellation, it is only Europe that can do it. (Žižek, 2005a)

The moment when postliberal sovereignty could emerge never crystallised: without a firm strategy for a hegemonic Europe the referenda could not convey a common global vision for Europe. Such a strategy is needed to transform current transnational Europe into a global postliberal project and to instigate a European attempt to hegemonise the hegemony of the globalised transnational space.

Instead, the referenda were used by different political forces in order to articulate their opposition to the ongoing transnationalisation of European institutions. For example, many traditional left social movements and organisations, such as national and European trade unions, the Association for the Taxation of Financial Transactions to Aid Citizens (ATTAC), and most of the left parties represented in the European parliament, that is the Confederal Group of the European United Left – Nordic Green Left (GUE/NGL), used the internal political contradictions in single nation states, especially in France and in the Netherlands, to oppose the ratification of the proposed EU constitution. Fear was the dominant element circulating in the public debates leading to the European referenda. This was mobilised by the phantasms of an omnipotent neoliberal hegemony, of a Europe with permeable borders, of a multiculturalism out of control.

However, there is nothing subversive about fear, it only solidifies a transcendent relation between people and the polity by reactivating the double-R axiom. It encapsulates people within the national territory and confines them to its institutions of representation. Fear excludes everything which threatens this transcendent mediation between people and nation. That is, it excludes all these political actors who are external to national sovereignty, but are nevertheless crucial players in a transnational Europe. The EU constitution was not rejected because this was either an effective means to oppose neoliberal policies (as if European national governments are not enforcing such policies) or a means to intervene in the freedom of movement in Europe (as if the Schengen Agreement is not in force). It was rejected because of the fear of new social actors entering the terrain of local national politics: other groups and communities of Europe (remember the Polish plumber in Aix en Provence), the new Muslim citizens of Europe (remember the painful negotiations between the EU and Turkey), illegal migrants (remember the Mediterranean Euro-African space).

The target of the 'No' campaign was to prevent the ongoing trans-nationalisation of European states. But this proved to be a weak strategy, because blocking the ratification of the European constitution did not question the process of transnationalisation at all. The left social movements and organisations which participated in the 'No' campaign had neither the power nor the will to effectively oppose a series of major policies which have already made transnational governance in Europe a reality; such as the Schengen Agreement for the creation of common migration, border and surveillance policies across Europe, the Bologna process for the creation of the European higher education area, the Lisbon Agenda for innovating Europe's economy, etc.

The politics of fear simultaneously dissects the European transnational space into nationally regulated segments and negates the postcolonial constitution of this one Europe. As Balibar (2004a) notes, the denial of the postcolonial condition of Europe disrupts any possibility for understanding the meaning of otherness and the problem with the ongoing make-up of European citizenship today (Balibar, 2004a, p. 46). Although the failure of the referenda did not have any serious effect on the transnationalisation of Europe, the 'No' campaign celebrated this failure in the name of the European people as a univocal synthesis which, they claimed, was absent in the proposed constitution. But the very form of the referendum is the moment at which political sovereignty mobilises people as a nation; the referendum is, par excellence, the materialisation of the idea of national coherence.

And exactly this reinstatement of a nation-centred logic in left politics was heavily critiqued by a series of other left social projects and movements across Europe, such as the Eurowide network against precarity (EuroMayDay), various border activist campaigns and migrant groups. These movements remind us that politics which refer to European people as a *Volk* come to forget that it is impossible to think people outside of nation, i.e. without deploying a notion of a political subject bounded to national sovereignty. Euro-sceptic political movements and traditional left organisations return us to the terms of national sovereignty. In so doing, they undercut the possibility for creating a common European social space which operates *beyond* the institutions of the nation state and creates a viable alternative to transnational neoliberal governance (and neither do they offer any tools for thinking about or beyond the regime of control which concerns us in this book – postliberal sovereignty). Moreover, Euro-sceptics invoke a notion of European people through the discourse of a betrayed European nation. And it is on the basis of this betrayed univocal notion of European people that otherness is constructed in and expelled from the current political landscape. Consider for example the 'moral panic' which shook the Netherlands after the assassination of Theo van Gogh in 2004 (Mak, 2005). The declaration of the state of emergency and the pogrom-like raids which followed these events questioned thoroughly and irrevocably the established status of inclusion of migrants in Dutch society. A new form of exclusion of otherness is underway in current European politics. This exclusion is not primarily organised as a form of white supremacy (although in many cases this is happening) but it is the result of the creation of the illusionary paranoia of the univocal category 'European people'. The fiction of the notion of European people, which is nothing other than the annulment of the colonial and postcolonial past and present of Europe, manifests in conflicts around the Eurocentric limits of integration (as the rebellion of the *banlieues* during the French riots of October–November 2005 showed), and in conflicts over the freedom of movement across the new borders of Europe (consider the September 2005 crisis in Ceuta and Melilla, which is literally the first collective attack on a European border wall by transiting migrants from Africa).

In conclusion, the resulting picture of the situation in Europe after the 2005 ratification failure has two aspects. Firstly, the dominant neoliberal forces did not manage to create a postliberal global project for Europe out of the ongoing process of European transnationalisa-tion. And secondly, the traditional European left failed to challenge neoliberal transnationalisation: rather, fancying the logic of national sovereignty, they returned to a melancholic Keynesianism, or better, 'left conservatism' (Connery, 1999).

An Apocalyptic Passage to Postliberal Sovereignty

The apocalyptic rhetoric of George W. Bush suggested a completely different picture regarding the emergence of postliberal sovereignty: he employed a universal language for the aggressive postliberal project of a global neo-corporativism. If the reappearance of neo-conservatism on the political scene has had a meaning, this meaning must refer to the installation of a postliberal project of local and global sovereignty. Here, we do not only mean the influence of neocon think tanks and foundations on the Bush administration – such as the American Enterprise Institute, Heritage Foundation, Project for the New American Century, Koch Family Foundation, Scaife Foundation, etc. Rather, we are interested in understanding social control; specifically, forms of regulation produced by the elaboration of a neo-conservative policy which primarily attempts to unite various parts of American society and different global actors on the global scale in a new solid, effective, and virtual vertical aggregate.

It has been argued that United States foreign policy during the Bush administration is serving to consolidate a new imperialism (Harvey, 2003). However, the role of the United States in the formation of a new global system of power is the main point of divergence between those attempting to grasp the current geopolitical situation (Arrighi, 2003; Atzert and Müller, 2003; Hardt and Negri, 2000; Panitch and Gindin, 2003; Wallerstein, 2003). In the case for characterising the United States as a new imperialistic power, the United States is thought to reoccupy the power vacuum left after the collapse of the Soviet Union, claiming unipolar leadership. According to this position, the United States no longer performs Bill Clinton's multilateral hegemonic geopolitics, but a unilateral politics of violent dominance. But what this account of the new imperialism fails to understand is that if unilateral power is not part of a broader global, postliberal aggregate, it then takes the form of naked power. And naked power blocks and cancels transnationalist horizontality between global social and economic actors. This is something which nobody can afford today. The United States – more than anyone else – needs a viable transnational, horizontal, hegemonic system that frees capital flows and access to both resources and to technological innovation. A neo-imperialist strategy could possibly impose domination in order to restore superiority when a rupture in the actual balance of power occurs, but the productivity of such an imposition is bound to be limited. A neo-imperialist strategy signifies the opposite of what the United States is actually striving for today: globalised markets, circulating culture, travelling technoscience.

The United States is not striving for neo-imperialist dominance but for a system of postliberal sovereignty. It functions, not as a nation trying to represent its own interests, but as an administration which seeks to change how politics operates. The United States tries to effect this shift by working to consolidate a series of postliberal vertical aggregates on a global scale, which contest and effectively compete with other emerging vertical aggregates in the Euro-Asian, east Asian or Southern geopolitical space. Only by continuing to promote a transnational field criss-crossed by permeable, horizontal connections, is it possible to instate fluid, global vertical aggregates which incorporate different social actors in common hegemonic formations. These actors can vary immensely and can rarely be reduced to nation states. They are much more polymorphic, fragmented, energetic, and diversified than a massive bloc of a series of nation states. The United States is not undertaking nationalist-based geopolitics; rather it attempts to create a strong formation of alliances with many different actors (not primarily nation states) using existing transnational multi-centred networks of power. The United States does not dominate globalisation; it attempts to hegemonise the already hegemonic structure of globalisation. And the United States is striving more than ever before to build up such a postliberal vertical aggregate, not because it wants to consolidate or expand its power; rather, it tries to do this because it is losing power as other new postliberal aggregates emerge and contest the power of the United States on a global scale.

This necessitates a very different form of subversion from either a simplistic anti-imperialist approach or the traditional left position which we described earlier in the case of European politics. The main problem with reductionist anti-Americanism, formulaic anti-imperialism or left conservatism is that they define themselves in the negative. They fail to connect with the productivity of power and they condemn resistance and subversion to melancholy (Brown, 1995). Subversion then becomes the constitutive outside of what it tries to negate.

Firstly, any response to this situation involves acknowledging that postliberal sovereignty is an emergent project; hence, part of the difficulty of recognising its form and function lies in the fact that it may not be solidified, and therefore evident, in the sense that national or transnational sovereignties have been. Secondly, there are new emerging counter-hegemonic projects (Santos, 2001) which contest postliberal sovereignty and are reappearing on the socio-political scene of the nascent third millennium. Our immediate future contains the proliferation of both postliberal vertical aggregates of power and of unsettled and escaping subjectivities interrupting and refusing the operation of sovereign powers in whatever form they take. In this chapter, we have gestured towards this future by examining shifts in sovereign power and identifying its emergent forms. In considering the passage from national to transnational sovereignty, we want to emphasise the primary role of imperceptible subjectivities, subversion and escape in these transformations. But we have not yet identified contemporary forms of escape, nor the ways in which they contest postliberal sovereignty. This is the objective of the book: to understand the current face of escape as it is forcing transnational sovereignty to transform itself into postliberalism and as it challenges the emerging vertical aggregates of postliberal sovereignty. In Section II, we trace the genealogy of escape, analysing different ways in which unsettled and subversive subjectivities force responses out of the existing regimes of control. Then, in sections III, IV and V, we examine three central fields in which both postliberal sovereignty and the immanent forces of escape are at work: the specific fields of life, mobility and labour.

Section II
ESCAPE!

4 VAGABONDS

The Primacy of Escape: the Vagabonds' Coercion and Freedom

There emerges, in the course of the fifteenth and sixteenth centuries, an army of the poor, beggars and robbers; people who have neither land nor paid work, since the masses of peasants forced off the land could not be absorbed into manufacturing, which was almost inexistent at this moment. They were treated as criminals and accused of no longer wishing to work under their former conditions. The poor laws, with their brutal punishments (ear amputation, branding, whipping, slavery), served to control the sudden mobility of the population while attempts were made to coerce the vagabonds into work.

The establishment of the early capitalist mode of production is founded, not only on an invention of a new system of labour productivity, but also on the necessity of reconstituting wandering bodies as a disciplined and industrious class – the working class. The coercion needed for the production of the working class involves attempts to incorporate the wandering mob's surplus of freedom into a diverse regime of control involving: a system of mobility control; a system of punishment and coercion; and a system of disciplining the body into that of a wage labourer. Over the course of several centuries, we can see national and local authorities seeking to prevent the free movement of the poor, beggars and workers by constantly refining this threefold regime of control, whether as part of measures to control the poor, or by disciplining their habits, or by directing their work to manufacturing.

This flight of the poor from labour during the birth of capitalism can be seen as an important site for a newly strengthening form of control, i.e. biopower (Foucault, 1991, 2004a, 2001). In contrast, from our vantage point, their mobility primarily appears as subversion, as a force which escapes the immediate conditions of life and then forces a response in the form of biopolitical population control (Federici,

2004). The fragmented history of vagabondage is not just a marginal story in the history of sovereignty; it is a symptomatic case which exemplifies how the primacy of escape provokes the conditions of its control in the realm of production and labour in the modern nation state (Hardt and Negri, 2000). In vagabondage we see a paradigmatic image of the constant drift out of biopolitical discipline, a drift which simultaneously forced the development of some of the core strategies for the control of migration which we encounter today (these strategies will be discussed in Section IV, on migration).

We want to use the story of vagabondage in order to continue our exploration of the tension between escaping subjectivities and control. In the first section we argued that national sovereignty, transnational governance and postliberal aggregates each emerge as historically and geopolitically concrete configurations of control and productive formations of power; in different ways they harness and channel the singular uncontrollable, escaping potentialities of people. This account of power will serve as the background against which we can now develop the main argument of the book: we cannot understand social change and people's agency if we always see them as *already* entangled in and regulated by control. We can understand the formation of power only from the perspective of escaping people, not the other way round. People's escape, flight, subversion, refusal, desertion, sabotage, or simply acts which take place beyond or independently of existing political structures of power, force sovereignty to respond to the new situation which escaping people create, and thus to reorganise itself. Sovereignty manifests in response to escape. People do not escape their control. People escape. Control is a cultural–political device which comes afterwards to tame and eventually to appropriate people's escape. Social struggles come first. Thus, we had an analytical purpose when we described transformations of sovereignty as a matter of internal evolution in Section I. The rest of the book will show how these transformations – and in particular the contemporary emergence of postliberal sovereignty – are meticulous and difficult adjustments to people's evacuation of the places of a given regime of control.

Changing perspective on the relation between escape and sovereignty offers a new lens through which to view biopower. Both Foucault's (1978, p. 474) notion of biopower as the ubiquitous tool used to establish control through the twin poles of subjectification and population regulation and his analysis of the productivity of power offer invaluable insights which travel with us at every moment throughout this book. Nevertheless, now is the moment when a different approach to biopower could develop, and is needed. Where Foucault sees the constant refinement of biopower as the means of making people productive, we see it is a *response* to people's escape, to trajectories which take them beyond the regulatory practices of biopolitical control. That is, biopower explains, not the great confinement and control of free subjects, but the co-option of the powers of escaping people. Here, we exemplify this shift by discussing the example of mobility – in particular that of the vagabond masses in the transition period between feudalism and early capitalism. In the next chapter we discuss theoretical tools for conceptualising escape. Finally, in the last chapter of this section, we present our understanding of escape in the conditions of postliberal sovereignty.

Wandering Poverty

Vagabondage makes its first appearance in France in about 1350; it is a term to describe undesirable forms of mobility which begin to become punishable under a series of decrees and laws (Geremek, 1994; Sachße and Tennstedt, 1986, 1998). It is only one of a number of names bestowed on a previously unlabelled problem: vagabonds are also referred to as paupers, beggars or idlers. These terms reflect the negative light in which feudal society viewed this force of uncontrolled mobility. In a society where the means of control is based on the sedentary nature of the population, mobility challenges the very possibility of control. The types of mobility recognised as legitimate by feudal society are the pilgrimage and some more or less tolerated forms of nomadism. The crusades also belong to these forms of mass social mobility that begin to emerge during the eleventh century and which partly at least form waves of emigration. The so-called People's Crusade of 1096 initiated by Pope Urban II, for example, was originally planned as a military pilgrimage to Jerusalem. But it subsequently developed into a mass migration of about 100,000 impoverished peasants (Mayer, 1988).

Paupers, beggars, idlers, crusaders, pilgrims, nomads, vagabonds. The borders separating these categories were often rather blurred. Nomads referred to themselves – in order to legitimise their mobility – as pilgrims from Egypt, which in English then became 'gypsies'. These were often joined by others who were then referred to as 'counterfayte Egyptians', as bogus or disguised 'gypsies' (Lucassen and Lucassen, 1997, p. 231). Although one can differentiate between the 'gypsies' with their own culture, language and codes and seasonal workers prepared perhaps to settle in one place, the border between the two is indistinct. And the authorities oscillate between attempting to differentiate between these groups and identifying them, because of a lack of appropriate instruments (documents, identification papers), as a single group. In addition, the streets of the late middle ages are also populated by jugglers, fable tellers, smiths and soldiers.

The [English] Vagrancy Act of 1744 assembled together categories of social condemnation that had been accumulating in various statutes since the days of Elizabeth and added new ones to bring it up to date with the labor discipline needs of eighteenth century masters. Besides giving magistrates the power to whip or imprison beggars, strolling actors or gamblers, gypsies, peddlers, and 'all those who refused to work for the usual and common wages' it empowered magistrates to imprison wandering lunatics and 'all persons wandering abroad and lodging in alehouses, barns and houses or in the open air, not giving a good account of themselves'. (Ignatieff, 1978, p. 25)

Starting from the late Middle Ages the term vagabondage became increasingly broad until it eventually included all types of migration and nomadism. And the uncertainty around these categories was to last for many centuries.

Deterritorialisation (1): Exodus From the Land

Long before the violent proletarianisation of labour in proto-capitalist economies (Polanyi, 2001; Marx, 1988; Wallerstein, 1976), the wandering mob and the flight of the peasants expressed a struggle against the feudal rent system. The centuries before the Great Plague (1665), generally considered to form a watershed in the emergence of a pre-capitalist labour market, were characterised by an increase in the expenditures of feudal households. Everywhere in Europe peasants were leaving their estates 'illegally'. This flight from the land either spurred on the rapid growth of towns, flowed into colonisation movements towards the east or led the peasants to the life of the vagabond. In the passage from the fifteenth to the sixteenth century the feudal system was plunged into permanent crisis, not by the need to remunerate peasants, but by the flight of the peasants (Dobb and Becker, 1972).

Everywhere in Europe, whole districts and villages were abandoned. In Middle Germany, peasants became colonists; the colonised Slavs had been almost exterminated and hence the need for labour was great (Dobb and Becker, 1972). In some French provinces the resulting freedom enabled the emergence of free rural communities with their own mayors and systems of justice. The flight and the associated shortage of peasant labour allowed the peasants as a whole to demand rights and privileges. Feudal lords reacted to these demands and the scarcity of labour in different ways. One quite widespread strategy was to introduce monetary payment for services in place of feudal obligations (Wallerstein, 1983). Another strategy was to lease land to peasants. Whilst a minority of migrating peasants were 'won back', this flight from the land was crucial to the end of feudalism.

The feudal lords' reaction to this flight was, however, not uniform. While in some parts of Europe concessions (payment, leasing of land) were made to the peasants, in others the nobles reacted with an intensification of labour services. Especially in Eastern Europe, peasants who absented themselves were 'recaptured' and feudal obligations extracted by force (Dobb and Becker, 1972). At times this politics of immobilisation indicated an attempt to return to the feudal order. For example, where there was an absolute shortage of labour the feudal lords resorted to coercive means in order to tie labour to the means of production. In effect, the two types of immobilisation (mild in the case of concessions and violent in the case of coercion) mutually supported each other: in many cases, indeed, it was the same feudal lords who employed concessions to try and stem the flight from the land who soon made recourse to coercion in order to tie the fugitives to the land.

The many different attempts during the late Middle Ages to suppress mobility and to stop peasants from flowing into towns failed to restrict vagabondage (Sennett, 1994). Instead, growing numbers of paupers and peasants caused the towns to erect dams to prevent people flowing into their territories. Now, the peasants became *brassiers* (*braceros*), who entered the market by 'renting' their arms for a daily wage (Moulier Boutang, 1997). The vagabonds were still not proletarians able to work. In order for them to become unemployed workers who could exert downward pressure on wages they first had to have either the desire to work or be subjected by force (Castel, 2003). This was where projects of disciplining and incarcerating paupers and beggars in poorhouses and workhouses, but also in monasteries, galleys and armies, began to emerge – i.e. the institutions which, in subsequent centuries, would be charged with solving the problem of the mobile classes, the 'mob'.

For the first time, a more systematic regime of control emerged as a response to the vagabonds. This was an attempt not so much to return the masses to the feudal system, but to capitalise on their mobility and to absorb its potentials into a new system of accumulation of bodies and capital. Manufacture and proto-capitalist production followed the wandering masses. The new regime of control emerged to tame the escaping mob. The genesis of a docile industrious worker can be located in these disciplinary efforts. The new regime of control responded to vagabondage in three ways. (1) It tried to make poverty and the wandering masses visible and controllable by institutionalising poverty and territorialising mobility. (2) It attempted to control mobility (and only when mobility became dangerous did the new regime attempt to suppress it completely by introducing harsh laws for its punishment). (3) Finally, it tried to transform the habits and the bodies of the wandering masses by incarcerating them in workhouses in order to transform the energy of mobility into an energy of productivity.

Controlling the Vagabonds (1): Institutionalising Poverty

It is true that nomadic life was already considered undesirable during the early Middle Ages. The differentiation between legitimate beggars (on the grounds of being unfit for work) and those beggars who were fit for work and thus illegitimate, can already be found in the clerical debates of the time. However, the expansion of the money economy in Europe from the beginning of the twelfth century onwards resulted both in growing criticisms of wealth and in the establishment of charitable institutions (such as the mendicant orders) able to mediate productively the contradictions between ownership of wealth and the Christian ethic (Ignatieff, 1978). The Christian ethos of poverty emerged in reaction to the accumulation of wealth on the part of the church (Geremek, 1994, p. 35) and expressed itself in the *fuga mundi* or asceticism. Asceticism was tolerated by the church as long as it remained an individual expression or, where it became collective and thus a potential threat, it was channelled through the foundation of mendicant orders. Thus, during the twelfth and thirteenth centuries an increasing number of charitable institutions were founded, allowing both access to salvation through charitable works *and* the display of wealth. There was now a division of labour between the occupational poor and wealthy Christians. The doctrine of poverty and the praise of alms served to legitimise wealth. The ritualisation and institutionalisation of poor relief turned poverty into an occupation; the recipients of alms were listed in town tax rolls as tax payers. For instance in 1475 in Augsburg, out of 4,485 tax payers 107 were registered as beggars (Geremek, 1994).

This ritualisation of poor relief was loudly criticised long before the Reformation. Christian poor relief was seen to make begging attractive: it did not differentiate between the really poor and those fit for work, too many alms were distributed and, finally, it was pointed out that praise of poverty ran contrary to the Christian obligation to work. These discussions would have been purely scholastic had they not been coupled with social and economic processes that lent them a certain significance and sustained relevance. The organisation of poverty as a constitutive element of the social politics of the feudal order entered a period of crisis. As described above, the deterritorialisation of poverty, its quantitative growth, and the concomitant development of new forms of work led to the emergence of wandering poverty. In response, in the fifteenth and sixteenth centuries, practices of poor relief, care and surveillance undertaken by charitable institutions mainly assigned to the church gradually transformed the wandering mob into the identifiable mass of the poor. Now a new differentiation between local and foreign vagabonds absorbed efforts to regulate poor relief (Sachße and Tennstedt, 1998, p. 43) and with it there was an attempt to institutionalise poverty by reterritorialising the wandering masses.

Controlling the Vagabonds (2): Punishing Vagrancy

The Black Death, in the mid fourteenth century (Mottek, 1974), accentuated struggles over the distribution of the feudal rent. As a direct consequence of the epidemic, the *brassiers* became 'scarce', leading to an increase in their wages. The rise in labour costs varied by branch and region. In Paris the wages of builders' labourers rose by 100 per cent while the wages of agricultural day labourers in England were 2.35 times higher during the plague than at the beginning of the century. Yet daily wages for English building workers rose by only 20 per cent during the period (Mollat, 1986). Around 1350, edicts were issued throughout Europe – in particular in England, Portugal, Castile, Bavaria and Aragon – against the wage increases due to the labour shortages. For instance, in 1351 an ordinance was issued by John the Good in France directed against vagrants who did not wish to take up their former work, introducing the threats of pillory, branding and banishment. Some years later, in 1354, traders justified their high prices on the grounds of labour costs (Geremek, 1994).

In England in 1349, the *Ordinance of Labourers* was issued, stipulating compulsory labour until the age of 60 and the requirement to accept wages fixed at the levels prevailing in 1325. Workers who had fled their place of work could not be employed elsewhere (Castel, 2003). Breach of contract by servants, i.e. running away from work, was punishable by a prison sentence. It is apparent that such measures alone could neither solve the problem of mobile workers nor effectively suppress them. In every case where edicts to restrict mobility were issued, new ones soon followed with either the same or modified content. These policies were continued until well into the fifteenth century and beyond.

The limitations of such strict measures cannot be fully explained by recourse to arguments about flaws in the local apparatuses of control. The widespread failure of cooperation of the people as well as the masters and lords was vital. The incarceration and punishment of paupers and beggars was rejected by ordinary people, who began to actively support beggars who resisted their imprisonment, at times to the point of instigating riots (Geremek, 1994; Linebaugh, 2003). The alliances forged between townspeople and beggars would suggest that townspeople recognised the fluidity that the dividing lines of laws and edicts attempted to mask, and that they saw the draconian measures directed against the beggars and the vagabonds as an attack on themselves. Moreover, this solidarity shows how widespread the phenomenon of vagabondage was, indicating that the laws could only attempt to control it rather than eliminate it. It was simply impossible to eliminate the deep manifestation of vagabondage in the everyday culture of the time.

Thus, the increasing mixing of what had formerly been distinct categories of beggars, paupers, nomads and vagabonds is an index of the de facto blurring of these categories in social life. The workers, for whom as yet no term existed, moved between these categories. It is evident that they made use of different elements of these ways of life.

The uncertainty of life from one day to another, and the very real possibility that they, too, might at any moment find themselves amongst the ranks of the unemployed, reduced to begging for a living, naturally bound the working population to these paupers. (Geremek, 1994, p. 227)

Controlling the Vagabonds (3): Discipline and the Workhouse

Whilst population numbers returned to their pre-plague levels after about 50 years, the 'vagabond' phenomenon did not disappear. As late as the eighteenth century, the towns, villages, streets and not least the political debates of Europe were filled with paupers, beggars and vagrants. This is because a new form of mobility appeared alongside vagabondage: forced mobility following expulsion from land (Allen, 1994). With the enclosures of common land in England and its conversion to grazing, the peasants were driven from the land to form a new, unwilling army of paupers and beggars (Polanyi, 2001; Negt and Kluge, 2001).

These enclosures began at the close of the fifteenth century, lasted for 150 years and increased again in the eighteenth century, this time in legal form under the 'Bill for Inclosure of Commons'. Aside from the mobilisation and transformation of peasants into proletarians, these enclosures created, on the one hand, tenants' growing dependence on landlords, and on the other, an enlargement of the agricultural land of the new owners that was accompanied by a revolution in agriculture (Marx, 1988). In *Das Kapital*, Marx writes about the new 'free proletariat', that is those thrown off the land faster than they could be incorporated into manufacturing:

They were turned *en masse* into beggars, robbers, vagabonds, partly from inclination, in most cases from stress of circumstances. Hence at the end of the fifteenth and during the whole of the sixteenth century, a bloody legislation against vagabondage was enforced throughout Western Europe. The fathers of the present working class were chastised for their enforced transformation into vagabonds and paupers. Legislation treated them as 'voluntary' criminals, and assumed that it depended on their own good will to go on working under the old conditions that no longer existed. (Marx, 1988, p. 723)

The numerous and often draconian measures used to torment the beggars and vagabonds of Europe over many centuries – branding, flogging, the death sentence – can all be understood as efforts to discipline the former peasants into wage labour (Marx, 1988).

Looking back over the course of the seventeenth century, Foucault sees the new disciplinary power coalescing, a power that subjugates and harnesses the body. In contrast to monastic discipline, aimed more at renunciation, this form of power is a machine that divides the body only to reassemble it again. Discipline produces a double result: on an everyday level, training the body's powers yields an increase in productivity and usefulness; on a political level, this usefulness corresponds symmetrically with social submissiveness to the given order of power (Foucault, 1977, p. 138). Discipline superseded the mechanisms of feudal power and established forms of power oriented towards the production of value. Foucault (1977) explicated this element of the subjugation of the productive body by examining the workhouse, a model institution whose mission was to re-educate beggars and young idlers. Workhouses used temporary incarceration to train a new attitude towards work and mobility. In the eighteenth century the workhouse also appeared as an answer to the problem of chain deportations (the 'dangerous' wandering masses were being expelled from one territory to others). 'Delinquency' legitimised the regulation of the population as a whole through the incarceration and surveillance of its 'dangerous' edges (Foucault, 1977, p. 278). The individualisation of the whole society was enabled as the prison expanded to the workhouse and then a disciplinary system formed an ever widening series of circles around this core. Thus, individualisation, i.e. localisation in space and time, formed the basis for the regulation of mobility. Disciplinary control came as a response to the wandering masses.

Contrary to what Foucault might say at this point, it was not that disciplinary power produced subjects to be tamed and trained. Rather disciplinary power followed the escape of people from soil, feudal rent and poverty. And it followed it because this escape of the vagabonds was a constituent force which challenged the feudal regime of control. It was not feudal power but disciplinary power which came to make this force productive. And this is particularly important: disciplinary power does not simply attempt to block and strangulate the escape of the vagabonds. Disciplinary power does not produce its subjects. Rather it *responds* to the escape of these subjects transforming them into a productive force for the establishment of a better system of control. This new system of control is wage labour.

Reterritorialisation: *Labore Nutrior, Labore Plector*

This is the line: *escape from feudal immobility – mobile vagabonds – discipline – wage labour*. Foucault (1977) would invoke the primacy of discipline in telling this story. There are others who usefully try to oppose Foucault's obsession with discipline and tell the story from the perspective of wage labour (Castel, 2003; Geremek, 1994; Ignatieff, 1978). But their approach is wrong: they eliminate the novel forms of agency which become evident in the moment of escape and social transformation, fixating instead on the continuities between the different forms of social organisation. These positions assert that beggars and paupers were often day labourers, i.e. they were *already* workers, so it is doubtful whether disciplining and training for work were the driving forces behind the foundation of the workhouses. Although this point is correct it neglects the fact that the vagabonds were primarily *fleeing from work*. Thus the line: *escape from feudal immobility – mobile vagabonds – discipline – wage labour* is the only option which gives us purchase on the formation of control, because neither the discipline-oriented nor the labour-oriented position can properly conceive of the phenomenon of vagabondage. Disciplinary power achieved the appropriation and reterritorialisation of the force of mobility into the strictly regulated system of wage labour. Control transforms the energies of escaping people; it does not produce people through discipline, neither does it expand on their already existing capacities to be workers. The social formula of escape: escape creates a form of energy which is potentially rupturing the equilibrium of an existing regime of control; then, a new regime of control needs to be established in order to appropriate this energy and transform it into a new manageable social subjectivity. Escape is about energy, whilst discipline is about rule and labour is about static abilities. The art of escape is the art of constructing an indeterminate form of energy from the encounter and interference with a regime of control. The art of control is not to destroy this energy but to transform it to a new form of energy, one amenable to regulation.

Begging and vagabondage were forbidden not for moral reasons but because they were escapes from feudalism and wage labour. The laws directed against the poor were both a reaction to uprisings (a whole series from 1378 on) as well as an attempt to control the mobility of labour (Castel, 2003). For instance, in France, at the end of the fourteenth century, a domestic passport in the shape of a certificate was introduced that was mandatory for any person wishing to leave their borough. The certificate had to detail the reason for the journey and the date of return to the area of residence. Such attempts to limit the mobility of labour evidence something of the force of flows of mobility. What is clear is that the paid labourer, working under a contract in conformity with the law, received permission to move. Thus, it is not the journey that was problematic but mobility without a labour contract, mobility which threatened the means then available to control both the level of wages (of particular interest to the emerging apparatuses of control) and the work carried out (of particular interest to the town corporations and therefore the guilds). Throughout the sixteenth century, poor laws and those laws directed against vagabonds became more intense, more severe and more innovative (e.g. with the introduction of branding, first on the chest, then on the forehead).

In the seventeenth century we see an increasing coupling of mechanisms of indenture and bondage with legal judgements specifying fines (Breman, 1989; Potts, 1990; Moulier Boutang, 1998; Emmer, 1986). Fines were paid by a master to bind an employee to his service. This so-called 'parish slavery' suggests that the increasing deployment of slavery in the American colonies during the same period was not an exception at all but rather part of a broader move to fix populations and workers. This same law also stipulated that whoever lived at least 40 days in a parish without recourse to begging should receive a regular residence permit. So a certain acknowledgement of workers' mobility definitely existed even if it was heavily limited and framed within the compulsion to have a recognised domicile (which represented an impossible hurdle for the poor, who could not afford a lease or rent). Of course, one way to avoid this control over mobility was through marriage. And just as with slavery, a precise legal framework had to be developed regulating dependants of the subjugated: the children, the marriage partners and other relations of the poor. The aim was to reduce the number of assistance seekers and to limit the possibilities of mobility offered by familial relations.

Deterritorialisation (2) (Short Preview): Maritime Communities of Exodus

During the course of several centuries, national and local authorities sought to prevent the free movement of the poor, beggars and workers, whether as part of measures to rein in poverty or to direct labour to manufacturing. This escape – this flight of the poor from labour – may also be seen as a revolt in the face of a politics of forced labour and a politics of wage limits. Here, we encounter a second drift away from control. The first is the escape from feudal immobility which became tamed by disciplinary efforts in order to consolidate the conditions of wage labour. However, the tension between escape and control continued to be active and to trouble the establishment of the system of wage labour. The escape of the vagabonds was not simply neutralised and effaced through discipline and punishment. It continued to occur, against the system of wage labour which the workhouse attempted to establish; the escape of the vagabonds later becomes an escape from labour. The line continues: *escape from feudal immobility – mobile vagabonds – discipline – wage labour – escape from salaried work*.

We can trace this story in the communities of exodus established on the sea. It is no coincidence that the strongest challenge to the disciplinary techniques for taming the mobility of the vagabonds and the wandering poor came not from manufacturing or the workhouse, but from the ships of the British Empire. Across the turn from the late sixteenth into the early seventeenth century, more people worked on these ships than in the manufacturing industry or than were to be found in workhouses; ships were the first prototypes of the factory. In them we can find all the organisational principles of the later industrial architecture of production – a large workforce which is required to cooperate and coordinate, the processes of being made a slave to a machine, and the wage system of remuneration (Linebaugh and Rediker, 2000).

Gangs and vagabonds do not simply represent the marginalised or the outcasts of society. Rather than robbery and theft, they instigate and participate in tumults and uprisings and their situation often fuels the demands and slogans of these acts of subversion and occasionally revolt (Mollat, 1986; Linebaugh, 2003; Castel, 2003). These multiple and localised forms of vagabond insurgencies anticipate the later fugitive communities, such as the maroons and pirates. The vagabonds are a precursor of the 'dangerous classes', as Louis Chevalier characterised the working class of the nineteenth century (Chevalier, 2000). *Communities of exodus* that parallel the movements of revolt were formed during the whole period from the Renaissance up to the beginning of the industrial age. These included pirate ships, laboratories where slaves, serfs or sailors established alternative societies beyond compulsory wage labour (Linebaugh and Rediker, 2000). Their aim ranged from the 'attempt to live in common poverty without differences of rank' (Mollat, 1986, p. 207) to establishing a 'law of the privateers' of the seventeenth-century Caribbean, which was oriented towards the utopia of a classless society and contained practical forms of a collective social and political democracy.

The pirates were African runaways and indigenous people as well as former indentured slaves or free workers who had been more or less kidnapped by the press-gangs in the ports of the transatlantic empire and forced into galley service. They paid into a form of retirement fund and elected their officers. Similar to escaped slaves everywhere on the American continent, they formed communities of maroons who collaborated to escape the tyranny of both slavery and wage labour. As with the poor, who were the ultimate losers in any direct confrontation with lords or town patricians, these communities of exodus had only a limited chance of survival. Their production system was a combination of robbery and hunting–gathering – only possible in areas that had not been colonised. As their moral economy was partially based on theft, the pirates were not only economically dependent on a society they rejected but could also be easily criminalised. Piracy was not only tolerated for a long time but was in fact commissioned in the battle carried out among the colonial powers for influence, territory and political and economic power. England employed pirates in the Caribbean to weaken the Spanish territories and colonial trade. The pirates were only declared enemies when they increasingly began to reject this instrumentalisation and establish themselves as an alternative model to the forced labour and exploitation aboard the imperial fleet (Linebaugh and Rediker, 2000).

The wandering workers were not only an economic and political problem. They were a practical and symbolic threat to the dominant order. The fugitive communities of exodus, pirates, maroons, runaway slaves, vagabonds, wandering poor, uprising peasants and mobs in harbour towns and colonies made up the rebellious forces which, despite their ultimate decline, challenged the regime of labour and mobility control to the extent that it had to transform itself in order to become an effective tool for controlling the escaping mob. It is no coincidence that the word mobility not only refers to movement but also to the common people, the working classes, the mob. In the next chapter we examine how the subversive unruliness associated with the escaping mob functions and we consider how best to conceptualise this engine of social and political transformation.

5   OUTSIDE REPRESENTATION

The Subject-form and the Tension Between Escape and Representation

The histories of vagabonds' mobility described in the previous chapter are histories of escape; they illustrate how the concept of escape changes our understanding of social conflicts and their biopolitical regulation. Social and political thought usually considers acts of escape – for example refusal, desertion, betrayal, sabotage, exit and subversion – as individual deviations from collectively organised forms of social conflict, or as uninspired, exasperated reactions to intolerable pressure (Jane Bennett, 2001). Escape is frequently considered to be a passive, weak and irresponsible way to deal with an unfolding social conflict or one's own situation. We argue the opposite: escape brings us to the heart of social conflict, and it constitutes a form of creative subversion capable of challenging and transforming the conditions of power.

The vagabonds encounter a regime of control which functions by trying to impose immobility. Immobility disciplines bodies and renders them productive; it captures bodies and channels some of their potentials into the labour force. Bodies become territorialised; people become subjects of a specific territory, of a sovereign power. Their mobility is not a reactive move against territorialisation, rather the forces of territorialisation are imposed on people's mobility. What was previously sheer movement now exists as an energy traversing in a new field, it becomes escape. People moving – territorialisation – vagabonds escaping. So, although escape necessarily relates to the terms of control, it is not constrained by a given regime, the seeds and means of escape exist prior to control. In the case of the vagabonds, we saw that the regime of control becomes productive only through its capacity to seize on and capture the energies and forces stemming from unsettled bodies, from people's mobility. The relation between control and escape is one of temporal difference: escape comes first. Unsettled bodies move, they become vagabonds who escape, they leave the stage of forced immobility; power reorganises itself in order to respond to their exit.

Sovereign power mobilises representation to organise and contain social conflict. Representation is nothing other than a means to render the forces partaking in a social conflict visible to the gaze of power. Moreover, power relations operate by making social actors representable within a regime. As we described in the previous chapter, only when escaping people are represented as a dangerous class or codified as a mobile workforce do they enter the order of power. More precisely, in response to the wandering masses power is forced to reorganise itself. Control encounters escape with representation. This is the formula of power. Already in the first section of this book (in particular in the discussion of the double-R axiom in Chapter 1) we argued that the main target of the political machinery of representation is the production of particular kinds of subjects. It is through the process of representation that people become subjects amenable to being managed by power. If, for a minute, we distance ourselves from the immediate social, cultural and political conditions we have described in Section I and try to understand the very constitution of the subject in the historical time of national and transnational sovereignty, we can recognise a series of recurring patterns which make up this subject. These patterns pertain to the role of production, the relation between sexuality, social relations and the body, and finally the relation between people and polity. On the level of production, the subject is constituted by the very fact that he or she is the immediate producer of the material existence of society through labour activities: the productionist subject. On the level of the body, social relations and sexuality, the subject is constituted through his or her participation in a compulsory heterosexual matrix which sustains phallocentric dominance: the heteronormative subject. Finally the relation between people and polity is constituted through subjects who understand themselves as capable of social transformation to the extent that they identify and strive to achieve a position which has predominance in society: the majoritarian subject. It is on all these three levels that representation turns people into subjects of power.

The conjoining of these three dimensions shapes the very idea of the subject, the *subject-form* as we call it in this book. The subject-form could be understood as the amalgamation of these three different historical determinants of social existence. Our argument is that escape is an attack on the productionist, heteronormative, majoritarian subject-form. It may be that certain forms of escape primarily work against one or other dimension of the subject-form, but the practice of escape is a force which challenges the very coherence of the subject-form. Power encounters everyday practices of escape from the subject-form by intensifying the inclusion of people through processes of representation. In this sense we could say that escape and representation are the centrifugal and centripetal forces revolving around the subject-form and securing its central role in the organisation of political power. Representation is a form of power organised as spectacle. For Debord (1994) the spectacle is not just a collection of images, representations and abstractions; rather these images and representations mediate every single social relationship. The subject-form is not an abstract category. It is steadily constructed and reconstructed through the continuous process of representation in every single social relationship, even those of the briefest, most uneventful kind. Escape attempts to break out from this fastidious construction of the subject and to dissolve the spectacle's domination through representation. This chapter traces the tension between congealed formations of representation and amorphous energies of escape which subvert the productionist, heteronormative and majoritarian subject. Our analysis of these strategies of escape from the subject-form enables us to identify possibilities for politics outside representation. These will be described at the end of the chapter as a means of introducing the exploration of contemporary politics of escape in the rest of the book.

Exodus in America in the 1870s

Vagabondage was a system. The case of the escaping vagabonds is not unique. For example, labour was something of a paradox in America in the late nineteenth century. Migration meant that the country had to invest relatively little in the production of a labour force: it seemed as if America was receiving a constant stream of ready-made, adult workers. Yet, wages were high and it was difficult to find workers for waged-labour. 'The excess of people', according to Benjamin Franklin's diagnosis of the problem, followed their desires and moved away from wage labour and into agriculture (B. Franklin, 1840/1794; see also Virno, 2005). As long as land acquisition was a possibility, people pursued it. The mobile frontier of this young nation marched west with the people. In the last chapter of the first book of *Das Kapital* Marx (1988) asked what had been interrupting the logic of capitalist wage labour since the turn of the eighteenth century. All the right conditions seemed to have been imported from Europe with the colonisers, the money for investment, the technical and business expertise and the absence of a feudal hold on people. The people too were there. However, what had failed to take hold was their relation to the labour market; the subjectivity of the worker did not develop and take a secure hold in these conditions. The opportunities presented in this new land were many; one of them was the opportunity to escape from relations of dependence between workers and employers by acquiring and farming land. Thus Franklin, in the attempt to ward off industrialists' requests for assistance in setting up new businesses, wrote that 'labor being generally too dear there, and hands difficult to be kept together, every one desiring to be a master, and the cheapness of lands inclining many to leave trades for agriculture' (B. Franklin, 1840/1794, p. 467), thus preventing the growth of manufacturing industries.

There is an ordinary reflex on hearing this story about people's escape from labour: this is to see in the escaping worker the fate of a body which later will become subject to disciplinary power. The escaping workers seem predestined to be contained and punished.

Such a reading could be easily bolstered by drawing on Foucault. As we said in the previous chapter, when Foucault looked at workhouses (1991) he saw vagabonds who tried and failed to follow the trajectory of escape, and became the raw material of disciplinary force. But looking at America's tales of labour exodus, Marx saw something different: 'The wage worker of today is tomorrow an independent peasant, or artisan, working for himself. He vanishes from the labour market, but not into the workhouse' (Marx, 1988, p. 756). For Foucault, mobility was constrained through the disciplining of bodies. Marx saw, in his momentary glance towards America, the failures of these efforts (Erickson, 1984). And efforts were made: slave labour; negotiations with the British colonial government to increase the price of land so as to force people back into wage labour; the introduction of contract work; finally, the coolie system of importing indentured slave-like labour. But after all these impositions had been introduced what was evident to Marx was the desire to move, not with industrialisation and the rationality of productivity, but with the frontier.

At this moment, for Marx, the rebellion against immobilisation is not only a search for a better future but a praxis of political significance which questions the very foundations of the conditions of production in this historical moment: wage labour. Of course no escape is constituted as a pure subversion. Escape is always a situated and ambivalently arranged process. Moving with a frontier takes people beyond the repressive character of the factory system, but at the same time it is a move which proceeded along a great racial divide in the brutal process of the American conquest (Allen, 1994; Todorov, 1984). In the words of Bernard Bailyn (1988, p. 114), 'it was the juxtaposition of the two – the intermingling of savagery and developing civilization – that is the central characteristic of the world that was emerging in British America'. Thus, escape is always singular, it is a local historical process, one which is variously connected to simultaneously creating new forms of oppression as well as freedom. The history of escape is plural; those who flee American capitalism are the colonisers of the West and simultaneously the forerunners of the contemporary 'cult of mobility' (Virno, 2005, p. 18).

Refusing Work

In the 1960s and 1970s, the politics of everyday life fuelled various practices of escape – exits from hegemonic conditions of work, from patriarchal social and sexual relations, from national subordinations of ethnic minorities to mention only a few. In Italy and some other Global North Atlantic societies at this time, the flight from work was politicised as a strategy of refusal (Tronti, 1966). Workers leave the factories, and seek new forms of work; part-time, flexible work (Bowring, 2002; Thoburn, 2003). Together with students and the jobless, they actively cultivate ways of living in precarious conditions. Their mobility destabilises hegemonic labour relations, provoking a political crisis in Fordist society. They refuse to assume and act in accordance with subjectivities based in work and productionism, escaping the disciplinary powers of the factory system and subverting the very idea of labour (see the magnificent work of Krahl, 1984). They constitute a social movement which tries to transform everyday life, rather than to gain representation in state politics. Their refusal is not simply a refusal to work, but a refusal to translate their social struggles into a set of demands addressed towards the redistributive capacities of the welfare state (Tronti, 1966). In this form of escape we see a direct link between the practices of refusal and the negation of representation, and with it the negation of the double-R axiom. The Italian movement (and a similar movement in Germany) was important for rethinking subversion not so much because it entailed escape from the factory, but because it refused to reconnect this escape from the factory to some form of representation which would reintroduce the struggles back into the national social compromise (discussed in Chapters 1 and 2). The refusal of work is in fact a refusal of representation. It is a refusal to re-enter the constitutive productionist dimension of the subject-form. The movement out of the factories explicitly severed assumed connections between state politics and everyday life. People were only able to participate in the national social compromise to the extent that they held, or aspired to hold, full-time normal employment. However, when people start investing in efforts to transform everyday life, in creating a multiplicity of modes of existence, trajectories and desires, the normalising function of the national social compromise becomes increasingly evident and with it the irrelevance of state-targeted politics. This brings Fordism to its limits and, even if it was for a very short historical moment, it exposes and challenges the very idea of productionism as a core moment of everyday existence.

Whilst the passage to post-Fordist labour conditions is often characterised as a transition initiated by employers seeking to expand the conditions of work, the story of the Italian Operaist (and later autonomist) movement suggests something else. Capital is creative

(Hardt and Negri, 2000; Virno, 2003), it follows escape, using it as the engine of its own development (Tronti, 1966). This is why Moulier Boutang (2001a) describes the powers of refusal as 'terribly efficient' in fuelling the evolution of capitalism. The history of capitalism is a history of regimes of control being fragmented by escape, transformed and fragmented again.

Our interest in escape is not that it culminates in a *better* configuration of life. Rather, the concept enables us to examine the often neglected engine of transformation which occurs without a master plan and without guarantees. Escape is a means, not an end (Agamben, 2001). It is means without ends in action. Escape has no morality (the American runaways exit work by exterminating indigenous people). But it entails the desire to evacuate an oppressive morality; escape follows this desire. Not every 'no' constitutes an escape; passive or reactive departures change little. Escape is a creative, constructive move, one which radically alters the very conditions within which struggles over existence are conducted (Virno, 2003). This creativity entails working with the surplus of what has been harnessed by regimes of power (as the vagabonds did when they acquired licences to travel for the purpose of marrying and used them only to travel); by returning to potentials which have been neglected, misrecognised and remain unannounced (Irigaray, 1985b). Escape is about dissent and construction, it is not protest. It is made up of everyday, singular, unpretentious acts of subverting subjectification and betraying representation.

When looking more broadly at the social movements of the 1960s and 1970s, the Italian experience of the autonomist movement and the refusal of work seem to be only one of the many elements of a wider strategy of escape (Neilson, 2005). Local historical contingencies rooted in the social and cultural idiosyncrasies of the Italian left movements, meant that the Operaist concept of exit was restricted to escape from the productionist, Fordist regime of work. But this refusal of work was part of a broader movement of escape from the subject-form prevalent in Global North Atlantic societies. And these acts of subversion entail forms of escape which are provoking a much deeper challenge to the very notion of the heteronormative, productionist, majoritarian subject-form.

Escape from Phallocentric Modes of Subjectification

In feminism we find the most thorough discussions of the subject-form on the level of the material constitution of the body and its discipline (Gallop, 1988; Scarry, 1985; Bordo, 1993) as well as on the level of the social and political meaning of escaping the masculinist, heteronormative matrix (Haug, 1992; Butler, 1990; De Lauretis, 1987; Rubin, 1984). Here, though, we want to focus on a particular feminist position which in the most radical way problematises the process or representation and the escape from its dominance. Writing in the 1970s and 1980s, Irigaray (1977, 1985b, 1985a) was part of sexual difference feminism which contested the attempts of liberal feminists (e.g. Steinem, 1992) to ensure the inclusion of women in public, political life. Demands for equality do not question the terms against which equality is measured. Through their eagerness to play the game of the double-R axiom, liberal feminism fails to contest the very representations which materially constrain the embodiment of the feminine. Thus, by attempting to fuel the radical social trans-formation necessary to subvert patriarchy, liberal feminism risks contributing to a 'power to *reduce all others to the economy of the Same*' (Irigaray, 1985b, p. 74). We understand the 'economy of the Same' as the function of the subject-form which sustains the continuity of dominant forms of representation and precludes attempts for radical transformation. This happens because woman, the feminine, is present in the phallocentric economy, but she is always represented as one of two positions sustained by the subject-form – phallic and masculine or passive and feminine. In contesting these representations, Irigaray moves to interrogate the function of representation altogether.

Whilst some subjectivities and bodily potentials are excluded in the social imaginary, some feminine potentials still flow through and materialise in the bodies of both men and women. This 'feminine' is distinguished from representations of the feminine in the social imaginary, which are constrained by phallocentric fantasies. Thus, sexual difference feminism seeks to address the chasm between the feminine potentials which circulate through everyday social spaces and relations and the misrepresentations of the feminine which are commonly deployed in attempts to describe or work on those spaces and relations (Whitford, 1988). The problem is to understand and contribute to these feminine powers to initiate change in the absence of forms of representation within which they can be recognised (Braidotti, 1993). This calls for the capacity to work with and continue creating amorphous, fluid modes of existence which, although they are lived, cannot be articulated at the present moment – a capacity, we argue, which is central to the politics of escape (see Chapter 9 for further discussion).

The embodied experience of the feminine acts as a disruptive excess to the phallocentric economy. These feminine pleasures, embodied modes of relating to others and to the world, remain unrepresented. Working with these bodily potentials involves, first, tackling how the oppression of women is conducted at the level of bodily sensation and perception. To this end, Irigaray develops an alternate lens through which the body is sensed – and she does this without claiming to give a true account of feminine bodily sensations (Grosz, 1989a). One criticism of sexual difference feminism holds that it is founded in essentialist notions of the body. But this criticism entails reading Irigaray as attempting to represent the potentials inherent in female anatomy (e.g. Moi, 1985). However, any such endeavour is explicitly rejected by Irigaray, on the grounds that it could only ever play into the fetishised desire to reveal the truth of the feminine, to reinsert it into the subject-form, and would result in the 'recuperation of the feminine within a logic that maintains it in repression, censorship, nonrecognition' (Irigaray, 1985b, p. 78).

By turning to the multiplicity of auto-erotic sensory pleasures experienced by women – *'woman has sex organs just about everywhere'* (Irigaray, 1981, p. 103, emphasis L. I.) – she refuses the patriarchal gaze which reduces women to passive objects of pleasure. The masculine ascription of the feminine as 'not one' is subverted without being negated. Irigaray presents here a central moment of the politics of escape: it is not about negation but about betrayal. It is about betraying all those representations which eternally bind us to the masculinist economy of the sexes. This betrayal cannot be accomplished simply by developing alternate representations of the feminine and by playing them against the masculine representations. Rather, by using representation against itself, Irigaray strives to develop a lens which can be attuned to absence, multiplicity, simultaneity and non-identity (Grosz, 1986, 1989b). The feminine is unrepresentable. The betrayal of the subject-form as a core moment of the escape from phallocentric modes of subjectivity works by tracing the ruptures which emerge in current representations, by following the lines which expose their inability to address the suppression of the feminine. Irigaray's work offers an account both of the mechanisms of representation through which a patriarchal regime of control disciplines the body and of the feminine potentials which exceed control and remain unrepresentable. By harnessing the unrepresented feminine, which arises in the tension between discipline and excess, she denaturalises phallocentric notions of the body and renders them meaningless.

Feminist politics goes beyond the fight for inclusion within a regime of control. Inclusion is exposed as inclusion within a patriarchal regime of control, an expansion of patriarchy. However, subverting existing representations of the feminine does not amount to articulating a positive feminist project. Subverting the phallocentric construction of the body necessitates a radical move; it demands that we think betrayal and escape as forces which materialise in the creation of new relations between bodies (relations which exceed phallocentric sexualisation) – Irigaray's work brings us to this point, but does not make this move. This move to materiality is simultaneously a move beyond the predominance of language and the symbolic. What is important, then, is not only to betray existing representations, but to escape them by constructing new bodily experiences and modes of connecting. As we already said earlier in this chapter, the practice of escape is not an abstract strategy, but a singular activity which accompanies us through the everyday.

Bodily Constructions/Speculative Figurations

In her investigation of possibilities for feminist politics, Donna Haraway makes the move beyond the realms of language and the symbolic by interrogating the very material constitution of bodies. The ubiquitous representationalism of the common dichotomies between sex/gender and nature/culture is contested as she relocates them into a non-linear intermingling of human, animal, and machinic bodies. In so doing she cultivates the conditions for exiting from the fixed and closed representations of the Global North Atlantic subject-form. The result is an ingenious exploration of the material processes of production through which bodies make themselves and construct their own relations to each other. Haraway's concept of the 'apparatus of bodily production' (1991a, p. 208) connects both the critique of productionism (as articulated in the escape from labour) and the critique of heteronormativity (as articulated in the escape from phallocentric subjectification). Haraway's move against the fixed representations entailed in the subject-form is grounded on the level of everyday materiality: neither bodies nor objects nor their relations among each other pre-exist as such. Rather bodies, things, relations are in a continuous process of passionate construction through their own interdependent activities. This is the apparatus of bodily production, a process through which we not only create semiotic devices to deal with the world but also material bodies which exist and transform our lived worlds. The making of bodies is a matter of facticity and efficacy.

Facticity means that these bodies are simply there and invite us to engage with them in a way which did not exist before. Their very existence entangles us in a process of co-constitutive action, a process in which we and other things do not simply inter-act with each other as external and autonomous entities, but each exists through the process of action. We, other bodies, things do not enter into the process of mutual action as pre-existent and pre-constituted entities; we exist because we are entangled in action with other bodies and things – Karen Barad (2007) calls this intra-action. Other bodies and things do not merely respond to human action. They are there de facto as part of a co-constitutive action. Their facticity is the result of the fact that they contain embodied and incarnated forms of actions, as Ernst Schraube (1998) says, which cannot simply be controlled or manipulated by an external observer. There is a 'still pedagogy' (Bourdieu, 1987, p. 128) which a social field – that is comprised of bodies, things, practices – exercises on people participating in it. Facticity means that we cannot avoid being part of or in the process of action. And it is through this process that things and objects are constantly incorporating and producing other things (and therefore the world we live in); in the words of Günther Anders, 'objects are thirsty' for more materiality and for more action (cf. Schraube, 2005). We cannot encounter the facticity of things and bodies other than with concern. Concern here has simul-taneously a threefold meaning: interest, care and being concerned. We enter into the process of intra-action not as the knowing subjects or as abstract cognisers, but as interested, careful, concerned actors (Papadopoulos, 2005). The construction of new bodies, their facticity, is not an epistemological problem. It is an ontological one. The world appears not as an object to be known but as the ontological unity of intra-actions, as a wholeness of possibilities, involvements and mutual metamorphoses. The process of a material construction of other bodies, things, relations is indicated by the term efficacy.

We encounter the world in an immanent process of intra-action because the facticity of other bodies has a direct effect on us and our immediate relations, that is they change de facto the whole constitution of our existence. Haraway calls for an ethics of concern and accountability, not as an abstract moral principle of responsibility, but because of the very fact that our everyday engagements produce bodies and relations which have a certain efficacy on the world (Puig de la Bellacasa, 2008b). Haraway's apparatuses of bodily production are not simply manufacturing events, they are onto-political engagements with the world. They produce material changes which cannot be avoided, negated, bypassed or simply neglected, because these bodies change the very *terms of our experience* and create new situations in which we find ourselves. The efficacy of other bodies and things does not result from the fact that other bodies and things act independently of us; rather, it means that through mutual action new conditions and configurations of experience emerge (see Chapter 8 in Stephenson and Papadopoulos, 2006; see also Middleton and Brown, 2005; Caygill, 1998). We become entangled; subjects and things merge in a new ontological unity, changing the fundamental structure of experience – in Whitehead's terms this is an actual occasion (Stenner, 2008). In this process we become inventive, creative, constructive. The escape of the subject-form is thus not a retreat and disengagement from the world; rather, escape instigates an intensification of committed constructions and efficacious interventions. Escape is not a ghost, merely a protean trickster. It is a means to experiment and to initiate speculative ways to deal with the immediate and concrete facts which dwell in our worlds, because our experience cannot simply neglect their stubborn persistence and their inescapable efficaciousness (as developed in Whitehead's speculative metaphysics, see Whitehead, 1979; see also Gare, 1999).

It is through this speculative process that Haraway creates new feminist figures which exceed representation, which 'cannot, finally, have a name; they cannot be native. Feminist humanity must, somehow, both resist representation, resist literal figuration, and still erupt in powerful new tropes, new figures of speech, new turns of historical possibility' (Haraway, 2004, p. 47). Going further than Irigaray, Haraway sees these new speculative figurations as emerging in literal, material processes of the creation of new bodies, relations, organisms, objects and things. These figurations are both literal and fictional (Puig de la Bellacasa, 2008a). Literality and fictionality, reality and imagination, reality and virtuality are always simultaneously present in experience. Thus Haraway's speculative figurations do not bluntly oppose given configurations of experience, they rather escape them by creating new actual forms of experience, in the Whiteheadian sense – in Chapter 9 of this book we call this experiential constructive form of escape *continuous experience* (see also Stephenson and Papadopoulos, 2006). Escape from compulsory representationalism is simultaneously real and imaginary. It is the creation of new speculative figurations, new deliberate actual constructions, which puts us right in the heart of new experiential configurations. Günther Anders' call to train our capacity for 'moral fantasy' and Walter Benjamin's 'speculative experience' are behind the ideas presented here. In his book *The Outdatedness of Human Beings* (Anders, 2002, pp. 271ff.) Anders discusses the inadequacy (what he later develops as a philosophy of discrepancy) between our feelings and the unforeseeable effects of things, and demands that we train the elasticity and capacity of our imagination (see Ernst Schraube's exceptional analyses of this in Schraube, 2003, 2005). Walter Benjamin discusses also the magical and spiritual language of things in his text *On Language as Such and on the Language of Man* (Benjamin, 1996b) and develops a programme of a 'speculative experience' as a means of recognising the immanent wholeness of life beyond a naive utopian idealism or blunt versions of materialist dialectics (Caygill, 1998). Incorporating speculative figurations into the practices of escape undermines both the unworldly utopianism of many left traditions as well as the unbearable historicist realism which we encounter in many post-Marxist approaches, especially the traditions of refusal of work as described earlier in this chapter (see also Badiou, 2005b, pp. 42ff.).

By working with the imaginary and the fictional as a creative material sensibility, Haraway opens up possibilities to rethink the tension between escape and representation. If escape is the construction of experience on the ground of speculative figurations, then we can start developing a better understanding of how escape is blocked, policed and controlled. If escape hinges on the knot of fictionality and literality to construct and materialise new forms of experience, then it is exactly this knot which becomes the target of control. Escape is captured and controlled when the entanglement between literality and fictionality is interrupted by power. This happens by attempting to insert acts of escape into the process of representation. Representation attempts to excise escape's fictionality and virtuality by delegitimising it as impossible, quixotic or impracticable and, simultaneously, it tries to make its reality and literality productive (as we saw for example in the case of the vagabonds: see Chapter 4). Power works by policing the border between the fictional and the real, by interrupting their constructive force to harness and create actual occasions of experience outside representation. This policing of the speculative figurations of the imaginary is pervasive, so deeply has it been inserted into the very heart of politics that policing has become a substitute for politics.

Politics, Policing

Any project of escape is wary of co-option, the ever-present risk that efforts to initiate or participate in radical social change might be diverted in another direction and appropriated in the existing system of representations. Co-option is not an anomaly, it is a mode of capture pervasively employed by sovereign power. As Wallerstein says, 'the revolutions never worked the way their proponents hoped or the way their opponents feared' (1998, p. 13). But co-option may not always be the result of an intentional act. It can be the outcome of misrecognition. The problem lies at the level of perception, or sensory experience (and, as we illustrated in the earlier discussion of Libeskind's *Garden of Exile and Emigration*, different forms of sovereign power train the senses to perceive distinct modes of connectedness to the world). To say that the potentials of subjectivity and escape are unrepresentable means that they remain invisible to those whose sensibility can identify neither excess, nor absence, nor speculative figuration. Attempts to harness and work with these imperceptible potentials will be misrecognised and translated into the given terms of representation. And it is precisely this form of limited sensibility which proliferates through policing (Rancière, 2000).

For example, the terms deployed to speak of migrants (asylum seeker, *Gastarbeiter*, illegal migrant) constitute them as a homogeneous social group and function to police their insertion into broader society. The policing effected by these terms is historically situated. For example, the French term 'immigrant', has served to hide and expel the name 'worker' from political debates (Badiou, 2005b). 'Immigrants' are a rather new species of subject in France. They used to be called

migrant workers or just plain workers. Today's immigrant is first a worker who has lost his second name, who has lost the political form of his identity and of his otherness. ... What he has lost is his identification with a mode of subjecti-fication of the people, worker or proletarian, as object of a declared wrong and as subject giving form to his dispute. (Rancière, 1998, p. 118)

Certain social groups, such as migrants, are rendered visible and accountable through policing. Policing stands in for politics in contemporary times. It results from attempts to found political actions and decisions in an egalitarian principle which holds that all should be included as equals and partake in a majoritarian realisation of politics. But egalitarianism is, of course, only a principle, not a description of the societies in which we live (Rancière, 1998). All societies consist of different parts, of people who are seen to contribute different skills, forms of wealth or knowledge. The paradox of working with the egalitarian principle is that it demands that all should have an equal role in sustaining and governing society, but it cannot transform the fact that people's capacities to partake in society are perceived as *un*equal (Balibar, 1997). The capacities of the mother, the migrant, the worker may be simply undetectable for some. Moreover, being included on the basis of the egalitarian principle, rather than on the basis of what one can offer, compounds any perceived lack of capacity. Working with the egalitarian principle cultivates sensibilities which ignore what lies beyond immediate perception: society appears to consist of self-evident groups or parts – of people who occupy the space that has been allocated to them and no other. Naming and representing – the core moments of the egalitarian principle – are the primary political tools for controlling society. They reinsert excluded social actors into the subject-form by constructing them as majoritarian subjects. That is, they construct them as subjects who are entitled to participate in politics because their own position *might* become those of the majority in the governance of the social. Formal equality is thus a mode of inclusion which effectively creates social minorities with the promise that these minorities can aspire to become majoritarian subjects and to change politics. Naming and representing under the guidance of the political principle of equality are thus the main means of restraining escape and of reincorporating it into the workings of power. The result is that what typically stands in for politics in contemporary times is, in fact, policing: the realm where the normalising functions of inclusion and co-option are enacted.

Outside Politics

To escape policing and start doing politics necessitates dis-identification – the refusal of assigned, proper places for participation in society. As indicated earlier, escape functions not as a form of exile, nor as mere opposition or protest, but as an interval which interrupts everyday policing (Rancière, 1998). Political disputes – as distinct from disputes over policing – are not concerned with rights or representation or with the construction of a majoritarian position in the political arena. They are not even disputes over the terms of inclusion or the features of a minority. They occur prior to inclusion, beyond the terms of the double-R axiom, beyond the majority–minority duality. They are disputes over the existence of those who have no part (and in this sense they are disputes about justice in a Benjaminian sense of the word, Benjamin, 1996a). Politics arises from the emergence of the miscounted, the imperceptible, those who have no place within the normalising organisation of the social realm. The refusal of representation is a way of introducing the part which is outside of policing, which is not a part of community, which is neither a minority nor intends to be included within the majority. *Outside politics* is the way to escape the controlling and repressive force of contemporary politics (that is of contemporary policing); or else it is a way to change our senses, our habits, our practices in order to experiment together with those who have no part, instead of attempting to include them into the current regime of control.

This emergence fractures normalising, police logic. It refigures the perceptible, not so that others can finally recognise one's proper place in the social order, but to make evident the incommensurability of worlds, the incommensurability of an existing distribution of bodies and subjectivities with the principle of equality. Politics is a refusal of representation. Politics happens beyond, *before* representation. Outside politics is the materialisation of the attempt to occupy this space outside the controlling force of becoming majoritarian through the process of representation.

If we return to our initial question of how people contest control, then we can say that when regimes of control encounter escape they instigate processes of naming and representation. They attempt to reinsert escaping subjectivities into the subject-form. Outside politics arises as people attempt to evade the imposition of control through their subsumption into the subject-form. This is not an attempt simply to move against or to negate representation. Nor is it a matter of introducing pure potential and imagination in reaction to the constraining power of control. Rather, escape is a constructive and creative movement – it is a literal, material, embodied movement towards something which cannot be named, towards something which is fictional. Escape is *simultaneously* in the heart of social transformation and outside of it. Escape is always here because it is non-literal, witty and hopeful.

Of course, outside politics is embroiled in the very problem of representation it tries to contest. As we show in the following chapter, this is not a limitation in and of itself. However the question arises as to whether the figure of escape can activate the imaginary of outside politics. Because the figure of escape is indebted to twentieth-century politics and resides in twentieth-century fantasies, it invokes an agonising historicist realism in conjunction with a salvation-driven utopianism. Beyond this, we want to look for escape in the amphibious and alkaline transformations people make against the metallic melancholia of twenty-first-century postliberal sovereign power. In other words, following the trajectory cultivated by late-twentieth-century feminist work, we trace outside politics in the most intimate, we say imperceptible, niches of the everyday and the body – and this is the topic of the next chapter.

6 IMPERCEPTIBLE POLITICS

The Predicament of Resistance

We find ourselves in a predicament in doing politics, writing about politics: the predicament of resistance. It is a timely predicament. From the beginning of the twentieth century until the 1980s the value of traditional forms of organising resistance (especially in the forms of party and trade union politics) was self-evident. But they no longer seem to offer a viable radical form of resistance. In response, the social movements of the 1960s and 1970s – identity politics, micropolitics and cultural politics, in particular – have had a major role in taking us beyond the state-focused terms of traditional forms of resistance and in re-energising our potentials for action in everyday life. But now resistance in these movements seems to be increasingly compromised by their entanglement in neoliberal forms of governance, by the crisis of multiculturalism and by the fact that some have become productive forces in the new capitalist economies of knowledge and culture in Global North Atlantic societies (we discuss these various forms of resistance more extensively in the next three sections of the book; see also Stephenson and Papadopoulos, 2006).

The 1990s was an important period of cross-fertilisation between familiar modes of resistance which target the state and struggles which seek to transform social experience. Strategies for resistance commonly employed in party and trade union politics were irrevocably exposed as reproducing inequalities by failing to question assumptions about universalist (and nation-oriented) notions of a good life. At the same time, the risks of an exclusive focus on the politics of the everyday became increasingly evident. Seeing *all* experience as political can fold back on itself and become a depoliticising move. This is particularly the case when recognition of difference stands in for redistribution of resources and reallocation of positions, muting the imperative to refigure radical alternative sensibility (Rancière, 1998; Santos, 2001).

We passed through the 1990s, all of us involved in various forms of organisation and resistance, and we exited the decade in a form of speechlessness. Experimental forms of subversion, new social movements, have emerged in the first few years of the new century (Chesters and Welsh, 2006). We are part of these experiments. This book is an experiment to think politics after the predicament of resistance; to think, with Hoy, of resistance as both an 'activity of refusal [and] ... an attitude that refuses to give in to resignation' (2004, p. 9). We find ourselves in a situation in which people participating in state-targeted forms of resistance do not want to go on in the old way and those involved in the politics of everyday life are unable to go on in their way. If the times were Leninist we would be on the threshold of a revolution which would revolutionise existing forms of resistance. But the times are not Leninist; they seem to be quiet. What is audible is the predicament of resistance and the indeterminacy of experimentation with various forms of subversion. Or maybe we could raise the volume on something else – a form of politics which employs modes of resistance that are already materialising in our current postliberal sovereign conditions: *imperceptible politics*. We use the term imperceptible politics to designate everyday cultural and practical practices of escape.

Imperceptible Politics Transform the Body

We have an ally in writing this book: time. Writing at the beginning of the twenty-first century we are not simply making reference to the present. The current times allow the book to happen. In the beginning of the third millennium, we are precariously situated on a rather aseptic, sober, glamorous facade, with lots of neglected agony beneath. This book could easily be fuelled by mourning and lament (as criticised by Brown, 1995), or it could strive to culminate in some kind of genealogy (N. Rose, 1999) or critical deconstruction of the present (Žižek, 2005b). It could even attempt to refuse despondent visions of the future by promising that agony is, in principle, translatable into euphoria (a mode of engagement critically analysed by G. Rose, 1996). But we are writing not as active and watchful observers of our times; we are not even writing in the flow of time, as its loyal handmaidens. Rather, time – with all its stubbornness and smoothness, its warm reliability and its disorienting absence of synchronicity – fuels these micro-electrical firings which govern the muscles of our fingers on the keyboards of our sleek laptops. Time both writes us and yields material with which we can address the predicament of resistance.

New tools of subversion are emerging, but they have not crystallised, they are ungraspable. This describes our encounter with imperceptible politics; it is not simply situated in our present conditions of postliberal sovereignty. Of course, imperceptible politics is demanded by our situatedness. But at the same time, it is imaginary and outside of the present historical chronotope. It is only possible to work *on* the real conditions of the present by invoking imaginaries which take us beyond the present. And this trajectory away from the present is achieved by working *in* time, by *intensifying* the present.

Imperceptible politics works with the present. Time is fractured and non-synchronous – the historical present can be understood both as containing residues of the past and as anticipating the future (Marvakis, 2005; Bloch, 1986). Yet it is impossible to identify either the past or the future by moving backwards or forwards in time. Neither move is possible. Time forces us to work in the present, by training our senses to examine what appears evident as well as what is absent. This sensibility enables us to perceive and imagine things and ourselves in unfamiliar ways, to follow open trajectories. Time contains both experiences of the world which have been rendered invisible and the seeds of experience which may be possible to realise (Santos, 2003). Imperceptible politics can be neither perceived nor conducted from a transcendent perspective; that is, elaborating a 'metaphysics of the present' (as criticised in Adam, 1995) can reveal nothing of the mode of engagement with the present we are describing. This engagement entails experiencing time in a subjective and embodied way, being forced to transform ourselves in order to deal with this current predicament of resistance. Situated in the present historical regime of control, imperceptible politics involves *remaking the present* by *remaking our bodies*: the ways we perceive, feel, act. Imperceptible politics transforms our bodies.

Loving the present, existing in the present, imperceptible politics is practised in the present. It works with social reality in the most intimate and immanent ways, recalling the whole history and practice of escape, as we described earlier, and rethinking it anew. Doing imperceptible politics entails the refusal to use our perceptual and action systems as instruments for representing the current political conditions of resistance. It functions through diffraction rather than reflection (Haraway, 1997, 1991c): diffraction creates 'effects of connection, of embodiment, and of responsibility for an imagined elsewhere that we may yet learn to see and build here' (Haraway, 1992, p. 295). In this sense imperceptible politics is more concerned with changing the very conditions of perception and action than with changing what we see. Only such bodily, lived transformations are sufficient for interrupting the pervasive sensibilities being shaped by sovereign powers.

A Constituent Force against Postliberal Sovereignty

Postliberal sovereignty seizes power by creating vertical aggregates on a transnational level. In Chapter 3, we described these aggregates as hegemonising the transnational space of global flows. Aggregates cut across and absorb selected segments of traditional horizontal social structures such as class, gender, race, social position, economy, institution, the market, technology. Borders are inserted between people (often unobtrusively), actants who might previously have worked on a horizontal plane. These boundaries are not simply geographic; they do not delimit companies, industries, governments, NGOs or community alliances (Sassen, 2000), nor do they just scatter and isolate. Rather, they mark out the distinct elements of these different entities which are to be recombined in vertical alignments of power with each other.

Like capital, postliberal sovereignty is inherently unethical and opportunistic. In this unscrupulous enterprise, so characteristic of the Bush–Blair era, resistance becomes just another structural element contributing to the erection of postliberal aggregates. We already know that the very conditions for resistance are always directly entangled in power. But such entanglement, so brilliantly described by Hoy in his analysis of post-structuralist understandings of resistance (2004), does not necessarily block the development of effective strategies of subversion. Of course, sovereignty digests resistance: active forms of resistance are continually co-opted. But this twin movement of flight and capture only appears catastrophic if we insist that there must be an ultimate solution to social conflicts. We do not. Certainly, resistance is frequently absorbed by power after its initial eruption. Movement – co-option – resistance – capture happens all the time. The particular problem with the fate of state-targeted and everyday micropolitical forms of resistance in the era of postliberal sovereignty is that they lose their *constituent* powers. Their eruption no longer pushes power to reconsider and reorganise itself, to move to new directions (see also Chapter 14). While these familiar forms of political engagement can certainly trouble and interrupt the seamless unfurling of postliberal sovereignty, they lose their power to trigger change (Negri, 1999). And exactly this force is crucial for our understanding of escape. As we discussed in the previous chapters, the primacy of escape is that it is a constituent force of change.

Escape is not opposed to or against the regimes of control in which it emerges; escape betrays the regime of control by carefully evacuating its terrain; as it becomes a constituent force of social transformation it forces power to follow the line of escape and reconstitute itself. But how is this done in the everyday? What kind of cultural and material actions sustain escape? Earlier we called imperceptible politics the everyday practices which make up escape. Certainly imperceptible politics addresses postliberal sovereignty and entails developing strategies for exiting postliberal representationalism. But this is neither their main intention nor their main target of action. Their targets pertain to the specific social struggles and social conflicts in which they are located. Imperceptible politics changes sensibilities, it changes the immediate social realities of existence in these fields in ways that, after a certain point, become impossible to ignore. This is what makes it a constituent force. Imperceptible politics changes society without ever intending it. It becomes a constituent force because it constructs new material realities where it operates, not because it strives to erect a better society in general. Imperceptible politics does not believe in a future to come, it believes in its everyday actions, it loves the fields in which it operates, it traces the future in the present, it cunningly subverts everything which is there to maintain the integrity of a given field of power.

In this sense imperceptible politics does not necessarily differ from or oppose other prevalent forms of politics, such as state-oriented politics, micropolitics, identity politics, cultural and gender politics, civil rights movements, etc. And indeed imperceptible politics connects with all these various forms of political engagement and intervention in an opportunistic way: it deploys them to the extent that they allow the establishment of spaces outside representation; that is, spaces which do not primarily focus on the transformation of the conditions of the double-R axiom (rights and representation) but on the insertion of new social forces into a given political terrain. In the previous chapter we called this form of politics *outside politics*: the politics which opposes the representational regime of policing. Imperceptibility is the everyday strategy which allows us to move and to act below the overcoding regime of representation. This everyday strategy is inherently anti-theoretical; that is, it resists any ultimate theorisation, it cannot be reduced to *one* successful and necessary form of politics (such as state-oriented politics or micropolitics, for example). Rather, imperceptible politics is genuinely empiricist, that is it is always enacted as ad hoc practices which allow the decomposition of the representational strategies in a particular field and the composition of events which cannot be left unanswered by the existing regime of control.

If imperceptible politics resists theorisation and is ultimately empiricist, what then are the criteria for doing imperceptible politics? There are three dimensions which characterise imperceptible politics: objectlessness, totality, trust. Firstly, imperceptible politics is objectless, that is it performs political transformation without primarily targeting a specific political aim (such as transformation of a law or institution, or a particular claim for inclusion, etc). Instead imperceptible politics proceeds by materialising its own political actions through contagious and affective transformations. The object of its political practice is its own practices. In this sense, imperceptible politics is non-intentional – and therein lies its difference from state-oriented politics or the politics of civil rights movements, for example – it instigates change through a series of everyday transformations which can only be codified as having a central political aim or function in retrospect. Secondly, imperceptible politics addresses the totality of an existing field of power. This seems to be the difference between imperceptible politics and micropolitics or other alternative social movements: imperceptible politics is not concerned with containing itself to a molecular level of action; it addresses the totality of power through the social changes which it puts to work in a particular field of action. The distinction between molar and molecular (Deleuze and Guattari, 1987, p. 275) has only analytical significance from the perspective of imperceptible politics. In fact imperceptible politics is both molar *and* molecular, because by being local *situated* action it addresses the *whole* order of control in a certain field. Imperceptible politics is located at the heart of a field of power and at the same time it opens a way to move outside this field by forcing the transformation of all these elements which are constitutive of this field.

In this sense, imperceptible politics is a driving force which is simultaneously both present and absent. We described this in the previous chapter by exploring the importance of speculative figurations for the practice of escape. On the everyday level of escape (a level we called in this chapter imperceptible politics) speculative figuration can be translated into trust. This is the third characteristic of imperceptible politics; it is driven by a firm belief in the importance and truthfulness of its actions, without seeking any evidence for, or conducting any investigation into its practices. This is trust. Imperceptible politics is driven by trust in something which seems to be absent from a particular situation. Imperceptible politics operates around a void, and it is exactly the conversion of this void into everyday politics that becomes the vital force for imperceptible politics.

Before discussing further the question of the absent centre of political action and the problem of the void and trust, we want to describe how these three characteristics of imperceptible politics become a constituent force of change in the three fields of life, mobility and labour. In the second part of the book we trace the tension between postliberal sovereignty and imperceptible politics in these three fields (see Figure 11). A field crosses various disciplinary domains and social spaces, and these crossings are held together as 'boundary objects' (Leigh Star, 1991) which exhibit a relative autonomy in their constitution and function (cf. also Bourdieu, 1990). Pandemic influenza, for example (see page 127), traverses the terrains of biomedicine, public health, the pharmaceutical industry, international health agreements and organisations, farmers and agribusiness, border control and border activism, national and international security agendas, the management of the bodies and everyday lives of millions of people. All these different terrains make up the field of pandemic influenza.

We use the term *regime of control* to designate the conjuncture of different institutions and actors which operate in the attempt to control power in a specific field. A regime of control is an unstable but effective alliance between forces of power. It is always historically specific. For example, in Chapter 4 we described how the regime of mobility control emerged as a response to vagabonds' flight in the field of labour in pre-capitalist north European societies. But fields are not solely dominated by regimes of control. Fields are regions of the social world held together by a pervasive regime of control but also by distinct forms of social cooperation and expressions of social conflict. A field is not a coherent unified system of operations. Rather, it contains distinct, independent, sometimes conflicting elements.

Analytically a field contains all those institutions, discourses and practices which sustain a regime of control but also all those experiences and practices which escape it and force control to transform itself. As discussed in previous chapters, forces of escape are always located in and start from a concrete field. Escape is always grounded. But where is it grounded? There is a surplus of sociability produced in each specific field, an excess which lies outside the existing forms of representation operating in that field. It is this excess of potentials that creates the possibility of escape. And more specifically it is imperceptible politics – that is, the everyday cultural politics of escape – which are practised in and fed by this excess of social relations. Imperceptible politics arises from the tension in a given field between the dominant regime of control and social relations of excess which emerge in that field. Excess is the necessary precondition of imperceptible politics. And imperceptible politics gives birth to lines of flight which attempt to escape the regime of control in a certain field. These are the relations of power which we will be analysing in the second part of this book in the fields of life, mobility and labour (see Figure 11).

politics (section I–II)	emergence of postliberal sovereignty (chapter 1–3)	outside representation (chapter 4–5)	imperceptible politics (chapter 6)
↑ FIELDS ↓	↑ CONTROL ↓	↑ EXCESS ↓	↑ ESCAPE ↓
life (section III)	regime of life control: Formation of Emergent Life (chapter 7–8)	the haptic (chapter 9)	continuous experience (chapter 9)
mobility (section IV)	regime of mobility control: Liminal Porocratic Institutions (chapter 10)	excessive movements (chapter 11)	autonomy of migration (chapter 12)
labour (section V)	regime of labour control: Precarious Life and Labour (chapter 13)	embodied experience of precarity (chapter 14)	inappropriate/d sociability (chapter 15)

11.   Diagram of the relation between control, excess and escape in the fields of life, mobility and labour

What is important to highlight here is that while imperceptible politics is grounded in the unrepresentable relations of excess in a certain field, it simultaneously opens a way to move outside this field. This move is enabled by trust (which we discussed earlier in this chapter and expand on here). Where does imperceptible politics' trust in this fictional, imaginary, excessive dimension of escape come from?

Addressing a Void With Imagination: Subversion, Escape, Becoming Everyone

Imperceptible politics is driven by imagination and fictionality – the imagination required to address an absence, as Santos (2003) describes it. As discussed above, representation diminishes the senses. Not only does representation dictate the terms of inclusion in political disputes of a certain field, it blunts our capacities even to perceive the multiple realities of bodies, people, desires – inappropriate/d forms of life (Trinh T. Minh-ha, 1987). These inappropriate/d modes of existence, this excess of social relations, remain after the existing regime of control has dissected and transformed subjectivities into controllable objects of discourse: bodies become identities, people become *demos*, desires become demands. Imperceptible politics starts from this excess of inappropriate/d modes of existence which from the perspective of the regime of control constitutes a void (Badiou, 2005a), a void residing in the political system of representation.

As Badiou (2001, p. 68) says about the void, it is the very heart of a particular situation around which 'the plenitude' of social and material relations making up this specific situation is organised. This plenitude is mirrored, managed and regulated through procedures of representation (it is policed, as we said with Rancière in the previous chapter). Consider, for example, the surveillance and control of highly patrolled passages of migrational flows through the porous borders of Global North Atlantic countries. There is a plenitude of laws, practices, institutions, customs, migration police and border patrols, rituals, detention centres, informal migrant networks, knowledges, life projects and much more, which makes up this situation. This abundance is structured around an absence: the embodied and unrepresentable desire which people follow as they cross borders despite the regime of control which tries to close them off or to constrain and control them. When they enter into the language of the plenitude, these people are called illegal migrants. They are treated as a problem, an economic, social or humanitarian problem, which has to be solved through deportation, revisiting legislation or negotiations with other states. What is absent is their actual movement, what people become as they navigate the fissures of nation states and borders. The absences of the inappropriate/d migrants and their desire constitute a void, a void around which this situation is organised.

When all these inappropriate/d modes of existence beyond identity and passports become represented, it is only to be measured, policed, and finally, controlled. But they *do not always* become represented: when the void becomes an action, it does so as a force which challenges the existing organisation of plenitude in a certain field. Because it cannot be accommodated in the current situation within existing conditions of control, it is a constituent force pushing for a radical change. The imperceptible politics emanating from the void cannot be ignored. The millions of inappropriate/d bodies render borders permeable de facto, throw the current regime of control into disarray, force sovereignty to reassemble itself – everyday imperceptible politics becomes escape from a regime of control.

Imperceptible politics is the moment when the void of mobility (or labour or life, as we show in the next sections) becomes subversive. Some may want to use the word resistance instead. But here we understand subversion (or resistance if you prefer) in a positive way: as the desire to depart from the plenitude which organises control in a certain field. Or better, as the trust in something which is absent and unrepresentable, and yet operative and constitutive of a specific field. This desire comes from the very heart of the situation, but leads directly and unconditionally beyond it. Desire. Trust. Escape! This is the only understanding of resistance which is relevant for imperceptible politics, and it is indeed the only understanding of resistance which escapes the melancholic uptake of Foucault's work in neoliberal times. This is the reason why we prefer to talk of subversion instead of resistance in this book. Drawing on Johannes Agnoli's (1996) intriguing exploration of the historical metamorphoses of this concept, we understand subversion as the process of reclaiming a form of praxis which is there but is forgotten, suppressed and rendered seemingly absent. It is an act which cannot be understood as critique, or as a form of dialectical negation of negation, or even resistance but it stands there as 'negation sans phrase' (Agnoli, 1996, p. 16), that is conceptual and theoretical work which obtains its efficacy only through 'laborious mole-work' (Agnoli, 1996, p. 226). Subversion is that which is banished and eradicated through political representation, yet never completely. As an act of reclaiming, the subversion entailed in imperceptible politics is located in the everyday and precedes and prepares the practice of escape itself.

Subversion remains imperceptible to the representational policing of a field and works with an excess of social relations which spring from the 'absent centre' of this particular field. This is the fictional and imaginary character of imperceptible politics. It is only by conjuring up the speculative and fictional qualities (see previous chapter and Haraway, 1992, 2004) of a situation that it is possible to address something which is absent and yet there, something arising from the core of the situation but which is yet to emerge. Imperceptible politics is here, always present within a regime of control, cultivating trust in speculative figurations of a radically different future in the present. Imperceptible politics is here.

Imperceptible politics unfolds as a continuous break from existing forms of representation. But how do people actually do this in their everyday lives? How do people deal with the constant pressure of policing and representation, undo their fixed positions and enter into processes of dis-identification? How do people move beyond themselves as they connect to each other in the situated process of escape? Becoming is a political practice through which social actors escape normalising representations and reconstitute themselves in the course of participating and changing the conditions of their material corporeal existence. This is not only a force against something (principally against the ubiquitous fetishism of individualism and against sovereign regimes of population control) but also a force which enables desire. Every becoming is a transformation of multiplicity into another, suggest Deleuze and Guattari (1987). Every becoming intensifies and radicalises desire, creating new modes of individuation and new affections. Becoming is a drift away from representation, but neither a wild, arbitrary move nor a teleological progression along a chain of hierarchically organised transformations (as Patton points out in commenting on Massumi's interpretation of becoming, see Patton, 2000, p. 82). Becoming, for Deleuze and Guattari, starts 'from the forms one has, the subject one is, the organs one has, or the functions one fulfils' (Deleuze and Guattari, 1987, p. 272).

This ceaseless process of diversification and transformation neither fabricates an infinite series of differences nor has a predefined end. Becoming has no fixed telos – but Deleuze and Guattari are no 'difference engineers' (Ansell-Pearson, 1997). They are meticulous manufacturers of unity, a unity without subjects. There is no 'final analysis' in this unity! Differences, individuations, modalities are only the starting point; they are the building materials of the world. So, interestingly enough, the end of all becomings is not the proliferation of difference, it is its elevation into a process of becoming everyone. It is a process which creates a unity of multiple singularities. Becoming indiscernible, impersonal, imperceptible occurs when 'one has suppressed in oneself everything that prevents [one] from slipping between things and growing in the midst of things' (Deleuze and Guattari, 1987, p. 280).

Becoming everyone occurs anew in each moment, in every place. Becoming everyone is a universal strategy because it prevents a certain form of becoming from being held up as a universally acclaimed endpoint. Becoming everyone is a move based on respect and care of the worlds we are creating when we leave behind marked and secure social positions and selves; the everyday politics of escape is based on these modes of constructing new imperceptible sociabilities. In this sense, becoming everyone is becoming imperceptible because it is a move of dis-identification, a decisive move leading outside of the subject-form, as we described it earlier in Chapter 5, towards the construction of new bodies and relations.

Becoming everybody/everything is to world, to make a world. ... It is by conjugating, by continuing with other lines, other pieces, that one makes a world that can overlay the first one, like a transparency. Animal elegance, the camouflage fish, the clandestine: this fish is crisscrossed by abstract lines that resemble nothing, that do not even follow its organic divisions; but thus disorganised, disarticulated, it worlds with the lines of a rock, sand, and plants, becoming imperceptible. (Deleuze and Guattari, 1987, p. 280)

Imperceptible politics is based on a continuous process of leaving behind all those forms of representation which constrain the connections between people and attempt to condense them into the next policing node of postliberal aggregates of control. This takes us beyond our current predicament of resistance, to work with modes of subversion which are already unfolding without announcing themselves.

PART II

A CONTEMPORARY
ITINERARY OF ESCAPE

Section III
LIFE AND EXPERIENCE

7 THE LIFE/CULTURE SYSTEM

The Historical Emergence of the Regime of Life Control

In the *Birth of the Tragedy* Nietzsche captures the core of what was broadly conceived as the most liberating feeling against the darkness of the years around the turn of the twentieth century: a cheerful and resolute affirmation of life. Of course from the perspective of a century's end, things always look nastier than they really are. The promise of a better century to come is a major relief when contemplating the weighty number 100. Promises ease feelings and channel your attention to the future, away from the past 100 years of ineffectiveness. A promise always has an object: revolutions, revelations, innovations, inventions, expansions, occupations, discoveries. What Nietzsche has done is to disconnect the idea of promise from a particular object. Life itself is the promise. 'Ich will dich: du bist werth erkannt zu werden' ('I desire you: you are worth knowing'), Nietzsche invites us to say to life (Nietzsche, 1999, p. 115). This disconnect is so sudden, unexpected, stupendous. But Nietzsche lies more than 100 years ago; he is part of the last century and the one before that and we know from the perspective of an ending century that things always look nasty.

Nietzsche's investment in life itself is distinguished by the way it devalues any promise that appeals to an outside of the present world: promises are enchanting and captivating not because of their reference to a possibility beyond, but because of their worldliness. But what is really extraordinary in Nietzsche's thought is that it rehabilitates banality, or better that it elevates banality to something astonishingly superhuman: life is the solution for the problem of life. The exodus from the lived life is to be found in life itself. Pure banality in the form of sublime heroism. With Nietzsche you always return to where you are. This is immanence. With Nietzsche, if you act correctly in life, you can joyfully affirm how your actions return life to you. It is the banality of the solution that makes it so marvellous.

The warmth elicited from this idea is what makes it so appealing: the ordinary life is not an enemy, it is the object of desire and the ultimate place to be. And even a life which is not worth living is a desirable life which can be changed. Life is the appropriation, expansion, accumulation of energies; life means overpowering life (and others), means will for ... , you already know. Activism, the will to do, is equally connected to negativity as to pleasure, to pessimism as to optimism, to beauty as to barbarity, to the sublime as to the ordinary. With Nietzsche the lived life and the logic of life come together. As Simmel says: 'Life, in its flow, is not determined by a goal but driven by a force: hence it has significance beyond beauty and ugliness' (Simmel, 1968, p. 17).

What Nietzsche introduced with his concept of life again dominates the plane of social and political theory as the twentieth century turns to the twenty-first. The long twentieth century is the century in which the concept of life grew immensely. But what is the meaning of the concept of life? No *Oxford English Dictionary* here, no citation and juxtaposition of the etymological and canonical definition of the concept. Much more, we are interested in how the concept travels through various contexts and landscapes, how it spreads over different social biotopes. While organisms disseminate, they vary; or better, as they mutate and recombine, they disseminate. And so also our concepts, these energetic denizens of our socio-scientific worlds which order our views in their own ways. There is for example a widespread cultural imagination today that we possess the capacity to fundamentally change the conditions of our existence. This new master narrative of changing 'life itself' pertains, on the one hand, to the technoscientific objectivist optic of being capable of monitoring, controlling and transforming processes of life in their entirety. On the other hand it is germane to many critical accounts in social theory which assert that we have entered a historical phase in which there is nothing outside of agonistic efforts to change life (Agamben, 1998; Deleuze and Guattari, 1987; Rabinow, 1996; N. Rose, 2001; Virno, 2003; see also Lorey, 2006; Fraser, Kember and Lury, 2005; Greco, 2005). Both trends constitute what we call the regime of life control.

The regime of life control is the attempt to systematically manage and control the field of life; that is, human experience, the human body as a biosocial entity, and, finally, the everyday. All these three dimensions constitute the field of life as it emerged historically at the end of the nineteenth century. This section starts with a historical investigation of the emergence of the regime of life control. We focus on Germany at the turn of the 1900s, because Germany of this time resembles a unique laboratory in the Global North Atlantic socio-political space for elaborating a systematic regime of life control. We call this early form of the regime of life control the *life/culture system*: changing life is making culture, culture transpires out of the energetic flux of life, life is culture. Life is transformed in the name of life. After outlining this early attempt to establish a viable regime of life control (in Chapter 8) we move to the contemporary configuration of the regime. A hundred years after the emergence of the life/culture system, the predominant modes of controlling life today centre around disease, biotechnology and biosecurity. In the final chapter of this section we examine the role played by the regime of life control in the emergence of the new form of contemporary domination, the postliberal aggregates we described in Chapter 3. We ask: What are the existing possibilities for escaping and subverting regulation by the regime of life control? What is the imperceptible politics of escape in the field of life? But before discussing the contemporary regime of life control and its escaping forces, we want to trace the concept of life back to a moment where the first form of life control, the life/culture system, emerged.

The Concept of Life Around 1900; the New Human Synthesis; Industrialism; Expressionism Around 1910

In the first decades of the long twentieth century the notion of life became one of the most central, if not the most central, point of departure for the articulation of social, political and intellectual/ artistic claims (cf. Rasch, 1967). But the notion of life turned out to be more than simply a vehicle for the articulation of such claims: it emerged into a concept which transformed and organised central aspects of cultural imagination and political practice in Germany's first three decades of the 1900s. It is in the name of life (not of freedom, rationality, equality, nature, progress, etc.) that utopias – whether left or right – gradually arise. It is in the name of life, the untamed, uncontaminated, creative, immediate, genuine, total, vibrating, restless life, just to mention some common attributions to life of the time, that socio-political activity is performed.

Life becomes the way to liberate the people from alienation in the workplace, on the street, in public. The concept of life focuses primarily on the materiality of the individual existence. It is the source and the arrival point for any attempt to liberate the body, the movement, the gestures, the gaze, from civilisational exhaustion and to perform a new synthesis of individual and the community. The liberation of dance from the ballet form and the predominant separation between men and women as minds/choreographers and bodies/interpreters respectively initiated by Rudolf von Laban, Mary Wigman and others was intended as a means of establishing a new form of expression characterised by a new 'ethic of movement' and a new 'language of the body'. This new form of expression, sometimes called *Ausdruckstanz*, sometimes called *neuer Tanz* or *absoluter Tanz*, was meant to transgress the tyranny of the mechanical, rational, male-dominated arrangement of motion and action and to inaugurate a new utopia of the body: a 'bodysoul', in which archaic and mystic forces arising out of the 'kingdom of silence' amalgamate with the vision of a new liberated human being (cf. Schenck, 2008; and S. A. Manning, 1993; see also Banes, 1998; and more generally the beautiful work of Toepfer, 1997).

The concept of life simultaneously serves as a tool for analysing the sociocultural situation of that time and becomes a condition for imaging and organising possible alternatives to it. It becomes a source for the negation of the given and an inspiration for action. It captures the cultural imaginary. This is one of the first moves towards forging a vigorous connection between life and culture. Life enters the realm of culture. Life does not have to be explained, it is now the general *explicans*. Georg Simmel writes, around 1915:

The philosophy that exalts and glorifies life insists firmly on two things. On the one hand it rejects mechanics as a universal principle: it views mechanics as, at best, a technique in life, more likely a symptom of its decay. On the other hand it rejects the claim of ideas to a metaphysical independence and primacy. Life does not wish to be dominated by what is below it; indeed, it does not wish to be dominated at all, not even by ideas which claim for themselves a rung above it. (Simmel, 1968, p. 21)

Conjuring up life doesn't *simply* mean rejecting the instrumental rationality of the techno-industrial world, the growing rigidity of institutions and bureaucracy, the mass democratic annihilation of creativity, in favour of an interchangeable individuality. Summoning the uncontrollable powers of life challenges the new industrialism by appealing to a new form of cultural existence: collectivity. An organic, fluid collectivity, in which singularity is celebrated as the way to revive community and to build up society. The life/culture system is fascinated with the reorganisation of time and space through industrialism (cf. Kern, 2000). It is fascinated with speed, complexity and dynamism. At the same time, the concept of life attempts to reveal the limits of this situation; it attempts to dissolve the connection between rationalism and industrialism and to unveil how industrialism subjugates the creative forces of society.

Boccioni's painting *The City Rises* (1910) rehearses the struggles, turbulences, revelations of this process – the public space of the new metropolises as the battleground from which the new culture and the new human being would emerge. Monumental buildings are erected on the soil of life (Figure 12).

12.   Umberto Boccioni, *The City Rises*, 1910, oil on canvas, 199.3 × 301 cm, Museum of Modern Art, New York. Digital image © Museum of Modern Art/Scala, Florence 2008.

Urbanism is the by-product of life. Muscular horses – hybrids of evolution, the mythical Pegasus, the winged Nike of Samothrace – let civilisation blossom. Working men struggle to steer them, the deed is the result of the exuberant and inexhaustible power of life. They cannot domesticate these powers, they have to accommodate them, let their strength, greatness, physical and intellectual potencies emerge in this futurist, warlike depiction of life. And it is exactly this struggle with the power of life that can enable the new culture to emerge. The concept of life transforms during the first decade of the twentieth century into the scalpel to remove the 'carcinomas of the old society' and the means to create a new form of human existence: 'Der neue Mensch'.

I come out of this night – to go into night no more. My eyes are open never again to be closed. My blind eyes are sound – what I have witnessed I shall never forget: I have seen the New Man – This night he was born! – Why should it now be difficult – to go out of the city? Already in my ears is the rushing wave of those coming in their turn. I feel the turbulent flow of creation – about me – above and beyond me – unending! I am one with the stream of new life – in it I live on – and stride forth from today into the morrow – untiring in all things – in all things enduring. (Kaiser, 1971a, p. 130)

Georg Kaiser's most successful but highly ambivalent expression-istic plays of this time, which in the period 1917–20 alone had 17 premieres throughout Germany (Tyson, 1984, Vol. 2; Willeke, 1995), refer to a very peculiar, almost anti-humanistic, form of humanism. In the name of humanity (and of the human being, 'des Menschen'), they attempted to replace the existing human being with a new one. In a deserted life, humanity can only be rescued by humanity through its thorough regeneration. Kaiser's 'neuer Mensch', new human, in the play *Die Bürger von Calais* (quoted above), is a plea for a radical rejection of the world as a given. Only in a world of desire can the vision of a new human being appear. Expressionism calls for vigilance, because only through immense alertness can the resurrection of a new human being take place (nothing religious here: the regeneration of the human will be a secular affair, a celestial place surrounding living human flesh, apocalypse for the multitude, profane messianism). Expressionism's deep commitment to negating the given world and to envisioning a world of desire entails a push to withdraw from every act ensuing from a will to do, to withdraw from activism, to refuse to propose a way out, preferring pedantically to delineate the impossibility of the world. Impossibility is posited as the condition on which the world itself is constructed.

The concept of the new human being is the foundation of expressionist ethics and simultaneously it deconstructs any possibility for outlining the contents of these ethics (Kenworthy, 1957). Expressionist humanism is nourished by revealing how impossible are the reformation and the rebirth of the human being. But because of that, the call for human regeneration becomes more intense, pathetic, inescapable. Expressionism is precisely this: showing how impossible it is to grasp that which is unavoidable. 'Das Wort tötet das Leben' ('Words kill life') (Kaiser, 1971b, Vol. 2, p. 276; cf. also Kenworthy, 1980).

The Systematic Formulation of the Concept of Life: the Life/Culture System

Whilst the expressionist movement refused to combine critique, utopia and a hyper-energetic making of life, this combination gradually became the hallmark of a whole new movement for the regeneration of the human being. It was clear: the birth of the new human being was not simply a theoretical, or an aesthetic question. It required that the intellectual avant-garde be linked with political practice. There were certainly many intellectuals across Europe – Filippo Marinetti, Ernst Jünger, Drieu de la Rochelle, Gustave Le Bon, Gottfried Benn, Ortega y Gasset to mention a few – obsessed with the imminent apocalyptic new human synthesis (cf. Schenck, 2008). But, as we discuss below, more than a cultural or political tale of salvation, the image of the 'new human being' turned out to be a way of restructuring the everyday conditions of existence. The concept of the new human being presupposed the deep transformations taking place in social, economic and technological sectors of society in the early twentieth century (Peukert, 1987). At the same time, the new human being anticipated and prepared the ascent of new forms of socio-political organisation, forms on which fascism later thrived (Sternhell, Sznajder and Asheri, 1994).

The ideology of breeding the new human being, the rampant social antagonisms, the ongoing modernisation of society and the shaping of everyday existence – together, all these aspects were entangled in the production of a cultural matrix on which many different socio-political and intellectual movements arose. This matrix was the life/culture system: unrestricted life generates genuine, authentic, pure culture itself; the making of culture needs no other legitimisation than the promotion or at least the protection of the creativity of life. The life/culture system enabled an attack both of transcendence and of any pseudo-moralistic foundation of socio-political action, and *at the same time* it served as an unspoken explanatory principle for the malaise of the time as well as a maxim for future socio-political action. The life/culture system did not envision an improvement on current outdated forms; it was a radical redefinition of them. Simmel:

At present, we are experiencing a new phase of the old struggle – no longer a struggle of a contemporary form filled with life, against an old, lifeless one, but a struggle of life against the form as such, against the principle of form. (Simmel, 1968, p. 11)

Various utopias and ideologies of escape were grounded on this quest for reclaiming the totality of life: life is the sole source of all its contents, there is nothing outside. The life/culture system radically rejected any external foundation or legitimisation from beyond and simultaneously retained, exactly what it pretended to abolish, a complex device of mystical, utopian fantasies of liberation and action. Nietzsche in pure form.

The Basic Components of the Life/Culture System: Materiality, the Body

The project to reorganise society took place at the beginning of the long twentieth century in the name of the life/culture system. This was the case for many different social and intellectual forces, from militant communists to right-wing nationalists and fascists. From today's perspective the project to reorganise the social corpus, which Nietzsche and many other intellectuals of the time anticipated in their texts, was much more than a textual invention or a theoretical exercise. It was marked by a concern with materiality. This is what made the life/culture system so powerful and so efficient: its deep veneration for activism and for changing the material conditions of existence – the total mobilisation of human and technological resources and the celebration of the dynamism of material life. This commitment to materiality had two sides: firstly, there was faith in technological progress as a means of harnessing the changeability of human capacities; secondly there was a strong adherence to the idea that irrationality acts as a potent force lying at the heart of all technological developments and of the mastery of the body. The life/culture system was primarily characterised by the belief in irrational progress and in the mystical powers of materiality: only by this mystically driven will to do can progress take place.

Concerns with activism and materiality provoked a deep engagement with a specific notion of the body. And it is perhaps important to mention here that this idea of the body elicited a double connotation: the body of the individual and the body of a society or community. At the beginning of the twentieth century, these two meanings of the body were indissolubly combined together in cultural imagination and in socio-political practices associated with the life/culture system (Toepfer, 1997). If the process of the codification and the assemblage of a community or society as a unity, as the 'People-as-One' (Lefort, 1986, p. 297) is necessary for the constitution of a political subject (a process whose role in the consolidation of national sovereignty we have already mentioned in the first section of this book), then this process was disseminated into the reorganisation of the individual body, of *each* individual body involved. The most profound example for this is mass gymnastics (Burt, 1998) as the topos where the social and individual bodies collapse literally into each other, a topos which becomes a (socio-historical) body through the absorption, or better, cannibalisation, of individual bodies. This bodies' body was the soil on which the worship of the body's materiality, physicality, manipulation and invigoration took place between 1890 and 1940 (Segel, 1998). The turn to the body, in this dual individual–social connotation, was the path along which imagined unified communities emerge. An imagined community entailing the perception of the 'People-as-One' could only solidify through the alteration of the individual body's gestures, habits, movements, codes, everyday practices.

The Body of the Proletariat; the Worker's Body; the Workspace

The proletariat organises its body, literally: its body is organised as a subject of historical change and its body, better to say its bodies, as a living subject. Agitprop theatre (Hermand and Trommler, 1988), Erwin Piscator's theatre for the masses, left-militant dance (Weidt, 1968), collective performances (Toepfer, 1997), *Arbeitersport* (worker's sport) (Guttsman, 1990) are ways in which the body of the intended historical subject (the emerging proletariat as promise for social change) always and inescapably passes through the reorganisation of the singular living body. Compare for example a very popular book of the time in left-wing circles, *Der Staat ohne Arbeitslose: Drei Jahre 'Fünfjahresplan'* (*The State Without Unemployed People: Three Years into the 'Five Year Plan'*) (Glaeser, Weiskopf and Kurella, 1931), in which the representations of the worker's body (as the carrier of the will to change everyday life), the body of the proletariat (as the unified historical subject of action) and the national body of the Soviet Union (as the image of the desired condition to come) converge on each other and fabricate an image of the proletariat as the 'People-as-One' – a unity over time extending from the here and now of everyday life to life as possibility, to the 'life hereafter'.

Through such modes of mobilising the individual and social body, the primary configurations of the life/culture system gradually connected with interests in the artistic realm before and during the Weimar republic. This specific idea of the body circulated in music, film, theatre, architecture and, finally, into public life, and was expressed in the revolt against the Wilhelminian order after the First World War. As they disseminated, the logics of the life/culture system gave birth to the multiple avant-garde traditions of the 1920s (Willett, 1978). This is the backdrop against which the proletarian *Gegenöffentlichkeit* (counter-culture and public intervention) gradually emerged (Guttsman, 1990); organisations for workers' culture (e.g. Interessengemeinschaft für Arbeiterkultur), the workers' theatre association (Arbeiter-Theater-Bund), the mass choirs and the workers' singers association (Arbeiter-Sängerbund), the workers' radio club (Arbeiter-Radio-Klub), left youth and sports organisations and camps, people's theatre stages (Volksbühnen), the Marxist Workers' School (MASCH), the association of the proletarian–revolutionary writers and a series of new newspapers and magazines (e.g. Bund Proletarisch-Revolutionärer Schriftsteller or Arbeiter-Illustrierte-Zeitung, Linkskurve, etc.).

Oskar Nerlinger, a painter who among many other left intellectuals and artists of the time understood his work as a contribution to social transformation, made *An die Arbeit* (*Going to Work*) in 1929 (Figure 13). It is an apposite reaction to the cultural and social conditions of the Weimar republic, i.e. to the illusion that technological progress will change the conditions of labour, the mechanical and sterile existence in the workplace, the utilitarianism of the economy, and the growing unemployment. The painting attacks the prevalent subjects of the 'Neue Sachlichkeit' (New Objectivity) movement by reintroducing a radical critique of the social oppression and the alienation of labour represented as the subordination and disciplini-sation of the worker's body through the architectural constellation of the industrial space. On a figurative level it inadvertently and disturbingly anticipates the mass extinctions in the concentration camps in the name of labour.

At first glance, Nerlinger's *Straßen der Arbeit* (*The Streets of Work*) (1930; Figure 14) recalls *An die Arbeit*. We find a similarly solemn representation of an effective socio-technical environment which through the structural condensation of temporal and spatial order upholds the promise of technology. But they are not the same. The arrangement of lines in *An die Arbeit* reveals a closed spatial location. In contrast, the lines of *Straßen der Arbeit* seem to be timelines: they traverse the different planes of the human–machine landscapes and lead to something new, some kind of promise. Whilst the 1929

13.   Oskar Nerlinger, *An die Arbeit* (*Going to Work*), 1929, Tempera und Kasein auf Leinwand, 121 × 81 cm, Stiftung Moritzburg, Kunstmuseum des Landes Sachsen-Anhalt, Halle. © S. Nerlinger, Berlin. Printed with permission of Stiftung Moritzburg, Halle.

14.   Oskar Nerlinger, *Die Straßen der Arbeit* (*The Streets of Work*), 1930, Tempera auf Pappe, 79.5 × 159 cm, Stiftung Stadtmuseum Berlin. Reproduction: Stadtmuseum Berlin, Christel Lehman. © S. Nerlinger, Berlin. Printed with permission.

painting seems to be closed and folded into itself – evoking the enslavement of life – the later work appears to be captured by the centrifugal force of unfolding life. What we see in the second painting is that life itself is the promise.

The Body of the Nation; the Life of the Nation; Fascism

At the same time, many intellectuals were appealing to the German people, *das deutsche Volk*, for an opposition to the 'enslavement of life' (Krannhals, 1928, p. 223) that is evoked and implicitly critiqued in Nerlinger's paintings. The concept of life exerts here a similar influence in a very different body: the body of the nation. In a peculiar manner, the same utopian liberation of life simultaneously activates these two different social bodies, the proletarian and the national, and culminates in the eruptive polarisation between communist and national socialist movements after 1929. This polarisation was not only a political opposition but a deep sociocultural one:

'Modernity' was not the only factor on the cultural scene [during the Weimar republic]; the new art was by no means universally popular and accepted, traditional directions and forms were influential, and modernism was opposed by strong trends of pessimism and anti-modernism. Thus German culture at the time of the Weimar republic was a deeply divided culture – we may even say that there were two cultures which had scarcely anything to say to each other and were mutually alien and hostile, each denying (though with very different degrees of justification) that the other was a culture at all. (Kolb, 1988)

But the chasm between modernism/avant-garde and conservatism/ traditionalism that nourished the contradictory movements in the first decades of the long century of life destabilises neither the centrality of the utopia of the new human being nor the matrix of the life/culture system in the sociocultural imagination of the time. In fact, at this point, the life/culture system was the basic platform for the articulation of most major political movements' social claims.

In the first decades of the 1900s, the concept of life was taken up in philosophical and psychological thinking and provided fertile ground for the proliferation and the later metamorphosis of conservative ideologies into the fascist project. For example, in his book *Der Geist als Widersacher der Seele* (*The Mind as the Adversary of the Soul*) (1964, Vols 1–2; see also other shorter texts in Vol. 3), Ludwig Klages offers a psychological theory of the subject, which follows the paramount 'principle of life' (1964, Vol. 3, p. 43). Whilst the primordial condition of human being is the unity of human being and life, of soul and flesh and nature, Klages argues that this biocentric principle is threatened by the then contemporary logocentric and technocentric civilisation (cf. especially Klages, 1964, Vol. 3). Instead of mind being dependent on life, life lapses into being dependent on and inferior to mind. Klages advocates an image of the person in which the principle of life, the care of life, and the principle of will, the key feature of life, regain supremacy over the techniques of thinking and over rationalism (1964, Vol. 1). Life opposes here 'the decline of the soul' (1964, Vol. 3, p. 623).

Oswald Spengler in *The Decline of the West* approaches the same issue not from the perspective of subjective experience but from the perspective of a collective (of course, this means nationalist) history:

A power can be overthrown only by another power, not by a principle, and no power that can confront money is left but this one. Money is overthrown and abolished only by blood. Life is alpha and omega, the cosmic flow in microcosmic form. It is the fact of facts within the world-as-history. Before the irresistible rhythm of the generation-sequence, everything built up by the waking-consciousness in its intellectual world vanishes at the last. Ever in History it is life and life only – race-quality, the triumph of the will-to-power – and not the victory of truths, discoveries, or money that signifies. World history is a world court, and it has ever decided in favour of the stronger, fuller, and more self-assured life – decreed to it, namely, the right to exist, regardless of whether its right would hold before tribunal of waking-consciousness. Always it has sacrificed truth and justice to might and race, and passed doom of death upon men and peoples in whom truth was more than deeds, and justice than power. And so the drama of a high culture – that wondrous world of deities, arts, thoughts, battles, cities – closes with the return of the pristine facts of the blood eternal that is one and the same as the ever-circling flow. (Spengler, 1928, p. 506)

The same matrix of the life/culture system that we encountered earlier in looking at the organisation of the proletarian body emerges here, but with a different signification, a reactionary resentment that gradually gained power. This reactionary resentment is dominated by a similar concern with materiality – a concern that recurs again and again, forming a basic pattern of the life/culture system; here, the investment in materiality takes the form of a conservative traditional-ism which is linked with the denial of republicanism and liberalism, the revival of national consciousness and blood ideology, and the apotheosis of vitalism. We see again how the imagined community of the 'People-as-One' – which presupposes 'the oneness of things' and 'that men cannot be considered in fragments but only as one and indivisible' (Gentile, 1934, in Lyttelton, 1973, p. 301) – will contribute to establishing the dominance of national sovereignty and subsequently a widespread form of 'paranoid nationalism' (Hage, 2003).

Further Components of the Life/Culture System: Vitalism, Activism, Violence

Gentile: 'So we have established the first point in defining fascism: the totalitarian nature of its doctrine which is concerned not only with the political order and management of a nation but with its will, thought and feelings' (Gentile, 1934, in Lyttelton, 1973, p. 302). It is important here to clarify that the totalitarian moment in fascist ideology is the intention to change every aspect of society, to penetrate society in its entirety, to change life itself. Totality is a metonym for life in the fascist configuration of the life/culture system. Activism and vitalism are absolutely indispensable because they mobilise even the most remote parts of society, they infiltrate each single aspect of life. Now is perhaps the moment to say that it was on the issue of activism that fascism went far beyond expressionism and replaced the pessimist, visionary aesthetics of expressionism with a populist social tool for intervening in everyday life. Instead of expressionism's fetishisation of negation, fascism celebrated the will to do.

Anti-republicanism, vitalism, nationalism gradually transform into the basic ingredients of the ascending fascist ideology. During the first two decades of the twentieth century, fascism invented its historical subject (nation), its enemy (liberalism) and its organisational principle (activism). But fascism struggled to find a political strategy – how to ground the will to do and on which principles to found a doctrine of political practice remained open questions. These questions were resolved with the idolisation of violence and war. Of course violence does not appear at first sight as a political strategy, but in fascist ideology it gradually transforms into the means and ends of political action.

Marinetti and the Italian futurists (Boccioni among them; see the discussion above of his painting *The City Rises*) made enormous contributions to positioning war as a necessary element for sustaining the life/culture system through their aestheticisation of violence. Marinetti and many other futurists vehemently supported Italy's entry into the First World War:

The present war is the most beautiful Futurist poem which has so far been seen; what Futurism signified was precisely the irruption of war into art ... The War will sweep from power all her foes: diplomats, professors, philosophers, archae-ologists, critics, cultural obsession, Greek, Latin, history, senilism, museums, libraries, the tourist industry. The War will promote gymnastics, sport, practical schools of agriculture, business, industrialists. The war will rejuvenate Italy, will enrich her with men of action, will force her to live no longer off the past, off ruins and the mild climate, but off her own national forces. (Marinetti, 1914, in R. Griffin, 1995, p. 26)

In the futurist aestheticisation of violence, the myth of the new human synthesis was not so much a serious political target – it did not provide visionary features and demand that they be achieved; rather this myth was employed as an instrument for changing the immediate practices and language of politics towards a nationalist ideology which glorifies the use of violence (see Marinetti, 1913, in Apollonio, 1973; cf. also Aragno, 1980; Mosse, 1980). But the struggle for the New had, once again, unprecedented and ironic consequences: Boccioni enlisted in the Battalion of Cyclist Volunteers in July 1915 and some months later he was discharged and went back to Milan, but in July 1916 he returned to military service in an artillery regiment. On 17 August 1916 he suffered a fate that was certainly unheroic: he accidentally fell from his horse in Sorte, near Verona, and died the next day (Hulten, 1986).

War becomes a core element of the life/culture system; it is an internal feature of life, an anthropological constant, which remains 'unchangeable through all time and changes only in its forms and means' (Hitler, 1945, in Mann, 1958). Of course the coalescence of fascism and futurism and the aestheticisation and banalisation of violence are only part of the story of fascism's ascendance to power (De Grand, 2000; Lyttelton, 1991). But here we are particularly interested in the configurations of the life/culture system and the cultural/ideological phenomenology of fascism at the beginning of the long century of life. Because we can say – with Gramsci and Poulantzas (see Poulantzas, 1974) amongst others – that the crisis of hegemony which preceded the fascist seizure of power was not only a socio-economic one but also a crisis of political organisation and first and foremost an ideological crisis. New forms of cultural imagination, such as the palimpsest of the new human being, the vitalism of life, the mystical figure of an organic and pure collectivity and the glorification of violence and activism, these vehicles effectively questioned the existing dominant ideologies in crisis, neutralised their cultural significations and, as we discuss below, put new forms of sociocultural existence to work in everyday life.

In his insightful study of the genesis of fascist ideology, Sternhell describes the development of the theoretical resources of the fascist ideology from the 1880s onwards (Sternhell, Sznajder and Asheri, 1994). He argues that a crucial element of the formation of the fascist ideology was the abolition of an idea of violence as a mere tool for achieving political goals and the elevation of violence to a value in itself. Georges Sorel was a key figure in undertaking this task, in his transformations from a radical left-activist to an intellectual whose work was adopted as proto-fascist. Sorel established a new vision of militant political action – revolutionary syndicalism – based on a revision of Marxism and the rejection of its rational analysis of socio-economic relations. Here Sorel seems to be drawing heavily on Bergson's critique of progressivism and teleological thinking and his turn to the explosive creativity of unpredictable novelty and change. Furthermore, Sorel's militant programme is based on a radical critique of the decadence of the political, intellectual and moral order of bourgeois liberal society, and, finally, on the attempt to incorporate (independently of Bergsonian philosophy) James' pragmatism into his scheme of revolutionary myths (Sternhell, Sznajder and Asheri, 1994; see also Meisel, 1951; Curtis, 1959; Stanley, 1976). The only thing which Sorel kept almost entirely from Marxism was the idea of class struggle,

for it is only through struggle and action that the proletariats can achieve their goals. But what are the goals? Sorel has largely eliminated economic justice from his desired condition; remaining are those Proudhonian warlike virtues whose sublime qualities make the proletariat ripe for transforming European civilization into a civilization fit for heroes. (Stanley, 1976, p. 39)

In his 1906/1908 text *Reflections on Violence* Sorel proposes a logic of political action which resembles a condition of everlasting revolt and permanent violence (Sorel, 1915). But why do the ideas of activism and of violence become so central to the constellation of the life/culture system in its fascist version? Pure violence is not a tool of negation, destruction or change, as one might think at first sight. Pure violence has the opposite effect to dissolution: it tightens up all available resources, it energises the less active parts of a society, it stimulates and motivates, creates revolutionary myths, achieves unity of the social corpus; finally, it changes the totality of life, of the nation.

Violence as the Vehicle for Restructuring the Totality of Life

Fascism cannot be classified simply in terms of its position on the left–right spectrum (Sternhell, Sznajder and Asheri, 1994; Sternhell, 1986). Fascism is multidimensional, a new synthesis which merged ultra-right nationalism, ultra-left militant socialism and syndicalism, the rigorous rejection of liberalism (in both its liberal-democratic and social-democratic versions) and finally some mystical concepts of an organic collectivity involved in attempts to change the totality of life by direct action and violence.

In the period immediately after the first world war [and] ... preceding the second, the fascists clearly felt they were proclaiming the dawn of a new era, a 'fascist century' (Mussolini), a 'new civilization' (Oswald Mosley). And indeed, from its earliest beginnings, fascism presented itself as being nothing less than a counter-civilization, defining itself as a revolution of man, a 'total revolution,' a 'spiritual revolution,' a 'revolution of morals,' a 'revolution of souls.' For its ideologists, fascism – to use Valois's expression – was fundamentally a conception of life, a total conception of national, political, economic and social life. 'Total' was a word of which all fascist writers were extremely fond, and it was one of the key terms in their vocabulary: fascism was to be the first political system to call itself totalitarian, precisely because it encompassed the whole range of human activity. It was totalitarian because it represented a way of life, because it would penetrate every sector of social and intellectual activity, because it meant to create a new type of society and a new type of man. (Sternhell, 1991, p. 337)

The constant evocation of violence in fascist ideology represents the quest for the formation of a subject of history capable of thoroughly changing society and life's wholeness, its totality, as Sternhell says. Violence creates a social body; and it does that through the modification of each individual body participating in it. The emergence of the body as the main target of the sociocultural mechanics of fascism and the commitment to altering materiality in everyday life are coexistent with (and the means of) the attempt to transfigure the nation to a 'People-as-One' (Figure 15).

15.   *Wir gehoeren dir (We Belong to You)*, Olympiastadion, Berlin, 1939. Foto Schirner. Reprinted with permission of the Deutsches Historisches Museum.

At this point we have all the main elements contributing to the manifestation of national sovereignty, as we described it in Chapter 1. Which elements of national sovereignty become recoded in a fascist way and allow the emergence of the fascist state? What is the political significance of the (literally embodied) slogan 'We belong to you'? The target of state power is no longer the regulation of the social realm and the pacification of social conflicts, but the totality of life. State power wants to capture, secure and plan every single aspect of the life of everyone. This can only be performed by a total institution. National sovereignty transforms into the fascist state. Here is a substantial passage from Mussolini's and Gentile's (1932) key text, *Foundation and Doctrine of Fascism*:

But fascism represents the purest form of democracy if the nation is considered – as it should be – from the standpoint of quality rather than quantity. This means considering the nation as an idea, the mightiest because the most ethical, the most coherent, the truest; an idea actualizing itself in a people as the conscience and will of the few, if not of One; an idea tending to actualize itself in the conscience and the will of the mass, of the collective ethnically moulded by natural and historical conditions into a single nation that moves with a single conscience and will along a uniform line of development and spiritual formation. Not a race or a geographically delimited region but a people, perpetuating itself in history, a multitude unified by an idea and imbued with the will to live, with the will to power, with a self-consciousness and a personality.

To the degree that it is embodied in a state, this higher personality becomes a nation. It is not the nation that generates the state; ... rather, it is the state that creates the nation, granting volition and therefore real existence to a people that has become aware of its moral unity. ... The fascist state is no mere mechanical device for delimiting the sphere within which individuals may exercise their supposed rights. It represents an inwardly accepted standard and rule of conduct. A discipline of the whole person, it permeates the will no less than the intellect. It is the very principle, the soul of souls. ... Fascism in short, is not only a law giver and a founder of institutions but also an educator and a promoter of spiritual life. It aims to refashion not only the forms of life but also their content: man, his character, his faith. (Mussolini, 1932, in Schnapp, 2000, pp. 49–50)

The spiritual, anti-materialistic, anti-democratic cultural ideals of fascism developed alongside a violent culture of the body and the materiality of life (Falasca-Zamponi, 1997). And it is this activism, this will to change the body and culture and to create a cohesive social subject of action, that released the ideal of violence – creative, anti-rationalist violence, a virtue by itself. Violence as an everyday practice in the fascist seizure of the life/culture system has no other reason than the act itself. There is no other explanation for violence than that it is the accomplishment of the will.

The Life/Culture System as the Embodiment of Masculine Fantasies

In *Male Fantasies* (1987), a remarkable study about the Freikorps – paramilitary armies which came into being after the First World War with the aim of suppressing the revolutionised German proletariat – Klaus Theweleit shows that there was nothing hidden, no deeper structure in this violence than the fact that these men have simply done what they were willing to do. Violence is a matter of lust, virility, it pertains only to the subjective belief that it is necessary. Fascist violence is the liberation of desire 'in its most profound distortion: desire in the form that blood must flow' (Theweleit, 1987, p. 189):

Blood is the embodiment of the soldier's masculine desire for eruption and life, and the only thing permitted to flow within him. Blood appears repeatedly throughout fascist literature as a synonym for proper feeling. It may be substituted for almost any part of the fascist's psychic apparatus; blood is the productive force of his unconscious, the oil that pulsates through his machinized musculature, what boils when the motor runs ... The war-machine needs blood to continue functioning. ... War itself is attributed to the seething of men's blood ... (Theweleit, 1987, p. 185)

But what is particularly relevant from Theweleit's work for our discussion of the configurations of the life/culture system in fascist ideology is that the 'thirst for blood', for violence, for activism – this desire is embodied. The fascination with dynamism, materiality, the body, is *itself* an embodied phenomenon: it is a male concern, a male fantasy of excluding, suppressing and annihilating woman's body. The turn to the body in the life/culture system of the early twentieth century is a gendered one, a male body is realised through this form of investment in the body and its materiality.

In the last years of his life Boccioni made a series of sculptures devoted to introducing dynamism, plasticity, action, motion into static, immobile, moribund sculptural forms. The influence of the modernist inventions of speed, new machines, and the technological–military apparatus on Futurist and fascist art is well known (Hewitt, 1993; Kern, 2000). However, what is relevant here is not so much the reshaping of modernist aesthetics and visions of technological life to a fascist, anti-modern doctrine but that this process of transformation entails sexing the body of the new human being. The new human synthesis, this recurrent pattern of the life/culture system around 1900, was in fact the systematic production of a new *male* body. Needless to say, 'der neue Mensch', the new human being, is a new man, emerging out of the hatred and disparagement of women as the mere breeding biomachines of the nation. Women are the 'carrier of race and blood, and hence of the biological conservation of people' (Siber, 1933, in R. Griffin, 1995, p. 137) and the 'reproducers of the nation' (Caldwell, 1986). The new man emerges out of a deep contempt and 'scorn for woman' and out of the 'fight against feminism', as promulgated by Marinetti in his *Futurist Manifesto* (Marinetti, 1971, p. 42).

The Historical Failure of the Life/Culture System

Boccioni's sculpture *Unique Forms of Continuity in Space* (1913) depicts more the form of the new machine-like masculine warrior than the plasticity of the form of a human being that he tried to evoke (Figure 16).

16.   Umberto Boccioni, *Unique Forms of Continuity in Space*, 1913, bronze, 111.2 × 88.5 × 40 cm, Museum of Modern Art, New York. Digital image © Museum of Modern Art/Scala, Florence 2008.

Here is a lengthy excerpt from Maurizia Boscagli's (cf. also Kozloff, 1973, p. 192) apposite interpretation of the sculpture:

Boccioni's aesthetic program involved a dramatic redefinition of the human figure. The body, in his view, no longer maintains its anthropomorphic shape but rather becomes an agglomeration of matter in space. ... In Boccioni's theory and practice the human form is denied the stability that anchors the subject to a specific, individual body in order to privilege a drama of fusion with the surroundings. This machine-like and reified body is the visual translation of Marinetti's new man. ... By identifying with the motor, the Futurist male body goes beyond his human, organic possibilities to develop new capabilities and even new organs. ... [T]he new man is no longer an individual but a type and ... his body, replicating the different functions of the machine, is nothing more than plastic, transformable material. Human psychology, now obsolete, must be replaced with 'the lyric obsession with matter' as the Technical Manifesto of Futurism makes clear. ... [P]ropelled forward by the efficient energy of its tight muscles, [Boccioni's bronze] is an aerodynamic shape suggesting continuous movement. Individuality has been abolished from it: The head is a combination of skull, helmet (that still however retains a memory of the classical), and machine part; facial features have been erased. As mechanized matter, the Futurist man–robot must be devoid of any sign of individuality and humanity. The multiplication of man by the motor takes place through a process of synthesis, condensation, and elimination of the superfluous. To become a body without a residue, the Futurist type must divest himself of all emotions, ... and at the same time distance himself from the excessive, redundant, and useless elements of society, 'women, the sedentary, invalids, the sick and all prudent counsellors.' (Boscagli, 1996, p. 136)

In this and other sculptures of the time, Boccioni attempted to capture the dynamism of life, to break with traditional objective lines of interpretation and let the objects speak on their own. It is a magnificent idea. Boccioni and many other Futurists believed that the objects have a vitality and plasticity in themselves. They tried to escape the traditional objectivist gaze by working with forces in place of stable qualities, conflicts instead of representations: their object had 'no form in itself' but consisted of 'force lines' which 'enable us to see it as whole – it is the essential interpretation of the object, the perception of life itself' (Boccioni, 1913, in Apollonio, 1973, p. 90). Objects are located along a single plane of forces, on which the contradictions, the possibilities, the changes in their constitution take place. Nothing comes from outside, space is continuous, objects and environment fuse – 'let's split open our figures and place the environment inside them', cries Boccioni – materiality transforms under the pressure of the multiple forces extending across space. Boccioni's figures are mixtures of humans, robots, automata, animals, machines, environment. They are hybrids – indeed Boccioni's sculptures celebrate hybridity – and more than that: a hybridity which interferes with the observer. Boccioni fantasises that his sculptures are not only fluid forms of continuity *as such* but that they expand, and traverse, and cut through the actual space between sculpture and observer, through other bodies, objects, places outside of them: 'the cogs of a machine might easily appear out of the armpits of a mechanic, or the lines of a table could cut a reader's head in two, or a book with its fanned-out pages could intersect the reader's stomach', says Boccioni in his *Technical Manifesto of Futurist Sculpture* (Boccioni, 1912, in Apollonio, 1973, pp. 62–3).

With his sculptures, Boccioni rejected the taming gaze of tradition-alism; he wanted to let life itself produce – through his own hands – its appropriate forms. He saw his objects, himself, in continuity with life, 'in fact, we have life itself caught in a form which life has created in its infinite succession of events' (Boccioni, 1913, in Apollonio, 1973, p. 93). Life indeed spoke through the hands of Boccioni. But the continuity which arose crystallised in the cultural and political codes of a chauvinist, fascist and violent culture. Boccioni's hybrids were only transfigurations of masculinity, 'multiplied men' (Marinetti, 1971, p. 92). Boccioni's agonistic vision to traverse space ended up in the stupid and ruinous idolisation of violence and war; despite all its marvellous games with time and space and machines. Despite.

Boccioni's work is a metaphor for the historical establishment of a regime of life control, what we have called the life/culture system. His work invokes the will for liberation from the traditional objectivist and transcendent gaze, and is simultaneously captivated by the facticity of its own involvement in the creation of an infrastructure of death. In the beginning of the long century of life, in the time when life emerged as a way to generate society and culture, the life/culture system was inextricably entangled with a dramatic failure of a whole epoch in Global North Atlantic societies.

8 THE REGIME OF LIFE CONTROL: THE FORMATION OF EMERGENT LIFE

The Patriarchal Post-war Welfare State and Refusal in the 1960s

The Second World War saw the culmination of the life/culture system of the 1900s, and its wake brought the demise of this regime of life control as it had manifested in the realm of national sovereignty: vitalism, creativity, potential, virility, dynamism were viewed with suspicion; their historical connection to the aestheticisation of violence and warfare now appeared as an immanent quality of life itself. Attempts to privilege life as a driving force of social transfor-mation orienting us towards the future had to be defended against in the second half of the twentieth century. Just as the life/culture system had never existed in isolation, its repudiation did not occur in a vacuum. Life was disparaged as dangerous for the same reasons that it had previously been revered, that is on the grounds that it was an uncontrollable and mystical force. Instead, the state came to be valorised as an objective, accountable, manageable and governable regime of life control. This shift was effected in practices and techniques of government employed by state institutions, but, as we discuss later, it also pervaded everyday life.

In the post-war period, the public adopted a new mode of legitimising everyday political engagement. Rights, inclusion, equality, recognition; these are the interests that mobilise people and these interests seem to belong to the grand narrative of democratising social and political life against the malaise stemming from the impossibility of controlling life: 'Let's dare more democracy' was the echoing motto (and not only in Germany). The articulation of these interests fuels the development of the welfare state and the welfare state legitimises such claims. The grand narrative of democratisation and the grand apparatus of the welfare state came to replace, or better to domesticate, the uncontrollable anomaly of the politics which had been intimately connected with life in the period before the Second World War. The grand narrative of democracy evolved around the idea of protection: protecting society from itself, that is from the destructive forces of life lurking in the heart of society. The welfare state embodies the idea of protection, a patriarchal role which is fulfilled by developing more and better techniques for the management of risk.

Historically, risk has played an important role in the consolidation of nation states. Unlike an accident which is primarily considered as an individual event, risk affects populations and populations are constructed in specific ways. For example, Ewald points out that the nineteenth-century political technology of 'insurance contributes ... [to forging] a mode of association which allows [people] to *agree* on the rule of justice they will subscribe to' (1991, p. 207). Insurance against risk functions as a technology of association, constructing allegiance to and commonalities between members of an association. Importantly, when the state enters the field and guarantees the stability of social insurance it is 'equally guaranteeing ... its own existence' (Ewald, 1991, p. 209). As the state becomes the guarantor of social insurance, this protection against risk becomes a tangible and concrete means of securing the social contract.

Even as the welfare state was being solidified, and later defended, many different moments of escape in the post-war period served to question any collective faith in the promises of patriarchal protection. The 1960s illustrates these cross-cutting movements. For example, at the very same time that the notion of the welfare state was gaining some purchase in the United States (e.g. with the introduction of War on Poverty, food stamps and Medicaid) many people were investing in a world and future that was to threaten representations of Western nation states as reflecting the desires of their citizens. Certainly, Vietnam made for the United States international relations disaster with which we are so familiar now. But more than this, in the United States, the push to 'bring the troops home' resonated widely with other forms of refusal and disobedience and with the attempt to cultivate alternate forms of collectivity. In one sense, the call to 'turn on, tune in and drop out' had been made (and followed) in a multitude of counter-culture and civil disobedience movements in previous eras. This time its widespread resonances meant that counter-culture became a force of social change. As Connery (2005, p. 68) puts it, 'that these mostly marginal currents were brought into a culture industry that reached tens of millions, proclaiming an end to work on Maggie's farm and strawberry fields forever, is a victory, an inroad, not simple co-option'.

Once the population was manifesting as a collective with capacities for refusal, international relations disasters like Vietnam were no longer the main concern of Western governments: that spot was occupied by the re-emergence of mass disobedience on home soil. Democratic governments had spent two decades repudiating the celebration of life's creative potentials and channelling life into a specific mode of collectivity: an ensemble governable by democracy. They relied on the people's collective and active turn towards national government to distinguish themselves from 'totalitarian systems' (de Tocqueville, 1963). The widespread absence of this cooperation ruptured any faith that governments could bestow order and, more importantly, it enacted the knowledge that protectionism could not be enjoyed without the associated costs of exclusion. There is an escape taking place, a constituent force which pushes national sovereignty to transform itself in the effort to quell the epiphany of something which resembles a 'many-headed hydra'. In this chapter, we want to trace this force and the transformations it effected in the configuration of political organisation and sovereignty (as described in Section I). In particular we describe the new configurations for controlling life after the 1970s as we move from national sovereignty to transnational governance, and in the more recent move towards the emergence of postliberal vertical aggregates. Whilst the modes of securitisation employed by recent regimes of life control are polymorphous, there have been particularly marked developments in the alignment between health and security. The post-war period saw the intensification and proliferation of everyday practices and techniques and rationalities of governance all targeting the management of health and which, over the past two decades, have been increasingly linked to security. Hence, here we use the field of health as an entry point into exploring the new modalities, tropes and workings of the regime of life control as it emerges in its transnational and postliberal guises.

Uncontrollable Life, Permeable Bodies

HIV is many objects, has multiple significations, materialises in many different ways. When it erupted in Western gay communities in the mid 1980s, HIV initially triggered a moral panic, not over the deaths it caused, but over what it suggested about the vulnerability of the body – and of the body politic (Martin, 1990). This vulnerability was signified through a conflation of gay men with disease. HIV was a reminder to many that gay men, regardless of their actual sexual practices, subverted the masculinist fantasy of the intact body underpinning the heterosexual matrix (Crimp, 1988; Weeks, 1995) – the fantasy that masculine bodies (like the nationalist fantasy of sovereign states) are bounded and impenetrable (Irigaray, 1985b; Roberts et al., 1996). Homosexuality tweaks, no, wrenches, at a tension within the heterosexual matrix (Bersani, 1987). The acknowledged penetrability of a woman's body is not just evidence of her imagined weaknesses; it is a constant reminder of the insatiability of her desire and the possibility that – as she does not have the same finite capacity for sexual intercourse as her male partner – she may fulfil her desire by having sex with another man, other men. This anxiety troubles the masculine fantasy of sex as a form of conquering others, because it introduces the threat that, in the very act of exercising his autonomous, sovereign control over another person, a part of his body (his semen) might mix with that of another (Waldby, Kippax and Crawford, 1993). This nightmare of masculinity underpins the entrenched connection between sex workers, who 'publicise (indeed sell) the inherent aptitude of women for uninterrupted sex' (Bersani, 1987, p. 211), and disease (i.e. not only HIV: consider syphilis in the nineteenth century; see Spongberg, 1997). And of course, what has emerged is an everyday imaginary of infection in which penetrability *causes* disease (i.e., disease originates in women's bodies) and promiscuity *denotes* disease.

Homosexuality unsettles the hegemonic (but vulnerable) masculine fantasy of a bounded, intact, impermeable body. Add HIV to the picture, a disease of the immune system, and the virus appears to some as further evidence of the threat that permeable bodies pose to the health of the population, and more specifically, the threat that homosexuality poses to the body politic. The story is now familiar. In many Western countries the body's vulnerability to HIV initially unleashed widespread homophobia (Treichler, 1988). Of course, at the same time that this phallocentric fantasy of the body fuelled responses to HIV, alternative, already present imaginaries were being cultivated. Whilst phallocentric embodiment underpinned notions of sovereign, rational, autonomous subjectivity, this hegemonic fantasy's colonisation of lived embodiment was far from complete, as evidenced by the disparate experiences harnessed by feminist and queer theorists and activists (e.g. Rubin, 1984; Warner, 1999a; Grosz, 1994).

The same tension, between affirmation and defence of the bounded, impermeable body on the one hand and the problematisation of the connection between the body, individuality and sovereignty on the other, was being played out in responses to HIV in a very different arena: immunology. Emily Martin (1994) and Donna Haraway (1991a) discuss shifts in the way scientists were engaging with the immune system from the late 1960s through to the mid 1980s. Certainly, the hegemonic phallocentric notion of embodiment is there in immunology; the immune system is conceived as a hierarchical centre of command-control operations defending the body from invasion through its capacities to recognise 'outsiders'. But this 'biomedical imaginary' (Waldby, 1996) is also being disputed from *within* the discipline of immunology. There is an alternative characterisation of the immune system as an inherently conflicted network, a distributed system which no longer operates by discriminating between inside and out, self and other, protector and invader. Immunity is a self-managing relation between context and body: 'Context is a fundamental matter, not as surrounding "information", but as co-structure and co-text' (Haraway, 1991a, p. 214). Furthermore, in this biomedical characterisation, the immune system is not a system which monitors in order to protect by identifying invaders, rather its capacity to connect with the outside world hinges on its capacity to connect with *itself*: 'A radical conception of connection emerges unexpectedly at the core of the defended self' (Haraway, 1992, p. 323). The immune system is now an emergent double relation: a relation to its relation to the world. Hence, at the same time as HIV immunology was reproducing phallocentric notions of sovereign subjectivity (Waldby, 1996), alternatives were emerging from within the discipline and crystallising in the notion of an individual as a 'constrained accident' whose coherence, to the extent that it exists, is contingent (Haraway, 1991a, p. 220).

Looking back now at the field of HIV, what we can see is a series of challenges to normative notions of subjectivity, population and to processes of exclusion from the body politic. And we can see how these challenges contributed a transformation in the regime of life control that corresponds with the ascendance of a new form of political organisation since the 1970s, what we called in Section I transnational governance (of course these challenges took place in many different areas in the regime of life; we refer here to HIV as a paradigmatic event in this process). These challenges were motivated by different problems, led to different forms of intervention and were being posed on many different levels, from within immunology and science studies, from feminist and queer theory and activism and from PLWHA (People Living with HIV/AIDS) and HIV activists, such as ACT-UP. By questioning the promise that regulation can be achieved by a sovereign entity policing the borders between inside and outside, these different challenges collectively undermine promises which hinge on the controllability of life. The force that was initially suppressed in the post-war period by collective investment in protectionist thinking seems to be re-emerging – life. If the immune system becomes a figure which signifies the uncontrollability of the body (Martin, 1994), this is not because there is something unique about immunity, but simply because it moves with the times.

The Neoliberalisation of Life: Administering Populations, Managing Everyday Risk

Once the unpredictable, contingent, volatile nature of individual and collective bodies had been reintroduced into the foreground of both everyday life and political life, we see a transformation in the ways life is conceived and managed. After the 1960s and 1970s, life is not there simply to be suppressed; it increasingly becomes the matter and means of the effective management of large-scale populations. This intensification of the means to regulate life served to solidify the long emergence of risk society (Beck, 1992). The post-Second World War welfare state's interest in population health played an important role in the proliferation of practices designed to manage risk. The now familiar biopolitics of 'population security' – the components of which Foucault (1978, p. 120) traced as emerging in the eighteenth century (Pieper, 2006; Revel, 2006) – involves the identification of 'social pathologies', the calculation and distribution of risk across a collective and interventions in the form of social interventions (Collier and Lakoff, 2006). This is all done in order to suppress and contain life's uncontrollability, to transform its unpredictabilities into predictabilities. Risk becomes something to be managed, it loses all affirmative connotations as that which can lead to (or is even necessary for) positive transformation (Douglas, 1992). Risk is to be administered by predicting, calculating and 'colonising the future' (Beck, 2002, p. 40).

As this approach to managing uncertainty becomes increasingly central to population health in the post-Second World War period – a process which is intensified from the 1960s on with the transnationalisation of risk, as we show below – it travels through health, education, city planning, environmental management and beyond (Ewald, 1986). The state has a concrete, statistically assessable object – the population, an ensemble of living beings. However, although risk is deployed in the hope of securing a firm and expedient relationship between the state and its biopolitical object – the population – risk starts to turn against its own deployment. This shift is evident in the rise of surveillance medicine over the course of the twentieth century (Armstrong, 1995; Fearnley, 2006). As the medical gaze extended from the hospital to the population, so too its focus on the symptoms present in bodies expanded to include the risk factors inherent in the extra-corporeal spaces, both physical and psycho-social, in which bodies are situated. Managing risk became not so much a matter of identifying a 'fixed or necessary relationship to future' health threats as risk started to emerge, as that which 'simply opens up a space of possibility ... [and] exists in a mobile relationship with other risks, appearing and disappearing, aggregating and disaggregating, crossing spaces within and without the corporeal body' (Armstrong, 1995, p. 401). Much has already been said about one effect of this shift: risk increasingly becomes a matter of lifestyle, something to be consumed. But this neoliberalisation of risk is crucial to the second effect of risk's expansion, i.e. the transnationalisation of risk.

By the neoliberal 1980s and 1990s the responsibility for risk management was saturating everyday life and the task was all consuming. We know this individualising story – the story has been astutely told by Nikolas Rose (N. Rose, 1996a, 1996b). Individuals were enjoined to take responsibility for population health (Race, 2001; Rosengarten, 2004), for the labour market (Dean, 1995), for their youth (Kelly, 2006), for their use of drugs (Bunton, 2001) and even to take responsibility for things which were suddenly said not to exist – such as class differences (Walkerdine, Lucey and Melody, 2001; Skeggs, 1997). Life re-enters the social domain, not only as a result of the body's permeability coming to the fore, as we described earlier, but also as a way to address and to manage the everyday social realm.

The proclaimed aim of the neoliberal project is to reduce social and political life to a matter of the market (Harvey, 2005). It does this partly by rejecting the possibility of recognising the reality of what is to be governed – on the grounds that whatever that reality is, it is fundamentally uncertain, something which Hayek calls a 'spontaneous order' (Hayek, 1973, p. 35) that leads to 'unknown ends' (Hayek, 1976, p. 15). But perhaps this is not the definitive reason for the project's resounding success (despite its immense local variations, see Tickell and Peck, 2003). As Fredric Jameson points out, 'the reasons for the success of market ideology cannot be sought in the market itself' (1991, p. 266). The strength of the neoliberal project stems from the combination of post-Fordist strategies for the accumulation of capital with a transformation of social regulation which releases the government from its protectionist responsibilities for society and redistributes risk into the realm of the ordinary. The most pervasive effect of neoliberal governmentality is to proliferate into and to occupy the finest fissures of everyday life.

Governance now has to construct a non-controlled space of exchange, in which enterprising and competitive individuals participate and interact in their own interests and at their own expense, on the presumption that this mode of engagement is the most rewarding for individuals. According to this neoliberal doctrine, individuals as social agents have a stake, interest, and a possible return from their participation in this essentially uncertain space of everyday social exchanges (Buchanan, 1986; see also Burchell, 1996; Pieper and Gutiérrez Rodríguez, 2003). This form of governmentality, neoliberal governance, harnesses state politics – against which neoliberalism is only hypocritically 'allergic' – to achieve an 'artefactual' (Hindess, 1996) self-organising social regime which functions by distributing risk across the everyday.

The neoliberal break with the national sovereign mode of suppressing life is, as we have suggested in the previous paragraphs, a double project: on the one hand the post-war state intensifies a move towards the large-scale administration of populations, whilst slowly but steadily retreating from its function as a guarantor and protector of risk. On the other hand, risk is redistributed to members of society, who are expected to respond and regulate themselves when dealing with the uncertainty related to their lives – this is the subjectification of risk through technologies of individual self-regulation. This double move towards the neoliberalisation of life was taken up as the main pillar for controlling life in conditions of transnational sovereignty.

From International Life Control to the Transnationalisation of Risk

The 1986 Nobel prizewinner in economic sciences and decided opponent of the 'Keynesian episode in economics' (1998, p. 24), James Buchanan, classifies economy not only as a form of exchange, but also as politics. In so doing he introduces a fundamentally new optic on the idea of government; the politicisation of the market beyond state institutions existing within national borders (Buchanan and Tullock, 1962). Neoliberalism feeds off the challenge to the rational, contained subject of national sovereignty (evoked in the earlier discussion of immunity). Certainly, it deploys the legitimising figure of the subject as an autonomous individual capable of taking control – the notion underpinning many practices and techniques of national governance. However, if neoliberal modes of control seem to be fuelling an 'epidemic of the will' (Sedgwick, 1992), or the imperative to continually demonstrate individual control, this is precisely because neoliberalism arises as part of the response to the challenges to any notion of individual autonomy arising on multiple levels. Such challenges arise in diverse realms, ranging from the discipline of immunology (discussed above) to modes of state-governance which hinge populations and to societies which act as networks. Neoliberalism responds to the introduction of situated, porous, non-foundational entities that live and breathe uncontrollability, by *harnessing* these entities in place of sovereign agents. The fluid, networked and relational subject becomes both the object and the means of regulation.

Together, the neoliberal attack on the institutions of national sovereignty, the development of novel techniques for the administration of large-scale populations and the elaboration of non-foundational modes of self-relation, create the conditions to manage the social space of uncontrollability – a space which comes to be envisaged as a global transnational space. Regulating life on a post-national scale involves surpassing national sovereignty's rigid strategies for representing the population and risk, and creating a new system of representation. The network is the image which dominates transnational sovereignty (see Chapters 1 and 2). The challenge to state and individual sovereignty is mounted across many levels – it arises in exploding high-tech industries and imaginaries of the 1980s, in conceptions of risk proliferating in the surveillance and management of health, in everyday social relations and public imagination, in the 'free' circulation of culture and commodities.

A common problematisation arises from these countless attacks: i.e. the impossibility of reasonably presuming the nation state to be the dominant player in matters of risk management. This is sometimes discussed in terms of the nation state being weakened through processes of transnationalisation. For example, in their report on the policy implications of risk society, NATO's Parliamentary Assembly identifies tensions between national and transnational powers and 'tentatively concludes' that, although

states will remain the single, most important organising unit of political economic and security affairs over the coming decade ... governance will emerge as a major challenge ... [and] increased international dialogue, cooperation and action on an ever-lengthening list of transnational issues may prove the only way to reassert control over phenomena that might otherwise evade control. (NATO, 2005, p. 16)

This illustrates a common representation of the present, i.e. a situation in which the power of nation states is giving way to be replaced by international cooperation. In contrast, however, we suggest that the combined effect of the neoliberalisation of life and the transnationalisation of risk is leading to a *new* mode of life control – a regime which exceeds both national and transnational modes of sovereignty.

We want to illustrate how transformations in life control occur as effects of the neoliberalisation of life and of the transnationalisation of risk and its governance by returning to the field of health, and infectious diseases in particular. NATO is responding to a shift evident in the field of international health. International tracking and management of disease has a long colonial (and military) history (W. Anderson, 1996, 2002). But as the role of global health institutions intensified in the inter-war period (Bashford, 2006) and culminated in the establishment of the World Health Organisation (WHO) in 1948, there was an attempt to identify and locate risk on a transnational scale. WHO adopted methods of disease surveillance which, because they were designed to seek out pathologies in entire populations as opposed to individual bodies (this is obviously in accord with the neoliberalisation of life described above), contributed to constructing nations as 'nations of epidemics' (Fearnley, 2006). But as WHO took these techniques onto the global stage it encountered problems as to how best to envisage and manage epidemics which traversed national borders.

WHO's greatest success to date has, arguably, been the eradication of smallpox in 1978 (Tarantola, 2005b) – eradication barring samples held in laboratories. The smallpox programme was chiefly resourced and implemented by nation states; barely any resources were given by private donors and there was very little NGO involvement. Vaccination was mandatory and there were countries where people were not asked to consent, or it was simply forced on them. This success story illustrates how, in order to implement agreed programmes, international health depends on national governments' capacity and political will, one or both of which WHO found lacking in many subsequent attempts at disease management and eradication.

By 1978 a new approach to global public health came to the fore. The primary healthcare movement brought the emphasis away from programmes which focused on a single disease and back to the problem of developing broad-based (and community integrated) healthcare. This shift is manifested in the Declaration of Alma-Ata which defined health as 'a state of complete physical, mental and social wellbeing, and not merely the absence of disease or infirmity … a fundamental human right' (*Declaration of Alma-Ata*, 1978, p. 1). As with the rise of surveillance medicine, this effectively challenged a clinical, disease-focused healthcare delivery model – in this case through the introduction of an integrated, 'holistic' approach.

Nation states were certainly envisaged as being crucial to primary healthcare in Alma-Ata, but additional actors were introduced to ensure a networked system, to build the capacity of nodes in the network, to give due emphasis to prevention and health promotion and to represent the people. Now, healthcare

involves, in addition to the health sector, all related sectors and aspects of national and community development, in particular agriculture, animal husbandry, food, industry, education, housing, public works, communications and other sectors; and demands the coordinated efforts of all those sectors; [and] requires and promotes maximum community and individual self-reliance and participation in the planning, organization, operation and control of primary health care, making fullest use of local, national and other available resources; and to this end develops through appropriate education the ability of communities to participate. (*Declaration of Alma-Ata*, 1978, p. 2)

Alma-Ata set out to achieve an 'acceptable level of health for all the people of the world by the year 2000 ... through a fuller and better use of the world's resources, a considerable part of which is now spent on armaments and military conflicts' (*Declaration of Alma-Ata*, 1978, p. 3). The declaration's positive, holistic notion of health amplifies and diversifies risk and then distributes the responsibility across national and transnational networks of actors whose success hinges on their capacity to connect and cooperate. Whilst the techniques it invoked have been elaborated and widely deployed in the field of health, three decades later it is patently clear that Alma-Ata's set goal has not been achieved. Moreover, the neoliberalisation of life and the transnationalisation of risk which constitutes the regime of life control in conditions of transnational governance do not seem to be capable of addressing the power structures which are emerging and solidifying in global health. The political problem of health inequalities is ever present and at the turn of the twenty-first century, following the interventions of the International Monetary Fund and the World Bank into the budgets that countries of the South can allocate to health, the health status of populations of the South is considerably worse than in previous decades (People's Health Movement, 2000; WHO, 1998; Braveman and Tarimbo, 2002; Navarro and Shi, 2001).

The Pitfalls of Life's Neoliberalisation in Conditions of Transnational Governance

Approaches to health inequalities have shifted rapidly in the past two decades. The long-evident limitations of health efforts which rely on international agreements and cooperation are even more glaringly obvious now, in the light of a welcome influx of funds from non-state donors. Global funds are now some of the wealthiest entities in the field of health. For instance, by the end of 2007, the Bill and Melinda Gates Foundation had an asset trust endowment of $US 37.6 billion and had spent $US 8.5 billion on global health (with another $US 5.9 billion on global development and education initiatives in the United States). Their annual spending on global health is on a par with WHO's annual budget. Since 2001, another global entity, the Global

Fund to Fight AIDS, Tuberculosis and Malaria, has spent more than $US 10 billion, money donated by (more than 60) nations, as well as 'corporate partners', such as American Express, Apple, Carphone Warehouse, Converse, GAP, Giorgio Armani, Motorola Inc., O2, Orange UK, Tesco Mobile and Yahoo!. What is important here is that these global funds are marked, not only by the involvement of private entities as donors, but also by their willingness to give large grants to bodies which may not include any state actors at all. They are in a strong position to decide what health problems to address and how – and to draw expertise away from state ministries of health and into their own employment (Asante and Zwi, 2007). Whilst real advances in global health can be achieved with this massive influx of funds, there are also concerns that the process serves to further distance governments of countries of the South from important decisions and processes of health service delivery to their populations (Tarantola, 2005a; Garrett, 2007).

As global funds have been spending billions, WHO has been trying to strengthen its own capacities to harness the cooperation of its member states by developing the new International Health Regulations (IHR), implemented in 2007. These regulations consist of a legal framework to 'ensure international health security without unnecessary interference in international traffic and trade' (WHO, 2007a). Member states sign on to reporting and trying to stop international health emergencies (thus going beyond the designated diseases of cholera, plague, yellow fever and smallpox of the 1969 agreement that the IHR replaces), not only at national borders, but at their source. WHO discusses compliance in the following terms:

Although the IHR (2005) do not include an enforcement mechanism *per se* for States which fail to comply with its provisions, the potential consequences of non-compliance are themselves a powerful compliance tool. Perhaps the best incentives for compliance are 'peer pressure' and public knowledge. With today's electronic media, nothing can be hidden for very long. States do not want to be isolated. The consequences of non-compliance may include a tarnished international image, increased morbidity/mortality of affected populations, unilateral travel and trade restrictions, economic and social disruption and public outrage. Working together and with WHO to control a public health event and to accurately communicate how the problem is being addressed helps to protect against unjustified measures being adopted unilaterally by other States. (WHO, 2007a)

Clearly, although the new IHR is an international law, it does not carry much weight in and of itself. It is still articulated within the limitations of WHO's reliance on the cooperation and political will of its member states. Of course, there are good reasons to offer cooperation. It is arguably the case that Western governments are showing more interest in promoting global health now than ever before. This shift is occurring partly in response to nation states' increasing realisation that 'in the context of infectious diseases, there is nowhere in the world from which we are remote and no one from whom we are disconnected' (Institute of Medicine, 1992, p. v). That is, echoing WHO's rewriting of the IHR, Western nations translate the impossibility of stopping disease at national borders into the imperative to invest in trying to curtail disease before it arrives at the border. So nation states are active players in the intensification of the networked response to health management which is anchored in Alma-Ata – but not only through their support of WHO's IHR. Rather, WHO becomes just one of the players with which states collaborate. For instance, the United States Department of Defense–Global Emerging Infections Surveillance and Response System (DoD–GEIS) is leading the global response as it collaborates with military epidemiology units around the globe and at home, with NASA, the Centres for Disease Control and university based researchers as well as with WHO (Chretien, 2006a, 2006b, 2007). As competition for control of the networked response intensifies, we see a shift occurring in global health – a move beyond what we have called the transnationalisation of risk and towards a new regime of life control. We describe below the development of the *formation of emergent life*, which lies, as we shall argue, at the heart of postliberal polity and the verticalisation of power.

Vertical Control of Life's Circulation: the Case of Pandemic Influenza

It has been noted that global health is increasingly a market affair undertaken so as to ensure the circulation of commodities, medical products, technoscience and information (N. King, 2002). The beginning of 2007 saw a number of entangled developments regarding the potential market for a vaccine still in development for an influenza pandemic; problems arose around the 'free circulation' of virus samples necessary for the development of the vaccine. Interest in the future problem of an influenza pandemic has intensified since the emergence of H5N1 in birds in 1997. H5N1 is commonly discussed in the light of its potential to recombine with an existing human influenza virus and trigger an influenza pandemic in humans. Whilst it largely affects birds, by the end of December 2007 335 human cases of H5N1 had been reported to WHO, resulting in 206 deaths, the worst-affected countries being Indonesia (113 cases and 91 human deaths) and Vietnam (100 cases and 46 deaths). The prospect of pandemic influenza in humans has come to be seen as an increasing threat to global health, and WHO designates the current global situation as one of 'pandemic alert' (which lies between 'inter-pandemic phase' and 'pandemic'). For the past five years, WHO has been intensely involved in trying to identify ways to build capacity and strengthen early-warning systems, as called for by DoD–GEIS. This work includes developing guidelines on the use of vaccines and antivirals, supporting the development of preparedness plans worldwide and circulating virus samples used in vaccine research and production.

For those involved in the development and distribution of a vaccine for pandemic influenza there are a number of challenges – chief among them is the fact that their 'target' virus does not exist as yet so it is unclear exactly what the vaccine is being developed for. Moreover, whilst protecting health globally is estimated to require 6.2 billion doses of pandemic vaccine, current global production capacity means that it would be impossible to produce more than 500 million doses (Lancet, 2007). In 2004, at the height of concern that H5N1 might trigger a human influenza pandemic, WHO foresaw that in the event of such a pandemic, countries of the South would have either seriously delayed access to vaccines, or none at all (Lancet, 2007). For countries which might be able to afford access, there would be an inevitable time lag between an influenza outbreak of (or approximating) pandemic proportions and the manufacturing of a vaccine. To shorten this time lag, vaccine research development is proceeding on an 'as if' basis (i.e. 'candidate' vaccines are being developed), all of which means that pharmaceutical companies and other vaccine researchers need access to H5N1 and other influenza virus samples. WHO plays an important role through the work of its Collaborating Centres, which collect, identify and circulate virus samples. But in 2007, WHO's interest in the circulation of viruses came under powerful scrutiny.

In January 2007, days after GlaxoSmithKline applied to register a human H5N1 vaccine in Europe, the Australian-based pharmaceutical company CSL Limited announced that they had made a breakthrough in the development of a vaccine for a potential pandemic influenza. Shares soared. The event was reported as a national triumph in the Australian media. And in a way it was a national triumph. On its website, CSL advertises itself as 'a global, specialty biopharmaceutical company ... [w]ith major facilities in Australia, Germany, Switzerland and the U.S., [and] over 9000 employees operating in 27 countries'. But this is only its most recent incarnation; between 1916 and 1990, CSL had been the Commonwealth Vaccine Depot, later the Commonwealth Serum Laboratories and then the Commonwealth Serum Laboratories Commission. CSL's pandemic influenza vaccine development had been funded by \$A 7.7 million of the Common-wealth's budget (this in comparison with the \$A 6.5 million allocated to 33 separate university-based research projects in the government's special call for influenza research in 2005). The Victorian State government had contributed a further \$A 2.9 million to housing CSL, 'in recognition of how important a world-class influenza vaccine production facility is to the State of Victoria and to all Australians' (CSL Media release, 12 May 2005).

In early February, Siti Fadilah Supari, the Indonesian minister for health, made an announcement described in the Australian media as 'a highly unusual display of patriotism' (*Sydney Morning Herald*, 8 February 2007). Indonesia declared they would cease sending their virus samples to the network of WHO Collaborating Centres undertaking global influenza surveillance. The Indonesian strain of H5N1 has caused more human deaths than that found in Vietnam, and withdrawing it from Collaborating Centres would hamper their work in identifying the evolution and spread of influenza viruses, as well as in facilitating vaccine production for seasonal as well as pandemic influenza. Indonesia was in discussion with the United States-based company, Baxter, and threatened to give Baxter sole access to their virus samples in exchange for technological assistance and help in building capacity to ensure adequate domestic vaccine production. For their part, Baxter denied that they had made sole access to Indonesia's virus samples a condition for any prospective agreement. (As of the end of 2007, nothing but a memorandum of understanding had been signed.)

Although described in the media in the language of competition between nations or between transnational pharmaceutical companies, at the heart of this story lies a process of supranational verticalisa-tion in postliberal conditions (as discussed in Chapter 3). We are witnessing the forming of a vertical alignment around a transnational company from the pharmaceutical industry – an industry which is battling to retain its command as the world's most profitable line of business (in terms of return on investment) (Neroth, 2004) – the Indonesian Ministry of Health, Indonesian pharmaceutical manufacturers and scientists. Moreover, some NGOs, pharmaceutical activists and government representatives of countries of the South have been sympathetic to this strange alliance, despite the exclusion of other nations and actors from the process. The alignment between the Indonesian Ministry of Health and Baxter – more akin to an aggregate of stem cells than an open-networked system (see Chapter 3) – represents a move beyond existing global health agencies' failure to address health inequalities. Currently stalled, the continuing emergence of this process of verticalisation will result in new means of exclusion from access to vaccines. An Indonesia–Baxter monopoly might mean that fewer production plants are involved in addressing the conundrum of how to manufacture enough vaccine in a timely way and that vaccines are less affordable.

Prior to this announcement, Indonesia's struggles to contain H5N1 outbreaks in birds (culling without adequate funds for compensation is no easy matter) had been reported as evidence of the fact that Indonesia was posing a health threat to the rest of the world. So what was the rationale for squarely occupying this position of threat? Siti Fadilah Supari was clear on this point: Indonesia was objecting to WHO's role in providing influenza virus samples for commercial gain which benefited the North and not the South. She remarked that WHO 'sometimes forgets the good of the people in general and we want to change that' (quoted in Chan and de Wildt, 2007). It transpired that WHO Collaborating Centres had not been following their own guidelines (adopted in 2005) which required gaining the consent of donor countries prior to passing on vaccine samples (Chan and de Wildt, 2007). Whilst Collaborating Centres had neglected to enter into Material Transfer Agreements with donor countries of the South, they had not shown the same oversight when it came to their dealings with vaccine manufacturers, and patents had now been obtained for some influenza viruses (Khor, 2007). After freely providing virus samples to WHO, Indonesia had been asked (by a British institution) to sign a Material Transfer Agreement – despite the fact that the British Department of Health holds that countries which have provided samples for sequencing should have free access to those samples (TWN Info Service, 2007). WHO's assistant director-general, communicable diseases, David Heymann, tried to explain to a forum at the 2007 World Health Assembly that the organisation had replaced its own guidelines with a 'best-practice document' in late 2006; the new 'best practice' suggested that donor countries should make samples freely available and that WHO did not need to enter into any agreement about their use (Khor, 2007). However, this explanation quickly manifested itself as back-pedalling when it was reported, in the same forum, that the 'old' guideline document had been on the WHO website just two weeks before the May Assembly, i.e. WHO had the old document on their website many months *after* they had passed on virus samples without first gaining the consent of donors (Khor, 2007).

Throughout 2007, WHO convened a series of meetings in Jakarta (March), Geneva (April), at the World Health Assembly (May), and again in Geneva (November) at which Indonesia and some countries of the South repeated the demand that vaccine development be organised less by commercial gain and more by the need for equitable practices (Tangcharoensathien, 2007; Lawrence, 1956). After the March meeting in Jakarta, Indonesia agreed to come back into the fold of virus circulation and WHO agreed to review its laboratories' terms of reference so as to clearly outline procedures for virus sharing. WHO also committed itself to mobilising funding for a global stockpile and to developing equitable guidelines for its distribution (WHO, 2007b). The April meeting involved 15 pharmaceutical companies (including Baxter) as key players and further established the value and feasibility of a vaccine stockpile (WHO, 2007c). The challenge of H5N1 was serving to intensify the relationship between WHO and the pharmaceutical industry, as well as providing a trigger for WHO's own internal organisation. In May, resolution WHA60.28 was passed at the World Health Assembly urging the director-general to ensure mechanisms for the 'fair and equitable sharing of benefits' from influenza virus research (World Health Assembly, 2007). It was agreed that the terms of reference for Collaborating Centres would be amended so as to ensure 'application of the same standards and conditions to all transactions' and that any use of samples beyond the terms of reference would necessitate the agreement of the donor laboratories. Indonesia then pointed towards the ambiguous role of institutions *other* than the WHO Collaborating Centres in WHO's Global Influenza Surveillance Network, institutions such as government, military and private laboratories. Indonesia began asking questions about whether WHO's Collaborating Centres undertook the work of turning original samples into 'seed viruses' ready for commercial use, or whether this was being done by networked laboratories which would *not* be covered by the proposed changes. Although WHO has committed to reworking the terms of reference for its Collaborating Centres and for the sharing of virus samples, no agreement had been arrived at at the time of writing (December 2007).

If WHO does institute more equitable processes for virus sharing, questions remain as to the reach and effectiveness these processes can have in regards to the extensive network of collaborators involved in the Global Influenza Surveillance Network – pharmaceutical companies, health and military departments of national governments, and research laboratories. Neither World Health Assembly resolutions nor any WHO future terms of reference are legally binding, and it remains to be seen whether they will have any force. Their real strength will only be gauged in situations in which a national laboratory, a private pharmaceutical company and/or WHO Collaborating Centres find themselves in a position to profit from a virus sample which is in worldwide demand. That is, only in the actual event of a pandemic (or something approximating one) will we know whether 'free circulation' controlled by WHO and its collaborators or an alliance of the kind invoked by the Indonesia–Baxter aggregate will actually dominate.

However, we can see something of the effects to date of Indonesia's efforts to challenge the ways in which countries of the South have been excluded from the full benefits of entrenched international virus-sharing practices. By invoking the move beyond a transnational approach to risk, Indonesia has suggested a potentially productive means of refusing the inequities of international health agreements and alliances. The threat to opt out of international virus sharing has served to strengthen demands for health equity on the part of the South. Whilst continuing to insist on the importance of sharing viruses, WHO is currently being forced to reconsider what 'circulation' has entailed, and the expectation that laboratories of the South share their viruses free of charge whilst those in the North are able to profit from acting as middlemen in supplying samples to pharmaceutical companies. It remains to be seen whether this shift will come to be understood as triggering a series of events that ultimately strengthen international agencies such as WHO or whether it will be another piece of the story about exclusion from the emerging vertical aggregates which are coming to control life in the early twenty-first century.

Responses to the public-health problem of containing emerging infectious diseases, for example, align and segregate as they cut through sectors of (1) the pharmaceutical industry (the pharmaceutical industry has been the main recipient of Bush's Project Bioshield funding, designed to develop counter-measures to protect Americans from bioterrorism); (2) military researchers, working both domestically and in overseas postings and partnerships; (3) national governments (those who opt into the partnership approach to pandemic preparedness and those who opt out); (4) NGOs and the bodies of those who might provide precious samples of emergence itself. As transnational powers such as WHO are reinventing themselves in the battle to stay afloat, the parallel vertical alignment of actors in the field of public health signals a transformation from transnational to postliberal sovereignty.

The Regime of Life Control in Postliberal Conditions: the Formation of Emergent Life

When the head of WHO's Global Influenza programme said that '[t]he objective of pandemic preparedness can only be damage control' (*Weekend Australian*, 30 July 2005) he was not talking about the difficulties of organising an international response to this health threat, but referring to concerns about the catastrophic capacities of emergent viruses. Emergence was identified in microbiological research conducted in the 1950s and used to critique efforts to eradicate infectious disease as utopian; it suggested that war against infectious disease would inevitably be 'met with counter-resistance of all kinds' (Cooper, 2006, p. 117). But the critique did not take hold in the fields of biomedicine or public health at that time. Cooper argues that its acceptance coincides with an expansion in the notion of risk employed in financial and environmental sectors to include catastrophic risk – following which concerns about emergence re-enter biomedicine and public health. Catastrophic risk not only threatens calamity, as its name suggests, but it invokes the possibility of life being *made anew*, recombining and reassorting itself as it is destroyed. Like the catastrophic event, the specific mode of life's transformation is completely unpredictable. Hence catastrophic risk suspends us in perpetual alertness, and the ongoing rehearsal of the disastrous event. Life's emergence demands that people actively prepare for protecting themselves against a threat that arises from within, the threat of remaking from within. And, as we suggest below, the way to do this is not to avoid remaking life, but to engage in it. Moreover, the postliberal regulation of life circulates not only in public health and biomedicine, but also in biosecurity and warfare. The conduct of war is increasingly understood as a permanent affair involving vertical alliances of multiple players and the predominant use of guerrilla tactics by all actors (Cooper, 2006; Weizman, 2006), a situation which demands the pressing need to rethink what anti-war might now entail (Retort, 2005).

The contemporary spectre of pandemic influenza illustrates how notions of catastrophe and emergence are taking hold in public health. Some epidemiologists say that an influenza pandemic is likely to emerge unpredictably in the near future and to spread rapidly (e.g. Imperato, 2005). The intensity of WHO's response – particularly in terms of the time, expertise and energy invested in preparedness – seems to support such predictions. But, in the field of public health, predicting the course of infectious diseases is widely acknowledged as a nebulous affair. The United States surgeon general's claim in 1967 that 'it is time to close the book on infectious diseases' is a canonical moment of the kind which epidemiologists are cautious to avoid repeating. Add to this already blurred picture the spectre of a virus whose hosts respect no borders.

Pandemic influenza amplifies the paradox of a potentially catastrophic yet unpredictable threat to human health – and to global economic productivity (McKibbon, 2006) – and firmly locates it in the everyday. If the public appetite for the horrors of emerging infectious diseases in a globalised world was cultivated in the 1990s by writers such as Laurie Garrett (Garrett, 1994, 1996), it is now being well fed by stories about H5N1's potential for recombination and reassortment (Garrett, 2005). The work that goes into imagining emerging infectious diseases in pandemic proportions inserts a new vision into an old nightmare. There is the terrifying figure of the havoc to be wreaked by 'viral carnage': families holed up with stockpiles wondering if they will survive only to emerge to an invasion of fleeing foreigners bringing more disease and ensuring a scarcity of resources (Redlener, 2006). But the new twist in this nightmare is that the threat actually comes from within, from life. Infectious diseases are increasingly understood as emergent (Lederberg, 1996). Emerging viruses firmly insert the notion that life is an ingenious, uncontrollable threat into biomedical science and public health, but also into people's everyday existence. And this pushes at the limits of the neoliberal regime of life control, forcing it to transform itself in order better to grasp life's resurfacing in the field of health. It gives rise to a new regime of control, what we call the *formation of emergent life*. This contemporary regime of life control is emergent as it deals with life's inherent plasticity and creativity by working from *within* life, countering life with life. In this sense, the formation of emergent life has a double meaning. Firstly, it responds to formations of life which emerge as life moves and creates new unpredictable and novel configurations. Secondly, this regime of control involves developing strategies of intervention which *make* life as the regime develops new apparatuses to control life. The formation of emergent life is a means of allowing maximum control of life in highly uncertain conditions. The transcendent, transnational neoliberal regime of life control functions by seizing on life's potential and channelling it in the direction of power (Lazzarato, 2004). In contrast, the formation of emergent life functions by adopting the guerrilla tactics of an immanent player. From this immanent perspective the object of interest is not so much the population as vital systems. This shift translates into practices whose focus is on preparedness more than on risk itself.

By its very nature, emergence is hard to manage. It tests the limits of familiar public health responses which hinge on a rationality of insurance and entail strategies for transforming calculable dangers into risks which can be distributed across a collective and managed (Ewald, 1991). Because (as we described above) a rationality of insurance involves the attempt to manage how particular risks affect *populations*, the characteristics of those populations (extending at times to their situatedness) can become an important object of concern in conditions of national and transnational governance. Taking differences within and between populations as an object of inquiry can open opportunities for recognising and tackling health inequities, and it opens the terrain for arguing that biomedical interventions alone cannot suffice (Kippax and Race, 2003). Of course, in thinking about these strategies which target the population, it is still important to recognise that public health continually neglects its public; for example this neglect occurs in assuming that population statistics give an adequate representation of the public, or in overlooking questions about the importance of understanding how the public actively interprets information and develops unforeseen practices pertaining to health and illness. Notwithstanding this important critique, where public health uses these 'population-targeted' practices and rationalities, we at least find an opening for discussions about inequalities which affect the health of the population.

However, when the specific mode of life's transformation is being cast as completely unpredictable, we are witnessing the rise of practices designed to manage low probability, catastrophic, incalculable risk – strategies which ensue from what Collier and Lakoff (2006) call a 'rationality of preparedness'. In place of knowable risks, the rationality of preparedness deals with unpredictable, future events, *imagined* vulnerabilities. Public health is but one set of actors in a decentralised and distributed form of emergency preparedness which coalesces around a shared investment in being prepared. In addition to the intensification of disease surveillance, preparedness efforts privilege the coordination of 'vital systems security' with the involvement of state and non-state agencies (Lakoff, 2006; Rabinow, 2003). Vital systems include public hospitals, key governmental and non-governmental institutions (as in the market) and infrastructure such as water, electricity, communication lines and roads. Protecting them involves the development of warning systems (not only for disease but also for natural disasters and terrorist attacks) and the continuous rehearsal of readiness to respond to disasters through the networking of government and private agencies responsible for their maintenance.

Being prepared cannot be gauged by scrutinising details of the population's mortality and morbidity data, or by identifying and trying to address risk factors which render people vulnerable to disease. It is essentially an imaginary state, best established through imaginary exercises. For instance the Australian government conducted national exercises Eleusis and Cumpston in 2005 and 2006 respectively, to test and evaluate the nation's readiness for H5N1 and a human influenza pandemic. Press releases and conferences explained that there was an imperative to establish 'the effectiveness of the working relationships between federal and state governments and industry, administrative, public communications, operational communications and disease control policies' and the efficiency of 'the co-ordination between primary industry and health agencies in the advent of an outbreak' of H5N1 (*Courier Mail*, 29 November 2005); and to monitor 'interagency coordination and decision-making at the national and local level' (*Weekend Australian*, 4 November 2006). Notably, the security being offered here does not entail a direct focus on protecting a population, or even national territory. A new set of concerns take centre stage in the formation of emergent life: intra- and intergovernmental vulnerabilities, weaknesses in organisations and infrastructure. This is leading to an increasing development and deployment of public health strategies which entail fine-tuning techniques for addressing a multitude of potential emergency situations, ranging from bioterrorism through hurricanes to a pandemic. The vulnerabilities and health inequalities that affect a population are no longer of direct interest. As Lakoff puts it: 'although preparedness may emphasise saving the lives of "victims" in moments of duress, it does not consider the living conditions of human beings as members of a social collectivity' (2006, p. 272). Whilst people may have less direct purchase on rationalities and practices of preparedness, there are important ways in which this shift from population to preparedness infiltrates everyday life.

Imagining the Unimaginable; Being Enjoined to the Formation of Emergent Life

The formation of emergent life takes hold in the everyday through the reorganisation (or solidification) of social relations, processes which are not declared as such, but subtly effect the ways in which people are enjoined to this regime of control. For example, the case of pandemic influenza illustrates something of the differences between the familiar self-responsible, self-managing subject node of neoliberalism and the ways in which people are being enjoined to the verticalisation of life. A notable absence emerged in an analysis we conducted of Australian newspaper coverage (between January 2004 and January 2007) of H5N1 and pandemic influenza. Whilst we commonly think of the field of health as being thoroughly pervaded with the imperative for individuals to take responsibility for themselves, fewer than 5 per cent of the 333 stories analysed invoked the theme of individual responsibility for risk management. By comparison, each of the following themes were directly mentioned in around 20–25 per cent of the stories: Australia's pandemic preparedness; international relations; pharmaceuticals; the Australian or global economy; the broad problem of emerging infectious diseases, or zoonosis. Moreover, several of the stories which did mention self-management of risk indicated the limits of familiar imperatives in the context of pandemic influenza – for example, one story covered recipes for antiviral cinnamon muffins and anti-flu mushroom soup, and concluded with critical perspectives offered by a 'medical virologist'. The aversion to the imperative to self-manage risk is integral to the formation of emergent life, but this is not the only shift away from familiar modes of engagement with health issues.

The affects which accompany the formation of emergent life are not dominated by the sheer fear which has been identified as a contemporary mode of regulating populations (Massumi, 1993; Ahmed, 2003). Although Australians are being bombarded with the prospect of pandemic influenza – in recent years H5N1 has been one of the most intensely covered health stories in the Australian media (Chapman, 2003) – the media analysis of Australian pandemic influenza stories discussed above suggests that newspaper readers are being presented with vast amounts of uncritical reporting of the nation's preparedness prowess. This preparedness appears all the more necessary as it is presented against a backdrop of stories about the incompetencies and untrustworthiness of other governments in the region, and negative reporting of WHO's efforts to control disease transmission. People are enjoined not to demand protection, but to participate in both imagining the unimaginable and in the faith exuded by the government and uncritically reflected in media stories. A recent British study of pandemic influenza (Nerlich and Halliday, 2007) found that government figures reassuringly tended to play down the threat of H5N1 (i.e. by adopting the familiar stance of protection and defence). In contrast, the Australian Minister for Health and Aging, Tony Abbott, gave detailed warnings about the 'greatly increase[d]… chances for the avian influenza virus to swap genetic material with "normal" human flu strains and acquire the ability to spread easily between people' (*Australian*, 23 November 2005). The same minister *authored* an article outlining the threat to Australians of a pandemic. After presenting information about various predictions, including those of scientists who 'remain convinced an influenza pandemic is all but inevitable, and that the minor genetic shifts which have taken place show the H5N1 virus could change further and adapt to humans', Abbott adds weight to this position with the detail that '[a] person in Guangzhou recently contracted bird flu without any apparent contact with sick poultry' (*Sydney Morning Herald*, 5 July 2006). But Abbott has reassuring conclusions about the role that Australians are playing in the global response and 'the systems being put in place [by the government, that] will make *all future health emergencies* easier to handle' (*Sydney Morning Herald*, 5 July 2006, emphasis added). Even if a pandemic does not occur in the near future, Australians can rest assured that the nation's efforts are not being wasted on preparedness plans and exercises – we can be certain that there will be other catastrophes to confront in the future.

How the Formation of Emergent Life Works Through Everyday Recombination

If the formation of emergent life harnesses life's immanent unfolding, a second characteristic is that it works with life as recombinant. Life transforms itself by shaping and making life (S. Franklin, 2000; Haraway, 1997). This is a process of recombination: the formation of emergent life generates new combinations across all the multiple co-active levels of organisation – genetic, neural, organismic, environmental (Gottlieb, 1992) and affective, social, biological (S. Rose, 1998; Blackman and Cromby, 2007; Cromby, 2007) – and thus it transforms existence, introducing life forms which were not present before recombination. Current interest in emerging infectious disease illustrates something of these multiple levels: in the first issue of the journal *Emerging Infectious Diseases* (published by the United States Centres for Disease Control) the object of concern – viral emergence – is described 'as but one component of a dynamic and complex global ecology, which is shaped and buffeted by technologic, societal, economic, environmental and demographic changes, not to mention microbial change and adaptation' (Satcher, 1995, pp. 4–5). Processes of recombination change the very material conditions and elements of existence such that '[o]ne is not born an organism. Organisms are made; they are constructs of a world-changing kind' (Haraway, 1991a, p. 208). Consider how the resurgence of zoonosis is commonly explained as the result of recombinations triggered by the expansion of cities and the destruction of animal habitats, so that humans and animals find themselves in closer proximity. Whilst exotic animals and metropolises may seem to be poles apart, it is their intensified coalescence which explains the presence of new, shared microbiology. Our discussion of pandemic influenza, above, suggests something of how the formation of emergent life participates in processes of recombination. The current situation of unequal access to the expertise, manufacturing capacity and funds required for an effective vaccine might well shape H5N1's trajectory, as might the prospect of an Indonesia–Baxter vertical alignment and the privatisation of a virus.

However, here we want to stress that formation of emergent life does not only function by harnessing science and information technologies to change biological life (as science studies scholars might suggest, e.g. Rabinow, 1996). The formation of emergent life's control extends to a much broader domain than the liminal borders between nature and culture in technoscientific work. The recombination of life necessarily takes hold in the everyday through the reorganisation (or solidification) of social relations. Consider the family (Figure 17). Whilst much has been said about the idea that the family is under siege as an institution – morally, economically, politically – it is also evolving and expanding. And by this we do not mean that the family is a resilient institution capable of withstanding attack. Rather, this system of social relations is transforming itself.

17.   Honda Asimo Humanoid Robot (advertisement), 2002. © American Honda Motor Co., Inc. Printed with permission.

The Honda Asimo makes the perfect family portrait. They share the joke, the unexpected pleasure of the new arrival, and the smile relays between parents and children through Asimo. Not even the dog is put out; the new presence underscores the dog's friendly protectiveness. Asimo presents us with a domesticated vision of cyber-carnal recombination which affirms as it extends the heteronormative institution, celebrating the family's inclusiveness. Recombination could problematise essentialist understandings of persisting social institutions, such as the heteronormative family and its underlying assumption of kinship relatedness. But here the insertion of a foreign object seems to have the opposite effect: to shore up a heteronormative, liberal vision of the family as a bounded unit.

Reformatting Western kinship thinking is not just a question of rethinking biological links and shifting the boundaries between humans, animals and machines (Haraway, 2003; Strathern, 1992). It is a part of a broader order of social relations which also lie in the focus of the formation of emergent life control. This is the domain of the everyday. The formation of emergent life regulates life by inscribing emergent recombinant practices into people's everyday practices. The human–robot–dog articulation in the advertisement above operates on multiple levels of racial, gendered, sexualised and class-based configurations of everyday life – read in the Asimo ad: white, heteronormative, patriarchal, middle-class Euro-American family. We see the formation of emergent life as a regime which not only controls life by making life on a molecular, genetic or organismic level, but also by making life on the plane of ordinary sociality.

One might think that working on the immanent and contingent plane of making life would unleash many creative and subversive potentials which are connected to non-essentialist, anti-foundational or critical political ways of engaging with life. This can certainly be the case – many critical thinkers in the field of science and technology studies have stressed this (Haraway, 2007; Bowker and Star, 1999; D. J. Hess, 1995; Schraube, 1998; Winner, 1986). But it is not always the case. The formation of emergent life is innovative in its attempts to capture and dominate life – these attempts range from the new proposed means to control the circulation of vaccines to the embeddedness of recombinant practices in heteronormative social relations, as described above.

The Primacy of Experience

Whilst our discussion of Asimo and an as yet nonexistent virus might suggest that the formation of emergent life takes hold in the everyday principally through technological or biomedical developments, this is only part of the story. These new means of capture most commonly work in banal moments of life, a quality which is easily overlooked. In fact, we do not want to pose a duality between everyday experience and high-tech developments. In the next chapter, we offer an explanation of how experience is captured by and escapes the formation of emergent life which, following Whitehead (Whitehead, 1979; Latour, 2005), avoids such bifurcation of nature into the stuff of science and the stuff of subjective interpretation. We demonstrate that everyday experience is fertile soil for the operation of (and challenges to) the formation of emergent life; the regime seizes the immanent potentials of experience, potentials which are crucial to escape (as discussed in Section II).

Of course the same might be said of the life/culture system's fetishisation of activism and violence, which functioned by pervading the everyday imagination, or even of the welfare and neoliberal states' obsession with the proliferation of risk. However, in the next chapter we want to elaborate in more detail on the precise modes and processes of everyday experience being captured by the formation of emergent life, as well as those in which escape arises. Analysing the limits and reach of this regime's modes of capture demands that we differentiate between trajectories of immanent experience. Daily action, transformations in life, everyday experience are always immanent, non-totalisable, material and situated (Deleuze and Guattari, 1987, pp. 492–500; Haraway, 1991c). But very different trajectories can unfold *in* life's emergence and recombination. We use the term *optic* as a way to grasp the disembodied, objectivist, organicist trajectories which circulate in everyday action. Optic trajectories link the body's immanent relation to the world to established, policing representations of experience. The formation of emergent life functions through these transformations that take the form of optic trajectories, so that life is being continually dominated as it is remade. However, optic experience is bypassed by (or may divert or be diverted by) haptic trajectories which work with the same materials and moments but move in another direction altogether – haptic trajectories stem from and work with what is there and cannot be represented in the everyday (see the passages on speculative figuration in Chapter 5 and on the void in Chapter 6).

In the next chapter we examine this tension through a discussion of feminist tactics for politicising experience and tactics employed in politicising experiences of illness. No high-tech fantasies here – just illness narratives and autobiographies, stories that are typically valued to the extent that they can give meaning to lives and open possibilities for people to act agentically, to increase their capacity for action and to take some measure of control over their lives (Frank, 1995). But the accounts we consider actively oppose the imperative to analyse the meaning of experience, recognising the proliferation of optic trajectories in such practices. Instead, as we explain below, by staying close to and working with the immediate material conditions of experience, these accounts illustrate how haptic trajectories of experience can test the limits of the formation of emergent life.

The nature of experience is continually debated and commonly cast as universal, as either reified, situated or as lived (for an in-depth discussion, see Stephenson and Papadopoulos, 2006). These approaches understand experience as the property of a given entity (i.e. a subject); thus they solidify the subject, or cast experience as the end product of social regulation and positionality, privileging processes of subjectification. As we discussed in Chapter 5, a strong concept of the subject and taking subjectification as one's starting point for understanding experience both effect the policing of experience. That is they both incorporate experience into the logic of representation and neglect aspects of experience that cannot be accommodated within this logic; neither can elucidate dimensions of experience which subvert policing. Hence, it is impossible to subvert control without an operative concept of experience: what we call – in the next chapter – continuous experience, which explicates how people develop imperceptible ways of escaping the seizure of experience by the formation of emergent life.

We could draw on Benjamin's work on phantasmagoria to explain and analyse the workings of the optic mode of existence (Benjamin, 1999; Buse et al., 1999, pp. 59–70). Equally, we might turn to Debord's (1994) work on the spectacle, characterised in part as 'the common ground of the deceived gaze and of false consciousness' (1994, thesis 3). But, despite their importance for cultivating our imagination, there is a problem with these concepts: they invoke the optic as something external to what people do, as something which is added to people's actions as a means of subjugation and coercion. In these approaches, the representations and images which dominate and subjugate immediate sensual experience and material action seem to have their provenance in the notion of ideology. A top-down reality is invoked as dominating people's daily actions and experiences. We want to avoid this understanding of dominance functioning through the imposition of external images and representations over people's ordinary lives. Instead, we need tools for examining how the terrain of life is not always, already ensnared, nor a space where only familiar biopolitical and new postliberal modes of co-option and policing proliferate. Experience is captured, but experience is also the most fundamental point at which the politics of life itself breaks with policing. The imperceptible politics of escape from migration and labour control, discussed in sections IV and V, relies on tactics which release and play with haptic, continuous experience, and it is to these that we now turn.

9 EVERYDAY EXCESS AND CONTINUOUS EXPERIENCE

Politicising Everyday Experience

That the private is political might be familiar news, but the depoliticisation of the private or its total collapse into the political are also very ordinary stories. Feminists deployed the interrogation and affirmation of the politics of everyday experience in response to the imposition of an external, patriarchal, heterosexual gaze – an imposition which functioned to contain struggles over the regulation of sexuality and gender to the private realm (Haug, 1987; Gill, 2006; Crawford, 1992; D. E. Smith, 1987; H. Rose, 1994). For a time, the effects of this feminist strategy were electrifying, akin to the woman being drawn by Dürer's *Draughtsman* (see Chapter 1) standing up and throwing the grid out of the painting. These effects materialised in the emergence of new forms of social and sexual relations, in transformations in the workplace, in health services and in state politics. But today we are forced to reconsider the potence of experience, of the private and the personal.

In recent decades we have witnessed the increasing proliferation of starkly individualistic practices of everyday life and individualistic modes of relating to self and others. Following this neoliberal turn, even the subjective desire for freedom can be seen as a mode of individual regulation, i.e. 'the personal' becomes the means through which subjects are constructed as individually responsible for their own continuous self-invention (N. Rose, 1996b). Concurrently, we are witnessing the rise of a therapeutic and medicalised culture, involving modes of relating (to selves and others) which constitute subjects as traumatised, negated and in need of recognition (Frank, 1995; Orr, 2006). When such relations substitute affirmations of individual experiences for political action, political engagement is reduced to resentment and nostalgia (Brown, 1995). If the everyday is being laid bare as an active player in political change today, we must take account of the fact that the dominant trajectories at work in much politicisation of experience are the same optic trajectories through which the formation of emergent life operates.

Certainly, the widespread use of the political potential of experience has forced transformations in social and political life. But since the 1960s and 1970s we have seen the proliferation of this intimate form of power (see Chapter 2) which feeds off the wild insurgency of experience. The formation of emergent life functions through optic trajectories which link the body's immanent relation to itself to the game of representing and gaining recognition for identity and difference (Santos, 2001). Not only does the formation of emergent life need the personal; the more politicised that personal is the easier it is to absorb into intimate power. Now, demonstrating how the personal is already located in the public domain can solidify the very processes of policing that feminist politics of the left aim to subvert and rework. For example, foregrounding the personal realm can accelerate a collective, cultural turn inward in search of solutions to political problems. Simply representing the private and asserting the personal through collective actions is an increasingly inadequate response to the ongoing flows and mattering of patriarchal powers. Today this form of political engagement seems to be akin to micropolitics which, as we discussed in Chapters 5 and 6, seems to be incapable of addressing and challenging existing inequalities. The feminist declaration that 'the personal is political' has provoked a response. Once, an outright negation of the personal might have been a main defence of patriarchal power. But when life is regulated through the very paths carved out by feminist politics, feminism's target must include the patriarchal revaluing of the personal domain.

Rather than jettison the terrain of the personal and the private outright, we want to follow the trajectories opened by feminist and queer politics, which escape the imperative continually to represent experience, and return us to the problem of how to continue to devise ways of actively making the personal political without always being captured by life control. We do this by distinguishing between approaches to experience which identify the optic at work in the everyday (a useful but limited project) and those which seek to harness the productiveness of both the joyous and despairing excesses of experience, carving out trajectories which lead to imperceptible politics.

Capture in the Optic Trajectory: Self-esteem; Hybridity; Pink-washing

Something of the contemporary capture of experience is exemplified in the feminist discussion surrounding Gloria Steinem's (1992) *Revolution from Within: A Book of Self Esteem*. Taking what for many was an unexpected turn, Steinem argues that feminism needs self-esteem. Her rationale is that good self-esteem enables participation in the public domain, a prerequisite for effective political engagement. However, it might appear that there is a regressive dimension to Steinem's call to work on oneself. The imperative to transform oneself has long been a means of containing women's engagement to the personal, and not the public, domain (e.g. Walkerdine, 1990). Steinem appears to neglect decades of feminist work which targeted the pathologisation of women's subjectivities as unstable, unpredictable, emotional (e.g. Irigaray, 1977; Grosz, 1989a); work which attacked women's historical exclusion from the public domain on the grounds of inadequate personhood – as opposed to adequate personhood, defined in phallocentric terms (e.g. Hall, 1985). In advocating the importance of a particular psychological state (of esteem) as the basis of political action, Steinem seems to take a depoliticising turn.

This is an important critique, but it does not elucidate why actors (not only Steinem but her avid readers) who had been so central to subverting patriarchal notions about the inadequacies of feminine personhood now seem to be moving beyond their own insights. Perhaps the turn to self-esteem is not actually a backward step but a step which keeps abreast of and works with the intimate functioning of contemporary forms of experience in the regime of the formation of emergent life. Steinem's interest in self-esteem has been defended on the grounds that it offers a more realistic and more promising way of tackling contemporary depoliticising forms of the regulation of experience (Cruikshank, 1993). In this reading, the political relevance of self-esteem is that it instils a moral obligation to participate in public life and to shake off the apathy that accompanies democratic governance. Following de Tocqueville (1963), Cruikshank identifies the risk of depoliticisation which seems to accompany democracy. Certainly, de Tocqueville saw free people when he visited democratic America. But, to his eyes, the freedom and equality granted to isolated individuals entailed its own form of powerlessness: independent citizens are weak and in the absence of projects which bring them together there is a danger that their freedom will amount to nothing. De Tocqueville argued that democratic governance cannot function without people coming together and that governments need to take an active role in bringing people together:

In democratic countries the science of association is the mother of science.... If men are to remain civilized or to become so, the art of associating together must grow and improve in the same ratio in which the equality of conditions is increased. (de Tocqueville, 1963, p. 110)

For de Tocqueville, democratic governments can only be distinguished from despotic rule through their effective deployment of technologies of 'association', i.e., technologies of governance must extend into everyday social relations between people. Seen as a technology of governance, self-esteem can be understood as a means of engaging people with a regime of control. For contemporary theorists of neoliberal governance, self-esteem is a tool through which relations to the self are constructed, relations which enjoin people to others (it is hard to create and sustain relations without self-esteem), a prerequisite for active (supportive and contrary) engagement with others and with government.

Critics of *Revolution from Within*, Cruikshank suggests, fail to take account of the impossibility of developing a feminist politics which is located outside of neoliberal configurations of patriarchal power. From this perspective, it would seem that feminist struggles are best fought in and through the uneven, contingent and unpredictable course of continually emerging modes of regulation. Whilst acknowledging that self-esteem is a technology of governance which opens people to self-regulation (and opens women to patriarchy), it emphasises that, as a 'science of association', self-esteem also opens people to new forms of politicisation (and women to feminist politics).

However, in this reading of the value of self-esteem, political engagement is seen from the perspective of regulation only. It mistakenly conflates the political potence of social relations with the harnessing of bodily potentials through a 'science of association' to a regime of control. Such a reading illustrates how neoliberal governmentality theory is blind to the full realm of immanent potentials, seeing only those that reveal themselves as trajectories moving towards control. It is true that a feminist turn to self-esteem might elucidate the contemporary regulation of life; but by reducing politics to active engagement in governance (and self-regulation), Steinem is inciting feminists to follow optic trajectories, to play the game of policing.

Consider another example of the ambivalent effects of some contemporary critical forms of political engagement. This is the issue of hybridity, which has been so central for undoing racialising essentialist practices (Ang, 2003; Anzaldúa, 1999; Bhabha, 1994; Hall, 1994; Papastergiadis, 2005; Santos, 2001; Werbner and Modood, 1997; Young, 1995). Even notions of 'rhizomatic hybridity' (Wade, 2005, p. 606), which arise from engagement with recombinant genetics and the new era of biosecurity, are entering into discussions of hybridity. One might think that this denaturalisation of race would intensify anti-racism in our current political conditions. But the idea of hybridity seems to have rather ambivalent outcomes: it neglects the materiality of race and its importance for articulating effective anti-racist politics (for an extensive discussion of this issue see Papadopoulos and Sharma, 2008; see also Saldanha, 2006). The idea of hybridity seems to normalise subjectivities in transnational and postcolonial conditions by including them in shuddering multicultural societies (as discussed by Hage, 1998), or by aestheti-cisating otherness through the 'ambivalent coupling between racism and sexualized desire for the Other' (Sharma and Sharma, 2003, p. 5). And Sanjay and Ashwani Sharma continue:

Contemporary Orientalism appears less troubled with the danger of going native (and even miscegenation) in its relation to otherness, which may account for the 'frisson' of difference being harder to sustain now. Moreover, the encounter with the Other is no longer only one of a distant place or mediated through Orientalist representations; it has become an everyday occurrence in the Western multicultural metropolis. Nevertheless, while the racism of Orientalism has shifted towards a differentialist inclusion, we find that an assiduous preservation of 'the proper distance' from the 'Other' has become portentous. (2003, p. 6)

In all these examples we see how the immanent and situated trans-formations taking place on the level of everyday practices are easily absorbed into a distant and all encompassing system of representa-tions, a policing system which then pervades the everyday as an optic trajectory. Life is becoming coded and all the actual entities which make up experience are coralled into the form of an already determined and fixed entity (Whitehead, 1979; Braidotti, 2006).

The formation of emergent life establishes itself as a regime of life control by transforming one (pluripotent) mode of everyday existence into another (a clichéd mode of inhabiting the everyday). This is the depoliticising move of experience; a move which is made patently clear, for example, when Jain (2007) examines the 'pink-washing' of breast cancer partly through corporate investment in 'awareness' campaigns. One might consider that a 'breast cancer awareness' day would be a vehicle for engaging the public with women's suffering and deaths resulting from this disease or with the importance of identifying and contesting the prolific use of carcinogenic compounds. But Jain argues that instead of making breast cancer into a communal event of this kind, pink-ribbon day (sponsored by Estée Lauder) redeploys heteronormative, romanticised notions of women as innocent and reduces any political project of freedom to affirmation of individual women's survival of illness. As we mentioned above, one alternative to entering into these neoliberal games might be to negate the realm of experience altogether. However, we want to argue for a different strategy, one which draws on feminist and queer attempts to work from and with the movements of excessive trajectories in the everyday.

Jain hints at this in her insistence on the imperative to refuse the 'pornography of death', a form of pornography which involves the proliferation of images of titillating, violent deaths and renders ordinary deaths invisible (such as women's deaths through cancer). This refusal, she anticipates, must take the form of the 'material presencing' of the ordinarily unseen violence of death (Jain, 2007, p. 526). Whilst the material presencing of death may certainly be manifest in public demonstrations or performances of the kind Jain discusses, we argue that what is important is that it occurs in people's everyday lives – more than this, this materialisation begins and ends in the everyday. The private and the personal do not become political through being elevated to something public and extraordinary; it is not the spectacle that is politicising, but rather a process of return to and radical reorganisation of the very space in which ordinary, mundane experiences arise. The personal undoes itself and this is what makes it political. We examine this process below, through Gillian Rose's account of her own terminal cancer, in which the meanings and significance loaded onto her illness are refused and undone through the return to the ordinary. There is nothing exceptional in these ordinary encounters, their meaning is not given and pre-existent; their potence lies, rather, in the immanent unfolding of actual experiences.

Experience Beyond Representation

Feminist and queer politics have continued to develop strategies for making the personal political – strategies which test the current policing of the personal realm and trouble the very conditions in which subjectivity is produced. Repoliticising experience is not a matter of affirming subjective experience by trying to connect it with power. It entails developing alternative relations and modes of being, anxiety inducing relations (Chambers, 1998), modes of connecting which evade clichéd forms of capture, by working with the excess of the everyday.

This leads us to the central question of this section of our book: What is imperceptible politics in the regime of life control? How does imperceptible politics give birth to acts of escape from the optic trajectories employed by the formation of emergent life? In Chapter 6 we described escape as a form of subversion of regimes of control, rather than as a force which simply opposes these regimes. It is a betrayal which is enacted and performed in the everyday, a refusal to accept the pressure to adopt and operate with the given representations operating in the formation of emergent life. This subversion takes place in the heart of the regime, it operates with existing representations and at the same time it exceeds and annuls them. Betrayal and escape from the regime of life control occur as forces which materialise in the everyday by creating new forms of sociability beyond and below the formation of emergent life's regulation.

Imperceptible politics in the formation of emergent life exists and acts in the core of this regime. And the core of the regime is the everyday. As much as the formation of emergent life works in the immanent terrain of everyday life, there is an excess produced there, an excess of sociability, which lies beyond the representational structuring of the optic. Haptic trajectories circulate in the excess of everyday experience, segments and moments which do not yet coalesce into identifiable elements of the everyday; they undo representations as they materialise. There is a creative, imaginary quality to the pathways of escape they carve out of the everyday (which does not mean that their flights are ultimately unrealisable). With Debord (1981) we can say that this is the moment when everyday life turns against itself, becomes a betrayal of itself, changes itself, transforms and overcomes the optic trajectories which try to organise experience.

The excess uses something of the blasphemy deployed in the carnival (Bakhtin, 1984; Lachmann, 1997; Lefebvre, 1991) to invert, to twist, to mock the portentous and pontifical narrative of the regime of the formation of emergent life. It is in the carnivalesque, this 'world turned topsy-turvy', this 'play without a stage' (Bakhtin, 1978), that the limits of optic trajectories are encountered and their pretentious seriousness is unveiled. But the displacement enacted by trajectories of excess has nothing to do with a transgression of the everyday that has been celebrated in prior, phallocentric attempts to think transformation (e.g. Bataille, 1986). There is no transcendent move, it occurs in the everyday. Haptic trajectories are not extraordinary, but mundane and, as we discuss below, this is where their potence to betray the formation of emergent life lies. With Bakhtin (1984, p. 474) and his work on Rabelais, which has been crucial for our book, we say: 'All the acts of the drama of world history were performed before a chorus of the laughing people.'

The Haptic: Cancer and the Break of Illness Narratives

Like 'pink-ribbon day', illness narratives risk focusing on affirming individuals' strategies for survival and for exercising choice. Gillian Rose's (1997) *Love's Work* is an anti-narrative. She repeatedly refuses the myriad of different possible meanings well-intentioned friends and experts suggest she could attribute to her ovarian cancer. She recognises their (well-intentioned) efforts as policing. To make her illness palatable to others would be to negate the inside, immanent story of movement, to negate the contradictory trajectories being opened, criss-crossed and closed again and again as she navigates a terminal illness. She struggles to work with the dynamic fluidity of living and dying, of being close to death, of touching death. Gillian Rose refuses the invitation to relate to others solely through optic trajectories of experience, rather she engages with the haptic excesses of experiences circulating between herself and others; she moves with them and she works with them and against them from within. Haptic trajectories are connected to a specific configuration of the material presencing of existence (Jain, 2007); they do not pertain to meaning extracted from representations of individual experiences. Haptic trajectories start from the incommensurable. In the beginning was incommensurability. 'What is expressed' through these haptic trajectories, we can say, 'is the incommensurability of sense. This is politics at its best. A politics not of consensus or causality, but a sensing politics of bodies-in-movement' (E. Manning, 2007b, p. 119).

Rose disputes the notion that her cancer has a meaning, any meaning. She reintroduces that which is excluded in good illness narratives – her cancer is a random event: 'it has no meaning. It merges without remainder into the horizon within which the difficulties, the joys, the banalities of each day elapse' (1997, p. 72). There are no choices in *Love's Work*, there is only an interrogation of possibilities for harnessing experience to follow singular trajectories of excess, and to affect – to woo – others through continuous experience. Rose's experience works as an unfolding unruly, constituent force which moulds everyday transformation. In place of evoking the object of her experience, her cancer for example, for the reader's inspection, she invites us into the continuous flow of her experience.

Rose finds that others are affronted not only by the fact of her cancer, but more so by her energy for life, her vitality. And the reader has a sense of this vitality. The book is crafted so that before we read about the details of her illness we learn about Rose's relations with friends and lovers, with Judaism and Christianity, her work, her passions, her faith in destruction and recombination and construction – 'Let me then be destroyed. For that is the only way I may have a chance of surviving' (1997, p. 87). Without offering redemption, *Love's Work* gives us a sense of what Rose brings to a terminal illness, and how she is being remade by it.

After initial surgery and a summer of chemotherapy, an operation to remove a colostomy fails. Rose adopts the colostomy, embodies it. Noting the glaring absence of this long-established medical procedure in literature, she has little trouble in describing her new physicality: 'Tight coils of concentric, fresh, blood-red flesh, 25 millimetres (one inch) in diameter protrude a few millimetres from the centre left of my abdomen... Blueness would be a symptom of distress' (1997, p. 87). She cannot convey her everyday relation with this body without contesting its incongruity: 'I have trouble imagining, publicly or privately, that everyone is not made exactly as I am myself.... my routine is unselfconscious about the rituals and private character of your routines. Thus, I handle my shit' (1997, p. 89). Rose invokes and refuses how others distance themselves from her bodily functions:

Deep brown, burnished shit is extruded from the bright, proud infoliation in a steady paste-like stream in front of you: uniform, sweet-smelling fruit of the body, fertile medium, not negative substance ... This is to describe a new bodily function, not to redescribe the old. The organ of this fracture has achieved that pipe-dream of humanity: evacuation of the body is far removed from the pudenda, pleasure and pain. (1997, p. 88)

Handling your shit brings you closer to everyone, Rose argues; now she embodies everyone's dream of a new relation to shit.

Dis-identification

This strategy of dis-identifying with cancer might be – has been – read as a form of denial. Equally, Rose might be taken as exemplifying the 'difficult patient' – as Chambers (1998) reads Eric Michaels, discussed below. But neither is the case. She is generously appreciative of the skill and insight that others (friends and healthcare workers) bring to realising the malleability of medical knowledge and practices. One of her surgeons (she has two because her cancer spreads between different realms of expertise) says 'a beautiful thing' after the failed surgery: 'You are living in symbiosis with the disease. Go away and continue to do so' (1997, p. 93). But she is deeply and eloquently critical of those who lack such engagement.

Such discernment is simultaneously destabilising and promising. Rose repudiates colonising understanding and pastoral care; she indignantly destroys the very notion of 'unconditional love' well-wishers glean from alternative and new-age health movements and try to offer in their attempts to relate to her. Instead of aligning her experience with dominant narratives of illness, she seeks out uncertainty, the risk of relating and the painful confusion of life. The reader is drawn into the repoliticisation of her experience as she continually invites us to 'keep your mind in hell, and despair not' (1997, p. 98). This is no masochistic gesture. It is a refusal to be captured by the force of representational practices of illness (Robbins, 2005), a force which traverses and infuses everyday experiences of illness. A refusal is possible because this optic infusion is always incomplete, always accompanied by, haunted by, haptic trajectories which lie beyond the representational regime in the excess of sociability.

Rose works with experience beyond representation, the excess of everyday life. In so doing, she makes her departure from a form of power which enjoins individuals to employ redemptive notions of a good life as they connect with others. The move towards hell is promising because it enables an engagement with the present which is not always already colonised and transcended by a given better solution. In this way Rose can work with haptic trajectories, blocking the extension of intimate political power into the finest fissures of sociability and moving beyond clichéd renditions of the everyday. By dis-identifying with illness, she struggles to avoid simply playing the game of policing and capture of everyday excess. The effect is that her thanatography 'burns with its own form of radiance and hope' (Soper, 1996, p. 160).

Out of the 'Foucauldian Horror Show'

Rose evokes her body's recombination as 'everyone's dream' as she draws others into the haptic trajectories of embodiment that are neglected in the representational regimes of illness narratives. Eric Michaels (1990) employs a strategy which is similar in many ways. *Unbecoming* is an active struggle to push his bodily transformations out of the realm of the 'Foucauldian horror show' (1990, p. 25) of the hospital, and into public terrain, and to work these transformations as a series of events which fuel *others'* recombination and new modes of connectedness (Carrigan, 1995). This thanatography opens with an account of the 'clear and insistent' narrative which is traversing Michaels' body: Kaposi's Sarcoma is described as a set of 'morphemes, arising out of the strange uncertainties of the past few years to declare, finally, a scenario' (1990, p. 23). The virus's destruction is irrefutable – he is reduced to making a series of wish lists denoting the order in which he would prefer to lose his bodily functions, knowing that these lists will bear no relation to the course of the disease.

Trained as an ethnographer, Michaels is profoundly ambivalent about the process of representation and in the diary he keeps in the last year of his life (1987–88), a diary written for publication, he continually reflects on his own intent and the possible reception of the diary after his death. Chambers (1998) reads *Unbecoming* as an anxiety-provoking text: Michaels tries to destabilise us. He tries to draw his readers out of the safety of any 'concerned' connection with an HIV-positive gay man, a depoliticising mode of connecting which, like empathy (Jill Bennett, 2003), blocks transformation. And he does this be demanding some form of engagement with the new specificities of his embodied experience. He creates newness out of nothingness by investing in the materiality of his own experience as it emerges in the connections between his ill body, his relations to the gay community, HIV politics and the discrimination of the immigration authorities.

Michaels really hates Brisbane, where he went to take a job – a job for which the Department of Immigration is now refusing him a permanent resident's visa on the grounds that he is HIV positive. His status poses 'possible health risks for the general community and the considerable public health costs which will accrue from the treatment given' (letter from the state director of the Department of Immigration, quoted in Michaels, 1990, p. 170). Once his visa appeal has failed, the only thing preventing the minister from demanding his immediate departure from Australia is the deterioration of his health: Michaels is too ill to travel. But this means that he is trapped in Brisbane; he is no longer free to visit either Sydney or Alice Springs, where his friends and affinity to these places might make 'a few weeks extra [of life] seem worth it' (1990, p. 185). He rails against the situation and, in the last weeks of his life, is particularly incensed by the way Immigration pursues his doctor with questions about his capacity to travel whilst he is lying in a hospital bed. His final entry:

Can you believe this? ... They really insist on hounding me to death. ... Why would even the meanest bureaucrat be party to so mean a treatment?... That people willing to do this exist staggers me. That they can represent the official arms of the State depresses me more than I can say, or think. (1990, pp. 185–6)

Perhaps the potence of Michaels' work remains unrealised in the field of Australian immigration policy – in mid 2007 the prime minister of Australia announced a new proposal to prevent people (including refugees) with HIV and leprosy from entering the country on *any* visa, including a tourist visa. This announcement followed increases in HIV infections in the state of Victoria, which the Victorian Minister for Health blamed on migrants (it later transpired that these 'migrants' were largely people from New South Wales relocating to Victoria).

However, the challenges that Michaels poses to sexual politics, in particular his insistence on the need to develop an HIV-positive, gay politics, have travelled further. A postscript to the book, a previously unpublished document dated 1982, gives some insight into Michaels' trajectory in sexual politics. A participant in 1970s gay liberation, he simply states 'I liked being deviant' (1990, p. 191). The tense is past. Michaels vehemently disputes the wisdom of gay men's exchanging deviance for the comforts of normalisation – partly because the acceptance granted is only surface, but more pointedly because it means that 'being a faggot isn't very interesting anymore' (1990, p. 191). He tries (in 1982) to anticipate responses to this depoliticising normalisation, wondering whether people will be forced out of complacency by a swing to the 'lunatic right', whether with the passing of time gay men will look back and develop a more radical critique of the heterosexual matrix, or whether 'gay epidemic cancers and disease will mean we will have to learn the art of conversation again' (1990, p. 192). Conversation is important as a site for cultivating a gay aesthetic, but not *any* gay aesthetic, certainly not the aesthetic of the 'lavender prison' which Michaels sees gay men as constructing (1990, p. 191). It is a means of enabling the play of everyday excess in the connections developed between people. As such, the 'art of conversation' veers away from de Tocqueville's 'science of association', rupturing the policing of the everyday.

Unbecoming

For Michaels, betraying the means of everyday life control entails undoing every position (social, sexual and kind-of-identity position) which has become congealed and no longer sustains the elasticity necessary for a transformative move beyond itself. There is nothing solidified about sexuality in *Unbecoming*, it appears as immanent in social and sexual relations. He describes his own coming out

[i]n New York, 1971, [when] 'gay' was something impossibly chic, central to the cultural life of the city, a public rather than a private form, beginning to assume that enormous sense of importance that Western society would accord gayness in the 1970s whilst straights bungled their sexual politics and aesthetics. (1990, p. 28)

Michaels evokes his sexuality as both ordinary and highly contingent; this mode of becoming would have taken an entirely different course had he been born 20 years earlier or later.

As sexuality momentarily coalesces only to be continually rediscovered and remade, its political potence also shifts. Mardi Gras, 1988. Michaels writes about the parade as a fantastic spectacle of the kind only gay men could mount. But more exciting still was

the sea of partygoers ... tens of thousands of people flowing down the streets of Sydney for hours afterwards ... Astonishing and unarguably political, though it's impossible to venture a reading of what those politics might be or mean. The world really perched on the edge for a few hours, and could at any moment have collapsed into a black hole in the ground and disappear. As close to the 'Day of the Locust' as I expect to see! (1990, p. 108)

Whilst the political potence of this sea, this swarm, is marked by the fact of walking, of reclaiming city space and of entering into the carnivalesque everyday, it stems from the very moment of becoming with others. It is through such moments which break the logic of policing – so that experience is lived as 'play without a stage' and without a script, having the possibility of moving in many different directions – that becoming everyone acts as the constituent force of imperceptible politics.

As he himself is transformed by his sexual practices, by his ethnographic work with and relations to Indigenous people in central Australia, by HIV, Michaels continues to work with everyday experience as a means of questioning his social relations and the limited modes of political engagement he sees available to him. In the last months of his life, these questions turn to the problem of how to engage with the specificities of HIV and the forms of destruction and recombination it entails, the way these transformations are being embodied not only by positive individuals but by the gay community and beyond. On reading the cultural analyses offered in the (now canonical) 1988 special issue of *October* on HIV, Michaels reports finding most of the pieces depressingly uninspiring (with the exception of Bersani's paper, discussed in Chapter 8). In response to authors who wheel out familiar critiques of the pathologisation of gay men, Michaels retorts 'we already know nobody likes faggots, and hardly expect late capitalism to show much sympathy' (1990, p. 157). More pointedly, he suspects

a sort of liberal humanism infects these analyses which, by exempting gays from criticism, in its own way renders us passive, and so victims in terms of our own arguments. I stuck my tongue (and my arm, and my cock) into some pretty odd places during the 1970s and remain unsure about some of that. Desire rarely proved to be democratic. We continued to police the class structure as much by our sexual choices as our careerism. Is there no way to discuss these things, to evaluate them and possible complicities in our present conditions outside the tacky theologies of guilt and retribution...? (1990, p. 157)

This attempt to imagine an HIV politics which starts from and works with the virus and its remaking of sexuality is what finally legitimises the publication of *Unbecoming* for Michaels. That is, after months of questioning both his own purpose in entering into the questionable business of representing his experience, and his friends' reasons for continually encouraging him to write the diary, on reading *October* Michaels articulates a role for his own work: to subject himself, gay men, gay cultural politics to penetrating critique is Michaels' mode of journeying to hell. But unlike for Rose, there is no 'back' here for Michaels, no reconstruction, it is simply a continual process of movement, a becoming which never congeals, an unbecoming which materialises in new experiences and then moves again, challenging them. Imperceptible politics.

Love's Work and *Unbecoming*, living and dying, death as an ongoing engagement in life. Both Rose and Michaels appreciate (for what they are worth, i.e. the care of those who invoke them), mock and then jettison all the optic trajectories traversing the everyday that are offered to the sick – codified moments of ordinary life which are magnified as they are encountered in ill health, modes of connection which both recognise as deadly to those who participate. In different ways, each writes to break the rules of representation and integration, transforming the game into a political dispute over their very existences. The excesses of the everyday become palpable as haptic trajectories animate the experiences circulating between Rose's transformation, others to whom she is connected, 'everyone' who she has 'trouble imagining ... is not made exactly as' she and her own previous journeys to hell. As the haptic circulates between people in *Love's Work*, it is regenerative, it produces life out of death, it produces new experiences outside of the optic regulation which polices everydayness. Michaels too imagines a world beyond policing. Not a future world, but a world being actively made in the present, and his living is a part of this process. We have argued, in Chapter 5, that an escape is manifest as a material, irrevocable shift which changes the conditions of existence without negotiation. Here we want to add that escape, at its most basic level, is only possible with the transformation of experience. It is primarily an experiential trans-formation which fuels and lies at the core of the politics of escape. The third entry in Eric Michaels' diary marks his escape:

This is why I have AIDS, because it is now on the cover of *Life*, circa 1987. And this is why I can't believe everyone doesn't have it, because of the sense in which I believe myself hypertypical. And if any of this is so, then it explains why the world I look out on now seems so drear and painful, so devoid of joy, so mean and petty, not such a bad place to leave. The implications of an end to liberated sex and the death of gayness has truly miserable cultural/demographic/historical implications, even more than just a world of mean-minded hypocrites and wowsers shaking their fingers 'I told you so'. The reason I'm not terribly interested in living in such a world/future is not it isn't any fun. I haven't had, nor sought, any fun since 1975. It's the oppressions, the cathedrals of inequality and greed that are to be built out of that rhetoric of the failure of liberation that I have no great wish to see. (1990, p. 29)

Actual Occasions, Events and Continuous Experience

In Chapters 8 and 9 we discussed how the regime of life control involves the recombination of the body as a biosocial entity and attempts to disseminate these transformations into everyday sociality. The tool of this dissemination is experience. The optic trajectory of the regime of life control colonises and controls life by arriving in the most basic and ordinary fissures of people's lives: experience. It is in experience that we see how the remaking of the everyday and the recombination of bodies come together to create stable forms of controlled life. No regime of life control can operate and consolidate itself without capturing experience. Drawing on Gillian Rose and Eric Michaels, we described attempts to escape this capture – through the cultivation of haptic trajectories. But how do these haptic trajectories undo the control of life and reclaim life outside of the optic function? Addressing this question necessitates developing an understanding of experience beyond accounts of universal or situated experience. If experience is the ultimate target of the regime of life control, it is also the starting point for every politics of escape. Experience is the most contested point; it is where control and escape ultimately meet only to follow subsequently divergent paths of development. We could read this divergence as a gesture towards freedom – a topic which is so central in Benjamin's early writings (Benjamin, 1996c). Here we find a concept of freedom which is neither given in experience nor existing as a normative formal ideal outside of experience. Rather, experience constantly shapes and is shaped by the move to freedom. In his *Critique of Violence*, Benjamin points out that this move to freedom, or, in his words, 'divine violence', lies 'outside of law' (Benjamin, 1996a, p. 252); that is, outside the pernicious policing established by lawmaking and law-preserving violence. What is important for us here is that experience is neither simultaneous with nor independent of freedom; it is instead in a co-constitutive relation to freedom from policing (see also Chapter 6).

Experience evades the regime of policing and seizure of the optic through its dispersal across space as well as time. Dispersal means experience is scattered across different locales, across disjointed emotions, between disparate encounters among people, animals and things. Scattered in time and space, these discrete points are incorporated into the trajectories carved out in people's encounters and movements. Moreover, experience can never be fully unified as *the* experience which pertains to something, for example a historic event, or an illness. Against the optic understanding of experience as a form of enduring substance bound to a subject, we understand it as part of a process. Experience consists of actual occasions which arise from temporally preceding actual occasions. Here, we draw on Whitehead's (1979) speculative metaphysics and his distinction between determinate events – a moving body for example, or a reflexive, intentional subject – and actual occasions of experience – e.g. a footstep, a partial sensation, currents of a process, what Whitehead sometimes calls 'drops of experience'. The concept of actual occasions provides a useful tool for interrogating the haptic realisation of the building blocks of existence, of life, of potentiality; for Whitehead there is nothing beyond actual occasions. The process of their realisation is a creative one; nothing determines it apart from other, preceding actual occasions. 'Whitehead's creativity is ... manifest in the world, in the coming-to-be of all new actual entities. These constitute its accidental (non-predetermined) manifestations, and through them it has a merely contingent toehold on existence, despite its basic nature' (Simons, 1998, p. 388). Pertaining to sensation and not rationality, pertaining to process and not substance, these creative forms of experience are always either becoming, or perishing. They are not distinct components of larger entities: 'each actual [occasion] is a locus for the universe' or more specifically a locus of the 'universe which there *is for it*' (Whitehead, 1979, p. 80, emphasis A. N. W.).

How can the world exist in a fragment, a process of experience? Whitehead introduces the concept of an actual occasion in the attempt to refuse the ways experience is commonly thought – such that subject and object are split (for an extended discussion of this see Stengers, 2008). Instead, he insists that '[t]he occasion as subject has a "concern" for the object. And the "concern" at once places the object as a component in the experience of the subject with an affective tone drawn from this object and directed towards it' (Whitehead, 1933, p. 176). In this sense we do not have here the core enduring substance of a subject and the binarism between subject and object, but streams of actual occasions.

Although actual occasions can evade being captured in the substance of a subject-form (as discussed in Chapter 5) this alone is not why they are of interest and use in thinking imperceptible politics. Importantly, when actual occasions coalesce together into a nexus, or 'society', they are transformed into another mode of experience, what Whitehead calls events which have continuity and a degree of stability. But, as Erin Manning explains, events always 'remain invested' in the quasi-chaos of actual occasions' becoming and perishing, 'for they have been prehended from the indeterminacy of the forces which compose them. This indeterminacy is a living aspect of the event' (E. Manning, 2007a). That is, stable, representable modes of experience are always accompanied by, no enabled by, imperceptible worlds which exist *for* unrepresented actual occasions of experience.

Rather than thinking of these dimensions of experience as two sides of a coin, we use the term *continuous experience* to denote their co-existence. The passage of continuous experience – i.e. back and forth between a nexus of actual occasions and an event – is always unstable and dispersed across incommensurable processes, moments and spaces. Continuous experience only exists as a fluid movement between. Moreover, whilst events entail actual occasions they are not determined by them. Hence, the connections between a society of occasions are always contingent. This is continuous experience, the form of experience which pertains to the imperceptible politics of escape which addresses and forces transformations in the totality of power (as discussed in Chapter 6) of the optic regime of life control.

As discussed in the previous chapter, the formation of emergent life's fascination with recombinant life – that is the deep reorganisation of the material existence of bodies in the everyday – usurps the life/culture system's vitalism and turns into the stuff of techno-scientific experimentation which is then inserted into the everyday in an objectivist, optic form. Continuous experience betrays this optic transformation, not by baulking at or suppressing the potentialities included in these transformations, but by navigating the amorphous terrain of the everyday in ways which betray the fixity of meaning entailed in the optic regulation of everyday experience (an example of this fixity is Asimo, discussed in Chapter 8) and which reclaim experience as the process which evolves, reorders and recombines everyday life again and again. Continuous experience is always already recombining; recombination is its mode of existence, not something to be celebrated as a particular masculine omnipotent fantasy of changing the totality of the world and life itself.

These recombinant processes hinge on continuous experience's capacity to disperse not only across people, but between people *and* things. Again, Whitehead is useful for avoiding an understanding of experience which is based in an attempt to conceive of nature as homogeneous (Latour, 2005). Whitehead insists on the qualitative differences between different forms of life and between life and inorganic matter. Given this, he seeks to *understand* how relationships between different modes of existence, between people and things, can evolve and function. In this regard, the concept of actual occasions helps to elucidate what it means to claim that a thing experiences or can share experience. There are direct correspondences between some of the occasions studied by physicists and those experienced as part of a human's higher faculties. A 'physical occasion' involves the passing of energy between distinct entities. When a series of such moments coalesce they become a physical entity; Whitehead understands what has happened in the same terms as the concrescence of actual occasions into an event. As Stenner (2008) points out, a common difference between the physical occasions which make up, say, a stone and the higher grade actual occasions which make up some mental process is that the former do not express the creativity of the latter. In this way, Whitehead not only explicates the commonalities and the differences between people and things but concrete pathways, or occasions of experience, through which they are related. For Whitehead there is only one stuff out of which the world is made. But against other reductionist monist understandings of materialism, Whitehead argues that this stuff is not only matter but contains also experience of different grades (Whitehead, 1979, p. 109; see also D. R. Griffin, 1998; Lango, 2004).

As both Michaels and Rose emphasise, the subject is undone as she is constructed through the circulation of continuous experience. Continuous experience is the excess which occupies the same terrain as the formation of emergent life; it moves through, works with and reworks life's potential on all its different levels of organisation. But unlike the regime of control, it is open to unrepresented worlds as it works with haptic trajectories; it triggers processes of unbecoming, of undoing optic representational trajectories and congealed material arrangements. With Benjamin we could say here that 'experience is the uniform and continuous multiplicity of knowledge' (Benjamin, 1996c, p. 108). That is, the actual occasions of experience are the final constitutive element of the world and at the same time they are always diverse and in constant change, creating new material configurations of life.

Material Presencing and the Immediacy of Continuous Experience

If experience is beyond optic representation, this is not to say that it has no role in the transformation of life. Continuous experience is a force which works, neither through articulation nor through the bestowal of meaning, but through materialisation. It alters de facto the immediate material conditions of existence *without* needing to be interpreted as part of a given system of meanings. The politics of escape hinges on continuous experiences because this is the most basic and crucial level at which social change takes place. Continuous experience is a form of social change which exists long before it is codified as such, that is as a social movement which attempts to transform a given social order. Thus, when we say that continuous experience alters de facto the material conditions of existence, we mean that it creates new imperceptible everyday forms of bodily existence and sociability which only later can be classified as movements which challenge the stability of a regime of control. For example, we show in Chapter 4 how vagabonds escape the feudal system of labour in an everyday and imperceptible way before they are considered as a threat and then recaptured in a new regime of wage-labour control. Or in Chapter 15, we show how precarious workers create artefacts and social relations which remain outside capitalist modes of appropriation. Thus, they materialise their activities in ways which exceed the process of commodification. Continuous experience displaces hegemonic optic representations as it materialises in people's everyday lives. Continuous experience instigates a transformation which happens on the very immediate, mundane, ordinary, grounded sphere of our bodily shape, habits, perception and sociability. This is the reason why continuous experience is the most basic stuff of the imperceptible politics of escape.

Both Eric Michaels and Gillian Rose live their bodily transformations by engaging with the materiality of these experiences. After surgery Rose lives with a colostomy. But her experience of the colostomy is not determined by the colostomy itself. Neither is it the case that this experience is produced through her engagement with representations of her colostomy (in fact, she notes the relevant absence of representations). What Rose does is to follow the new sensations of her physicality, she moves with actual occasions of experience, observing the colours, the smell, the warmth: that is, her experience *is* bodily. And it is because she literally embodies the redirection of her shit that Rose's experience of her colostomy interrupts its medicalisation or the pitying gazes of her friends.

Materialisation opposes any representational function of language. People develop singular modes of existence by being embedded in continual processes of affecting others, of materialising experiences, changing bodies, creating new connections to things and animals. This is a process of co-evolution which gives birth to non-standardised experiences of being in the world and being in a certain body. But this body is not an organism, it is not representable in language. The body one has, the body one is, the environment in which one lives, the environment which exists in our bodies is always created and cannot be effectively denied (Csordas, 1994). It is not an option, it is always the real starting point in which all future transformations are located. Materialisation, thus, creates life which cannot be reversed, bypassed, forgotten, eliminated. It is there, you deal with it. Humans, things, animals evolve together, incorporating each other into the materiality of their existences. These relationships mean that there is an accountability to other people, forms of life, the environment which is central here (Braidotti, 2006). As Donna Haraway says, 'language is not about description, but about commitment' (Haraway, 1991a, p. 214).

In what senses can the immediacy of material presencing be beyond representation? In what sense can continuous experience unfold below the optic regime of life control? We want to note that imperceptibility does not amount to invisibility, or to being beyond sensation altogether (here we draw on Wolfe, 2006, in her reading of Deleuze). For Deleuze, as with Rancière, what is outside representation is so because it is incommensurable with a majoritarian commonsense. The imperceptible is an active force which becomes apparent by materialising in the body, such that 'the body's effort to endure always takes the form of a forcible communication between incommensurables, producing new intensities and reconfiguring the old' (Wolfe, 2006, np). Our argument, illustrated in Rose and Michaels' thanatographies, is that people actively participate in the circulation of intensities and the reconfiguration of those sanctioned by the regime of life control by working with actual occasions of experience as they materialise in our lived relations and as they undo stable, representable subject positions.

Betraying Time

Continuous experience flows through time, departing from the logic that experiences are discrete points on the timeline of individual's life story (Adam, 2004). Regimes of control employ a linear representation of time in order to function (for further examples of this in relation to migration and labour control, see Chapters 11 and 14). The formation of emergent life's imposition of normative discourses occurs in time, structuring time and controlling the flow and the figurations of everyday activities (Elias, 1978). But continuous experience retreats from this chronology. The exits it constitutes are not effected through practice, rehearsal or refinement. They are idiosyncratic and contingent, and can as easily fail as succeed. Above we said that actual occasions and continuous experience are contingent and not determined, but that is not to say that they cannot be anticipated. People invest in transformations which may or may not occur. They tarry with time – an idea which is intriguingly discussed by Michael Theunissen (1991); they enter into a different relation with time, taking distance from the imperatives of linear and reversible time (Sandbothe, 1998), turning away from the sense of events and towards the quasi-chaos of actual occasions. Tarrying is a means of engaging with this mode of being which is inextricable from others, from the situation – a move beyond the self and towards the world, enabling the permeation of experience with the world. Tarrying is intentionless, purposeless and targetless: it has no object.

Continuous experience unfolds without constituting a coherent intentional subject. Tarrying occurs before intentionality and entails the dissolution of the reflexive subject, disrupting any formation of a nexus of occasions. Continuous experience produces action as part of the social field in which it unfolds, not intentionality. Intentionality and intentional agency are relatively unproblematic for those working within a given regime of representation, with its predetermined rules and codes. But it is unhelpful if intentions cannot be articulated, or exist outside representation.

Continuous experience works with unrealised trajectories, possibilities which do not yet exist, potentials which may never manifest. Tarrying with time does not entail a concrete vision of an alternate future, but an expanded, slowed-down present which fuels new imaginary relations with other actants and new forms of action, possibilities people are compelled to explore, but which only later and unexpectedly will materialise in an alternative future. The effects of this constituent force can never be intended, but cannot occur without people's fidelity to change (Badiou, 2005a; see also Chapter 6). Continuous experience is both immanent and full of potentialities and fictionalities – it is speculative. It is incorrigibly present, mesmerised by suddenness (Bohrer, 1994). This is political action from the absent core of a situation, an active mode of being which prepares and evokes a change in the unfurling present as it permanently questions any possibility to restore a notion of the subject.

Subjectlessness

Continuous experience is a constituent force which undoes subjectivity – and this is precisely what Steinem fails to grasp in *Revolution from Within*. Subjectivity is variously conceived in different social or theoretical contexts: in the neoliberal market-oriented universe, subjectivity takes the form of the rational entrepreneurial individual; in mainstream psychology and dualist philosophy, we have the universal subject as a carrier of pre-organised mental structures; in humanist talk, we encounter subjectivity in the shape of a person's unique interiority; in discursive accounts, subjectivity is related to social or linguistic positioning; in theories of governmentality, subjectivity is recast as subjectification, that is subjectivity is ever made anew through power-pervaded social relations; finally, in cognitive neuroscience, subjectivity is constructed as a disembodied activation pattern of the brain's network.

All of these approaches conceive of subjectivity as a way to interrogate how the subject is produced in particular social relations (Papadopoulos, 2008). In other words, all of them cast sociability as a homogenising unifying force which fabricates subjects. They can account for a group of individuals who come together representing a common standpoint or social position (e.g. humanist and discursive approaches to subjectivity); or for a social group constituted as such through the forces of regulation (e.g. governmentality theory); or for a group of people who are connected through pre-existing disembodied similarities or qualities (e.g. universal and cognitive approaches to subjectivity). But they cannot account for the specific forms of heterogeneity entailed in collective modes of existence, for the incommensurable dimensions of any nexus of actual occasions which lie beyond common sense and common sensibilities. None of these approaches to subjectivity manages to conceive of sociability, or the connections between people, in terms of singularity. Because of this, we prefer to talk about experience, and more precisely continuous experience, instead of subjectivity.

In contrast to all these approaches, with Spinoza we can understand sociability as a move along a trajectory of increasing differentiation, without characterising the connections forged between people in terms of some overarching unity. Here, plurality is an enduring feature of existence, and collectivity is cast as a network of individuals in which singularity emerges (Negri, 1991). Singularity is neither universal nor particular, but occupies the terrain between these two poles. In Whitehead's terms, singularity would be the unique perspective of an actual occasion on the multiplicity of other actual occasions. For the most basic elements of which the world is made up are actual entities, segments of experience in which a multitude of many different things acquires an individual unity. Whitehead calls this process concrescence and insists that the conditions for the unity of actual occasions lie entirely within and for themselves.

Now, the importance of sociability can be grasped in terms of its role in the production of singularity, not in terms of its role as a catalyst for the production of subjects. More than this, interrogating sociability can be the only means for understanding how the irreducible differences of singularities 'can be extended close to another, so as to obtain a connection' (Deleuze, 1991, p. 94). This marks a radical shift from collective forms of existence thought as individuals aggregated in the form of a homogenising unity. Unlike individuality, which enjoins subjects to representing some notion or aspect of themselves into a collective universe, singularity exceeds representation and interrupts self-coincidence (Patton, 2000). Singular connections are not based on commonalities, but on shifting relations of affinity between concrete, material others. Singularity emerges from sociability rather than acting as its foundation. Thus Rose and Michaels' jarring insistence on the incommensurable dimensions of their experience is not, in our understanding, evidence that they are despairing or difficult patients; rather it is a fundamental element of modes of sociability which strive towards shattering majoritarian commonsense. In contrast to approaches to subjectivity which cast sociability as a homogenising and relational force or process, we understand continuous experience as fuelling a mode of connecting with the world as a non-unifiable singularity. Certainly, continuous experience moves through subjectivity; but it is incommensurable with the subject. It does not seek to transform subjectivity, or to invest in the emergence of 'new subjectivities'. It simply materialises.

The (reassuring or terrifying) containment of self-reflection – thought as an 'I' reflecting on a 'me' or even a 'we' – is shattered by the flow of continuous experience. As it washes through the connections between people, animals and things, continuous experience exposes the internal incommensurability of actual occasions of experience, and the sheer impossibility of being a 'subject' in any kind of stable, predictable relation with oneself, others or the world. Continuous experience collects singularities, binding collectives of those who belong nowhere, those who are in a process of becoming everyone.

The process of becoming everyone is akin to a subjective death, in the sense that subjects are irrelevant as individuals with subjectivities. But their experience matters more than anything else; actual occasions that test the limits of commonsense materialise in and between bodies. Experience lives. Continuous experience evokes a fictional understanding of people's relations to each other and the world; in this way it fuels the imaginary necessary for embodying alternate modes of sociability, modes which refuse the optic exclusions of the formation of emergent life. Hence, experience matters because it is through experience that the connections between people are refused, reworked and reimagined. Continuous experience directs the focus on imperceptible politics towards these small-scale events and moments, which are germane to how people move, walk, touch each other, feel, sense.

In the following sections we describe how this mode of imperceptible politics deployed in the regime of life control is also an important means of escaping the regulation of migration and of work. We examine how the relations between those involved in migration contest contemporary sovereignty and how the excess of sociability entailed in precarious labour destabilises the configuration of productivity today. Any form of imperceptible politics necessitates remaking the minutiae of everyday connections between people. And the most basic steps in this politics are the actual occasions of continuous experience – in Whitehead's words the creation of 'novel togetherness' (Whitehead, 1979, p. 18). As continuous experience flows between people, it corrodes the fixtures and aspirations regulating people's vision, it eats into eyes which see only control; it cuts through flesh and travels on by literally remaking our bodies. Can you imagine a world without the constrictions of subjectivity?

Section IV
MOBILITY AND MIGRATION

10   THE REGIME OF MOBILITY CONTROL: LIMINAL POROCRATIC INSTITUTIONS

The Regime of Mobility Control

The current European regime of mobility control and the process of the Europeanisation of migration policy exhibit less the traits of transnational governance and more those of postliberal policing (as discussed in Chapters 2 and 3). The European Schengen process, we argue, is a paradigmatic laboratory for experimenting with the vertical aggregates of postliberal sovereignty; these postliberal processes exist both within and parallel to transnational European integration. Approached from a historical perspective, we can see how the Europeanisation of migration policy does indeed result from European Union integration efforts. However, the policy process has now advanced to the point that it has become a central, generating moment of the new postliberal transformation of Europe (Walters, 2004; S. Hess and Tsianos, 2007).

It is no coincidence that in this context Etienne Balibar (2004b) refers to the double-edged nature of the 'institution of the border' in Europe: on the one hand, it functions as an instrument for the regulation of people's movements and, on the other, this border institution is only seldom subject to democratic control. In her exceptional work on European border policy, Enrica Rigo (2007) has pointed to how European migration policy leads to the diffusion and stratification of borders across Europe. In accord with many other critical researchers (Walters, 2002; M. Anderson, 2000; Lahav and Guiraudon, 2000; Revista Contrapoder, 2006) Rigo (2005) refers to a 'deterritorialisation' of state sovereignty. In certain cases, the knock-on effect of third-state regulations, the 'police à distance' as Didier Bigot and Elspeth Guild (2003) call it, expands the Schengen space of control into countries which are not members of the European Union. The notion of third states stems from a German asylum compromise developed in 1992, according to which a refugee who enters Germany (and now the European Union) by way of a 'safe' third country (i.e. one in which he or she is not subject to political persecution) may be deported to that country. This has led to so-called 'chain deportations', because the safe third countries that surround Europe are increasingly declaring neighbouring countries to be safe third countries as well. It also indicates how the control of mobility, which used to be an explicit national responsibility, has become the focus of a multitude of national and transnational institutions. The 'deterritorialisation' of sovereignty illustrates the postnational character of contemporary European migration politics.

The postnational process of border displacement should not, however, be understood as resulting from the actions of sovereign states attempting to extend their power. Rather, it has been effected by a complex struggle in which the existing regime of mobility control is itself challenged by fluid, streamlined, clandestine, multidirectional, multipositional and context-dependent forms of mobility. That is, it is necessary to understand the Europeanisation of migration policy from the perspective of the subjectivities which force it to emerge.

Behind the migration flows, the overloaded ships and the increasingly strict border controls, we can find events which point to the constituent force of escape. At first glance, this may seem like a heroic glorification of migrant ruses and tactics best suited to the egoistic, neoliberal ideal type of the Homo economicus or to the 'ground staff of globalisation', as Sabine Hess (2005) has called migrant workers. However, the importance of escape becomes evident when transformations of sovereignty are apprehended as the result of global migrant practices, practices that tend to undermine the basis upon which sovereignty has hitherto functioned. Research on trans-nationalisation and on new migration economics (Basch, Schiller and Szanton Blanc, 1994; M. P. Smith and Guarnizo, 1998; Morokvasic, Erel and Shinozaki, 2003) undermines notions of the migrant as single, economically driven, male Robinson Crusoe (Andrijasevic, 2004; S. Hess and Lenz, 2001). These studies stress the importance of households, families, companionships and friendships, kinship structures and other networks as the contexts within which migration and decisions about migration take place. As we show in the next chapter, migrants never reach the border on their own. But before moving to this we want to trace the formation of the contemporary regime of mobility control.

The concept of a regime of mobility control is increasingly deployed in discussions about shifts and weaknesses in national sovereignty and contemporary transformations from transnational governance to postliberal sovereignty (as described in the first section). Where one often used to speak of migration *systems* (Hoerder, 2002), the term *regime* allows the inclusion of many different actors whose practices, while related, are not organised in terms of a central logic, but are multiply overdetermined. When the concept of a system is applied to migration, the primary focus of analysis becomes the means to control practices of migration – all else is cast as an effect of control. In contrast, the concept of the regime allows us to investigate the relation between the actions of migrants and those of agents of control without invoking a simplistic relation between subjects (cast as agents of control) and objects (understood as migrants or those who assist migrants) of migration. According to Sciortino,

> [t]he notion of a migration regime allows room for gaps, ambiguities and outright strains: the life of a regime is a result of continuous repair work through practices ... the idea of a 'migration regime' helps to stress the interdependence of observation and action. (2004, p. 32)

The focus of regime analysis, then, lies on the 'third space': the plane of negotiation lying between and across the segments of interwoven political and economic transnational processes, processes that are no longer simply intergovernmental, but emerge with the installation of the regime. The issue here is how to encapsulate relations that are, by their very nature, extremely unstable, and that cannot be assumed to be externally regulated or safeguarded (by the state, for example). Rather, the processes through which social relations are regulated emerge from social conflicts that, again and again, result in innovation (or overthrow) of institutional compromises. Thus, at the core of the processes entailed in the Europeanisation of migration, we find social conflicts which trigger transformations in the regime of mobility control.

Transnational Mobility and the Europeanisation of Migration Control

Together, the partial loss of the ability to control and manipulate national migration policies and the increase of transnational migrational flows have led to a shift from national or bilateral control of the recruitment of guest workers (who were granted limited residency rights) towards the control of illegalised labour migration. We can trace the insignia of this shift in the European

Union's migration policy. Certainly, European Union policy still focuses on the freedom of movement of European Union labour migrants, on the partial integration of resident third-state immigrants (i.e. non European Union nationals) within social legislation and on a common restrictive policy towards migrants who are not in possession of documents. However, it has also expanded to encompass new forms and strategies of mobility control. These primarily entail the externalisation of the control of migration beyond the Schengen borders in Morocco, Mauritania and Libya. Thus, beyond the borders of the European Union we find heterogeneous and hierarchised spaces of circulation with stepped zones of sovereignty: spaces that can neither be governed through the inner-European principle of Schengen territoriality (homogeneous spaces with equal rights), nor through the national double-R axiom (see Chapter 1). One result of extending migration control in this way is that the margins of the European Union become centres of gravity of a new government of border crossing. Increasingly, the classical transit countries such as Turkey, Libya, Morocco, or the countries of the former Yugoslavia, are becoming the final destination for migrants on their way to north-west Europe (Anthias and Lazaridis, 2000; R. King, Lazaridis and Tsardanides, 2000). This clearly illustrates not only how their function has changed – from a source of emigration, to a transit route, to, finally, a destination for would-be immigrants – but also shows the 'productivity' of the European migration and border regime. The more difficult migration to north-west Europe becomes, the more attractive as potential immigration destinations the peripheral economies of south, south-east and eastern Europe become. As Ayse Öncü and Gülsun Karamustafa (1999) conclude, this migration is both a precondition and a motor for a specific form of peripheral globalisation of the economies at the edge of Europe.

Migrants' transnational mobility strategies bring with them new forms of subjectivity, subjectivities that permanently transgress the political borders of the nationally regulated labour market (Ong, 1999). Positioning is flexible both spatially and in relation to the specific labour market; it takes place in the context of the mutually intensifying dynamics of the imposition of discipline and the attempt to evade it. Diverse migration strategies can be understood as creative responses to situations where the chances of gaining official residency appear extremely remote (Salih, 2003; Andrijasevic, 2004; S. Hess, 2005; Morokvasic, Erel and Shinozaki, 2003; Cyrus, 2001).

Up until now, the focus of transnationalisation research has habitually concentrated on migrants' transnational practices and networks – regarded in most studies as 'counter-hegemonic political space' (Appadurai, 2000; Augustin, 2003; Chatterjee, 2004). From this perspective, migrants' transnational networks and practices figure as both a defiant answer to and an unintended consequence of restrictive migration policies, policies which are posited as unsuccessful attempts to counter migrants' practices. However, the risk of such an emphasis on the apparent 'failure' of political measures of control is that the 'productivity' of the new forms of migration control gets overlooked. This 'productivity' can be apprehended if we avoid considering the Schengen process as simply that which governs migration from above. Instead, if we view Schengen as part of a broader social struggle around migration, we can recognise how, for example, the security measures of the Schengen border space have generated the means of their own overcoming. That is, migrants continually develop temporary mobility tactics and abandon new transit solutions as soon as they have been discovered by the border guardians and recodified as problems of border security.

Mapping Schengen

The Schengen Agreement has become the central official policy instrument for achieving uniformity of border policies across the European Union. It is not our intention here to reconstruct in detail the complex evolution of the contemporary European border regime that has been forced along, both within and outside European Union institutions, over the last 20 years (for a detailed genealogy of the Schengen process, see Düvell, 2002; Geddes, 2002; Groenendijk, Guild and Minderhoud, 2003; Leuthardt, 1999; Walters, 2002). Rather, we want to investigate how the Schengen process has become integral to the social conflicts out of which the current regime of mobility control in Europe has emerged. The history of the Schengen Agreement exemplifies the general modus of the Europeanisation of migration policy. It has its roots in an informal meeting of five government heads that took place in the Belgian town of Schengen in 1985. This meeting was held to discuss measures to unify European markets, especially ones aimed at removing internal border restrictions. Here, the five founding countries, Germany, France, Belgium, the Netherlands and Luxemburg, deemed it appropriate to initiate compensatory measures for the disappearance of national border controls, and invented the 'common European border' (M. Anderson, 2000; Tomei, 1997). However, this outward redeployment of controls is only one element of the policy initiated for the restructuring of border controls. Schengen also brought an extension of internal border zones. An increasing number of internal spaces such as railway stations or motorways were redefined as 'border areas' (on the reconfiguration of internal and external borders see the significant contributions in Revista Contrapoder, 2006; see also Lahav and Guiraudon, 2000). It was only with the Treaty of Amsterdam in 1997 that the hitherto multilateral Schengen Agreement became part of official European Union policy (Leuthardt, 1999): *'Schengen-land'* with its *'Schengen visa'* becomes now a constitutive element of the legal order of the European Union.

Broadly speaking, the Schengen Agreement contains three main features: entry control is shifted to the outer borders; entry regulations and asylum policy are brought into line with one another; and measures directed against illegalised immigration and trans-border organised crime are put in place (Fungueiriño-Lorenzo, 2002; Niessen, 2002). Security considerations also shaped the Europeanisation of migration policy from the outset. Thus, in the 1980s, the first EU-wide bodies such as the TREVI group – an informal and secretive round of meetings between police chiefs and senior officials from the interior ministries – began to formulate a European migration policy that was closely linked to policies on terrorism and organised crime. This security matrix has rendered the Schengen process amenable to simple and speedy popularisation. It is particularly useful for recoding migration in terms of organised criminality, as illustrated by the anti-trafficking discourse which simplistically divides the movement of migration into evil traffickers and smugglers on the one hand and their poor victims on the other (Andrijasevic, 2005, 2007; Doezema, 2005; Luibheid, 2002).

Schengen has involved formal and informal advisory talks, meetings and conferences and a series of papers dealing with strategy and concepts that are constantly being produced and filed away. The ongoing non-linear development of the Schengen process cannot be grasped by means of a simple chronology. The maps created by the artist–activist collective MigMap (artists from Labor k3000 and militant researchers from the project Transit Migration) exemplify the complex intertwining of various discourses and legal policies. 'Governing Migration: a virtual cartography of European migration policy' (www.transitmigration.org/migmap) was motivated by the desire to create a situated cartography of European migration policy since 1989 (as opposed to a cartography of migration policy which reproduces the territoriality of the European borders). Map 3, on the Europeanisation of migration policy, uses a form reminiscent of a subway map to show the decentred and continual variations of 'observing' and 'action' (Sciortino, 2004) at the transnational, multi-level system of governance (Figure 18).

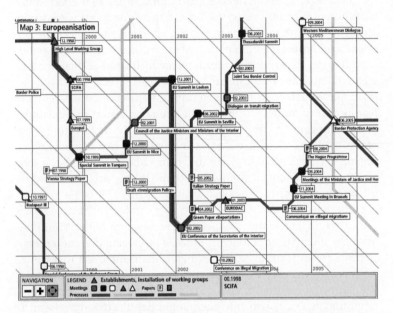

18.   Labor k3000 in collaboration with Transit Migration, MigMap (Mapping European Politics on Migration), Map 3: Europeanisation (detail), 2006, www.transitmigration.org/migmap (last accessed 23 May 2008). Printed with permission of Labor k3000, Zurich.

In Map 3 we can follow the emergence of particular strategies and operative concepts: how they are followed up for a time and begin to overlap with parallel projects, until the debate takes an abrupt turn thanks to the arrival of new ideas or the exigencies of the political concerns of the day (Spillmann, 2007). Moreover, the implementation of particular strategies relies heavily on underlying discourses which are not always apparent when one follows a linear chronological of the Schengen process from the perspective of its institutionalisation. Another map developed by Labor k3000 (Map 2, the discourse map), depicts the most important discourses being employed in recoding the axioms of migration policies, discourses that provide the arguments used in favour of particular policies (see www.transitmigration.org/migmap/home_map2.html, last accessed 23 May 2008). Discourses of human rights, security, asylum law, trafficking and the war on terror all compound, displace or submerge one another like meteorological turbulences.

The events of 11 September 2001 intensified the impetus to recode migration policy in the framework of a broader security discourse by explicitly linking questions of migration control to the military complex. The new European Union security and military policy also extended to entail a clear migration policy component. Here, the wars in Kosovo, Afghanistan and Iraq illustrate how an anti-migration policy can fall back on military intervention as an instrument. At the same time, these wars illustrate how migration containment has become part of military strategy and how the new warriors now have their own refugee-protection troops.

Even if the migration and border control regime which emerged through the Schengen process constitutes an attempt to impose a fluid and uniform instrument for the transnational governance of European borders, its implementation is not without problems. Despite the establishment of various European information systems and centres, information sharing and operational cooperation still remain deficient – not least on account of incompatibilities between nation states. Thus a Commission study on illegal migration from 2004 came to the conclusion that a lack of reliable and compatible data actually renders a common political strategy impossible (Communication from the Commission to the Council, the European Parliament: 'Study on the links between legal and illegal migration', 4 June 2004). At a Council meeting in Brussels in 2004, heads of government admitted that the aims of communitisation – that is the harmonisation of the different legislations on admission and residence conditions for non-EU nationals by aligning them on national and community levels in accord with the 1999 agreement of the European Council in Tampere – had not been met. For instance, the decision to transfer complete responsibility for migration policy from individual states to the Commission had not been implemented. The year 2010 has been set as the new deadline.

In the light of the unwieldiness of such top-down approaches to communitisation, measures agreed at the level of transnational governance are tending to force the pace of the Europeanisation of migration policy. These include measures implemented at European Union level on German insistence, such as the 'first safe country' regulation mentioned above, and the designation of safe countries of origins for refugees (since 1993); tightened visa regulations – the carrier sanctions – whereby airports and airlines have to take on the role of border police; or the invention of so-called 'Readmission Agreements' (Angenendt and Kruse, 2003).

Nevertheless, the Schengen Agreement is an extremely productive element of the Europeanisation of migration policy. Its inclusion in the Treaty of Amsterdam means that it is part of the *acquis communautaire* that accession candidates to the European Union must fulfil. It makes the adoption of the so-called *Schengen acquis* mandatory and links it to other political areas and financial programmes, meaning that failure to comply may lead to wide-ranging consequences for the candidate states (Cholewinski, 2000; Lahav, 1998). The policy of deterritorialisation, however, extends well beyond the circle of European Union accession state candidates. Thus, measures such as equipment aid and the provision of mobility control know-how are not just limited to the circle of European Union accession states, but form part of the European Union regional treaties such as the *stability pact* for the Balkan states, the *MEDA programme* for the Mediterranean area or the *Phare programme* for the states of central/eastern Europe. In addition to core measures in place at the supranational level, *Schengen acquis* bilateral agreements have facilitated the extension of European Union migration policy. As well as 'advice', these agreements involve technical, administrative and training assistance for the expansion of border security; exchange of information; and the provision of Immigration Liaison Officers (ILOs), who may also be operationally active locally (Holzberger, 2003).

The Emergence of New Forms of Mobility Control through the Schengen Process

The development of the Schengen process raises questions about the political constitution of Europe. The European Union is often recognised as a new type of entity, one that is neither a new 'super-state' nor merely an intergovernmental agreement (Jachtenfuchs and Kohler-Koch, 1996). Variations on this general position oscillate between perspectives which focus more on the nation state and those which emphasise supranational institutions. The former ascribe particular interests to individual states and track their realisation on the European level. The latter place supranational institutions in the foreground and position multi-level, transnational networks as central to the matrix of a new form of political government.

The processes of developing common European migration policies are understood as processes of 'harmonisation', i.e. the politically driven alignment of the migration policies of the individual European Union nation states on a supranational level. Harmonisation is commonly considered a zero-sum game: more European Union alignment means less regulation at the national level. However, Ulrich Beck and Edgar Grande criticise this functionalist approach, arguing that it mistakenly assumes the individual steps towards integration and unification of policies to be the consequence of some master plan. However, the aim and concrete realisation of European integration has been left deliberately open and Europeanisation 'happens' more-or-less as the result of 'institutional improvisation' (Beck and Grande, 2004, p. 62). Moreover, many of the results of this regime are better understood as unintended 'collateral effects', rather than as planned outcomes.

When we attend to the 'collateral effects' of Europeanisation we can see that the process is a not a zero-sum game, but a positive-sum game. The expansion process of transnational sovereignty produces *more* unintended effects at all political levels and for all political actors, effects that cannot be apprehended from a perspective fixated on individual nation states' loss of control. The 'more' resides precisely in the ability to govern the 'collateral effects', the unintended consequences of the process. A new type of politics evolves here, one that deploys new forms of political practice. For instance, Beck and Grande (2004) argue that the 'decoupling of decision making and public controversy' is constitutive of new modes of European Union governance. They write:

[o]n the one hand, this (temporal, spatial and social decoupling) relegates the actors of democratic consultation and control to preventive post-hoc; on the other hand, the so-called 'momentum' of the Europeanisation process is now politically generated and implemented in direct executive cooperation between governments and European institutions. (Beck and Grande, 2004, p. 64)

Pushed to the background in the light of the controversies around the European constitution and thus receiving scant attention from a wider public, *The White Paper on European Governance* – which was adopted by the European Commission in July 2001 (http://ec.europa.eu/governance/governance_eu/index_en.htm, last date accessed 3 February 2008) – reads like the script for Beck and Grande's understanding of European policy making. It calls for the strategic participation of civil society, the strengthened use of 'expert knowledge', the use of 'agencies' to implement measures in a decentralised way, and the demand for 'multi-level governance' so as to involve national, regional and local actors more closely in European Union policy making. Earlier we described this approach to governance in the context of transnational sovereignty (Chapter 2) and we discussed Alma-Ata's emphasis on community-based health services as an example of the neoliberalisation entailed in this shift (Chapter 8). Here, following the work of Sabine Hess and Serhat Karakayali (2007; see also Walters, 2006), we want to assert that transnational governance has been crucial to designing and implementing the Schengen process in its initial phases. The Schengen process and the broader Europeanisation of migration policy combined a variety of political actors in a networked form to deal with societal processes that nation states either never could, or no longer can, control. Transnational governance reflects the impossibility of having an external monopoly of force dominate in any single field. The mainstream debate about 'governance of migration' revolves around this precise problem, a debate that is fostered, notably, by the actors associated with international institutions.

While it is true that transnational migration was an issue for intergovernmental and transnational institutions long before the European Union governance debate, only since the 1990s have these institutions recognised migration as a genuine global phenomenon. Prior to this it was primarily national governments who tried to control mobility. All decisions concerning migration were taken by national Interior Ministries, and intergovernmental cooperation had a consultative function only. This changed with the emergence of transnational governance of migration; new transnational institutions were established, whose role is not only consultative but executive. The debate on a 'General Agreement on Movements of People (GAMP)' led by the staff of the International Organisation for Migration (IOM) is a characteristic example of this development. In 1951, in the context of the cold war, the United States and Belgium initiated the International Migration Conference to organise migration from Europe. The focus was on those people who had left socialist countries after 1945. The result of the conference was the establishment of Intergovernmental Committee for European Migration (ICEM) at the beginning of the 1950s. But it is only since the 1980s that these global bodies for governing the logistics of migration movements were transformed into effective tools for transnational governance of migration – and it is in this context that the IOM emerges in 1989 (Düvell, 2002; S. Hess and Karakayali, 2007).

While the transnational governance approach has been central to the Europeanisation of migration policy and to the Schengen process, here we want to assert that the limits of this approach become evident where the unintended effects of transnational European sovereignty collide with new forms of transnational mobility. These new forms of increased transnational mobility push the balance that migration governance has achieved to date to its limits, in regard both to the regulation of internal European Union migration and to the relation of the European Union to other non-EU countries. The central postnational project leading the Europeanisation process, namely the creation of a common internal market with freedom of movement, is already subject to multiple limitations. The so-called 'inner European space' is spatially segmented. The postponement of freedom of movement for workers from the new east European member states until seven years after accession is only one, very obvious, example. Moreover, there is a fragmented understanding of citizenship and residency that produces differing standards for different types of migrants (for example, the failure to harmonise or even implement comprehensive residence, education and employment rights for third-country nationals who are long-term residents in the European Union). The balance of transnational European governance is destabilised not only by the segmentation of the internal European space, but also by the pressures emerging in the relation between EU and non-EU countries. The European Union operates an aggressive policy for the control of migration by deterritorialising sovereignty outside of its own borders to neighbouring countries. Furthermore, irregular migration is increasingly treated as being beyond the realm of citizenship policies and negotiated as part of global governance agreements. In all these cases we see the emergence of a new form of mobility control, one which is no longer the result of transnational governance; rather it is designed and implemented by a series of institutions – we will call them *liminal porocratic institutions* – which lie and operate beyond public negotiation and beyond norms and rules instituted through governance.

Liminal Porocratic Institutions

Today we see the emergence of new forms of mobility control which operate in the liminal spaces between the public, the state and supranational organisations. These liminal spaces are regulated by institutions which largely attempt to close off possibilities for public participation in their management of migration. Crucially, these liminal institutions establish news forms of sovereignty, postliberal sovereignty (as we called it in Chapter 3), which extend beyond European borders through agreements with neighbouring countries. Both the liminal character of the new control institutions and also the deterritorialisation of sovereignty characterise what we call liminal porocratic institutions. Whilst these institutions have emerged in the context of European governance, like the regime of the formation of emergent life (as discussed in Chapter 8), they strive to establish new forms of postliberal control. In this context, several European Union institutions have emerged out of the Schengen process to date: the European police force, Europol; the Schengen Information System (SIS) for European-wide data comparison; the Centre for Information, Discussion and Exchange on the Crossings of Frontiers and Immigration (CIREFI), which organises an early-warning system for global migration movements; and the External Borders Practitioners Common Unit, which has since been attached to the border police agency known as FRONTEX. As concrete operational collaboration has proved difficult, the last two bodies are now supposed to improve cooperation and information exchange between the national agencies involved, as well as supporting them in efforts to implement the European Union measures more quickly and effectively through training programmes and common projects. To provide financing, a programme by the name of ARGO was initiated, an 'action program for administrative cooperation in the fields of external borders, visas, asylum and immigration'.

The concept of liminal porocratic institutions allows us to concentrate our analysis on these institutionalised aggregates which observe and act within the migration and border regime, and whose productivity entails transforming circulation along the border zones into circulation zones of graded sovereignty. National sovereignty strives towards a homogenisation of the population included within the borders of a sovereign nation, and transnational sovereignty strives to establish rules for the regulation of mobile populations achieved through global governance. In contrast, the postliberal space of liminal porocratic institutions can be understood as a flexible regime of control which attempts to regulate mobility flows by forging contingent border zones wherever the routes of migration make the existing regime porous.

Transitory border areas are secured by surveillance and control procedures whose aim is to fix the fragmentation of the Schengen space territorially by creating separate zones, each distinguished by specific spatial practices of social cohesion – a 'differential homogeneity' accompanied by a dehomogenisation of rights. The close linkage between Europol and numerous ad hoc European Union committees, and informal (even paramilitary) international contact meetings, clearly demonstrate how these *liminal institutions* of refugee and migration policy can emerge in spaces where even parliamentary oversight is difficult. This logic of policing mobility and the politics of military containment at the Schengen external borders emerged even more clearly during the war in Kosovo in south-east Europe with the use of the Italian navy against refugee ships in the Adriatic since 1977 and the creation of Macedonian and Albanian refugee camps in locations in the immediate vicinity of the border (i.e. the war zone) during the NATO bombardment. The illegal mass deportations on Lampedusa and the use of weapons in Ceuta by the Guardia Civil (a unit with an explicit military status) are also indicative of the militarisation of policing mobility.

Thus, in summary, we use the term *liminal* for describing two aspects of the new emerging tools for mobility control in postliberal sovereignty. Firstly, liminal refers to how institutions which control mobility operate in fluid, transit spaces on and around the European borders. Secondly, it indicates that as these institutions are constantly changing themselves their public visibility becomes impossible. Below we describe the key function of the liminality of these institutions and in the next chapter we discuss their porocratic attributes. Like the formation of emergent life, liminal porocratic institutions are not directly concerned with the management of populations. Rather they attempt to control migration flows and to regulate the porosity of borders. Whilst the porosity of the border regime is commonly seen as a security deficit, in the next chapter we try to show how liminal porocratic institutions work with (instead of against) porosity and to a certain extent participate in the creation of a porous system of mobility. Their goal is not to stop migration movements, but to control flows of movement by regulating the pores of the European borders. Before elaborating on this we want to describe the most important functional elements of liminal porocratic institutions: first, cyber-deportability, which hinges on the knowledge based cyber-technological management of migrational flows; second, the virtualisation of borders, which consists of deterritorialising border controls and externalising camps.

Cyber-deportability: the Virtual Imprisonment of Migrants

The most common manifestation of the border in Europe is not to be found along the geographical border line of the Schengen area, but rather in digital records on laptops belonging to the border police; in the visa records of European embassies in Moscow, Istanbul, Accra or Tripoli; in the checkpoints of Heathrow, Tegel, Paris Charles de Gaulle or Mytilini Odysseas Elytis airports; in the German central register of asylum seekers (ZAST); in the online entries of the Schengen Information System (SIS), where the data on persons denied entry to the Schengen area is administered; in the Eurodac, the data system administered by the Commission, where the fingerprints of asylum seekers and apprehended illegalised migrants are stored.

The centrality of the concept of 'mobility flow' for liminal porocratic institutions denotes the affinity between the fast, flexible multidirectionality of the mobile subjectivities of migrants and the knowledge-based cyber-technologies used for their surveillance. The denaturalisation of border control has the double function of politics at a distance and virtual data collection. It deploys a logic of an extraterritorial net of control which denaturalises not only forms of surveillance but also forms of punishment by extending the risk of deportability within and beyond state boundaries. Here we use Nicholas de Genova's (2005) extremely important concept of deportability in conjunction with the increased usage of cyber-technologies for migration control: cyber-deportability. Access to mobility is often via the computer screen and in the same way the threat of deportation or imprisonment in a detention centre is often regulated digitally through high-tech networks of control. In this sense, we can see how irregular migrants come to inhabit a 'virtual prison' (Diminescou, 2003).

Crucial to cyber-deportability is the creation of knowledge databases of migrants' movements. The implementation of cyber-deportability is possible only through the constant actualisation of existing data. This necessitates that liminal porocratic institutions take a very different approach to the relation between knowledge collection and implementation of border and migrant control operations. This new approach consists of tightening the feedback loop between observation and action, so as to enhance the flexible adaptation of observation and action to the specific modalities of clandestinised border-crossing mobility. According to Sciortino (2004), the aim of migration regimes is not so much to combat transit, rather it is to establish *anticipatory* strategies to target the flexible, unstable, temporary tactics of border crossing. This is achieved through the deterritorialisation of control, that is, the establishment of flexible surveillance and control technologies outside of the 'natural' borders of the European Union, in the very places where border crossing occurs and new migration routes emerge. Cyber-deportability relies on a constant loop between observing and acting, enabled by the deterritorialisation of control and the establishment of virtual borders as illustrated below.

'*People Flow: Managing Migration in a New European Commonwealth*' (Veenkamp, Bentley and Buonfino, 2003) is the title of one of the countless position papers produced by think tanks close to the European Union, such as the British think tank Demos, or the European Policy Centre (EPC) headed by Theo Veenkamp (also the head of strategy of the Dutch Ministry of the Interior). Published in 2003, *People Flow* sounds like a slogan of European anti-racist and migration-oriented left social movements. Central elements of this paper can be recognised in recent political recommendations on the deterritorialisation of camps made by the British government. This and many other similar position papers have long since recognised that migration is essentially uncontrollable. They refer to the need for a pragmatic approach to the 'humanitarian dilemmas' produced by the binary political division between the categories of 'genuine refugees' and 'genuine migrants'. In the process, migrants should be addressed as 'responsible partners'. Primarily, however, these papers foreground an understanding of the dynamic of migration – in their rhetoric, the 'autonomous migration drive'. They call for 'a network-based regime' to supplant a 'rule-based regime' and propose to utilise migration streams in ways that will be economically beneficial for target countries. *People Flow* suggests the establishment of a network of 'European Union Mobility Service Points' in the countries south of the Mediterranean. These service points should serve as reception centres for asylum seekers wishing to come to Europe, akin to international employment agencies along the transit routes. European Union officials then have the role of 'diverting' migration routes: bringing them into line with the needs of the target countries as well as those of global migration control. In addition, the authors suggest that asylum applications and granting of protection should be the responsibility of 'open' facilities, also outside of Europe.

The suggestion goes that migrants and asylum seekers could pay back the help they have obtained either through work services or through low-interest loans to be repaid after arrival. In general, *People Flow* formulates a globalised immigration regime that is completely relocated to the countries of origin.

However, it would be incorrect to reduce the role of think tanks like Demos to mere ideological agents of liminal porocratic institutions. On the contrary, their strategies of knowledge production rely on the same virtual data collection which is crucial for the executive operations of liminal porocratic institutions. The virtualisation of knowledge about migration movements and routes is a key element of the new regime of mobility control. This relies primarily on the construction of mechanisms of cyber control designed to react in an immediate way to the changes taking place on the ground.

Virtual Borders and the Deterritorialisation of Control: the Case of Maritime Borders

We want to exemplify the loop between the cyber-surveillance of mobility – deterritorialisation of control – and the virtualisation of borders by referring to the case of the European maritime border control. At an informal meeting of European Union interior ministers on 14 February 2002 in Santiago de Compostella, a 'comprehensive plan to combat illegal migration and people trafficking' was discussed. This preceded and formed the basis for the resolutions of the European Union summit on increased effectiveness of the European external maritime border in Seville in June 2002 (see the report Council of the European Union (2002): 'Presidency Conclusions at the Seville European Council', III, Paragraph 33 and the report on clandestine mobility: Council of the European Union (2002): 'Advances made in combating illegal immigration', 10009/JAI 141, Migr 56, Brussels 14 June 2002). Such treaties on trade, aid and support coupled with threats of penalties and sanctions are intended to pressure countries of origin and transit states to accept a 'common management of migration flows' and the return of their own citizens, as well as transmigrants, who are unwelcome in Europe.

In 2003, at the behest of the European Union interior and justice ministers, the French Interior Ministry think tank, CIVIPOL, produced a feasibility study on intensification of European maritime border controls (Council document 11490/1/03, 19 September 2003). CIVIPOL delineates three possible maritime entries to the European Union: harbours (entry as a stowaway); geographically favourable sea routes (so-called focal routes, such as Gibraltar, Lampedusa and the Aegean Islands, used by migrants picked up on the coasts of the European Union); and random routes (where traffickers land their clients on random coastal areas). CIVIPOL operates on the basis of a concept of 'virtual borders'. Accordingly, border controls are to be relocated to the origin and transit points (coasts and harbours) of transit states. On the basis of the CIVIPOL feasibility study, in November 2003 the European Council decided on a 'programme of measures to combat illegal immigration at the maritime borders of the European Union' (Council document 15445/03, 28 November 2003). What this involves, among other measures, is the pre-emptive interception and inspection of suspicious ships on the high seas. Where illegalised migrants are found, the intercepted ships are to be returned to the harbours of the third (non-European Union) countries from where the migrants' transport has begun. The European Union intends to create reception centres in these transit states where those picked up at sea can be held in 'humane conditions' until they are returned to their countries of origin. However, the policy of deterritorialisation of mobility control necessitates strict border-regime institutions that are capable of translating the measures agreed by the Council of Interior Ministers into the trans-border coordination of plans and their implementation.

The multilateral framework of the Baltic Sea Region Border Control Cooperation (BSRBCC) regularly coordinates operations that build on the experiences gained by Europol in so-called High Impact Operations, operations that seek to interrupt the routes used by migrants and to apprehend traffickers. For example, the Triton action plan involved border and customs police from Italy, France, Spain and Greece carrying out an intensive operation between 4 and 7 March 2003, based on an operations plan devised by Greece. In the course of this short operation, over 200 ships were inspected and 226 migrants and 6 traffickers apprehended. Initially, they were taken to European Union territory. A centre for risk analysis (RAC) was established in Helsinki to compile regular reports on individual case analyses. The RAC has an operational arm (European Intelligence Centre – EIC) that develops and helps implement surveillance and border control activities in cooperation with Europol and with the Immigration Liaison Officers (ILOs). On the basis of the 'proactive' use of the ILOs – who are European Union citizens attached to the Foreign Ministries of European Union member states and charged with gathering strategic and tactical information to be passed on to

Europol via member states' Foreign Ministries – the European Union assesses third countries that 'do not prove cooperative in combating illegal migration'.

The detailed planning of such actions is carried out in the forums of the Western and the Eastern Sea Borders Centres (WSBC und ESBC) founded in 2003. The Madrid-based WSBC coordinates actions in the Atlantic, the English Channel and the North and Baltic Seas. Based in Piraeus, the ESBC specialises in the timely and proximate implementation of plans for maritime control in the Mediterranean area as well as in the registration and assessment of situation reports from ILOs. They report on information about border crossing, including interrogations of migrants being held in the camps and of their helpers along the route. In this way, the virtualisation of borders and the deterritorialisation of control feed back knowledge which is crucial to the overall cyber-control of migrational movements. Taken together, these Sea Borders Centres form Schengen's organisational framework for future European maritime border control, whose restructuring began in 2005 with the establishment of the 'European Agency for the Management of Operational Cooperation at the External Borders of the European Union Member States' (FRONTEX). FRONTEX is designed to establish a cyber-database of migrational movements and to coordinate the whole area of external border control. The aim of such 'agencies' is to improve cooperation, exchange and the transmission of European Union directives into national political practices (e.g. the coordination of return operations/deportations, obtaining travel documents and formulating training programmes and guidelines).

Over the past four years, it has been singular, media-saturated 'humanitarian catastrophes' that have acted as the driving force for this new direction in European Union migration policy. While the official decision-making structures of the European Union seem extremely cumbersome, and the community aims decided at Tampere in 1999 have yet to be achieved, ad hoc processes that use the opportunities produced by humanitarian crises seems, on the contrary, to be highly productive. Despite their productive, cyber-technological/military dominance, liminal porocratic institutions are less concerned with expanding internal border controls than with pressuring transit and migrant countries of origin to collect and forward information which is crucial to the cyber-control of mobility. We have discussed above how the cyber-control of mobility functions through the virtualisation of borders, and this in turn is achieved through the deterritorialisation of local agencies of control. One key dimension of the deterritorialisation of control is the externalisation of camps.

The Humanitarian Pretext and the Externalisation of Camps

By 2003 the British government had already promoted the so-called 'home-based' erection of Regional Protection Zones or Transit Processing Centres, places where both migrants in transit and refugees deported from the European Union could be held outside of the European Union. Initially, however, this initiative of the United Kingdom was criticised by individual states (such as Germany). The European Union Commission, on the other hand, promoted the slogan 'to bring safe havens closer to the people' at the summit in Thessalonica in 2003. Orchestrated in the summer of 2004, the widespread public criticism of the failed rescue attempt of shipwrecked migrants from the *Cap Anamur* helped to galvanise the debate and finally ensured a breakthrough by successfully creating a broad liberal consensus. In the light of the increased public interest, the German interior minister, Otto Schilly, together with his Italian colleague, were then able to revive the idea of the externalisation of camps. They presented it as a necessary humanitarian reaction to the deadly consequences of the increased militarisation of the borders; the pair represented their initiative as resulting from indignation 'about the large numbers setting out for Europe, often in unseaworthy boats, and thereby risking their lives' (German Federal Ministry of the Interior press release on the occasion of Schilly's meeting with Pisanu in Lucca, Tuscany, 12 August 2004). Following their example, Austria demanded the construction of camps in the Ukraine for refugees from Chechnya. The UNHCR also entered the debate with their own externalisation concept, which really only differed to the extent that they called for the camps to be erected within the borders of the European Union, on the territory of the new member states. The IOM – an organisation that maintained an extraterritorial camp for Australia on the small island of Nauru – also got involved in this debate. In fact, the idea of establishing camps close to countries of origin was really not such a new one, as there were already a number of such camps in existence: one financed with Italian money in Tunisia, the north Iraqi protection zone, or the camps that were established in the context of the war in Kosovo, for example.

   Over the following two years, the southern European border and the Mediterranean remained in the focus of politicians and liberal public opinion. In the summer of 2005, images of hundreds of African migrants storming the high-security fences around the Spanish enclaves of Ceuta and Mellila in Morocco brought migration to the forefront of international media attention. The images had barely faded when in 2006 international cameras captured the arrival, day after day, of small, overloaded wooden boats as they landed on the Canary Islands. Since the intensification of controls on the Straits of Gibraltar following the events in Ceuta, African migration has been forced to seek ever more distant coasts, which of course mean longer passages. Again we saw the same mix: humanitarian indignation in the face of human tragedy and horror scenarios and an ensuing flurry of activism on the part of European Union ministers. And as with the events of the preceding years, the narrative of the new humanitarianism was pressed into service with demands for a deterritorialisation of borders and the externalisation of camps in the interests of avoiding a human catastrophe.

Going further, the logic of the new humanitarianism also includes an imperative to act – similar to a regime of exception. It allows the European border-regime strategists to implement actions and evade laws to an extent that would be impossible during 'peacetime'. These events have served to integrate transit countries from ever further inside the African continent into the European Union border regime. (For instance, African transit countries and countries of origin sat around a table in Morocco in June 2006, together with the European Union and the largest non-state actors of migration management, such as the IOM, to agree controls close to the country of origin). The humanitarian pretext and the moral panic it creates is also an excellent opportunity to generate billions for new border control projects. For example, following the case of the 9,000 migrants arriving on the Canaries, the European Union Commission managed to secure €1 billion for surveillance in addition to funds designated for re-equipping drones to secure the borders. Much of this funding has been directed to the controversial European Union border control agency, FRONTEX, that began operations in Warsaw in 2006; FRONTEX can now prove its usefulness by coordinating the support of European Union member states for the Spanish government. At a conference on this theme held in Hungary in 2007 – the 14th International Border Conference, attended by over 40 states from Europe, Asia and Africa – eight European Union states were able to agree to common patrols along the West African coast, involving warships and helicopters. If this common border patrol troop is a success, there is a plan to deploy it in other migration flashpoints; so a common border patrol troop will have been created that bypasses the European Union parliament, which had rejected exactly such a measure only three years previously.

The European Union's most recent efforts regarding the externalisation of camps have been anchored in the Hague programme, passed by the chief ministers in 2004 after an evaluation of the 1999 Tampere programme. While they had to conclude that the aims of Tampere and the communitisation of migration policy had not been achieved, they now proclaimed a new phase in asylum and immigration policy. This new European Union programme also proceeds from the understanding proposed in *People Flow*, that the 'international migration movement will continue to exist'. In order to confront this in reality, a 'comprehensive' and pragmatic approach is required. First and foremost, the 'external dimension of asylum and immigration' needs to be addressed. In plain terms, this implies further moves to externalise migration controls that include readmission agreements and the accelerated establishment of camps. Pilot projects are being undertaken to create regional security zones in third countries. These zones are being created – in the terminology of the European Union – in 'partnership' with the authorities of the countries involved and in close cooperation with the UN High Commissioner for Human Rights.

The emergence of such institutional aggregates, who are leading the way in the development of surveillance techniques, the administration of cyber-deportability and the deterritorialisation of borders, is plainly evident when we take the European Union as a case study. However, postliberal aggregates of mobility control, which are connected without being reduced to state and transnational governing bodies, are by no means restricted to the European Union. But rather than developing our analysis of liminal porocratic institutions by elaborating on different regional instances of their global emergence, our primary concern now is to examine the role of migration movements in the social and political struggles out of which these postliberal aggregates are arising.

11   EXCESSIVE MOVEMENTS IN AEGEAN TRANSIT

The Aegean Transit Space

The map of the Aegean archipelago (or the Straits of Gibraltar or the Channel of Sicily) denotes a geographical territory of sovereign control; but, defined as international waters, these spaces also guarantee the circulation of goods and freedom of movement. Greece did sign the UN Protocol against the Smuggling of Migrants by Land, Sea and Air, supplementing the United Nations Convention against Transnational Organized Crime, on 13 December 2000. However, it has yet to be officially ratified. Greece's ambivalent stance is an expression of the will to control borders on the one hand and their de facto permeability on the other. It is an expression of the clash between control and escape in postliberal conditions.

One of the most important results of the meeting of the European Council in Thessalonica on 19 and 20 June 2003 was the emphasis on the importance of controlling sea borders. But according to the Greek Ministry of Merchant Marine, the protection of the Greek seaboard involves a number of difficulties, primarily arising from its geographical specificities. The usual practice is that as soon as the harbour police discover unidentified ships in Greek waters they attempt to move them back into Turkish waters. Sometimes the ships heed these calls and turn about; however, it is likely that the ships make further attempts to reach Greek territory as soon as the patrol boat has sailed on. In other cases, migrants try to reach the islands on inflatable dinghies which cannot be detected by the security cameras. Dinghy occupants have reacted to threats of expulsion into Turkish waters with a risky manoeuvre: they overturn or sink their boats. At such moments the role of the harbour police is transformed into a 'rescue mission', since as soon as drowning people are found in Greek territorial waters, it is the duty of the coastguards to come to their aid. Those rescued are brought to land and handed over to the police.

Border control in the maritime sector is becoming almost impossible in most of the Greek islands. Attempts have been made to send castaway migrants back to Turkey from the island of Lesbos using cruise ships. However, this practice caused a 'diplomatic problem', since Turkey then accused the Greek state of organising and facilitating 'illegal migration'. Lesbos and Bodrum lie 8 km apart as the crow flies. The commander of the coastguard in Izmir explained to us during our visit there – like his Greek colleague, off the record – that the maritime border with Greece is not only in practice uncontrollable, for geographic reasons, but that the coastguard cannot really keep up with the speed and ingenuity of the 'transport business'.

The Turkish Aegean coast has become a transit space where the diverse dynamics of a transnational social space clash. Paradigmatic of this field is the way hotels such as the Hotel Almanya are used.

Like many such pensions and hotels on the Turkish Riviera, it is used by the Turkish authorities. Here, you can find not only German and Russian tourists, but also transmigrants being held by the police until their status can be determined and they are either set free or deported. Here, migrants from Iraq, Afghanistan, Syria, Liberia and Sudan are held in cramped conditions. Many of them possess a wide knowledge of migration matters, such as possible further routes, or the best places to apply for asylum and how best to go about it.

There are many such improvised 'deportation camps' in schools, empty factories and police stations. They are used by local authorities as temporary prisons in the absence of a state migration and asylum policy and of appropriate infrastructure. Many things can happen in this rather dubious system. For instance, migrants are packed off to Syria irrespective of whether they came from there or not. Alternatively, this situation can mean that a flu outbreak or a purported marriage leads to release from custody. There is also a market for fakes and frauds. The merchandise consists of fraudulent accounts of escape, faked papers or torture videos. Not only is use made of the categories of European Union migration policy, but it is clear that there is also a wide knowledge of the conditions of migration; how to make another believe that you are not coming from a 'safe country' or how to satisfy the documentary requirements of the European asylum process.

'Sheep Trade': the Wild Sheep Chase in the Aegean

In contrast to the well-known tourist destinations along the Turkish Mediterranean coast, Ayvalik is a small and almost sleepy resort that lies only a few kilometres from the Greek island of Lesbos. We visited Ayvalik as one of the sites of our militant research project of border camps in the south-eastern Balkans in 2003–04 (cf. Transit Migration Forschungsgruppe, 2006). Talking to people in Ayvalik about 'migrants' can be somewhat confusing: 'Migrants – göcmen? You want to research the stories of the exchange of Greeks and Turks in 1923? Yes, there are some people living here who were driven off Lesbos.' It was only when we ask for accounts of refugees, mülteciler, that we were told:

Yes, only last week our cleaning lady told us about a ship that sailed out with 23 people on board and capsized somewhere nearby. Only three survived. The coastguard doesn't bother to raise the sunken and stranded ships anymore because there are so many of them. I can bring you to one.

The journey did not lead to a stranded ship, but to another person who knew the 'sheep trade' from personal experience. Just a few years previously the man had helped 800 migrants board a tanker. It happened the way it always does. He got a call from Istanbul to let him know his help was needed. They actually succeeded in transporting the 800 people to the sparsely populated coast and from there to the tanker which was to take them directly to Italy. Unimaginable that 800 people could remain undiscovered on this strip of coast where the only land route to the next town is a gravel path. 'Nothing is really secret or goes unnoticed here', remarked our interview partner. A day later he got the news that they had captured the tanker. 'That's the risk in this business. We here on the coast just drifted into it. It all started at the beginning of the 1990s, at first very small and secret until now it's a big sector'.

The transport began when an Iraqi couple moved to Ayvalik and took a holiday home on the coast. At first they helped a few of their relatives to flee the Gulf War.

Then, in the middle of the 1990s the Kurds also began to show up, and now they're arriving from all over. In the beginning they all travelled by public transport; then they were brought with minibuses and eventually with three or four big buses – until the police began to notice. So now they are moved in trucks, squashed together like sheep.

He got involved in the business himself when two young men approached him in his hotel one day and asked him if he could help. The boat they had travelled on from Istanbul had been seized by the police. They needed help quickly as there was a group of migrants waiting in a forest nearby. They asked him to try and get their boat back for them. When the men led him into the forest he was shocked and could not believe his eyes. Because there – it was December, cold and wet – he saw men, women and children who had been waiting for days to make the crossing. They could not light any fires for fear of discovery. He decided to become involved and even to buy a boat if necessary. A few days later the refugees set out to sea but they were found and arrested a short way from Lesbos. The two men kept their word and pretended that they had stolen his boat. Still, he had wanted to get his money; after all he 'was no good Samaritan'. That was why he had gone to Istanbul – the central trans-shipment point and business headquarters – to try to get his money back; but with no luck.

The story told by another smuggler, an old fisherman, sounded similar. He also traced the beginning of his involvement in the business to his contacts with the Iraqi couple. What started out as a favour led to more and more people asking him for 'help', until eventually he was arrested three years ago. It was only during his two and a half years in prison in Greece that he realised that the 'sheep trade' had become big business on the coast, he told us with a smile. Much like the hotel owner, he wanted to help the 'poor migrants', but was quite happy to make a bit of money on the side.

As long as there is war and destruction in the world, people will take flight – that's the way it is. If people can only choose between death and hunger, they'll try and escape, even if it's dangerous ... and so I help them.

When we told him about how the former East German border was commonly discussed in Germany as an impenetrable border he laughed: 'I tell you people will always try and escape and others will always help them.' Nevertheless, the situation has become more difficult because the checks have increased. The 'sheep trade' continues, however, and the only problem is that there is always another police unit waiting around the corner that has not been bribed yet.

A professional smuggler in Greece told us of his experiences with the practice of border crossings: 'The payment only comes at the end of the deal.' That's the security that the customers or their relatives have. The deal is always a verbal one. The captain is 'trustworthy' because he suffers recurrent financial problems and needs the money. When the captain has been contacted and the agreement made then the date is set, the 'heads' are counted, and finally the price and method of payment is determined. The price varies according to the number of 'heads' and the type of journey. The captain can earn up to €15,000 per 'transport'. 'Sometimes, during the summer, we are finished in five minutes.'

Excessive Movements

The social relations amongst those in the immediate vicinity of the border zone are closely tied to the current developments in the metropolitan areas of West Turkey, as our chance encounter with Mike in Bodrum shows. Mike lived for a number of years as a transmigrant in Istanbul and then made his way along the coast with a small photo in his hand looking for a friend of whom he had lost track after a failed attempt to cross the border. 'Any other questions?' asked Mike somewhat reservedly during a second meeting in Istanbul. Years ago he had gone to Lebanon with his friend as a basketball player. They had managed to find a job there; a temporary work permit was not a problem. However, after years of civil war, Lebanon was a chaotic and difficult country. Both of them set out for Europe with forged passports and €1,500 in their pockets. They then arrived in Turkey via Syria. From there they made three attempts to continue their journey: with a visa and a scheduled flight to Poland, to Croatia and by ship to Greece. Every attempt failed – there was not much money left. It is very difficult to save money in Istanbul. Mike complained that they only rarely found work, had to pay exorbitant rents and had to change their accommodation frequently. The areas in which they lived were particularly prone to raids. Mike often spent days and months in prison. He still found ways and means of getting out of prison – not just because the deportation flights to Africa were expensive and the state infrastructure underdeveloped in this area. He could not remember, he told us with a laugh, under how many names he had been arrested.

Luis, too, was released from custody some time ago. He travelled with an official student visa, but was soon unable to pay the student fees, which meant his visa was no longer extended. Like many holders of forged passports, not having the option of buying a flight ticket, he set out for the Aegean coast, but the minibus from Istanbul was intercepted and the group was imprisoned in an empty school. Again, he had to decide in which category of the official migration and mobility policy to place himself. Should he stay in Istanbul and eke out a meagre existence, or return to Ghana and from there apply for a new visa or, even better, asylum – this time in Germany? Or perhaps attempt to reach Germany via illegalised routes? But, as he said, Greece would really be enough. Greece is in fact the first Schengen point of entry in this region, where the hubs of the migration routes are being linked under new conditions.

Resa, a migrant from Bangladesh, was involved in organising a transport from Lesbos to Italy. In the summer of 2004 he was detained in the main city of Lesbos, Mitilini, on suspicion of 'trafficking'. He used a dwelling on Mitilini to quarter the migrants, whom he recruited in the camp in Pagani. He flew to the island after he was contacted by phone by a Palestinian living in the camp in Pagani. He informed the transmigrants in the camp that the 'transport' to Italy, including the initial accommodation in Mitilini and Athens, would cost €500. About 750 people were stuck in the camp in Pagani

– guarded by eight policemen. A clothes donation organised by the local refugee support group on Mitilini offered a chance to visit the refugees. As soon as Resa caught sight of the camp, the prefecture official driving the truck with the clothing and medicines exclaimed with genuine enthusiasm: 'It's great here, just like in prison.' Most of those detained knew that they would have to stay in the camp for three months and then go to Athens. They asked for telephone cards and telephone numbers of NGOs in Athens. When asked if they needed anything, it was a surprise to hear the confident response of one of the migrants in the camp: 'Yes, an English grammar book. ... We want to go to Canada, you know!'

Apo was another inmate of this camp which was built as a so-called 'reception centre'. He told us that he was a 'guest worker' who had lived with his relatives in Stuttgart since the beginning of the 1980s. In the 1990s he had gone back to the Turkish mountains to fight with the PKK. When the PKK called a ceasefire he had withdrawn to Iraq. He had already spent some months trying to return to Germany, eventually managing to reach Lesbos from the Turkish coast. He could not return directly to Germany since – according to the stipulations of the German Aliens Act – his legal residency was no longer valid due to his long absence. So although he had lived in Germany for 25 years, Apo would be illegal in Germany. Now he was trying to contact his relatives in Germany so they could get him out of the camp and back to Germany in some way or another. Although he would qualify as a political refugee, he did not want to apply for asylum on Lesbos. He felt the procedure was too uncertain and took too much time. The acceptance quota in 2004 was 0.6 per cent and waiting periods of up to two years are not uncommon. If Apo applied for asylum in Greece, he would also have to be registered in Laurio – a camp for victims of political persecution, especially from Turkey, erected about ten years ago south of Athens. If he were to be registered in Greece as a refugee, however, his first arrival data would be registered in the Schengen Information System (SIS). According to the Dublin Convention for asylum and visa issues, which regulates first-country provisions, this would rule out travelling on to Germany since he would have to reckon with his being sent back to Greece in case of arrest. However, since Apo wishes to live in Germany, he accepts the risks entailed in crossing borders illegally. He is counting on being able to leave Greece illegally with the help of his family networks. He also does not wish to apply for asylum in Germany. As an asylum seeker he would automatically be sent to an asylum seekers' hostel, where he could neither work nor, due to the strictures of the residency regulations, live near his family. He just wants to live illegally in Germany.

On Crete, we find a repeat of this scenario in a hotel near to the oppressive and dull United States military base. A few years ago one would have found high-ranking NATO generals in residence here; today the hotel is host to 140 migrants. The decor is the same as in the camp in Lesbos; bored, card-playing naval officers drinking *frappé* with two migrants. The spokesperson for the detainees, who was a teacher in Egypt, tells us that half of the detained migrants are Palestinians who have applied for asylum, while the other half do not wish to make an application. Actually, they are only in Greece by mistake. They really want to go to Italy. Their only demand was to help them free 'their brother', who had been identified during an interrogation as a 'trafficker', only because 'they needed someone to blame'. According to a naval officer in front of the hotel, the four 'traffickers' had actually not been apprehended yet. 'The migrants know exactly what they want', said the Amnesty International activist from Hamburg responsible for the case, who showed little surprise:

The Palestinians, or those who apply for asylum as such, don't come from Egypt. For those who do come from Egypt and wish to go to Italy, however, it is better not to make an application for asylum, since, after their certain repatriation, they would end up in prison in Egypt as traitors. But this would mean not being able to make another attempt at immigration. And they always want to try again!

When viewed from a theoretical perspective which emphasises repression and regulation, the camps would appear to provide the ultimate proof for the efficacy and the misery of 'Fortress Europe'. However, the stories told by Mike, Resa and Apo provide exemplary evidence of the porosity and failure of this self-proclaimed panoptical and omnipotent 'fortress'. The counterpart to the discourse of Fortress Europe is smuggling. Security needs fear, repression needs risk, policing needs criminals, smugglers and illegalised migrants alike. The figure of the 'trafficker' or smuggler is like a blind spot in the current analysis of migratory networks – rarely researched and the most criminalised (with a few brilliant exceptions though: see Karakayali, 2008; Andrijasevic, 2004). The mafia-like veil covering the transport networks is criticised in the few existing studies only as a factor of transmigrants' exploitation (Icduygu and Toktas, 2002; Sciortino, 2004). Such an emphasis on exploitation is mainly used to prove the necessity for better border protection and stricter migration policing and to devalue migrants' agency (for a thorough critique of this understanding of trafficking, see Andrijasevic, 2004).

But something else is happening in the turbulent Aegean transit space. Something imperceptible. Mike's, Resa's and Apo's active embeddedness within criminal networks of cross-border mobility, as well as their perseverance and the multidirectional flexibility with which they manage their biographies, prompt an alternative understanding both of the supposed impermeability of borders and also of the function of trafficking. From the standpoint of migration, borders and trafficking are both part of the same structure of oppression. Migrants deal with this by incorporating borders and trafficking as necessary factors of their movements (Andrijasevic, 2003). They do not oppose them, they undo them by moving to the next city, the next country, the next continent. Migrants undo them by incorporating them into their imperceptible excessive movements. In what follows we want to exemplify this in regard to the function of camps. When viewed through Mike's, Resa's and Apo's eyes, camps are nothing more and nothing less than tolerated transit stations, even if these spaces seem to oppose the very core of migration: excessive mobility. Camps are heterotopias, in Foucault's (2005) words – that is, spaces outside of all spaces, although they exist in reality. What makes the imperceptible politics of migration so powerful is that it incorporates, digests and absorbs these spaces through the excessive movements of mobility.

Transit Camps

The function of liminal porocratic institutions (as described in the previous chapter) clearly illustrates current tendencies in the transformation of sovereignty. The process of the Europeanisation of migration policy and its result, liminal porocratic institutions, not only attempt to erect a rigid executive alliance for policing migration, but they also construct a space for a new form of migration regulation. While statist–legalist thinking understands undocumented and illegal migration as a criminal crossing of borders, it is, in terms of its local realities across Europe, a complex field potentially amenable to management and control.

Transmigrants caught at the borders are confined to the camps on the islands until their nationality has been accurately determined. Because of pressure from the European Union, a treaty of repatriation between Greece and Turkey was established in 2001, replacing the previous, ineffective bilateral repatriation agreements. However, this treaty is practically redundant due, at least in part, to the established human rights regime. European Union threats of penalties and sanctions are meant to force countries of origin and transit states like Greece to accept a 'common management of migration flows' and the return of their citizens or transmigrants who are unwelcome in Europe. However, when it gets translated into the actual practice of border institutions, the application of the treaty diverges radically from the Schengen deterrence scenario.

Those actors involved on the ground include not only the migrants and the militarised border patrols, but also those in the intervening negotiation space in which various NGOs strive to implement European asylum law. In Greece, repatriations are illegal following a human-rights perspective which deems that 'just-in-time' sanctions against illegal border crossings are secondary compared to a general presumption of a right to asylum or humanitarian assistance (administrative deportation according to §50 of Statute 2910/2001 on leaving and entering Greek territory illegally). The clarification of this procedure normally lasts 70 days. The Turkish–Greek treaty only works in cases where migrants can be classed as clearcut labour migrants from Turkey, and are either already registered in the Schengen Information System (SIS) as the result of a previous illegal border crossing, or they decide to 'out' themselves as illegal so that they can make a renewed attempt at the border crossing from Istanbul or Ayvalik under better conditions. For migrants from Afghanistan, China and Africa, repatriation is even more difficult, since such migrants must be handed over to the bordering country of origin, insofar as it is a 'third country'.

The illegal border crossing is usually registered by the coastguard or border police and on arrest the police order an immediate administrative deportation on the grounds of illegal entry. However, the state prosecutor suspends this provisionally by not filing an individual case against the illegalised migrant. This is a reaction to the fact that the police are unable to provide asylum procedures in the camps and, therefore, the illegalised immigrant cannot be immediately deported, because of a presumed right of asylum. As a rule, those not wishing to or unable to apply for asylum, or those clearly identified as, for example, Iranians or Iraqis, are transported as quickly as possible to the detention camps in the northern region of Evros (Lafazani, 2006). In the worst case, these migrants are 'clandestinely' sent back across the waters of the Evros river border – mostly under threat of violence. Those among the camp population who have not been immediately deported leave the camp after three months with a document that requires them to leave the country 'voluntarily' within two weeks. Here, the subordinate clause in the 'document of release' is of interest – it states: 'in a direction of your choice'. Apo and other transmigrants may, after obtaining permission to leave the camp with their 'release permit', travel on to the mainland. The law states that whoever claims asylum, either verbally or in writing, may not be repatriated. The applicant is supposed to be interviewed within three months, but in practice this phase lasts from one to three years.

This administrative practice documents a political calculus that is an open secret: the migrants will waive their interviews, remain illegalised and move on. Until 1992 the responsibility for both the recognition of the right to asylum and the financing of initial reception lay primarily with UNHCR. The official policy on asylum was characterised by the political credo that Greece was only a transit stop on the way to the European heartland. The implementation of European Union legal standards on asylum, mainly due to the intervention of NGOs, serves to put a brake on restrictive border controls and to a certain extent legalises the dynamics of mobility and transmigration. It could be termed a paradox that the Greek Ministry of the Interior refused to finance the construction of a large internment camp in the border triangle of Evros that was decided upon by the European Council in Thessalonica in 2003, and was to have had a capacity for 2000 inmates. It is a common belief of the local authorities in the region that a mega-camp of such dimensions would transform the border area into a favoured rest route for transnational 'migration flows'. The area would act like a magnet, upsetting the balance of control over the existing 'corridors'. It was deemed preferable to repay the sums of money allocated by the European Union for the camp.

So, transit camps mark a provisional topography of stations along the various migration routes. The camps along the Aegean function less as a blockade directed against migration and more like an entrance ticket into the next leg of the journey. Whereas on the Turkish side, before the gates of the 'fortress', the emphasis is on *immobilising migrants*, the focus on the Greek side is on the opposite: *institutionalising mobility* (Panagiotidis and Tsianos, 2007). The improvised camps on the Turkish side cannot be understood simply as the results of the deterritorialisation of the cordon of camps to extend beyond European borders. They mark places where the directionality of a migration route towards the side of the Greek transit camps is only temporarily 'diverted'. These diversionary tactics continue within the Schengen space on the other side, in Lesbos, in London, in Amsterdam, in Berlin. In the context of the Europeanisation of migration policy and liminal porocratic institutions, it is not simply that the heartland of Europe determines the general parameters and the south is then liable for local implementation. The European Union countries of the Mediterranean play an active and central role in this process.

The changes we have described to the function of the camps of southern Europe represent, at least in part, the beginnings of a productive transformation of migration control managed by liminal porocratic institutions. It would be a mistake to see the emerging migration and border regime in the Aegean zone as simply the product of European Union migration bureaucrats or of 'Balkan corruption'. The implementation of European Union migration policy across the whole south-eastern European area, with its informal cross-border economies, is more a mode of transit regulation than of transit blockage. This observation implies the necessity to rethink both classic migration theory as well as European integration studies; in particular it means that the necessity to rethink the concept of the 'camp' is unavoidable.

Camps as Regulators of Migrational Flows: Porosity and Permeability

Lesbos lies precisely at the emblematic overlap of two maps which are critical of current migration policies. The 'Atlas of Globalisation' from *Le Monde Diplomatique* maps fatalities and mistreatment at the new external borders of the European Union in homocentric circles, while the 'Camp Atlas' of the Project Migreurop (www.migreurop.org) marks the edifice of Fortress Europe with dots indicating detention centres. They form an almost continuous line on the south-eastern edge of the European Union. The highest concentration of camps in southern Europe is in the Aegean. But what exactly is a camp? Both critical and affirmative sides of the debate on camps talk about the fortress that Europe has erected against migration, evoking associations of a field of battle.

These associations are particularly important for ideological and political debates about migration. The migrants in the camp and the critics in the metropolises, rely on a human-rights discourse that seems, at present, to be the only vehicle capable of articulating migrants' interests (we develop an alternative approach to the human rights discourse on migration in the next chapter). When we visited the camps in Lesbos, the detainees immediately referred to the scandalous and inhumane living conditions and explicitly requested that we photograph the inadequate sanitary facilities. However, a militant research project and analysis of the border space cannot afford to replicate in its research the usual imperatives of political control which are implicit in the association of camps with battlefields or with humanitarian disasters. It is rather a question of producing a conceptual framework to elucidate how the spatialisation of social relations functions in the relation between camp and regulation. The concept of the camp – the ultimate symbol of sovereign power over life itself, for Giorgio Agamben (1998) – cannot be separated from these associations with battlefields and humanitarian disasters. These associations are deployed as the evidence for Agamben's approach. It is no accident that the official titles for the camps in countries such as Italy or Greece are 'Welcome Centres' or 'Barracks'. In Greece in particular, the association with concentration camps cannot be avoided: 30 years ago, the military junta maintained such camps for communists and republicans.

When Agamben talks of camps and invokes a Foucauldian perspective, camps seem to represent nothing other than repressive regimes of incarceration – even if this does an injustice to Foucault. He examines relations between sovereignty, the state of exception and the camp to explore the meaning of the camp within a changed political order. He is interested in an analysis of the political against the backdrop of its current crisis of representation, i.e. precisely the new political space that opens up when the political system of the nation state is in crisis. The definition of sovereignty as the power 'to decide on the state of exception' has become tediously commonplace (see also Chapter 1 of this book for a discussion of this). The state of exception as an abstract juridical dimension, however, requires a location: for Agamben, it is the camp. Camps are understood as areas of exception within a territory that are beyond the rule of law.

Moreover, Agamben's camp is the place where the biopolitical dimension of sovereign power becomes productive. It lays hold of interned subjects, and by denying them any legal or political status – as is the case in refugee or prison camps – it reduces them to their physical existence. Agamben elaborates on how this temporally or geographically limited state of exception becomes the norm, describing the camp as a place from whence new forms of law emerge in response to the lawlessness pertaining therein. The camp is a type of catalytic converter that channels the abolition of one order into a new permanent spatial and legal order. The suspension of order transforms itself from a provisional measure into a permanent technology of governing. The state of exception that manifests itself in the different forms of extraterritoriality becomes the new regulator of the contemporary political system.

Various authors, such as Ferrari Bravo (2001) or Mezzadra (2001), criticise Agamben's concept of 'bare life', because it focuses only on a legalistic understanding of the function of camps and excludes the question of the regulation of labour power. Such approaches reverse Agamben's concept: the question now centres on the mode of articulation between camps and the restructuring of the global labour market in contemporary capitalism. In his critique of Agamben, Sandro Mezzadra recasts the figure of the contemporary camp as a type of 'decompression chamber' which functions to disperse the pressure on the labour market, sectorally, locally and exterritorially (Mezzadra and Neilson, 2003).

Although the thesis of the 'decompression chamber' is important for understanding the relation between camps and labour, it offers only a productionist reading of mobility as bounded primarily to capitalist accumulation (we return to this in the next chapter). Instead, we want to foreground a far more crucial function of camps, one which consists of reinserting migrant movements into the time-scapes of specific societies. Previously, in Chapter 9, we argued that regimes of control function by imposing a particular, linear, notion of time and then controlling the passage of that time. Here we see that the key dimension of camps is that they connect mobile subjectivities with the regulation of migrants' time (discussed below). This happens as camps regulate the flows of migrants through the pores of a specific society. In the post-war period, migration was commonly controlled through the rotation principle: limited work permits were issued to low-skilled migrant men and women in order to avoid their long-term inclusion in the double-R axiom which constitutes the foundation of citizenship in European societies. But the rotation principle of the Fordist *Gastarbeiter* era failed, due to the uncontrollable nature of migrant mobility. Just as this failure resulted in an institutional compromise involving the temporal inclusion of the guest workers, the 'failure' of the camp cordon is connected to the post-Fordist attempt to institutionalise a new compromise involving the flexible inclusion of 'irregular' migrants (Willenbücher, 2007). What takes place now within the legalised spaces of camps is the transformation of undocumented labour migration into controllable migrational flows.

If one is to believe the official estimates of Europol, 500,000 undocumented migrants enter Europe annually via the south European/Mediterranean route. This represents one fifth of the total estimate of undocumented immigration to Europe. Under such conditions, the camps of south-east Europe are not there simply to restrict or block migration. By assigning to their detainees the subjectivity of the illegalised worker without any residence or labour rights, camps facilitate a differential inclusion of these workers into the system of labour. Differential inclusion means here that because these people remain in the country without any rights whatsoever, they are primarily employed in the unregulated shadow and informal economy. Under the threat of cyber-deportability, these people enter the labour market under the worst possible conditions. But differential inclusion performed by the camps not only reinserts people into the global labour market; it also externalises most of the reproduction costs of the camp detainees. They rely on their own informal networks to organise their lives, support, healthcare, etc. In conclusion, camps facilitate the entrance of people into the regime of labour and at the same time they outsource any responsibility for the maintenance of their life conditions to the detainees themselves.

We can see that camps are in no sense places of totalitarian immobilisation. Their relative porosity and the temporary nature of residence give them the function of stopover points. The camps are fields of various forces which permeate the migration politics of the European Union countries along various axes. Within them, migrants are subject to what appears initially to be a rigid system of mobility control, but which they seek to bypass where they can with microscopic 'sleights'. The camps represent less the paradigmatic incarceration milieu in the age of authoritarian neoliberalism than the spatialised attempt to temporarily control movement, i.e. to administer traffic routes; to render regulated mobility productive. Their porosity is thus an expression of an institutionalised border porosity that evolves through relations of power; relations of power where the actions of the migrants and their carriers play just as much of a role as the clearly discernible population policy intentions of the European Union.

Deceleration: the Temporal Control of Mobility

As we have already mentioned, the camps that are meant to temporarily freeze migration movements form an element, not only of contemporary migration regimes, but also of the political and philosophical debate about sovereignty and nationality, as the work of Agamben testifies. Our approach involves examining the dynamics of mobility and immobilisation, and points in a different direction. Is it possible to think camps 'from below'? The catastrophic functionalism of Agamben's position can be challenged; drawing on Paul Virilio (1986) we want to question the political disciplinary connotations of camp confinement and exclusion by using the notion of *decelerated circulation* of mobility. That is, viewing the camps from below reveals a constant flow of migrational mobility. Camps appear as the spaces which most drastically attempt to regulate the speed of this circulation and to decelerate it. Rather than stopping the circulation of mobility, camps reinsert a distinct linear time – one which is commensurable with contemporary tools of regulation which function in time – into migrants' movements and subjectivities. They bring illegalised and clandestine migration back into society by making it visible and compatible with a broad regime of temporal control. Decelerated circulation is a means of regulating migration not through space but through time.

The camps of liminal porocratic institutions created through the Schengen process are less panoptical disciplinary prison institutions than, following Virilio, speed boxes. Camps as they appear in *Fortress Europe*, Želimir Žilnik's film, are markings on the map of travel, communication and information centres, rest houses and, not infrequently, informal and unregulated credit institutions which act as banks for those on the move. Against the background of Foucault's *Discipline and Punish*, it would also seem important to examine the figure of decelerated circulation, and to ask how camps alter the relation of time, body and productivity (a relation we discussed in Chapter 4 regarding vagabonds' mobility, the contemporary version of which we examine more concretely below). The centrality of temporal over spatial regulation for understanding migration today is also clear when we consider how the time regime of the camp is distinguished by the disassociation of the body from its direct economic utilisation. Previously, mobility was rendered productive by territorialising movements and inserting them into a spatial regulation of bodies. Consider for example the workhouse (as described in Chapter 4) or the situation of the first foreign worker hostels of the *Gastarbeiter* era, which territorialised mobility in order to create a productive workforce (von Oswald, 2002). However, with the current configuration of camps, this seems to have changed.

Camps do not attempt to make migration economically useful by making migrants productive in a spatial order, rather they make migrants productive by inserting them into a global temporal regime of labour. This regime is not based on disciplining bodies and regulating whole populations. The temporal regime of global labour follows the movements of people and invests where it finds a productive workforce in a state of flux. This allows global capital to thrive on labour and life conditions which are in a state of transition and, most importantly, are primarily unregulated, informal and cheap (Sassen, 2006; Ong, 2005). With this global temporal regime of labour, the moving and changing workforce is rapidly embedded into capital's productive structure. However, global capital also quickly abandons those recently and opportunistically embedded workforces as soon as new possibilities for exploitation emerge elsewhere. Importantly, this is a *temporal* regime rather than a spatial regime because the spaces where global capital invests did not exist as such previously; they constantly emerge and vanish as people move, migrate and change their lives.

How should we understand migrants' waiting, hiding, unexpected diversions, stopovers and settlements; the refusals and returns; the possibility of a fatal end to the journey? As the camp regulates the speed of migration, it reintegrates the global vagabonds of the third millennium into a new temporal economy; an economy they have long since deserted on their journey. The main function of camps is to impose a regime of temporal control on the wild and uncontrol-lable unfolding of the imperceptible and excessive movements of the transmigrants. Camps do not suppress migration; they attempt to make people's escape productive, by reintegrating them into a global system of time management through their regulation by the postliberal liminal porocratic institutions. The proliferation of camps is a response to people's escape. Escape comes first, not power. Power and control follow. Changing perspective like this points towards the autonomy of migration – a thesis we interrogate in the next chapter – where the undocumented lives of the transmigrants succeed in imposing other uses, temporalities and turbulent geographies of mobility right there where the 'fortress' looms. As in the halls of Ellis Island, where migration biographies were hastily assembled, names and ages were invented and further routes were planned, camps, these new heterotopias of transnational living labour, can be seen as deceleration machines, temporarily delaying the arrival and in the process producing new subjectivities of entry.

Porocracy

Liminal porocratic institutions' governance of dynamic migration movements involves steering migrants into scaled time zones so as to produce governable subjects of mobility from ungovernable streams. Time is mobility. The humanitarian dilemma of the European border regime lies in the need to institutionalise the difference between sanctioned, cross-border labour migration on the one hand, and asylum law and juridical protection measures on the other. This in turn generates camps as heterotopias of sovereignty from which criminalised labour, new migrational experiences and biographies emerge. Various studies on the US–Mexican border (De Genova, 2005) and on the south-east European area (Andrijasevic, 2006) illustrate that the productive function of the border regime does not primarily consist of the capacity to stem or block migration flows. Rather, the effective governing of border porosity operates through registering movement and disciplining migrants in the camp stations as subjects of flexible, postliberal social order and labour. This form of governing is what we call porocracy, achieving global inclusion in the realm of productivity through the deceleration of migration flows.

At this point, we want to highlight a side effect of the Greek legalisation that is often neglected and that points to a displacement of functional elements of the migration/border regime. In the course of the mass registration accompanying applications for legal residence permits, information about mobility is gathered: records are made of transmigrants' routes and networks (Fakiolas, 2003). The drafting of controls and their restrictive premises are increasingly anticipatory. They are aimed less at hindering existing immigration and more at collecting information which will help to identify points where there may be some future loss of control over cross-border transit routes and migration flows, and not least uncontrolled repatriation.

The porocratic dimension of regulation by liminal porocratic institutions seems to be extended in the new Greek law on 'Entry, Residence and Social Integration of Third Country Nationals in the Hellenic Territory' (Law 3386/2005). This new law applies to those who did not receive documents in the course of past legalisation measures on account of invalid residence titles; in particular, migrants whose applications were turned down on grounds of illegal entry, as well as rejected asylum seekers, holders of 'pink cards' and those called upon to leave the country 'voluntarily' (cf. Walters, 2002). What is crucial however in this law is that the interviews that have been developed for this legalisation process (similar to those used in other European Union member countries) involve detailed registration and reconstruction of the local points of entry and the exact migration routes followed, in order to uncover the networks which organised the entry into the Greek territory. In this sense, what this law really regulates is the transitory function of the camp cordons in the Aegean zone.

The institution of the Greek–Albanian border is an exemplary case of this regulatory understanding of the camp. It can be delineated less by its topography than by the way it organises the relation between access to the national labour market in destination countries (Greece in our example, as part of the European Union) and modes of mobility in their extraterritorial spaces (Albania). This relation is regulated in a porocratic manner, that is by attempting to control the speed and magnitude of migration in a totally flexible and liminal way. Camps are only one possible way to achieve porocratic control. This is how we can explain the riddle of the missing camps. As is well known, there are no camps to be found along the numerous border crossing routes on the Greek–Albanian border, although migrants from Albania constitute the biggest immigration group in Greece. Nor were there any camps at the time of the mass exodus from Albania in the 1990s. The Greek–Albanian protocol from 1998 was consistently used for the massive deportations – the protocol explicitly rules out asylum. Albanian migrants caught, for example, on Corfu were repatriated within one hour. This renders impossible the establishment of a human-rights regime akin to that found in the Aegean transit zone.

It is certainly the case that camps are spaces beyond law; they are recognisable as such spaces and become the target of humanitarian critique (consider the discussions about the Guantanamo Bay detainment camp). However, camps are only one of the ways liminal porocratic institutions control migrational flows. The case of the Greek–Albanian border shows that there are many other possibilities which go much further in order to attempt a liminal porocracy. Here we want to emphasise again the double meaning of *liminality* in relation to *porocracy*. Firstly, porocratic control is undertaken by quasi-state institutions which are highly flexible and continually altering, since their function is constantly changing according to the contingencies of migration. Hence – this is the second meaning – these institutions are liminal in terms of their social visibility and of the opportunities which arise for public accountability. The barbarous raids of the Greek police on migrants at the end of the 1990s remained mostly unidentifiable, because the migrants were never institutionalised in a spatial way. They functioned, rather, as temporal measures which cannot and are not designed to stop or fully control migration; instead they attempt to regulate the inflows. Porocratic regulation is a highly undemocratic, repressive, violent – in a truly postliberal way – form of mobility control. It is not bare life that becomes the object of the porocratic regime of governing transnational migration, but rather the truly desubjectified naked subjectivity and labour power that is on the run from *Las Migras* of this world. It is not only migrants' knowledge, their bodies and their experience of the border space that is registered in the camps; the time of their mysterious arrival is also regulated; and the time of the arrival of their fellow travellers also. Liminal porocracy is how postliberal power tries to capture the excessive movements of contemporary migration escaping its control. This is the autonomy of migration.

12   AUTONOMY OF MIGRATION

Migration as a Constituent Force of Contemporary Polity

To speak of the 'autonomy of migration' is to understand migration as a social and political movement in the literal sense of the words, not as a mere response to economic and social malaise (Jessop and Sum, 2006). When migrants become illegal they are commonly conceived as people forced to respond to social or economic necessities, not as active constructors of the realities they find themselves in or of the realities they create when they move (for a typical example, see Jordan and Düvell, 2002). The autonomy of migration changes this perspective: migration is autonomous, meaning that – against a long history of social control over mobility as well as a similarly oppressive research in the field of migration studies – migration has been and continues to be a constituent force in the formation of sovereignty.

Engaging with the autonomy of migration is primarily a matter of acquiring a different sensibility – we talked, in Chapters 6 and 9, about how an embodied commitment to imperceptible politics entails the reformation of our senses. If we employ a new sensibility, we can see how power inhabits the everyday, tries to control and fabricate modes of subjectification and to seize on the multiplicity of continuous experience by working with optic trajectories. We can also see escape from the zones of misery as a political articulation and a genuine social struggle which works with the excess of experience. If we follow Toni Negri's plea to write the history of capitalism from the perspective of workers' mobility (see also Chapter 4) we will probably draw the contours of a historiography of autonomy of migration along the uprisings of the slaves and the serfs, the flight of the vagabonds and the pirates and the many insurgent movements proclaiming the refusal of work (Moulier Boutang, 1998; Mezzadra, 2001).

The autonomy of migration approach does not, of course, consider migration in isolation from social, cultural and economic structures. The opposite is true: migration is understood as a creative force within these structures. This shift challenges the holy duality of orthodox migration theory: i.e. the economistic thinking of the so-called new economics of migration versus the humanitarianism of both communitarian thinking and refugee studies. It also subverts the liberal discourse of the new migrant as a useful and adaptable worker as well as the logic of victimisation prevalent in NGO paternalistic interventionism.

While we talk of the autonomy of migration as a contemporary form of escape that challenges and betrays the present-day domination of postliberal power, we also see this concept as a tool for rereading the history of mobility. Mobility and escape play the role of protagonist in challenging and forcing each particular historical configuration of social and political control. Seeing the constituent power of today's migrational movements as they escape postliberal control allows us to investigate the genesis of the present from the perspective of mobility instead of the perspective of its control. We already discussed this perspective in Chapter 4 on the history of the vagabonds: this is the perspective of the moving masses, or better, a perspective that follows the directionality of the moving masses. Historically, the systematic control of the workforce's mobility was the reaction to the masses' escape from their enslavement and indenture to the guild. The establishment of wage labour is the attempt to translate the freedom of the vagabond masses into a productive, utilisable and exploitable workforce.

Capitalism Follows the Flight of Migration

In his landmark book *De l'esclavage au salariat*, Yann Moulier Boutang (1998) shows how wage labour emerged out of the flight from indenture and slavery. Moulier Boutang explores how mobility becomes the first and primary area of control and gives birth to the system of the labour market (which is based on free wage labour). The freedom to choose and to change your employer is not a fake freedom or an ideological liberty, as classical working-class Marxism suggests, but a historical compromise designed to integrate the newly released, disorganised and wandering workforce into a new regime of productivity.

In fact, Moulier Boutang's work suggests that from the outset wage labour is more of an ordering principle of workers' surplus freedom than a mere mechanism of oppression. Only later and gradually, with the emergence and consolidation of capitalist production, does wage labour become an oppressive constraint on workers' potential freedom (Ewald, 1986; Federici, 2004). Wage labour transforms the worker's liberty to be mobile into a fixed and stable workforce market. (One of the most significant consequences of the territorialisation of the workforce is the exclusion of women from the production process.) Capitalism transformed the force of the freedom of mobility into competitively organised upward social mobility.

On the grounds of his genealogy of mobility, Moulier Boutang argues that there was absolutely no historical necessity to organise wage relations as *free* wage labour. Consider some examples: Ewald describes how widespread the system of patronage economy was at the beginning of the nineteenth century; Wallerstein describes the slave mines of Scotland in the eighteenth century; Max Weber reminds us how the workers of the following century were bound in chains; similarly, Geremek argues that modes of slavery such as the 'second serfdom' in eastern Europe in the eighteenth century did not represent some obsolete historical model, but a widespread extreme form of labour immobilisation – see Chapters 4 and 5 for more discussion of these examples. Thus, wage labour might also have existed as serfdom, forced dependent labour, indenture, patronage economy, or as plantation slavery. And all this was based on a system of forced migration (Christopher, Pybus and Rediker, 2007).

The worker movement is not indifferent to slavery: after all, the abolition of the salaried worker, conceived as slavery, has figured into the statutes for some years, and has been suppressed only lately. However, Marx treats slavery as one page of the prehistory of capitalism, as a moment in the primitive accumulation of capital, before this absolute origin that he situates in 1789, or at the formation of a working class. Therefore, if we bring up, like Wallerstein or Braudel, the formation of capitalism toward the fourteenth or fifteenth centuries, we brutally reintegrate slavery into this history.... In other words, capitalism did not institute right away the free market in labor; it first invented the slave market, the repartition of serfs, the subordination of freedom to property. The interesting point is that at the moment when political economy begins to think of labor-value, everything begins to fall apart. Haiti, the island that produced half the sugar in the world, initiated a decolonization that lasted two centuries, got rid of the whites, and abolished the slave economy. Between 1791 and 1796, it was done: Toussaint L'Ouverture defeated Napoleon Bonaparte. The plantation economy was undoubtedly efficient; the problem was that it was unstable. If capitalism abandoned slavery as a strategic perspective, it is because its own existence was menaced by the instability of the market that it put into place: if there had not been the Jamaican insurrection of 1833, the English Parliament would never have abolished slavery. The struggles of the slaves in the two centuries of modern slavery are worth ten times more than the struggles of the working class: they were more violent, more virulent, more destabilizing than the worker movement. (Moulier Boutang, 2001a, pp. 228–9)

What does it mean that wage labour becomes *free* wage labour? How does the autonomy-of-migration approach understand this transformation? The difference between the slave market economy and the labour market economy does not mean the absence of middlemen or intermediaries in selling one's own labour power. The slave uprisings as well as the flight of the vagabonds rendered the coercive regulation of forced immobility or forced migration ineffective and, finally, obsolete. From this point on, labour could only be regulated through contractual agreements (that is no longer through non-economic violence) and it became free labour; that is, the freedom to choose your employer. So, the difference between the slave market economy and the labour market economy means something much more important than the absence of middlemen. It means that the possibility of changing employers becomes an indispensable feature of the capitalist market. Thus, 'striving for freedom' is the fundamental element of the capitalist labour relation.

The freedom to choose your employer becomes so important for capitalist labour that it simultaneously becomes the main focus of control. The freedom to move is the main source of productivity and the main target of control. The spectre of the workhouse always hovers over free labour. The freedom, which is so central for the circulatory function of the market, needs always to be under control and surveillance. In this sense, free labour, that is, self-determined, autonomous mobility, is always under the threat of immobilisation and territorialisation. The control of mobility is a social issue for capitalism, not just an issue pertaining to some atypical mobile workers.

According to Boutang, labour as an identifiable individual capability is a fiction. It is the wage form itself that creates the illusion that it is labour itself that is sold. What is sold is not individual capacities to work but rather a social, collective power that is able to set the capital relation in motion. The wage form is the method of remuneration best suited to managing the basic insecurity inherent in the whole process of production and value creation. This insecurity results from the possibility that workers might decline to provide capital with the most necessary ingredient for its functioning: labour power. So, from the perspective of the social conflicts pertaining to labour, any 'non-contractual' freedom – that is any form of mobility which is not regulated by the salary system – can only be understood as the refusal of the worker to work and, even worse, to valorise capital. The worker is free to sell his/her labour power, but he or she is not free to leave the position of dependent labour.

From the perspective of autonomy of migration, the possibility of escaping the position of the seller of labour power represents the essential threat under which capitalism developed. The threat has a name: mobility. This is the reason why mobility has been such a concentrated target of state regulation and state intervention. In early capitalism, when wages only covered a small part of the reproduction of labourers and when they had the possibility to return back to subsistence production, the need to patrol and intervene in workers' mobility was crucial for the establishment of capitalism (Federici, 2004). The freedom to enter a dependent labour relation was simultaneously the freedom to leave such a relation. So, capitalism is very much organised around the conflict of mobility:

[C]apitalism is characterised by a structural tension between the entirety of subjective forms of practice, mobility of labour is one such practice, ... and capital's endeavours to despotically control them ... This tension gives birth to a complex dispositif which simultaneously valorises and restrains labour mobility. The specific forms of subjectivity which pertain to the mobility of labour are also part of this dispositif. ... One could, thus, say: there is no capitalism without migration. (Mezzadra, 2007, p. 187, our translation)

Rethinking the Concept of the Autonomy of Migration

The autonomy of migration foregrounds the primacy of mobility for the emergence of capitalism, but this does not mean that the history of escape and mobility writes the other history of capitalism from below. The history of mobility is much more than a history of capitalism. Historical capitalism is just a specific form of the capture of mobility. For example, in Chapter 4 we discussed the control of mobility in the late Middle Ages on the threshold to the proto-capitalist social organisation. Whilst we agree with Moulier Boutang that the autonomy of migration is an escape from the system of plantation and slavery which gave birth to the wage labour capitalism, we also understand it as more than this.

Moulier Boutang's work usefully disarticulates the process of 'primitive accumulation' and the formation of early capitalism from the process of the proletarianisation of the masses in Europe. He challenges any notion that free wage labour is a 'natural phenomenon' or a 'structural necessity' in the history of capitalism. Instead, he develops an autonomy-of-migration approach which highlights the roles both of the 'wild anomaly' of the slave uprisings and of the impossibility of governing the escaping masses in the emergence of capitalist wage labour. Nevertheless, there is an impasse resulting from the attempt to think the development of capitalism from the perspective of mobility, as Moulier Boutang and Mezzadra conceive it. This lies in the equation of subjectivity, which evolves in the practices of mobility, with a generic potentiality of labour power to become productive. Hence, the subjectivity of escaping migration is not only translated into, but reduced to a subjectivity of capitalist production. This reading reduces mobile subjectivities to a productionist subjectivity of capitalism, and ends up *separating* mobility and its embodied experience (that is, the practices of migration are separated from the myriads of subjectivities which arise when people move). Moreover, migration is translated into the paramount subjectivity of mobility, which is then presented as the matrix and very form of capitalist production. The result is that the specificities of countless localised, embodied, situated experiences of migrants are elided at the expense of focusing on the single subjectivity of the one productive subject of capitalist production (in this sense, this approach reinforces the prevalent subject-form of contemporary sovereignty as described in Chapters 5 and 6). Deleuze and Guattari describe this elision as follows:

And in fact when Marx sets about defining capitalism, he begins by invoking the advent of single, unqualified and global Subjectivity, which capitalizes all of the processes of subjectification, 'all activities without distinction': 'productive activity in general,' 'the sole subjective essence of wealth...' And this single Subject now expresses itself in an Object in general, no longer in this or that qualitative state: 'Along with the abstract universality of wealth-creating activity we have now the universality of the object defined as wealth, viz. the product in general, or labor in general, but as past, materialized labor' (Marx). Circulation constitutes capital as a subjectivity commensurate with society in its entirety. But this new social subjectivity can form only to the extent that the decoded flows overspill their conjunctions and attain a level of decoding that the State apparatuses are no longer able to reclaim: *on the one hand*, the flow of labor must no longer be determined as slavery or serfdom but must become naked and free labour; and *on the other hand*, wealth must no longer be determined as money dealing, merchant's or landed wealth, but must become pure homogeneous and independent capital. (Deleuze and Guattari, 1987, pp. 499–500)

If the autonomy-of-migration approach ends up identifying the experience of mobility as the subjectivity of capitalist production, it ultimately restores the subject of capitalist polity which it tries so hard to dismantle. That is, it glosses over the productive tension inherent in experience which we discussed in Chapter 9. On the one hand, there are haptic trajectories and actual occasions of experience which defy representation and are always becoming or perishing; on the other there are optic trajectories and events, coherent subject positions which make sense in the game of representation. We suggested earlier that the latter are always in a process of undoing, unbecoming – i.e. the productive tension of experience. Throughout this book we employ the notions of escape and imperceptible politics to defend and to articulate the constituent power of escaping people when they evacuate the fixed spaces of the subjects of sovereignty (and of its very functioning principle, the subject-form). More than anything else, escape addresses a vacuum at the heart of contemporary sovereignty, one which arises when the double-R axiom assigns rights and representation to a coherent, indivisible, distinguish-able subject (and not to those who fail or refuse to present in such a manner). The reductionist (to capitalism) and productionist (to labour) readings of mobility which we described above as approaches to the autonomy of migration actually invigorate reinvestment in the double-R axiom. They encapsulate the escaping people of mobility into a game about the extension and expansion of rights and rep-resentation in contemporary North Atlantic societies. In this sense these approaches reterritorialise escaping subjectivities, rendering them into a function of contemporary sovereignty. The result is that migration movements are cast as just another political force participating in the negotiations for shaping contemporary policies on migration. From this perspective, the subjectivity of mobility appears as a molar power always tied to addressing the institutions of postliberal power. Against this we propose an understanding of mobility as a form of imperceptible politics of escape which effects the deterritorialisation of mobile people and dissolves the subject of the double-R axiom. Such imperceptible experiences of mobility haunt the worst nightmares of those subjects who fit the double-R axiom and whose new clothes are manufactured in the sweatshops of this earth.

The long history of the regulation and control of imperceptible experiences, the history of bodies and their mobility, is not the other history of capitalism, but the other history of the uncanny symbiosis between subject and sovereignty. The flight from this symbiosis is the refusal of subjectivity to be governed as subject. In today's postliberal conditions, this has an important consequence for reconsidering the meaning of autonomy of migration. By entering into the terrain of immanent experience and harnessing optic trajectories, postliberal sovereignty attempts to dissect the subject and to reincorporate it as a functional moment of the vertical aggregates of power. Earlier in this section we described liminal porocratic institutions as the postliberal regime of mobility control which tries to get rid of the rights-protected subject and population and to regulate migration as flows and passages. Postliberal aggregates are interested neither in protecting human rights nor in securing migrants' everyday social reproduction. Postliberal aggregates externalise their legal and social responsibility to the transnational communities sustaining migrants. Migrants, in particular undocumented migrants, rely on their informal networks for maintaining their daily existence. Under the gaze of postliberal sovereignty, migrants are always in transit, even if they dwell for many years or even decades in a certain country. Liminal porocratic institutions perform a double function: on the one hand, they regulate the pores of postliberal, transit spaces and the speed of passage of the migrational streams; on the other hand, they invest in cyber-control – that is, they externalise camps, virtualise borders and deterritorialise control – so that they bypass the implementation of human rights and social protection.

Postliberal sovereignty is nurtured by mobility. Mobility is a highly appreciated capacity. What migrants bring with them is not their labour power but their mobility, and postliberal control knows this.

In fact postliberal control is a form of sovereignty which is very much organised around mobility and migrational flows. Postliberal power thrives on mobility, needs it more than anything else. Postliberalism not only recognises the importance of, but also invests in, mobility. The concept of the autonomy of migration, which highlights the primacy of mobility, finds itself in a position at which postliberal power has also arrived! This is the predicament of resistance and subversion in the field of migration today. In response, in the rest of this chapter we trace the formation of a new understanding of flight and escape, one which enables us to grasp how the autonomy of migration functions as an imperceptible, constituent force which challenges and escapes postliberal power.

Documents

Although the arrival of Sir Alfred Mehran has been registered in many European police departments of immigration affairs, his figure remains an enigma. Sir Alfred Mehran's biography seems to be emblematic of the nomad (Mehran and Donkin, 2004). His desire was to come to Britain on a refugee passport with his original name Mehran Karimi Nasseri. In 1988 he flew from Brussels via Paris to London. In London he was refused entry into the country and sent back to Paris. But France also denied him entry and Brussels did not accept him back. Since then he has lived in the transit area of Terminal 1 in the Charles de Gaulle airport in Paris. When he finally got a UNHCR passport and was able to travel again and to leave the transit space, he declined to acknowledge or sign these documents arguing that the person Mehran Karimi Nasseri does not exist any more. This person existed in 1988; today he is Sir Alfred Mehran.

This course of events is typical of nomadic life. What characterises the nomad is not his or her passage through enclosures, borders, obstacles, doors, barriers. The nomad does not have a target, does not move or occupy a territorial space, leaves nothing behind, goes nowhere. The enigma of Sir Alfred Mehran's arrival does not result from his multiple displacements and final capture in Paris, rather it refers to the fact that this very moment of arrival has lasted 20 years. Arrival has a *longue durée*, it covers almost the whole life of the nomad; one is always there and always leaving, always leaving and always manifesting in the materiality of the place where one is.

You never arrive somewhere. Sir Alfred Mehran's spectacular story breaks with a classic conception of migration as a unidirectional, purposeful and intentional process. In this version of the notion of migration – typical of Fordist societies – the migrant is the signifier of a particular conceptualisation of mobility: the individualised subject laboriously calculating the cost–benefit ratio of his/her trip and then starting an itinerary with fixed points of departure and arrival. But migration is not an individual strategy, nor does it designate the option 'exit'. Rather, it characterises the continuous shifts and radical re-articulations of singular, individual trajectories. Migration is not the evacuation of one place and the occupation of a different one; it is the making and remaking of one's own life on the scenery of the world. World-making. You cannot measure migration in changes of position or location, but by its increasing inclusiveness and the amplitude of its intensities. Even if migration sometimes starts as a form of dislocation (forced by poverty, patriarchal exploitation, war, famine), its target is not relocation but the active transformation of social space. By being embedded in broader networks of intensive social change, migration challenges and reconstitutes the sovereign population control which functions solely through the identification and control of the individual subject's movements. Sir Alfred Mehran represents in the most radical way a non-representable migrant: the person who starts the journey is not the same at the end, the space which one inhabits is not the one intended, your new documents do not refer to who you are or who you were but to whom you become in the journey. Travel becomes the law, becoming becomes the code.

Nomadism's dictum 'you never arrive somewhere' constitutes the matrix of today's migrational movements. Below, we delineate various modes of mobile becomings which govern migrants' embodied experiences: becoming animal, becoming women, becoming amphibious, becoming imperceptible. Finally, in the last part of this chapter, we discuss how these volatile transformations escape the ubiquitous politics of representation, rights and visibility. This escape confronts today's configurations of postliberal political sovereignty with an imperceptible force which renders the 'walls around the world' irreversibly porous: this is the autonomy of migration.

Animals

The 'coyote' is more than a *Canis latrans* on the borderline of the United States and Mexico. It designates all those commercial 'guides' who are able to cross the national borders and to organise illegal migrational movements and undocumented mobility. British sailors call the elusive helpers of stowaway passengers 'sharks'; on the Greek–Albanian border their name is 'korakia', ravens. In Chinese they are called 'shetou', snakehead, a person who is as cunning as a snake and knows how to use his or her agile head to find a way through difficult situations. 'Shetou' was also the name of the Chinese network blamed in the public debates about the Dover tragedy, the death of 58 illegalised migrants in a container lorry at Dover at the beginning of this millennium.

The official anti-trafficking discourse is bound to a sovereign conception of border politics: it individualises border crossing and presents migrants as victims of the smuggler mafia. In the sovereign public imaginary, migration is an illegally organised scandal with only two players: lawbreaking migrants and criminal smugglers. But the criminalisation of border crossing and the reduction of the complex and polymorphic networks which sustain migrational movements to a one-act, two-actors play covers over something. It hides how the alleged humanitarian doctrine 'save the people' is nothing but a violent, sovereign fixation on the politics of 'save the borders' from unchecked intrusion. Migration is not a unilinear individual-choice process, it is not an effect of the push-and-pull mechanics of supply and demand for human capital. Migration adapts differently to each particular context, changes its face, links unexpected social actors together, absorbs and reshapes the sovereign dynamics targetting its control. Migration is arbitrary in its flows, de-individualised and – as we discussed in Section I and Chapter 10 of this section – constitutive of new transnational spaces which exceed and neutralise the attempts to establish postliberal sovereign aggregates. Migration is like big waves: they never appear precisely where they are expected, their arrival can never be predicted exactly, but they always come. They are of a magnitude capable of reordering the entire given geography of a seashore: the sandbanks, the seabed, the maritime animals and plants, the rocks, the beach.

In Turkey trafficking with illegalised migrants, *koyun ticareti*, 'sheep trade', is more than an affair of corrupt policemen and has little in common with the phantom of a globally active 'smuggler' mafia. The coastal 'sheep trade' is a whole regime of mobility, a whole informal network in which hundreds of different actors participate, each one with different stakes, to make borders permeable. Migration makes material and psychosocial spaces porous, a Benjaminian porosity, where public and private intermingle, deviance and norm are renegotiated, zones of exploitation and justice are rearranged, formal and informal situations are reassembled. Rendering states' apparatuses and borders porous is the tactic migrants deploy to oppose the control of desire. Becoming animal is not a mere metaphor for the transactions undertaken in the current regime of mobility, nor is it just a new academic theoretical trend; it is the cipher for the corporeal substratum of migration in times of a tenacious regime of forced illegality imposed by liminal porocratic institutions. We want to illustrate the importance of becoming for the migrants by turning to border crossings in the Straits of Gibraltar.

Brûleurs

The distance between Tangier and Tarifa is rather short. Changing continents takes less than two hours. In Tangier the harbour and the nearby streets are packed with people – people from North and West Africa, arriving in the cities of Maghreb, seeking a chance to come to the coastline and to cross the sea. Transmigrants. Marrakesh, Beni-Mellal, Rabat, Casablanca, Quadja, transit cities. The southern frontiers of Europe: Tarifa, Sebta, frontiers reaching as far as Lampedusa, Crete, Lesbos. Both trajectories together, the European frontiers and the Maghrebian transit places, mark the outlines of a living and breathing transnational space extending in many concentric circles around the Straits of Gibraltar.

Many border-activist networks around Europe and the world make maps of migration and mobility in an attempt to produce cartographic visualisations of the multiplicities of the social spaces within which migrants live and move: routes of migration, transit and rest stations, information channels, employment possibilities, illegal networks of trafficking, militarised spaces, places of increased electronic surveillance, detention centres, prisons, deportation centres. (For a wonderful collection of different projects and approaches, see the *Atlas of Radical Cartography*, Mogel and Bhagat, 2007.) The 'Map of Migrational Flows in the Estrecho de Gibraltar' (Figure 19) which was developed in the context of the activist event Fadaiat for freedom of knowledge and freedom of movement in South Spain – is very different from Debord's psycho-geographic maps of Paris (discussed in Chapter 2). Instead of a fragmented experiential perception of urban space and the visualisation of processes of subjectification, the 'Map of the Estrecho de Gibraltar' represents spaces of pure sociability in movement (regarding this, see the compelling publication on the Fadaiat event: Monsell Prado et al., 2006). These asubjective maps of migrational flows seem to visualise a space which oscillates according to the power of postliberal sovereignty and yet develops in spite of it. If postliberal sovereignty hegemonises transnational space, then the

asubjective sociality of the mobile body infiltrates into transnationalism by means of a counter-hegemonic project from below.

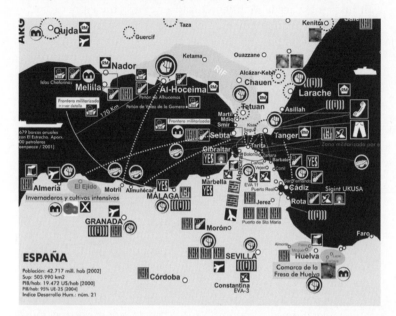

19.   Hackitectura.net, Map of Migrational Flows in the Estrecho de Gibraltar (detail),
2004,   mcs.hackitectura.net/tiki-browse_image.php?imageId=580   (last   accessed
23 May 2008). Printed with permission of José Pérez de Lama/Osfa and hackitectura.
net, Spain.

The 'Map of the Estrecho de Gibraltar' opposes the logic of
conventional maps, which convey an abstract and geometric truth,
and it simultaneously opposes a simply subjective, existential and
autopoietic vision of the social and the political (Casas-Cortes and
Cobarrubias, 2007; see also Monsell Prado et al., 2006; Black, 1997).
The map conveys truth, a common and universal truth, a truth which
is simultaneously abstract and situated. It is not a transcendental
truth like the truth of universal human rights. This truth is defined
by the common asubjective struggle to establish it (see also Chapter
6). This is truth from the embodied standpoint of praxis. Nomadic
motion is not about movement but about the appropriation and
remaking of space. The nomad embodies the desire to link two points
together, and therefore s/he always occupies the space between these
two points. Both the nomad's body and the space s/he occupies
transform equally; co-evolution of body and space: becoming.

In 1991, Spain imposed a visa requirement for migrants from the Maghreb region. Since then migrants from Morocco, Mali, Senegal, Mauritania, etc. gather in Tangier waiting for an appropriate moment to cross the Mediterranean. They are called *los herraguas*, the burners, people prepared to burn their documents when they reach the Spanish Schengen border in order to avoid being resent to their country of origin. In the documentary film *Tanger, le rêve des brûleurs* (Morocco/ France 2002), Leila Kilani follows the paths of Rhimo, Denis and others and documents the de-individualised dreams and practices of all these burners (Kuster, 2006a; Kuster and Tsianos, 2005). The strategy of dis-identification is not primarily a question of shifting identitarian ascriptions; it is a material and an embodied way of being. The strategy of dis-identification is a voluntary 'dehumanisa- tion' in the sense that it breaks the relation between your name and your body. A body without a name is a non-human human being, an animal which runs. It is non-human because it deliberately abandons the humanist regime of rights. The UNHCR convention for asylum seekers protects the rights of refugees on arrival, but not when they are on the road. And we already know, the arrival has a *longue durée*, migration does not really concern the moment of arrival but the whole trip, almost your whole life. This is how migration solves the enigma of arrival. As the burners say in Leila Kilani's film, if you want to cross the Spanish borders, it is not sufficient to burn your papers, you have to become a dog, to become an animal yourself:

In 1950 this route has existed. Some people ... our forefathers ... in this route. Moving this route. We are not the first people moving on this route. We go with information. We make our journey to the desert. Among our way to the desert ... we find many things in the desert. So what I believe in this route that whatever you want to make on this route you don't have to do it with money. Because some rogets, some bandits in the route. So that they can collect your money. You have to make the route without money. Whenever you get to your last destination you call for money and the money will come for you. Millions of people die in the desert, in this movement, in this journey when they plan to go to Europe when they died. All people who made it on this route they are dogs. And people who live roget life. What to understand by roget life? Roget life means people who can live without nothing, not have money, not to have nothing in your pockets, but you have cigarettes, you smoke cigarettes, you drink water, something. You don't bloody care. Even if they died you forget your ... you get me? You get me? You get me? People who made this route is dogs. Dogs. What I mean by dog. That is people who don't, who – who believe that anything

can happen. You understand me? I believe that anything can happen. By the god
... we get our last destination, no problem. (Kilani, 2002, minute 28.40)

Becoming is essential to mobility. The trope of becoming animal is
only one of the tactics migrants employ in order to claim their freedom
of movement. Becoming woman, becoming child, becoming elder,
becoming soil, becoming fluid, becoming animal is the migrants'
answer to attempts to control their desire.

Imperceptibility

Consider for example the 'eternal' becomings of one interviewee
– we met him doing fieldwork for the project on transnational
migration routes in a camp in northern Greece, discussed in the
previous chapter (see also Transit Migration Forschungsgruppe, 2006;
Frangenberg, Cologne Kunstverein and Projekt Migration, 2005) – a
Chinese man on his way to France. He was forced to stay in Romania
for some time, married and got a residence permit there, applied
for a European Union visa, was rejected, reapplied and got a three-
month work permit which brought him to Paris. After overstaying
his visa for more than twelve months, he was caught and deported
back to Romania (which meant that he was not eligible to apply
for a European Union visa for a period of ten years). In Romania he
changed identity and gender, married again, as a woman this time,
applied again for a European Union visa, travelled to Paris, changed
identity again and married in France, where he finally got a residence
permit. Some time later this person sent us an email that he or she
– the grammatical conventions of this sentence oblige us to choose
a pronoun – had arrived in Canada.

Becoming is the inherent impetus of migration. Migrants do
not connect to each other by representing and communicating
their true individual identities, nor by translating for others what
they possess or what they are. Migrants do not need translation to
communicate, migration does not need mediation. Migrants connect
to each other through becomings, through their own gradual and
careful, sometimes painful transformation of their existing bodily
constitution; they realise their desire by changing their bodies, voices,
accents, patois, hair, colour, height, gender, age, biographies.

But as we argued already in the section on escape and imperceptible
politics at the beginning of this book, becoming does not initiate a
process of eternal diversifications and differences. Rather, migrants'
becoming creates the indeterminate materiality on which new

connections, sociabilities, common lines of flight, informal networks, transit spaces thrive. Becoming is the way to link the enigma of arrival and the enigma of origin in a process of dis-identification. We mean here dis-identification literally, as the way to become more than one.

Migrants' material becomings do not end in a new state of being, rather they constitute being as the point of departure on which new becomings can emerge. Being is similar to the transit spaces where migrants rest for a while, reconnect to their communities, call their relatives and friends, earn more money to pay the smugglers, collect powers, prepare their new becomings. Being is nothing more than becoming's intermediate stages. If being is a passport number, migrants' becomings are countless. The multiplication of beings. Two, three, many passports! Dis-identification = being everyone. Because, you must be everyone in order to be everywhere. In Chapter 6 we talked about Deleuze and Guattari's consideration of the cosmic formula of multiplicity: becoming imperceptible. The imperceptibility of migration does not mean that migration itself is imperceptible. On the contrary, the more migrational flows become powerful and effective by materialising the practices of becoming, the more they turn out to be the most privileged targets for registration, regulation and restriction by sovereign power. Becoming imperceptible is an immanent act of resistance because it makes it impossible to identify migration as process which consists of fixed collective subjects. Becoming imperceptible is the most precise and effective tool migrants employ to oppose the individualising, quantifying, policing and representational pressures of the settled liminal porocratic institutions.

Visibility?

What kind of political subject does imperceptibility create? How is migration woven into the emergence of the policing system of postliberal power and how does it escape it? As we said in sections I and II, one of the major functional moments which solidify control in the context of postliberal power is the double-R principle. Migration was one of the main targets of the double-R axiom, even if it was treated differently in different countries. In the many European countries, for example, migration was assimilated in the form of *Gastarbeit*, temporary employment, which performs an inclusion of the right to work on the national level, without the extensive granting of equal political rights. Elsewhere, in countries which actively encouraged immigration, migrants were incorporated into the national social compromise (see also Chapters 1 and 2) by being accepted as an integral part of the national project in general. In this case migrants were granted not only full work rights but also political rights.

But despite the seemingly egalitarian treatment of migration in this second case, migrants came across the racist dispositifs prevalent in these societies. Equal rights did not mean the possession of equal symbolic capital in the politics of representation. Cultural studies and post-colonial theory (which, as we pointed out earlier, are primarily concerned with the critique of the representational deficit) initially arose in countries which had made efforts to incorporate migrants into the double-R axiom; they arose as the result of this particular historical experience, namely the coexistence between equal rights and racist treatment, between formal equality and de facto ethnic segmentation, and subsequently came to continental Europe. Despite variations in the way migration has been regulated, the main questions it has raised for researchers pertain to the assignment of rights and representational visibility to migrants. This is also the case for alternative politics and the politics of difference in the 1980s and 1990s which tried to address the living conditions of new and old migrants and to intervene in the given conditions of representation, to renegotiate and rearticulate them under the imperative that resistance is possible. But as we already argued in sections I and II, the politics of representation fabricates a form of resistance which, today, is incapable of escaping the forms of policing imposed by the current regime of migration control.

The decline of representation as the core politics of resistance and subversion means simultaneously the end of the strategy of visibility. Instead of visibility, we say imperceptibility. Instead of being perceptible, discernible, identifiable, current migration puts on the agenda a new form of politics and a new formation of active political subjects who refuse to become a political subject at all (rather than strive to find a different way to become or to be a political subject). Sir Alfred Mehran refused to use his original name when in 1999 he was offered a UNHCR passport which rendered him identifiable by the assimilationist logic of liberal–national administration (the semantic and practical code of the administration is integration). Many of the migrants in the border camps, instead of waiting for a decision regarding their asylum status, escape the camps and dive into the informal networks of clandestine labour in the metropolises. The migrants waiting on the north shores of Africa to cross the Mediterranean in floating coffins choose to burn their documents and enter a life which puts them de facto outside of any politics of visibility. Meanwhile visibility, in the context of illegalised migration, belongs to the inventory of technologies pertaining to liminal porocratic institutions for policing migrational flows.

Cunning

Of course migrants become stronger when they become visible by obtaining rights, but the demands of migrants and the dynamics of migration cannot be exhausted in the quest for visibility and rights. This is because both visibility and rights function as differentiation markers, establishing a clear link between the person and his/her origins, the body and an identity. And this is precisely what migrants want to avoid when they are clandestine on the road, when they are moving between places, cultures, religions, homes, continents. They do it differently: the mestiza way. Anzaldúa:

She is willing to share, to make herself vulnerable to foreign ways of seeing and thinking. She surrenders all notions of safety, of the familiar. Deconstruct, construct. She becomes *nahual*, able to transform herself into a tree, a coyote, into another person. (Anzaldúa, 1999, p. 104)

What migrants really want is to become everybody, to become imperceptible. They try to become like everybody else by refusing to be something, by refusing imperatives to become integrated and assimilated into the logic of border administration and cultural control. Migration is the moment when you prefer to say: I prefer not to be. And this is not something which characterises contemporary migration alone. It is only when social and cultural researchers (and associated public discourses and some social movements) employ concepts which are fixated on communitarian, humanist and identity politics that we are prevented from seeing migration as one of the biggest laboratories for the subversion of postliberal politics today.

Even the emblematic Ellis Island cannot be considered as the melting pot out of which the new American citizen was born, but as the space where endless stories of virtual identities were invented in order to make one eligible to cross the 'golden door' into the American country. The whole vision of an America welcoming everyone from abroad and as open to difference is based on an infinite series of inventions and lies. Valuable lies, nice lies, vital lies. America's history and the cunning of migration. Migration is the sister of transience, produces mixed forms, menwomen, coyotesheep, many new species. The cunning of migration breeds animals. How to register them in the clean and pedantic archives of the administration? How to respond to a sheep or a raven when it has the courage to encounter the gaze of the bureaucrat in a police department of immigration affairs and demand asylum? How to register all these liminal animals? How to record all these paperless subjects? How to codify all these continuous becomings? Impossible.

Migration's weapon of imperceptibility does not always succeed. It is a route without guarantees, it involves pain, suffering, hunger, desperation, torture, even the deaths of thousands of people in ships that have sunk beneath the oceans of the earth. But in this book we deliberately decided not to present migration once again as a humanitarian scandal or as a deviation from the evolutionist human rights doctrine of Western modernity. Is it a coincidence that the widespread images of migration in the media and public discourse of monstrous tragedies *equally* supply the ubiquitous humanitarian discourses as well as the xenophobic and racist politics of forced repatriation? Imperceptible politics attempts to change the perspective and to approach migration as a constituent force of the current social transformation, a flight from postliberal control, which is primarily sustained by cooperation, solidarity, the usage of broad networks and resources, shared knowledge, collective anticipation (Kuster, 2006b). This is the autonomy of migration in action; this is the imperceptible politics of escaping subjectivities.

Throughout this section, we have discussed some of the traits this flight takes today. In emerging postliberal conditions, migrants become imperceptible, enunciating their subjective lines of flight out of the current rigid and exploitative regimes of accumulation and Eurocentric culture. Migration is not intimidated by postliberalism's regulation of mobility, nor by its sophisticated, deterritorialised modes of cyber-control. Migration is at home in mobility. In this chapter, we have described how contemporary migration undoes the postliberal control of mobility: migration re-appropriates the postliberal capture of the subject and becomes dog, animal, manwoman, coyotesheep, everyone; migrants make use of the postliberal transnationalisation of their communities, transforming them into transnational communities of escape. Instead of waiting for a better concept of citizenship, migrants practise dis-identification; migrants reunite their mobility with the actual occasions of movement arising in it, and overcome the perennial separation of experience and the world which is germane to the productionist reading of mobility.

The moving packs of migrants traversing continents create uncountable continuous experiences, which are unlabelled, untamed, unidentified. People act together and make world without giving any permanent name to their alliances and conditions of existence, without ever intending to change the conditions of representation included in the double-R axiom. Without ever intending it, this multiplicity of subjectivities is tantamount to univocality. It is a moment where social control is exercised from below, where social change is subjectless, where the new elusive historical actors dwell in the world of imperceptibility and generate a persistent and insatiable surplus of sociability in motion, a new world in the heart of the old world of the liminal porocratic regime of mobility control and postliberal terror: World 2 (Papadopoulos, 2006). World 2 does not redeem this surplus of sociability by establishing a new totalising and messianic version of a better democratic polis, but it constitutes the imperceptible escape from the polis.

Section V
LABOUR AND PRECARITY

13   THE REGIME OF LABOUR CONTROL: PRECARIOUS LIFE AND LABOUR

What I have been able, with great difficulty, to discover, whenever the situation permitted it, in my conversations with the workers, is roughly as follows. A sub-proletarian, who 'invents' his work every day, has a precarious existence, but he does 'enjoy' a form of freedom and independence from all bosses. And in that sense he does feel himself to be free as a bird. This is why he looks down on the worker, for – as a comrade told me – he thinks: 'That bloke shuts himself up in a jail all day long, he turns himself into a slave, he agrees to obey a boss….' And when he sees a worker go off at a certain hour and return at a certain hour he reconfirms for himself that the worker's life is one of forced labour, made all the worse by the fact that the handcuffs and chains worn by the worker were put there voluntarily. His, the sub-proletarian's, life, on the other hand, is an independent one. And therefore he has no respect for the worker. If they meet on the street or elsewhere, they usually say nothing at all to one another. The sub-proletarian feels himself superior in intellect, inventiveness and, in general, in the art of living…. This is among the major reasons why the Neapolitan worker is so psychologically isolated. Any pride that may exist in having a steady job, a trade, is greatly diluted by the realisation which is constantly present before his eyes, that he has given up 'another way of life', which his neighbours lead, and which is a life full of great opportunities for adventure and the exercise of imagination.

Moreover, unlike the sub-proletarian, he lives in constant fear of losing his job. Hence even his prospects are severely limited, because the worker, without the factory, is finished. His existence without his job would be that of a cripple, given that he has never learned the petty trades of the street or, rather, that he has never learned to invent a 'business' or a way of making a living. In other words, he has no resources. Or else, even if he succeeds, his very success means his complete degradation as a worker. Thus we see that this sadness of the workers has another source: it stems from their renunciation of their entire external environment, where everyone lives all the year round in the open air, in the streets, walks there, works there, carries on his interminable disputes and fights his fights there, and so on. The worker, sealed up in his factory, is like a cloistered monk who has cut himself off from the world of others and renounced that life. In doing this, he is aware above all of having renounced the air, the environment, the rules and the means of the secular life, the philosophers of which are the lazzari, as the sub-proletariat is called.

> From a letter of a member of the Italian Communist Party
> to Louis Althusser, 1968 (Macciocchi, 1973, pp. 184–5)

Embodied Capitalism

In her research into the relation between subversion and exploitation among precarious workers in the United Kingdom, Amanda Ehrenstein shows the centrality of the body and of affective investments for sustaining the pressures and demands of work life (Ehrenstein, 2006b, 2006a). What is particularly striking in the accounts of the participants in this study, is that the centrality of the body arises in discussions about people's capacity to maintain their whole lives on a continuum (and not so much in relation to the imperative to maintain the productivity of work). Participants evoked a form of exploitation of the self, as opposed to an exploitation which is exercised from outside and pertains only to the limited realm of work. This exploitation of the self can be understood as the extended exploitation of one's own body and social relations required in order to remain active and potentially employable in conditions of structural insecurity in the labour market. Ehrenstein describes how this form of the exploitation of the body expands and colonises the continuity of the affective relations to the self and to others (see also Dowling, Nunes and Trott, 2007; Clough, 2007; Blackman and Cromby, 2007). For example Ehrenstein describes the range of strategies people develop, strategies which can be seen as the means to transform one's own self and social relations into a source for sustaining life:

investing energy in building up networks and enduring relationships of mutual support, constantly motivating people anew (themselves and others), creating welcoming atmospheres and stimulating surroundings in their projects for all the people involved, pretending emotions, perceptions and abilities that they did not have, overseeing feelings of despair by presenting themselves as successful, resourceful and optimistic even in hard times, not thinking about the future or problems they might face later on in their life, focussing only on the moment and the next few months, being prepared to become active and change plans quickly, so that they can deal with unforeseen opportunities and interruptions of their practice. (Ehrenstein, 2006a, p. 4)

Here we want to add the amounts of sheer energy required to cope with stress, anxiety, despair, as well as with the new forms of time management demanded of precarious workers. As Ehrenstein says:

The periods after important, time and energy consuming projects are seen as especially dangerous in relation to motivation and feelings of despair. To counter this problem they developed strategies of constant activity and persistent concern about the next job or the next project. Taking time out from work is not planned in advance; time-out is taken by chance or even loses its sense. (Ehrenstein, 2006a, p. 5)

In the previous sections of this book we highlighted the centrality of the body in postliberal attempts to regulate mobility and life. Today, the recombination of emergent bodies and materialities (Section III) and the porocratic control of mobility (Section IV) both become the sources and means of value creation. Here we want to interrogate the centrality of embodiment in the current regime of production in postliberal conditions. What is crucial to this regime of 'embodied capitalism' is that the body and its implicit connectedness to others and to the world is directly embedded in the process of value creation.

'Embodied capitalism' designates the centrality of the body and materiality in the current labour regime, and highlights the neglected embodied character of work. There are many exceptions to the omission of body in the sociology of labour and social theory, exceptions which are crucial for our understanding of the regime of labour control. The most important reside in the long tradition of feminist research on affects and bodies at work (Glucksmann, 2000; Wolkowitz, 2006; McDowell, Batnitzky and Dyer, 2007), on women's work and affective labour (Kessler-Harris, 1981; Morini, 2007; Hochschild and Ehrenreich, 2002) and on the relation between technoscientific practices and human bodies (Bowker and Star, 1999; Mol, 2002; Suchman, 2007). The creation of value in embodied capitalism occurs by recombining and intermingling matter: humans, animals, artefacts and things. Importantly, recombination also includes the workers' bodies; it reorganises their materialities, abilities, social relations, their capacities to affect and relate to other bodies, their potentialities, and, finally, it fractures this configuration and appropriates only specific parts of it. In Section III we discussed the recombinant dimension of postliberal control; here we want to consider how embodied capitalism either transforms or neglects continuous experience as it harnesses optic trajectories of experience into specific modes of labour. That is, we examine how labour is restructured in convergence with the transformations happening in the formation of emergent life and liminal porocratic institutions.

Our concern here is with how life's recombination necessitates the reorganisation of labour relations – and not with how life itself becomes a productive force (for example, see Section III; also Sunder Rajan, 2006; Waldby and Mitchell, 2006). There is a widespread assumption that productivity in embodied capitalism is the outcome of the 'cooperation between brains' (as the paradigm of cognitive capitalism or knowledge-based capitalism proclaims, e.g. Corsani, 2004; Gorz, 2004; Lazzarato, 2004; Moulier Boutang, 2001b). This idea hinges on the belief that the recombinant formation of life is the complex product of workers' intellectual and cognitive capacities. Against this, we argue that life becomes recombinant not only on the level of the product but also on the level of production itself. The recombinant formation of life is taken up in a new regime of labour control. The regime of *precarious life and labour*, as we call it, installs and assigns a very particular role to the body in current production: it is through the reorganisation of the body, that is of its intrinsic structure and of its connections to other human bodies, machines, animals, and things that the productivity of labour can be sustained in Global North Atlantic societies. The formation of emergent life constitutes life as a set of potentials to be worked with; the regime of precarious life and labour control designates *how* we work with the specific potentials of life; that is, it controls the labour process itself.

Precarious Labour

In the post-Second World War period, labour regulation in Global North Atlantic countries was chiefly a matter for the welfare state. The welfare state's productivity resulted from transforming the vertical asymmetry of the class conflict into a horizontal arrangement of rights and resources for protection of labour (Ewald, 1986; Castel, 2003). In addition to this, the welfare state's provision extended beyond the immediate regulation of normal wage labour to include protecting the life of the working individual (and his, and more seldom of her, immediate dependants) in non-working phases (Kaufmann, 2003). This regime of protection was based on the continual increase of labour productivity in the context of a nationally organised economy. The internationalisation of financial markets brought this form of labour regulation into perennial dysfunction

(Jessop, 1994). Productivity used to be driven by mass consumption, consumption which was regulated by the supply and demand of a certain national economy. The internationalisation of production and of financial markets rendered any nationally maintained order of labour relations increasingly inadequate (Hitz et al., 1995). This was a direct attack on the fiscal grounds of the nation's welfare systems. Capital's escape from national boundaries created new global spaces of transnational governance; and with this shift, nationally organised Fordist modes of regulating labour started to dissolve and sink into crisis (Lipietz, 1998). The neoliberal project attempted to transform socially guaranteed forms of labour protection into the individual duty of the solo-entrepreneurial labourer.

If neoliberalism is the market-driven institutionalisation of insecurity, its consequences are the decline of normal wage labour and the constant expansion of zones of insecure employment relations. Precarity designates this exact situation in the labour market. That is, precarity delineates how the multiplication of insecure and non-standardised forms of employment gradually become central to labour in contemporary capitalist conditions of Global North Atlantic societies. This trend affects workers' employment relations and social relations, their fears and desires, and avenues for people's participation in public discourse and civil society (Gallie and Paugam, 2003; Rodgers and Rodgers, 1989).

Contemporary sociological research on insecure employment relations casts precarious labour as the proliferation of atypical and irregular work relations which: (a) are contract based, part-time or short-term employment; (b) are product-oriented – usually in the form of subcontracted labour, project-based jobs, freelance work – and paid by the quality of the product the worker delivers; (c) are organised beyond existing structures of social welfare systems, such as unemployment benefit, social security, health insurance, services for maternity leave, etc; (d) are characterised by an increased mobility, global or regional as well as national; (e) intensify the trans-sectorial mobility of workers; (f) range from underpaid jobs (constituting the working poor) to highly paid executive jobs (elitist 'cognitariat'); (g) and finally, precarious work is understood as non-unionised, although there have been some attempts to connect with traditional trade unions.

Precarity is commonly regarded as the result of a multi-layered rearrangement of the production process in post-Fordist societies of the Global North Atlantic, occurring mainly through deindustrialisation, the feminisation of work and the rise of immaterial production. Firstly, deindustrialisation has meant redundancies for workers who were traditionally involved in industrial and serial production processes (Beynon, 2002; Revelli, 1999). Only a small proportion of Fordist workers subsequently re-enter similar production conditions. The turbulences of unemployment, the related destabilisation of the social bond and the failure to qualify for further employment pushes workers into a system of precarious labour – usually casual work (Campbell and Burgess, 2001), insecure labour (Heery and Salmon, 2000), informal labour (Chang, 2006; Williams and Windebank, 1998; Portes, Castells and Benton, 1989) – located in very different production segments or services from those in which they previously worked (Tálos, 1999). Seen from the perspective of deindustrialisation, precarious work *appears* as the end result of the flexibilisation and neoliberalisation of the labour market (Katschnig-Fasch, 2003).

Secondly, there has been extensive investigation of the feminisation of work, which is occurring alongside the reorganisation of employment relations. The Fordist gendered division of labour created a dichotomy of productive (production of goods) and reproductive activities (affective work, communication, caring, subjective work), with the latter being undervalued, primarily delegated to women and traditionally excluded from Fordist labour (Eichorn, 2004; Hochschild, 1983; Boudry, Kuster and Lorenz, 2000; Preciado, 2003). Now, the feminisation of work occurs, in part, through the incorporation of reproductive work into post-Fordist production processes. This incorporation largely occurs in the form of precarious labour. But this transformation does not mean that the patriarchal and gendered division of labour has come to an end (Nickel, Frey and Hüning, 2003; Skeggs, 1997; Walkerdine, Lucey and Melody, 2001; Gill, 2002). It only means that the lines of exploitation of female labour traverse the production process in different ways: new contradictions and ambivalences arise in tandem with the shifting configurations of gender relations and heteronormativity in the current division of labour (Bridget Anderson, 2000; S. Hess and Lenz, 2001; Mayer-Ahuja, 2004; Mirchandani, 2003; Pieper and Gutiérrez Rodríguez, 2003; Waldby and Cooper, 2008).

Thirdly, the proliferation of immaterial labour is considered to be post-Fordism's leading innovation in the production process (Lazzarato, 1996; Gorz, 1999; Marazzi, 1998; Bologna, 2006; Fumagalli and Lucarelli, 2006; von Osten, 2003). Immaterial labour is the production of commodities that are constituted by their cultural, emotional, creative or intellectual content. Immaterial labour can be understood as the process in which work becomes mainly subjective and communicative; the production of immaterial goods demands the whole investment of the worker's subjective and intersubjective abilities (Brinkmann et al., 2006; Moldaschl and Voss, 2003; O'Doherty and Willmott, 2001; Schönberger and Springer, 2003). Immaterial labour, especially in the creative industries (Ehrenstein, 2006b; McRobbie, 2004; von Osten, 2006; Raunig and Wuggenig, 2007), demands that workers blend their domestic, virtual and actual workspaces (Hochschild, 1997; Huws, 2003; Lohr and Nickel, 2005; Morini, 2007). The virtualisation of workspace is made possible by technoscientific innovations, principally information networks, global media cultures and new management and organisational structures (Eaton, 1995; Henry and Massey, 1995). For some, the rise of immaterial production appears as something to be celebrated (Pink, 2001; Florida, 2004) or at least as holding promise for the future (Atzert, 2005; Dyer-Witheford, 2001; Hardt and Negri, 2000). Alternatively, there is a pessimistic viewpoint which sees immaterial labour as part of the developments of modern societies over the last three decades which are triggering new unexpected levels of exploitation and the dissolution of social cohesion (Sennett, 1998; Boltanski and Chiapello, 1999; Rambach and Rambach, 2001; Lessard and Baldwin, 2003; Lovink, 2002; Castel, 2003; Giroux, 2002).

Beyond a Sociological Reading of Precarity: the Regime of Precarious Life and Labour

The concept of precarity carries its own risks. Our particular concern here is with its use as a sociological or cultural category, a use we have introduced in the previous paragraphs. Sociological analyses of precarity are useful to the extent that they articulate and describe the proliferation of features such as affective labour, networking, collaboration, the knowledge economy, etc. in terms that fit with mainstream sociological accounts of the network society (Lazzarato, 1996; Castells, 1996; Gorz, 2004). But this kind of sociological description is very different from an operative political conceptualisation of precarity which is situated in co-research and political activism (Negri, 2006; Colectivo Precarias a la Deriva, 2004) and which draws upon immediate interventions into the power dynamics of labour relations in contemporary European post-Fordist societies. When the sole use of the concept of precarity is to diagnose the present contradictions of production, the concept's role in conjuring up alternative modes of experiencing and in mobilising alternative forms of action in the present is neglected. If precarious workers have, like the sub-proletarian workers described in the letter to Althusser (above), their own distinct sources of pride, respect and autonomy, these are not being discussed or interrogated in contemporary sociological research on precarity.

Zora came to Germany on a tourist visa at the age of 19 following the war in the former Yugoslavia and lived for many years as a *sans papier*. She forged an existence through a wide variety of jobs, sometimes concurrent, in household services, the catering trade and boutiques. We want to present Zora's account of domestic work – an account which was gathered as part of the project on EU border control, described in Section IV – as illustrative of the inadequacies of concepts which cast the experience of precarious workers as the end product of relations of exploitation. After a while in Germany, Zora found herself being positioned in the labour market in a degrading way, her qualifications were being ignored and she also experienced the denigration and disdain associated with the racist 'Slav' tag. As she put it:

When I arrived in Germany I felt quite normal and then I noticed that I wasn't normal somehow. Here [in Germany], I am something ... bad .... Then there were cleaning jobs where people felt superior and they thought Slavs were inferior and me a cleaning lady and then from a crisis area, I was just rubbish for them. And I sometimes felt very bad, like I was carrying a heavy stone on my back as I washed the floors. At that time nothing could touch me. So I bent down and cleaned and felt bad, but at that time I just couldn't *allow myself* to think about it, like: 'Have I been badly treated or not?' Because I just mightn't have had the strength to come back again. I only started thinking about it much later, when I could allow myself.

If we read Zora's account with a view to understanding contemporary relations of production, we see only the particular forms of exploitation, the racism and the disdain to which Zora is being subjected (Pieper, Panagiotidis and Tsianos, 2008). From this perspective, not '*allowing [herself]* to think' seems like a form of denial on Zora's part. Whilst tragic portrayals of precarity can offer useful insights into contemporary labour control (for instance, see the work of Berlant, 2007), they can only neglect or misread people's gestures towards (or even concrete accounts of) experience lived *beyond* these relations of exploitation. In the midst of Zora's account of pervasive subjection, we have her startling contention that '[a]t that time nothing could touch me'. Rather than assuming that this is a tragic or naive claim of someone who is striving to maintain face, we want to maintain the possibility that Zora is generously sharing a tactic of dis-identification (as discussed earlier in Chapters 5 and 9). Through dis-identification, Zora reproduces and at the same time undoes the gendered and racialised orders which accompany every single minute of precarious labour.

What we read in Zora's account is the necessity to refuse the deterministic tendency to collapse the experiences of precarious workers into the conditions in which precarity is lived. (For an extensive account of this see the impressive discussion of Hannah Cullwick's diaries in Lorenz and Kuster, 2007.) For instance, by drawing on feminist discussions about sexuality, and in particular the concept of 'sexual work' (Lorenz and Kuster, 2007; Boudry, Kuster and Lorenz, 2000) we can acknowledge that although there is an inextricable link between Zora's sexuality and work, the relation is neither linear nor predetermined. Specific workplaces require not only precise skills, but also particular embodiments of gender and sexuality. Zora acts as a silent/silenced analyst of the present – as a modest witness, you could say – who renders explicit the 'unspoken contracts' through which the symbolic orders of ethnicity, national affiliation and heteronormativity are reproduced and negotiated in the workplace. So the embodiment of affect which Zora performs while working is not the result of the pure enactment of 'labour' skills or of information exchange or knowledge-oriented interactions (as many would argue; see for example Virno, 2003). Rather, this 'sexual labour' (Lorenz and Kuster, 2007) is permanently and inherently sustained through heteronormative and ethnicising/racist social formations. Hence, while working, we always create an indeterminate surplus of informal world-making investments which are not only related to work but also to its gendered and racialised order. However, Zora constantly decodes this order so that she can remain 'untouched by it'. In so doing, not only does she silently expose the relation between labour, gender and race which sustains domestic work, she also *exceeds* this mode of labour control by insisting on bringing aspects of 'untouched' experience to work, experience which remains beyond regulation. Moreover, as we discuss in Chapter 15, Zora experiences her precarity as a set of careful moves which develop new relations and spaces for action through a complex and unstable balance between freedom, desire, coercion and often violence (Kuster, 2006a; Kuster and Tsianos, 2007).

To avoid just another apolitical sociological category, we want to focus on the ruptures, blockades, and the lines of flight which are immanent in the configuration of precarious labour. It is misleading to assert that the sociological features of precarious labour, such as informality, cooperation, creativity, affectivity, etc., *constitute* precarious subjects. Today's emergent labour subjectivities do not coalesce into one unified social actor with the same position in production and the same characteristics. These subjectivities do not simply mirror the proliferation of precarity, nor are they the end product of shifts in the organisation of labour. Precarious subjectivities are the fluid substance through which labour is reorganised, in which precarity materialises. More than this, these emergent subjectivities are the ground on which the embodied experience of precarity is lived. The embodied experience of precarity *exceeds* the conditions of production entailed in precarious labour. When subjectivity is viewed through the lens of mainstream sociology, its flesh is corroded and its bare bones exposed.

Precarious subjectivities simultaneously evoke the contingent intensities of the production process and the intrinsic possibilities for overcoming its oppressive structures, akin to diabolical cartoons. There is always an excess of sociability and subjectivity in precarious lives which does not directly correspond to the immediate conditions of work. There is nothing mystical about this excess of sociability and subjectivity. It arises in the core of precarious conditions of work, i.e. when there is an unbreachable gap between work and its remuneration, a gap in which people have to live their actual lives. And by investing in this incommensurable gap, people create an excess to the work they do. People mobilise social and personal investments in order to produce (e.g. social relations, skills, informal networks, ideas) – some of this is entailed in the 'final product' of their labour, but much remains outside of it. Of course, this excess can be harnessed and redirected to create new forms of capital – the next product. But equally, this excess of continuous experience (as we have described it in Chapter 9) enables a form of politics which is not already absorbed into the regime of precarious life and labour. Thus, the new subjectivities traversing the archipelago of embodied capitalism are not identical with (or determined by) the conditions of post-Fordist production in Global North Atlantic societies. Today's composition of living labour arises in response to the risks imposed by embodied capitalism. What affords the emergence of these new subjectivities in post-Fordist societies is not the configuration of production – as for example Lazzarato (1996) or Corsani (2004) assert

– but the *embodied experience* of shifting arrangements of exploitation entailed in the regime of precarious life and labour.

This experience is a response to the crisis of social systems which were based on the national social compromise of normal employment (see the final two chapters and also Chapters 1 and 2). As work – in order to become productive – becomes incorporated into the non-labour sphere, the exploitation of the workforce happens beyond the boundaries of work; it is distributed across the whole time and space of life (Neilson and Rossiter, 2005). Precarity means exploiting the continuum of everyday life, not simply the workforce (Ehrenstein, 2006b). In this sense, precarity is a form of exploitation which operates primarily on the level of time (see Chapters 9 and 11 for discussions of the regulation of time by the formation of emergent life and liminal porocratic institutions in the fields of life and mobility). It changes the meaning of non-productive time and space.

Fordist regulation was secured in anticipation of workers' productivity, such that this mode of regulation operates independently of its immediate productivity. The protectionism of the welfare system functions through time management, by anticipating and securing the periods when someone becomes non-productive (through accident and illness, unemployment or age). In the regime of precarious life and labour, this lifelong scope in the process of time management disappears. It is eroded in part because the future is no longer guaranteed as before, but also because the future is already appropriated into the present (Ehrenstein, 2006b). Of course, the Fordist regime also exploits the future; but here the process of exploitation occurs in the employment contract which secures the possibility of exploitation beyond the moment of the present (for a history of the contract form, see Steinfeld, 2001). In contrast, in the post-Fordist regime of precarious life and labour we encounter a reconfiguration and intensification of the exploitation of the future (Priddat, 2002). As employment contracts become flexible and increasingly insecure, the exploitation of the future is sustained through the break of the bond of the contract, rather than through the contract itself. This results in an amplification of dependency: one is under increased pressure to ensure that one's future capacity to be 'productive' will be compatible with the demands of the market (lifelong learning, continuous acquisition of skills, expanded qualification and innovation are keywords in this process). So the absence of permanent (or even long) contractual employment increases exploitation: one is not only exploited by others but also by oneself: 'exploitation of the self' in Amanda Ehrenstein's words (Ehrenstein, 2006a). Self-exploitation happens in the regime of precarious life and labour when someone tries to anticipate and explore the future through its dissemination into the present and to intensify their own efforts to ensure that they remain competitive in the future. This post-contractual form of dependency is twofold: it is a dependency on the employer, who offers limited contracts, as well as a dependency on oneself to increase one's own capacity to get such contracts in the future. Zora's account exemplifies this: Zora can always refuse to work in a certain job but she can only do this if she has already secured, or at least planned, possibilities to sustain herself in the future through informal self-organised protection measures. Post-contractual dependency is the result of the exploitation of the future through the intensification of one's own efforts in the present to expand one's own capacity. This is what we mean when we say that the future is already exploited in the present. The regime of precarious life and labour is a means of labour control which appropriates this new form of the worker's productivity.

Precarious Subjectivities

How are individual workers affected by the breakdown of the national compromise of normal employment, the reordering of time and the new conditions of post-contractual exploitation in precarious life and work conditions? Above, we criticised the reductionism of mainstream sociological conceptualisations of precarious labour that considers workers as one unified social actor (akin to *the* working class), which mirrors the characteristics of post-Fordist productivity. Precarity is not a term for defining the new structure of production in Global North Atlantic societies. The investigation of work experience (see here the stimulating work by Charlesworth, 2000) and of the organisation of the everyday life of the working classes (see the painstaking work of J. Rose, 2001) is crucial to understanding the new social conflicts emerging in the regime of precarious life and labour. It reveals how new social subjectivities emerge through the embodiment of the social conflicts and ambivalences of living labour in the regime of precarious life and labour.

Precarious subjectivities represent the attempts to live with incessant neoliberal imperatives to transform the self, which proliferate in embodied capitalism. Of course, because experience itself is multiple, fluid and constantly changing, it is impossible adequately to characterise the subjectivities entailed in this labour regime. However, we want to sketch some connections between specific imperatives to self-transformation, and some of the predominant ways that we see these imperatives being taken up, reworked, embodied and lived. Our purpose here is not to attempt a definitive account of precarious subjectivity, but to prompt discussion of the complexity and multiplicity of modes of experiencing the regime of precarious life and labour. The subjective phenomenology of precarity, which we present below, draws on various militant research actions which took place as part of the EuroMayDay mobilisations in 2004–07, as well as on a series of research projects. Thus, our starting point for these thoughts is an analysis of more than 120 interviews from two research projects which took place in Hamburg between 2005 and 2007: 'Precarious Labour and Subjectivity' and 'Immaterial Labour and Migration' (research conducted by Marianne Pieper, Efthimia Panagiotidis and Vassilis Tsianos). Furthermore, the previously mentioned work by Amanda Ehrenstein (Ehrenstein, 2006b, 2006a) and the work by Brigitta Kuster on sexuality and precarity (Boudry, Kuster and Lorenz, 2000; Lorenz and Kuster, 2007) has been central to the development of the phenomenology of precarious subjectivities.

There is a tension between the neoliberal imperatives to transform the self which proliferate in embodied capitalism and the experiences evoked in these research projects of how these imperatives are embodied and lived in the everyday (see Table 1). We can see non-linear connections between: (a) embodied capitalism's ongoing flexibility, together with the absence of any form of protection and people's experiences of intense vulnerability; (b) the imperative to accommodate constant availability and precarious workers' hyperactivity; (c) the need to demonstrate the ability to manage the different tempi of multiple tasks and precarious workers' experiences of simultaneity; (d) processes through which one's own body is reorganised to accommodate multi-local environments, the crossing of various networks, social spaces and available resources on the one hand, and the embodiment of recombination on the other; (e) the constant reinvention of an adaptable, versatile, polymorphic but finally unquestionably heteronormative matrix and an increase in fluid intimacies between people; (f) the imperative to cope with and compress the overabundance of communication, cooperation and interactivity and feelings of restlessness; (g) the continuous experience of mobility across different spaces and time lines and people's unsettledness; (h) the centrality of emotional exploitation, or emotional intelligence, for the control of employability and multiple dependencies and feelings of affective exhaustion; (i) the imperative to be cynical, energetic, attractive, pragmatic, trained, all in all a professional arsehole, by being cunning, deceitful, persistent, opportunistic, imaginative, a trickster.

Table 1 *The relationship between neoliberal imperatives to transform oneself and people's embodied experiences of precarious subjectivities*

Neoliberal imperatives to transform oneself	People's embodied experiences of precarious subjectivities
flexibility	vulnerability
availability	hyperactivity
multitasking	simultaneity
multilocality	recombination
polytropic heteronormativity	fluid intimacies
communicative abundance	restlessness
mobility	unsettledness
emotional intelligence	affective exhaustion
professional arsehole	cunning

Challenging the Regime of Precarious Life and Labour: Excess, Freedom and the Embodied Experience of Precarity

How can escape be enacted in the regime of precarious life and labour? What is the imperceptible politics taking place in the regime? Throughout the book we have argued that escape is always the result of an excess created in the core of a regime of control. We want to call the excess which emerges in the tension between neoliberal imperatives to transform the self and precarious subjectivities the *embodied experience of precarity*. The embodied experience of precarity is a form of subversion and possibly a form of escape from the precarious subjectivities manifesting in the realm of the regime of precarious life and labour.

In order to elucidate this, let us follow a historical analogy. The vagabond masses escape the regime of immobility embedded in the guild, and their escape annuls de facto the regime of dependent and captive labour (described in Chapter 4). The vagabonds create the conditions of the free worker; that is, the worker who is able to choose where to sell her productive labour power. In so doing, the vagabonds create the structural conditions for the emergence of the system of free wage labour which, of course, comes to be a new means to tame and control the excess entailed in the exodus of the vagabond masses. (There is no ultimate solution in the history of escape.) The vagabonds create freedom and this forces capitalism to evolve into a new system for regulating free labour.

In contemporary times, the embodied experience of precarity signals the possibility of escape from the regime of precarious life and labour on the one hand, and on the other hand it becomes the direct target of contemporary labour control. The answer to the people's move away from the Fordist regime solidified as a new system of regulation in the 1970s and 1980s: neoliberalism. Thus, neoliberalism was simultaneously both a response to people's revolt against Fordism and a new order of domination. The productivity of neoliberalism consists in the deregulation of the labour markets and the systematic destruction of existing social protections of the labour force, in combination with an increase in individual productivity. But, as we described earlier, the neoliberal imperatives for self-transformation, which have been so meticulously embraced in the managerial biographies of the creative class and are so vividly described by Boltanski and Chiapello (1999), have a highly ambivalent effect on precarious life and work conditions. Labour is trapped in the neoliberal blockade of minimal protection and maximal individual productivity. This blockade seems to be socially unsustainable in the long term, something which is recognised even by the European Council (see, for example, the debates about flexisecurity, the new attempts to regulate mobility and the conditions of work; see also Gabriella Alberti's work (2007) on the reorganisation of recent European legislation on migration and employment. The regime of precarious life and labour is postliberalism's attempt to intensify, re-energise and redirect neoliberal governance so that it codifies and systematises precarity on a large social scale. Up to now precarity has been seen as the result of neoliberal market-driven deregulation of the labour markets and the dismantling of the welfare system; it has been cast as a treatment 'side-effect' which simply has to be endured. The postliberal shift entailed in the regime of precarious life and labour is that it attempts to institutionalise precarity.

As we write, we find ourselves in the middle of an unfolding situation concerning the reorganisation of labour relations as well as the conflicts and forces which create moments of escape. Precarious subjectivities are being contested from two conflicting sides: the regime of precarious life and labour aggressively tries to systematise the insecurity of precarious subjectivities; at the same time the embodied experience of precarity constitutes a drift leading away from these subjectivities. This experience is situated in the core of an open transformation taking place in the evolving postliberal regime of precarious life and labour. In other words, the embodied experience of precarity can subvert the manifestation of precarious subjectivities as the only possible vehicle through which to experience work in current conditions. This immanent mode of experience is ingrained in the very same move mobilised by the postliberal project (i.e. the move to respond to the neoliberal blockade by codifying and institutionalising it). *And*, at the same time, the embodied experience of precarity experiments on the terrain of its own freedom with new ways to expand and defend society. The excess which occurs in this experience is a surplus of freedom; certainly this excess can be (and is being) reinvested in new systems of postliberal domination; but it is also reinvested into emerging modes of escape, trajectories which move away from postliberalism.

What then are the potentialities for the political manifestation of the embodied experience of precarity? How can this surplus of freedom create possibilities for a line of flight from postliberal control? Who's afraid of precarious workers? It seems difficult to imagine that there could be anybody who is afraid of precarious workers. Is there a political significance to this excess sociability which does not necessarily flow into given modes of political representation proclaimed by the conservative and social-democratic parties alike in most countries of the Global North Atlantic? We would find it hard to answer this question in the affirmative were we, as discussed above, to approach the subjectivity of precarious workers as a unified social subject (or 'precariat') – we would neglect the possibility to interrogate the excess contained in the embodied experience of precarity. This is because we would enter a political logic, as described in Chapter 5, which incorporates subjectivity as otherness into the totality of political representation. Subjectivity is reduced to a part which is not yet included. Whilst such inclusion of subjectivity into political representation revitalises democratic politics, it does not question the regime of labour control and it sustains rather than subverts precarity. Such strategies neutralise the political excess of precarious subjectivities and work only with elements of subjectivity which can be incorporated as a manageable part of existing political regulation.

A subject included as otherness is and never was a frightening subject for the given political order. Rather, this subject is constituted as an anxious and afraid subject (Kuster and Tsianos, 2007). And, with Spinoza, we know that when the mob is frightened, it inspires no fear (Balibar, 1994). Hence we can say that fear is triggered by those who are unwilling to participate in the politics of inclusion and instead engage in acts of escape. But this raises a question about the possibilities of escape from the regime of precarious life and labour. In the next chapter we examine three organisational modes for mobilising labour subjectivities which have, historically, delivered fearsome and politically contentious subjects capable of challenging current forms of domination; and we consider why these have limited relevance for precarious workers today.

14   NORMALISING THE EXCESS OF PRECARITY

In the long social history of subversion we find three predominant forms of contentious political action related to labour subjectivities: the party, the trade union, and micropolitical strategies. Can any of these forms harness the excess of the embodied experience of precarity and deploy it in the evacuation of evolving postliberal regimes of control? In Chapter 9 we argued against assuming that experience is always already political, and examined the need to find new means to politicise experience. Here we consider these three forms of collective political engagement and argue that none is adequate to the task of politicising experiences of precarity. None can energise the imperceptible politics enacted through the embodied experience of precarity. In the final chapter of the book we open a discussion about the politics of escape from the postliberal regime of precarious life and labour.

The Party Form

One of most predominant occurrences of a frightening political subject in the history of the organisation of workers' subjectivity has been the revolutionary party. The main feature of this organised subjectivity is its militant character. The party transforms the subjectivity of workers into a war machine. The materialisation of revolution has as its primary target the extinction of antagonist class relations. The crucial goal here is to attack not only antagonist class relations, on the level of production, but also the wider institutions themselves which maintain the dominance of capital over labour – primarily state apparatuses. Without antagonist class relations, two means of regulating liberal national states are rendered void, namely rights and representation (as discussed in Section I). The party was the first and by far the most radical attempt to overcome the liberal political matrix of Global North Atlantic nations.

A crucial turning point in the actual history of the party form occurred when the organisation of workers' subjectivity (which had been so efficient in overturning the liberal matrix) was finally appropriated by the vertical organisation of the party form. This strategy of action had already been anticipated in the early years of the twentieth century in Lenin's conception of historical materialism. Lenin had one single goal: the revolution. This is truly phenomenal and unparalleled (albeit fatal). In the unsurpassable *What Is To Be Done?* Lenin (1902) claims that social conflict penetrates every corner of society, every social relation, every idea. Nothing is untouchable by class antagonism; it takes a partisan organisation and a revolution to change it. This is partisan philosophy and partisan practice. If Marx and Engels' monist materialism proclaimed the irresistibility of revolution on the grounds of a unified movement of matter and society, Lenin's dualist materialism elevated irresistibility to something even stronger, but on different grounds: the (party's) will. For Marx and Engels, freedom means subjecting oneself to the irresistibility of historical necessity; and Lenin added to that, subjecting oneself to political organisation, which is the only possibility to respond to historical necessity. As Arendt (1973, p. 53) says, modern revolutionaries regarded themselves 'as agents of history and historical necessity, with the obvious yet paradoxical result that instead of freedom necessity became the chief category of political and revolutionary thought'. The victim of the efficacious Leninist strategy of contentious political action was the most crucial element of revolutionary practice: workers' subjectivity itself. The insurgent creativity of workers' subjectivities which departed from the liberal matrix ended up in the facticity of the party's domination over society (Negri, 1999). A vampire-like optic domination absorbs the impulse of workers' subjectivities, disseminates it across society and then transforms it into the building material of a vertical organisation imposed from above.

The Trade Union Form

A further contentious collective form of political action in the history of workers' subjectivity starts directly from the workers' immediate relation to production. It differs substantially from the party form.

The clash between capital and labour was mediated and facilitated by the party's attack on the institutional manifestation of capital (and this manifestation was primarily the capitalist state as a whole). In contrast, trade union collectivity arose directly in the spaces where class dominance was experienced, namely in the factory. Even if the genealogy of the trade union form shows a parallel movement to the party form (see for example the events of 1918; by 8 November, workers' and soldiers' councils had seized most of Western Germany, laying the foundations for the so-called Räterepublik or Council Republic), at many historical moments trade union politics has been in direct contradiction to the party. Unlike the party form, the trade union form identified and organised workers' common interests according to their *immediate* position in the system of production and not against the whole system of capitalist political organisation around the state. If the party form engages in militant politics, the trade union form engages in politics of workers' protection, primarily in the form of syndicalism. If the party form is characterised by a historically unprecedented radicalism, the trade union form is characterised by a historically unprecedented moment of camaraderie and solidarity.

The trade union form is grounded on the principle of syndicalism, i.e. a belligerent sociability – belligerent towards the capital commando and sociable and protective towards its members. Labour struggles appear on the political scene in the late nineteenth and early twentieth centuries: the Paris Commune of 1871, the Noble and Holy Order of the Knights of Labour, the Industrial Workers of the World are just a few examples. But the protectionist character of trade union sociability was invested in the attempt to moderate the asymmetrical relation between capital and work. This led the traditional working-class movement, in particular in the inter-war and post-Second World War periods, to restrict its interventions into the realm of the state and to become encapsulated in purely productionist thinking. As segments of the working class gradually came to see their interests aligned with parts of the state, reformism became the political logic of trade unions. The trade union form of political action translated the surplus of sociability and solidarity of workers' subjectivity into institutionalised forms of state protection. Of course, this institutionalisation of sociability was not equally distributed across various groups of workers; and the national compromise of normal employment (as described in Chapter 1) was installed on highly uneven grounds. The statism of the trade union form radically changed the nature of the capitalist nation state. The protection of labour becomes an inseparable moment of the modern state and gives birth to the triptych: social protectionism, institutionalised regulation, welfare state.

The Micropolitical Form

The last and most recent form of a contentious social subjectivity stems from the radicalisation of the politics of everyday life. Here we encounter a departure from a political subjectivity which is primarily defined in terms of its relation to the production process. The micropolitical form returns to the immediate level of social life, in which experience gets under the skin and materialises, affecting selves and others. There is nothing exceptional to this functioning of the everyday. As Lefebvre (1991) says, it is the realm in which all extraordinary, specialised activity has been eliminated. Micropolitics recognises that the everyday is not identical with itself, it is the source and the target of change. Feminism, civil rights movements, identity politics, urban activism, anti-racism, all start from embodied experiences of exclusion on the level of the everyday and, at different points, these movements have all tried to rearticulate these experiences as difference, creatively cultivating difference and inserting it as a constitutive moment of the everyday. When politics becomes the politics of difference, the micropolitical form focuses on incorporating new social subjectivities into the established social compromise of the nation state – a compromise which has historically been organised along the lines of whiteness, heteronormativity, wage labour and property – by challenging the dominant conditions of representation (Laclau and Mouffe, 1985). The micropolitics of difference become a fight over representation. This political strategy finds its institutional equivalent in the concept of enlarged citizenship (Honig, 2001).

The politics of difference operates by first positing a radical externality that has yet to be inserted into society's institutionalised system of representations. By starting from spaces located outside dominant notions of citizenship, the politics of difference challenges factual forms of representation, and creates the conditions for new representations. Unlike the party form, which targets the militant decomposition of the liberal state as a whole, and the trade union form, which attempts to reduce existing asymmetries in the realm of the state, the micropolitical form positions itself on the neglected terrain of the everyday – a terrain which has been traditionally abandoned by the state – and from this very particular position attacks

established limited modes of inclusion into state institutions. But
in doing this, micropolitics contributes to expanding the terrain of
neoliberal state regulation into previously less codified and regulated
segments of life (Stephenson and Papadopoulos, 2006). Micropolitics
acts as the vehicle through which optic trajectories of neoliberal
regulation disseminate into the finest fissures of society and course
through the everyday.

'I don't have the time ...'

The question we posed at the outset is whether any of these political
forms could become the vehicle for the transformation of the subjectivities of precarious workers into a contentious subject of social
change against the regime of precarious life and labour. We want
to start by considering how the party form of political engagement
fails to harness the excess emerging from the embodied experience
of precarity.

Perhaps this is the first time in the history of workers' subjectivity
that the expression 'I don't have the time' becomes an explicit political
statement; it designates a form of collective subjectivity radically
different from that which fed the development of the party form.
The phrase 'I don't have the time' does not refer to an individualised,
personal time-management problem. Rather it is emblematic of the
collective experience that time is always already totally appropriated.
When precarious living labour is no longer confined to 'work time'
but colonises all of one's time, it fuels the embodied experience of a
restless movement between multiple time axes. (We discussed above
how production and reproduction are intermingled, as is the case
with work and non-work, work time and leisure time, the public
and the private.) The expression 'I don't have the time' is indicative
of the subjective internalisation of a lack of control over one's own
labour power.

Any liberation from the dominance of time over workers' subjectivities in post-Fordist production arises from the capacity to tarry
with time (as discussed in Chapter 9). Refusing to go with the flow
of time, inserting various speeds into the embodied experience of
time, tarrying with time – these are all ways to reappropriate the
productive means of precarious labour as they spill into and across
each and every moment of one's everyday life. These moments,
where precarious workers' subjectivities break the immediate flow
of time and avoid being constituted as productivity devices, escape
the dominance of the linear chronocracy which organises the

precarious work–life continuum (Bridget Anderson, 2007a). What is important for us here is that tarrying with time is a means to harness the constituent powers of continuous experience. It is a mode of engaging with the world that is purposeless in itself – tarrying has no object, it is non-organisable, it defies regulation. Tarrying with time is pure *potentia*, pure departure. In this sense it is the most powerful way to question the logic of precarity: it implodes the imperative to 'be creative'.

Party politics leaves no room for tarrying; it reproduces the over-determination of time by the existing system of production and in so doing reproduces its intrinsic inequalities. Let us explain. The party form is constituted as representing specific clusters or social classes in the system of production. Party politics is by definition the politics of subjects who share certain common interests according to their position in the production. If parties appear to represent the *commune bonum* or even to appeal to the totality of the national congregation – as we discussed earlier, in Chapter 1 – they reproduce the double-R axiom. Party politics is condensed social conflict; it attempts to intervene into a certain configuration of the double-R axiom, changing it in accord with the common interests of the subjects it represents. By doing this, party politics reproduces the injustices inherent in the double-R axiom and more specifically it reproduces the very structure of group and class representation. It attempts to shift the balance of power within an existing compromise between different forces. But what it cannot do is to question the overall logic of production as organised by the national social compromise in each particular moment. Party politics ends up reproducing social injustices by other means. In this sense we can read party politics as a means of policing the boundaries between productivity and non-productivity; those who participate are reified as particular subjects of production. Subjects can take part in party politics only to the extent that they belong to a certain group that can be represented in the national social compromise. But what about illegalised migrants and the *sans papiers* who cannot be considered as equal citizens? What about the rights of women at work, which still remain undervalued? What about the *favelas* and townships and the sub-proletarians (more than 30 million of them currently living in the United States alone)? What about the precarious subjectivities who are sometimes included in representation because they are 'creative' and 'hip' (the 'creative class') but never as refusing certain forms of work or social regulation? So, when people say 'I don't have the time to participate in politics', we can understand this as a refusal to participate, not in politics, but in policing the boundaries of production as they are sustained by the national social compromise.

Trade Unionism and the Vacuum of Protection

Trade unionism cannot harness the excess of the embodied experience of precarity, it cannot mobilise precarious subjectivities, simply because precarious workers' constitutive needs are, by definition, excluded from the national compromise around which the trade union form revolves. This is because the crisis of social welfare systems is nothing other than the end of a specific relationship between normal wage labour and state interventionism; a liaison which was nurtured by the trade unions. As we already know, the embodied experience of precarity is an escape from the system of wage labour. At the same time the neoliberal state has seized this trajectory of escape and harnessed it to the task of fuelling the proliferation of individuals' entrepreneurial activities beyond state regulation. This means that the two foundational moments of classical trade union reformism are absent in the terrain of precarity, i.e. statism of labour and interventionism of the state.

If we consider the basic conditions of precarious labour we can see how the embodied experience of precarity diverges from the trade union form. Precarious labour has a trans-spatial order, whereas the trade union form starts from the immediate space of production and mobilises workers according to their common spatialised interests (according to sector or geographical location). Hence a major obstacle to any classical syndicalism against precarity will be the trans-spatial movements of the precarious worker. (Regarding the problem of migrant mobility and new forms of organising, see, for example, Brekke, 2008; Milkman, 2000.) In the previous chapter we described two of the major characteristics of the embodied experience of precarity, i.e. hyperactivity and unsettledness. The embodiment of incessant movement across multiple locales destroys the possibility of the classic trade union organisation form based on a single locality.

The shift from the subjectivity of the wage labourer to the subjectivity of the neoliberal, entrepreneurial, self-managerial individual requires a new relation between the state and living labour and poses difficult questions for trade unions. Traditional trade unionism works to sustain a balance of power between segments of the working class and the state. What is important here is that only specific parts of the working classes can be included and represented to the state. For example, consider state interventionism into protecting the rights of the male workforce and establishing a hierarchical order of labour. Female and migrant 'dirty work' (domestic labour, undocumented labour, unskilled employment; cf. Bridget Anderson, 2000) are on the lowest level of this hierarchy. Historically, the attempts of trade unions to reduce the power asymmetry between labour and capital involved reproducing a hierarchical order between various kinds of labour subjectivities (Heery, 2005). Not all parts of the working classes are represented in the trade unions. Trade unionism normalised the subjectivities of some workers in normal employment and fractured de facto the everyday sociability of living labour into social groups which were accorded different values.

The early neoliberal policies of the 1970s amplified this fragmentation of the social by breaking down the traditional concepts of protectionism and systematically undermining the role of trade unions in the national compromise between labour and capital. The fruition of the neoliberal project elevated the fragmentation of living labour into a new regime of primary accumulation. Today, trade unionism cannot effectively protect labour and the neoliberal project no longer wants to protect it. The trade union form can ameliorate some of the problems workers face today, but it cannot effectively protect workers from the neoliberal attack against living labour.

We find ourselves in a vacuum of protection. The embodied experience of precarity very much reflects this vacuum; it is marked by an almost existential condition of vulnerability, felt in every moment of everyday life. The embodied experience of precarity calls for a new mode of protection which cannot be extended by trade unionist syndicalism. The income of the salaried worker used to be measured in relation to the quantification of an individual's labour power. This measurement was guaranteed and protected by collective trade union negotiations. But this no longer holds, simply because collective bargaining cannot protect something which is immeasurable. There is no monetary equivalent to the labour productivity of each individual precarious labourer (consider Dyer-Witheford's inspiring work (1999); see also Gorz, 2004) – and this despite fierce attempts to quantify and measure production outcomes of project work, intellectual labour, cultural products, affective labour, care work, domestic labour, etc. (for an example, see de Angelis and Harvie, 2006). It is increasingly evident that these intensive attempts to quantify the production of precarious work can only lead to suppression of resources and potentials invested by living labour (Negri, 2003). The singular productivity of the precarious worker is unquantifiable. Immaterial labour, in particular, confronts us with the impossibility of assigning an equivalent monetary value to creativity, affectivity and sociability. This leads us to say that life in precarious conditions needs a different form of protection, one which allows people to perform their everyday re/productive activities and at the same time guarantees an existential security when they are affected by the intensification of neoliberal (or postliberal) forms of exploitation.

New social movements against precarity (e.g. the EuroMayDay network, or the feminist collectives Precarias a la Deriva in Spain, Prec@s in Italy, etc.) stress this necessity and refuse to return to a form of politics which aspires to secure and protect precarious workers on the level of normal wage employment. In these European contexts the demand for basic income as the unconditional protection from the precarity of living labour has emerged as one of the immediate targets of movements against the regime of precarious life and labour (Fumagalli and Lucarelli, 2006). Unless unions are radicalised and accommodate demands beyond the logic of wage labour, such efforts will bypass them. The logic of wage labour is incompatible with the demand for basic income, because the latter calls for an uncoupling of wage from labour (i.e. the earning from the executed work). In this sense, overcoming the limitations of the trade union form entails a new form of syndicalism which starts with the embodied experience of living labour: *biosyndicalism*.

Biosyndicalism is the attempt to organise precarious subjectivities, by bringing together, into a new form of unionism, various contemporary experiments in collective organisation (e.g. networks of collective action, such as Precarias a la Deriva, www.sindominio. net/karakola/precarias.htm). This new form of unionism operates on a transnational level (it follows the transnational flows of labour mobility), it is trans-spatial and trans-sectorial (i.e. it does not represent a particular sector or a particular locale in the cycle of production), it is non-identitarian (i.e. it questions the predominant workforce identity as male and native), and finally and most importantly it questions the centrality of work time in the unfolding of the precarious worker's life. A syndicalism of this kind will preserve the most valuable and irreplaceable merits of the historical trade union form – i.e. caring, solidarity, and cooperation – and elevate them into new more complex forms of organisation (cf. Chesters and Welsh,

2006). It will be a truly life-oriented syndicalism (*bio*syndicalism), as it will operate on the immediate level of common life experiences. However, can this experimental syndicalism contribute to the creation of a fear-inspiring social subject against embodied capitalism? This can be answered by recalling a historical analogy: today the basic income for precarious workers is what the eight-hour day was for the working class before the turn to the twentieth century. Although the eight-hour day was absolutely crucial to the development of the working-class movement and to improving working conditions for those who could be represented by that movement, it could not contribute to the creation of a social actor who could challenge the system of production as such.

The Micropolitical Enterprise and the Failure of Representation

Can micropolitics go beyond the limitations of the party and trade union forms and politicise the embodied experience of precarity? It seems that there is an almost 'natural' proximity between the politics of the precarious workers and micropolitics. There are several reasons for this affinity. Firstly, both micropolitics and precarious politics share a common concern with the question of visibility. Micropolitics has proved a productive means of making visible what has previously been ignored. The embodied experience of precarity might seem like a candidate for such efforts; it is largely either rendered completely invisible in public discourse or flattened into talk of undeserving, irresponsible people or victims. Moreover, precarious labour has been effaced from the official agenda of the working-class movement and its institutions. Hence, it is either ignored, subsumed under the category of the service sector or disparaged as a synonym for the 'new economy' or 'human capital'; or, in the best case, immaterial labour is cast as 'knowledge work'.

Secondly, the proximity between micropolitics and the embodied experience of precarity arises out of their common situatedness in the everyday. Both start from and work on the immanent terrain of everyday life. The social struggles of migrant and feminist movements have made the issue of dirty work visible (Bridget Anderson, 2007b, 2001; Fantone, 2007). Importantly, the commonalities between the struggles of today's precarious movements and the social movements of the 1970s and 1980s which targeted the everyday are now energising the development of strategic coalitions of diverse forms of precarity-related activism.

Despite these commonalities and strategic alliances, there is an insurmountable difference between the two, one which prevents a micropolitical social movement against precarity from challenging the regime of precarious life and labour. This difference pertains to the failure of representational politics (as discussed in Chapters 5 and 6), a mode of engagement crucial to micropolitics. Today, representation is the means through which post-Fordism enacts its own exodus from the blockade of the existing national compromise of distributive rights. The shift away from the national social compromise is, partly, executed through a transformation in the relation between productivity (i.e. the creation of value) and property (i.e. the centralisation of accumulated value). Let us explain this. Precarious labour's productivity challenges post-Fordist modes of wealth distribution. In order to be productive, precarious labour needs unrestricted access to the resources of production (i.e. to the *netware*, such as networks, databases, visual data, health, culture, freedom of circulation, freedom of movement, access to educational resources). Hence, precarious labour becomes productive by blocking the capitalist principle of property. And, because the productivity of precarious labour is essential for the projects of both neoliberalism and postliberalism, this unrestricted access must be enabled. In response to this paradox a solution, of sorts, is arising, which, on the one hand, does not suppress the productivity, sociability, and creativity of precarious workers, and, on the other hand, reinstalls a new regime of wealth distribution – one which is based on establishing a new mode of regulating the property of netware (Moulier Boutang, 2001b). This mode of regulation is not founded on ownership of the means of production but only of its products (such as patents of intellectual goods and biodiversity; copyright; restrictions in up/downloading from the net; privatisation of health; mobility control, etc.). This is because the very means of production and of embodied productivity are not only the machines installed in factories or laboratories; they are the precarious worker's singular creativity, affectivity, sociability and capacity for mobility. The new system of property which emerges controls the products of labour rather than the means of production.

The change of the relation between productivity and property creates new problems for precarious workers, problems which pertain to the monetarisation and commodification of precarious workers' lives and resources. When life is rendered precarious, the failures of the national compromise of distributive rights are revealed: the regime of precarious life and labour restricts people's rights to participate in the established national compromise of normal employment. Of course, one response to this partial exclusion has been to engage in the politics of representation, to strive to activate multiple social actors and then attempt to initiate their inclusion in a new system of rights. This is the micropolitical New Deal of neoliberal societies.

The codification of the micropolitical New Deal in the neoliberal state takes the form of citizenship. In particular, cultural citizenship (Rosaldo, 1993) and flexible citizenship (Ong, 1999) are put forward in response to the crisis emerging out of the inadequate solution to the tension between labour and property described above. Flexible citizenship shifts the gaze from a hermetically and exclusively structured form of national belonging to a form of a residual belonging beyond the destabilised dominance of national identity (e.g. Sassen, 2004) and opts for a new extended foundation of democracy (e.g. Honig, 2001). It accounts for new social actors working on transnational, post-welfare representations of participative rights (e.g. Mezzadra, 2001). Despite its enormous importance for the political constitution of the present, the problem with the understanding of political representation found in the concept of flexible citizenship is that it cannot act *beyond* the already given ambiguous dynamics of the neoliberal project (as we discussed already in Section I in relation to the example of migrants' rights). Of course the new politics of transnational representation and flexible citizenship is crucial for today's social movements: it establishes de facto the right to escape dominant nationalist representations and the national compromise between labour and capital. Nevertheless it is defensive; it is primarily focused on challenging and expanding the limits of national sovereignty. Its target is to establish a new compromise between precarious labour and neoliberal capitalism. (The demand for flexisecurity is a typical example of this.) However important and necessary the politics of transnational representation and flexible citizenship might be, here we want to argue that it reterritorialises precarious workers' subjectivities in the matrix of a new postliberal statism. That is, it attempts to ameliorate the effects of the regime of precarious life and labour on precarious workers, instead of working and intensifying the politics of escape which is enacted at the heart of the embodied experience of precarity.

It seems, then, that neither the party, trade union nor micropolitical forms can work with the constituent force of precarious workers' continuous experience or harness this force in a move beyond the regime of precarious life and labour. These three dominant modes of politicising experience neutralise and normalise the excess of sociability which inhabits people's experiences of precarity. None is capable of distinguishing and working with the ambivalences and the specificities of embodied experiences of precarity. They mistake it either for the experience of a unified actor whose interests can be spatially located, or for experience bound by a linear chronocracy, or for unrepresented experience striving for visibility. What then are the processes of repoliticising experience which constitute a line of escape from the regime of precarious life and labour? In the final chapter we argue that, when seen as a multiplicity, precarious subjectivities constitute a radical form of imperceptible politics which points towards an escape from the contemporary regime of labour regulation.

15   INAPPROPRIATE/D SOCIABILITY

Value Creation in Embodied Capitalism

In the previous chapters, we described precarity as the mode of exploitation of life and labour in the regime of embodied capitalism. In contrast, approaching through the lens of embodied experience, we can grasp the myriad of singular experiences entailed in living and working in precarious conditions: the embodied experiences of a chainworker in a high-street fashion shop, of a student paying tuition fees by working as a security guard, of an illegalised migrant who works as a dishwasher, a domestic worker or a sex worker, of a qualified researcher who works on contract-based research projects, of an unemployed academic who works in a call centre, of an au pair who wants to stay in the country after the expiration of a contract, of a migrant computer expert who works as babysitter, of a non-unionised cleaner working on the tube, of a volunteer doing an internship in a cultural institution (and who not only works for free, but her working conditions are not covered by any collective framework whatsoever), of an architect who earns a living working on discontinuous projects, of a seasonal worker in the strawberry fields, of a cinematographer who works on three projects simultaneously and is paid (badly) for only one, of a single mother working part time, of a graphic designer whose work extends far beyond the ten hours she stays in the office. These experiences vary immensely, but they are all permeated by a pervasive social conflict: it is a conflict between high productivity and low protection, or else intensive creativity and deep vulnerability. That is, on the one hand, all these various embodied experiences of precarity constitute the primary terrain on which embodied capitalism's value creation takes place in Global North Atlantic societies. On the other, they are all confronted with the structural insecurity imposed by the system of a nationally organised compromise of normal wage labour (that is, full-time, long-term wage labour).

The system of wage labour and the corresponding welfare system produced a space-fixated work subjectivity (i.e. normal, full-time, wage employment) measured according to work time. Precarious labour implodes this subjectivity at various levels: it is not space-fixated – the precarious worker works in a multiplicity of locales; his/her work cannot be quantified and remunerated according to the system of wage labour measurement; finally, the experiences of precarious workers cannot be accommodated in the unified subjectivity germane to the national social compromise of normal employment. (We described these conditions in more detail in Chapter 13.) Precarious labour exists only in the plural, as a multiplicity of experiences variously positioned, exploited, and lived in the system of embodied capitalism, and not as a unified subjectivity or 'precariat'. Common to this multitude of experiences is that they all simultaneously suffer the postliberal intensification of the blockade of the system of wage labour whilst they are one of the primary sources of value in Global North Atlantic societies.

The creation of value in embodied capitalism is the result, not of the valorisation of labour power, but of the whole continuum of the embodied experience of precarity. In industrial capitalism, value is created by the appropriation of the strictly measured labour power of the worker. The worker is remunerated only for his/her labour power, not for the entirety of his/her life (e.g. domestic labour remains largely unpaid; little consideration is given to the support or the immediate social context necessary for sustaining the worker's ability to produce). In contrast, value in embodied capitalism is created by the appropriation of the whole of the worker's life and social relations, that is his/her relations of care, sociability, capacity to be mobile, ability to constantly expand his/her skills. But this needs some clarification because it is not completely accurate. There is a widespread argument about the transformation from industrial to post-industrial capitalism which describes the appropriation of labour as the appropriation of the worker's subjectivity in its entirety (Beck, 2000; Gorz, 2004; Schönberger and Springer, 2003; Sennett, 1998; Lazzarato, 2004; Virno, 2003). But this is not correct. The regime of precarious life and labour recombines the working subject and exploits specific segments of his or her everyday existence on a case-by-case basis. Embodied capitalism does not actually exploit the totality of the worker's experience; it dissects the subject and the entirety of his/her life and appropriates only certain parts of it. We want to suggest that it is through these very means of dissecting, selecting, appropriating and discarding subjectivities that control is achieved by the regime of precarious life and labour. Regulation entails abandoning the subject as a whole and recombining it, or parts of it.

What is recombined by contemporary capitalism is the worker's embodied experience (see Chapters 8 and 13 for discussions of how postliberal value creation operates by remaking life). In this situation, capitalism is no longer concerned with the calibration and management of the individual as part of a population, it is not even concerned with fabricating individuality in the guise of disciplinary institutions; rather, it attacks individuality *en gros* (see also Papadopoulos, 2004). Its new role is to dissect and dissolve the working subject and recombine it into new effective virtual compositions. Capitalism no longer deals with the link between subject, agency and power; it wants to get rid of all three and construct powerful composites which accumulate, in their bodies, different aspects of the public and the private, the natural and the artificial, the personal and the political. The individual only looks like an individual in its apparent bodily shape, but in reality it becomes a genetic source, an automated client, a host to a virus, a set of competencies, a self-creating assemblage of skills, a register and a code, a body capable of extreme mobility, an actant in a colony of stem cells.

Inappropriate/d Sociabilities of Precarious Life

What the regime of precarious life and labour appropriates and remunerates is not the whole subjectivity of the worker, but a de-individualised recombination of skills, qualities, and capacities. Think of Zora's account of domestic work as an illegal migrant (described in Chapter 13); what is appropriated is her capacity to perform subjection to the racism of her employer ('So I bent down and cleaned and felt bad'). However, through her dis-identification, what Zora brings to the work, 'drops' of her experience, are not entirely appropriated and regulated ('At that time nothing could touch me'). Precarity describes life in these conditions of recombinant embodied capitalism. Embodied capitalism needs the everyday, but it only needs and can accommodate small segments of what people do in their everyday lives. There is an excess sociability fabricated in embodied capitalism's conflictual process between value creation and recombinant exploitation, and this excess is overlooked. Consider the examples above: embodied capitalism profits from the mobility of the au pair, and neglects his or her social or political rights, since this person is considered to be in the country of work only provisionally. The regime of embodied capitalism regards migrants' bodies as naked labour power, not as mobile subjects of rights. At the same time this person utilises her capacity to be mobile as an au pair to gain the chance to enter the country *and* she uses her informal networks to stay after the expiration of the au pair contract (for some examples of this, see S. Hess, 2005; Morokvasic, Erel and Shinozaki, 2003; Salih, 2003).

Similarly, the creativity of the architect, the cinematographer or the graphic designer stems very much from their capacity to connect, socialise, produce beyond the project in which they are currently involved and for which they are paid. Whilst all these activities and experiences are necessary for work, at the same time they exceed what capitalist exploitation wants to and can appropriate. There is always a surplus sociability which remains unexploited in embodied capitalism. This surplus sociability destabilises social regulation, that is, it cannot be fully regulated, because it is incompatible with the current system of measurability of labour power (for examples, see Ehrenstein, 2006b; McRobbie, 2004; Vishmidt and Gilligan, 2003; von Osten, 2006; Widuch, 2005).

The illegal migrant dishwasher, the seasonal worker in the strawberry fields, the domestic servant and the sex worker all enter the highly exploitative and unregulated conditions of undocumented labour, conditions which embodied capitalism could tackle, by assigning unconditional rights for all workers, but refrains from doing so. At the same time, the existence of undocumented labour is the only way for illegalised migrants to sustain their agency, that is to sustain themselves, to cross borders, to establish a new life. It is this possibility to be on the road and at the same time to partake in transnational informal networks of life which cannot be regulated by embodied capitalism (for examples, see Andrijasevic, 2004; Bell and Berg, 2002; Faist, 2000; Kasimis and Papadopoulos, 2005). Moreover, sustaining networks can make it possible to *refuse* exploitation in undocumented jobs. Again, Zora's account illustrates this possibility. The repeated ironic remarks of the boss she had in a waitressing job, 'Oh, you poor thing, you got no tips again', after he had deducted them himself while helping out due to lack of staff, elicited this response from Zora one day:

then I, well, one day I'd really just had enough, so I gave in my notice and said 'there you go, now do it yourself, since you think you can do it all by yourself anyhow and its only *me that can't* because of the way *I am*, then help yourself, I am illegal, I don't owe you anything, so you have no rights over me, go ahead, just do it yourself, I'm gone' and I really left him in the lurch one evening, he just went crazy [grins].

The single mother, the unemployed academic working in a call centre, and the migrant computer expert working as a babysitter enter the job market in vulnerable positions in which they are underemployed. The gendered division of labour is mainly sustained by dismantling social systems of protection, a move which creates the conditions for the single mother's exploitation in a flexibilised labour market. Here, embodied capitalism dissects, extracts and appropriates, on an ad hoc basis, people's feminised social skills in undertaking affective and communicative labour; what is left behind includes people's multiple skills and abilities and the social inequalities which maintain the gendered division between feminised and masculine labour patterns (for examples, see Bridget Anderson, 2000; Parreñas, 2001; Shome, 2006).

The working student and the researcher on a contract employment also both actively participate in the production and reproduction of knowledge, while this knowledge is appropriated by senior members of staff and the institutions by which they are employed. Not only the student and academic, but also the single mother who works part time in a lawyers' office, the computer expert from Bulgaria who (because her diploma is not recognised in her new country of residence) works as a babysitter, and the unemployed English graduate who experiences the pressure to change his accent in order to hide his background from the international callers – all of them are variously exploited on a case-by-case basis according to the particularities of their lived embodied situatedness. Extreme insecurity and flexibilisation pertain not only to the experiences of the chainworker, but increasingly they come to characterise previously secure jobs in the industrial sector. Precarity becomes a highly adaptive pattern of labour regulation across different sectors of production. The entirety of all of these precarious workers' experiences and subjectivities is neither appropriate nor appropriated. Much is jettisoned.

All of these examples suggest how embodied capitalism extracts what is essential for creating value from the highly diversified subjectivities of these workers, and at the same time it retreats from any responsibility for accommodating the complexities of these workers' lives. There is an excess of social relations in the field of precarious life conditions, a plethora of inappropriate/d sociabilities, which is the main source for value creation, and, at the same time, this excess cannot be regulated by the regime of precarious life and labour. The term *inappropriate/d sociability* refers to a twofold form of sociability: on the one hand to a sociability which exceeds what can be appropriated for the purposes of value creation in embodied capitalism; on the other hand, to something which is incommensurable with, that is inappropriate to, the current regime of labour regulation. (See Chapter 6 for a general discussion of this concept; also see Trinh T. Minh-ha, 1987; Haraway, 1992.) The embodied experience of precarity exists and operates at the heart of the existing system of production, and simultaneously it entails something which is inappropriate/d because it exists in a vacuum of control; it exists in a new imperceptible world in the heart of the embodied capitalist world of control: World 2 (Papadopoulos, 2006). Haraway on what is 'inappropriate/d':

Designating the networks of multicultural, ethnic, racial, national, and sexual actors emerging since World War II, Trinh's phrase referred to the historical positioning of those who cannot adopt the mask of either 'self' or 'other' offered by previously dominant, modern Western narratives of identity and politics. To be 'inappropriate/d', does not mean 'not to be in relation with' – i.e., to be in a special reservation, with the status of the authentic, the untouched, in the allochronic and allotopic condition of innocence. Rather to be an 'inappropriate/d other' means to be in critical, deconstructive relationality, in a diffracting rather than reflecting (ratio)nality – as the means of making potent connection that exceeds domination. To be inappropriate/d is not to fit in the taxon, to be dislocated from the available maps specifying kinds of actors and kinds of narratives, not to be originally fixed by difference. To be inappropriate/d is to be neither modern nor postmodern, but to insist on the amodern. Trinh was looking for a way to figure 'difference' as a 'critical difference within,' and not as special taxonomic marks grounding difference as apartheid. (Haraway, 1992, p. 299)

The embodied experience of precarity exists *within* the matrix of labour in embodied capitalism and infuses new *constructive relation-*

alities into it. These are forms of sociability – informal networks of existence, cooperation and social reciprocity, the construction of socio-material artefacts, the transformation of the worker's flesh and abilities – that challenge the process of postliberal control as such. Consider, for example, Zora's account. Zora's constructive relationalities emerge in the complex grids of sociability which arise in conditions of clandestine mobility. Zora tried to come to Europe three times before she finally managed it. And she managed it through the constructive relationalities which emerged in her networks with other illegal migrants: these connections increased her agency in relation to organising jobs without papers, finding passports, meeting 'lads' who are interested in a fake marriage, identifying the cities in Germany where authorities 'tolerant' towards ex-Yugoslavians can be found, organising doctors at low prices. It is through these constructive relationalities that Zora can survive German society's racism, can sustain her body, can protect herself from police violence. These constructive relationalities are not, as many believe, just volatile social relations, but strong material and social spaces which cut across the plane of control which is imposed by the regimes for labour and mobility control.

Inappropriate/d sociability thrives on the real fleshly, material social actors of precarity as a force which interrupts the process of labour recombination and introduces assemblages of its own. This cacophony of precarious experiences, bodies and inappropriate/d sociabilities become a stream of decoding, a stream which places the excess of social, material, affective products created through the everyday life of precarious workers in an imperceptible space, a space which resides within, without being coincident with, the terrain of regulation. Inappropriate/d sociability is the flesh of the imperceptible politics of escape.

Decoding Use Value

Imperceptible politics is not an intentional or teleological act, but a means to harness and work with moments of refusal and creativity in precarious lives as people strive to escape the capture of productionism. Nevertheless, we cannot consider inappropriate/d sociability simply as a counter-power to the regime of control of embodied capitalism. We have already rejected this productionist model which considers the subjectivity of counter-power to be identical with the cycles and structures of production. That is, we cannot extract the subject of historical change from the subject of production. We are tired of this sort of Marxist reading of social transformation. The productionist model casts the subjectivity of the precarious worker as the end product of embodied capitalism. This model wants the exploited class to transform into a counter-power in the form of a class for itself, a class of total expressivity.

However, inappropriate/d sociabilities circulate among, not a unified social subject, but a multiplicity of actors who question the symbolic and material order of control by creating a new life within this order. What might be presented as a stable, representable subject of precarity actually arises out of (and glosses over) a myriad of imperceptible worlds which materialise in unrepresented actual occasions of precarious experience. The subversive potence of inappropriate/d sociability cannot be understood by positing it as a counter-power to a unitary power of the regime of labour control. Inappropriate/d sociability is not against the regime of labour control, rather it works with the potentialities entailed in it by creating spaces of sociability which constitute the ground of escape. This is the imperceptible politics in the field of precarity which could create a movement of escape from the contemporary regime of labour regulation. But we know that our considerations about this are not concrete enough to satisfy the people who will ask 'What is to be done today?' or 'How can we mobilise precarious workers?' We are writing at a moment when the possibilities for new collectivities are present and yet not formed. The collective form of organisation which can challenge the regime of labour regulation in the Global North Atlantic has yet to crystallise. As activists against the regime of precarious life and labour, we experience the difficulties of mobilising and organising precarious workers, bringing together different interests and positions and of developing a coherent strategy for intervention in the field of precarity. But at the same time we learn from these experiences that we can no longer think of the concept of class in Global North Atlantic societies as ultimately resulting from the structure of production (something that would make the fantasy of an emerging collective social actor more easily thinkable).

So although at this historical moment we cannot identify the social actor who will subvert and push the regime of precarious labour beyond itself, we know that this actor will not be formed according to its participation in the structure of production. We think, rather, that it will be shaped by the way people participating in precarious labour relate themselves to the products of their work and connect to each other by subverting the meaning of production as such and the content of their own products. The regime of precarious life and labour wants to select singular activities of ever expanding precarious life into a trajectory of production. Against this, the imperceptible politics of escape attempts to make spaces for the play of purposeless action. Imperceptibility is a form of decoding: decoding the product of its use value. It subverts attempts to recode the product as useful. Whilst Marx assigns the utility of a product to its intrinsic, almost naturalised, features, the continuously perishing 'actual occasions' of embodied experience of precarity call for the denaturalisation of living labour.

A non-natural process is never over-determined; it is immanent socio-materialising. Either it can be stabilised and coded according to the productionist regime of recombination in embodied capitalism or it can circulate in an unspecified space of purposelessness. Inappropriate/d sociabilities exist in imperceptible zones: zones where you can 'make yourself without purpose', cultures of 'doing it without yourself': DIWY. Precarity's moment of escape is the moment of being untouched by, of self-evacuation from, the permanent process of auto-commodification. This evacuation fabricates de-subjectified workers, fabricates spaces where activity cannot be appropriated. Purposelessness is not about creating 'irrelevant' products but about creating objects whose relevance is the very process of creation which is *outside* production. We envision imperceptible politics not as belonging to a certain class defined by its function in the production system, but as belonging to a community of people who find themselves in acts of escaping production. These people start from different grounds, follow different routes, their belongings are extremely varied, and finally they ultimately have nothing in common apart from the fact that their positioning as productive subjects makes them variously exploitable in the regime of embodied capitalism. That is, the contemporary regime of labour control exists as an attempt to stabilise the flux of continuous experience escaping precarity. But any stabilisation can only ever be temporary and is always threatened by the myriad of actual occasions of experience moving through and in the regime. In the present conditions of precarious life and labour we find the most sophisticated form of exploitation of the worker's body and simultaneously the speculative possibility of a new coming commons. This is the cunning of precarious workers. This is the cunning of escape.

REFERENCES

Adam, B. (1995). *Timewatch: The Social Analysis of Time*. Cambridge: Polity Press.

Adam, B. (2004). *Time*. Cambridge: Polity Press.

Agamben, G. (1998). *Homo Sacer: Sovereign Power and Bare Life*. Stanford, Calif.: Stanford University Press.

Agamben, G. (2001). *Mittel ohne Zweck: Noten zur Politik*. Freiburg: Diaphanes-Verlag.

Agamben, G. (2005). *State of Exception*. Chicago: University of Chicago Press.

Aglietta, M. (1979). *A Theory of Capitalist Regulation: The US Experience*. London: New Left Books.

Agnoli, J. (1996). *Subversive Theorie. 'Die Sache selbst' und ihre Geschichte. Eine Berliner Vorlesung*. Freiburg: Ça Ira Verlag.

Ahmed, S. (2003). 'The Politics of Fear in the Making of Worlds'. *Qualitative Studies in Education*, 16(3), 377–98.

Alberti, G. L. (2007). *Exploring the Relation Between Migration Management and the EU Strategies for Employment: An Ethnographic Study of the Policy Process in the European Parliament* (unpublished dissertation). School of Social Sciences, Cardiff University, Cardiff.

Allen, T. (1994). *The Invention of the White Race*. London: Verso.

Alpers, S. (1982). 'Art History and its Exclusions: The Example of Dutch Art'. In N. Broude and M. D. Garrard (eds), *Feminism and Art History: Questioning the Litany* (pp. 183–99). New York: Harper & Row.

Althusser, L. (1971). 'Ideology and Ideological State Apparatuses: Notes Towards an Investigation'. In L. Althusser (ed.), *Lenin and Philosophy, and Other Essays* (pp. 127–86). London: New Left Books.

Anders, G. (2002). *Die Antiquiertheit des Menschen. Bd.1: Über die Seele im Zeitalter der zweiten industriellen Revolution*. München: Beck.

Anderson, Benedict (1991). *Imagined Communities: Reflections on the Origin and Spread of Nationalism*. London: Verso.

Anderson, Bridget (2000). *Doing the Dirty Work? The Global Politics of Domestic Labour*. London: Zed Books.

Anderson, Bridget (2001). 'Different Roots in Common Ground: Transnationalism and Migrant Domestic Workers in London'. *Journal of Ethnic and Migration Studies*, 27(4), 673–84.

Anderson, Bridget (2007a). *Battles in Time: The Relation Between Global and Labour Mobilities, WP-07-55*. Centre on Migration, Policy and Society. University of Oxford.

Anderson, Bridget (2007b). 'A Very Private Business: Exploring the Demand for Migrant Domestic Workers'. *European Journal of Womens Studies*, 14(3), 247–64.

Anderson, M. (2000). 'The Transformation of Border Controls: A European Precedent?' In P. Andreas and T. Snyder (eds), *The Wall Around the West: State Borders and Immigration Controls in North America and Europe* (pp. 15–30). Lanham: Rowman & Littlefield.

Anderson, W. (1996). 'Race and Acclimatization in Colonial Medicine Disease, Race, and Empire'. *Bulletin of the History of Medicine*, 70(1), 62–7

Anderson, W. (2002). 'Going Through the Motions: American Public Health and Colonial "Mimicry"'. *American Literary History*, 14(4), 686–719.

Andrade, O. de (1990). *A utopia antropofágica*. São Paulo: Editora Globo.

Andrijasevic, R. (2003). 'The Difference Borders Make: (Il)legality, Migration and Trafficking in Italy Among Eastern European Women in Prostitution'. In S. Ahmed (ed.), *Uprootings/Regroundings: Questions of Home and Migration* (pp. 251–72). New York: Berg Publishers.

Andrijasevic, R. (2004). *Trafficiking in Women and the Politics of Mobility in Europe* (unpublished PhD dissertation). Department of Women's Studies, Utrecht University, Utrecht.

Andrijasevic, R. (2005). 'Problematizing Trafficking: A Case of Eastern European Women in Italy'. *Revue Europeenne Des Migrations Internationales*, 21, 155–76.

Andrijasevic, R. (2006). *How to Balance Rights and Responsibilities on Asylum at the EU's Southern Border of Italy and Libya*. Budapest: Central European University, Center for Policy Studies.

Andrijasevic, R. (2007). 'Beautiful Dead Bodies: Gender, Migration and Representation in Anti-trafficking Campaigns'. *Feminist Review*, 86, 24–44.

Ang, I. (2003). 'Together-in-difference: Beyond Diaspora, into Hybridity'. *Asian Studies Review*, 27(2), 141–54.

Angelis, M. de and Harvie, D. (2006). 'Cognitive Capitalism and the Rat Race: How Capital Measures Ideas and Affects'. Paper presented at the Immaterial Labour, Multitudes and New Social Subjects conference at the University of Cambridge, 29–30 April 2006.

Angenendt, S. and Kruse, I. (2003). 'Der schwierige Wandel. Die Gestaltung der deutschen und europäischen Migrationspolitik an der Wende vom 20. zum 21. Jahrhundert'. In J. Oltmer (ed.), *Migration steuern und verwalten: Deutschland vom späten 19. Jahrhundert bis zur Gegenwart* (pp. 481–99). Göttingen: V & R Unipress.

Ansell-Pearson, K. (ed.). (1997). *Deleuze and Philosophy: The Difference Engineer*. London: Routledge.

Anthias, F. and Lazaridis, G. (2000). *Gender and Migration in Southern Europe: Women on the Move*. Oxford: Berg.

Anzaldúa, G. (1999). *Borderlands = La Fronter: The New Mestiza*. San Francisco: Aunt Lute Books.

Apollonio, U. (1973). *Futurist Manifestos*. London: Thames & Hudson.

Appadurai, A. (2000). 'Grassroots Globalization and the Research Imagination'. *Public Culture*, 12(1), 1–20.

Aragno, P. (1980). 'Futurismus und Faschismus. Die italienische Avantgarde und die Revolution'. In G. Reinhold and J. Hermand (eds), *Faschismus und Avantgarde* (pp. 83–91). Königstein/Ts.: Athenäum-Verlag.

Arendt, H. (1973). *On Revolution*. Harmondsworth: Penguin.

Armstrong, D. (1995). 'The Rise of Surveillance Medicine'. *Sociology of Health and Illness, 17*(3), 393–404.

Arrighi, G. (2003). 'Entwicklungslinien des Empire: Transformationen des Weltsystems'. In T. Atzert and J. Müller (eds), *Kritik der Weltordnung: Globalisierung, Imperialismus, Empire* (pp. 11–30). Berlin: ID-Verlag.

Asante, A. D. and Zwi, A. B. (2007). 'Public–Private Partnerships and Global Health Equity: Prospects and Challenges'. *Indian Journal of Medical Ethics, 4*(4), 176–80.

Atzert, T. (2005). 'Multitudes. Über immaterielle Arbeit und Biopolitik'. In Verein zur Förderung Demokratischer Politik und Kultur (ed.), *Indeterminate Kommunismus! Texte zu Ökonomie, Politik und Kultur* (pp. 234–41). Münster: Unrast.

Atzert, T. and Müller, J. (2004). *Immaterielle Arbeit und imperiale Souveränität: Analysen und Diskussionen zu Empire*. Münster: Westfälisches Dampfboot.

Atzert, T. and Müller, J. (eds). (2003). *Kritik der Weltordnung: Globalisierung, Imperialismus, Empire*. Berlin: ID-Verlag.

Augustin, L. (2003). 'Forget Victimization: Granting Agency to Migrants'. *Development, 46*(3), 30–6.

Badiou, A. (2001). *Ethics: An Essay on the Understanding of Evil*. London: Verso.

Badiou, A. (2005a). *Being and Event*. London: Continuum.

Badiou, A. (2005b). *Metapolitics*. London: Verso.

Bailyn, B. (1988). *The Peopling of British North America: An Introduction*. New York: Vintage Books.

Bakhtin, M. M. (1978). *Literatur und Karneval*. Frankfurt am Main: Fischer.

Bakhtin, M. M. (1984). *Rabelais and His World*. Bloomington: Indiana University Press.

Balakrishnan, G. (2000). *The Enemy: An Intellectual Portrait of Carl Schmitt*. London: Verso.

Balibar, E. (1993). *Die Grenzen der Demokratie*. Hamburg: Argument-Verlag.

Balibar, E. (1994). *Masses, Classes, Ideas: Studies on Politics and Philosophy Before and After Marx*. London: Routledge.

Balibar, E. (1997). *La crainte des masses. Politique et philosophie avant et après Marx*. Paris: Galilée.

Balibar, E. (2004a). *Europe, America, the War: Reflexions on the European Mediation* (in Greek). Athens: Dardanos.

Balibar, E. (2004b). *We, the People of Europe? Reflections on Transnational Citizenship*. Princeton, N.J.: Princeton University Press.

Balibar, E. and Wallerstein, I. M. (1991). *Race, Nation, Class: Ambiguous Identities*. London: Verso.

Banes, S. (1998). *Dancing Women. Female Bodies on Stage*. London: Routledge.

Barabási, A.-L. (2002). *Linked: The New Science of Networks*. Cambridge, Mass.: Perseus Publishing.

Barad, K. M. (2007). *Meeting the Universe Halfway: Quantum Physics and the Entanglement of Matter and Meaning*. Durham, N.C.: Duke University Press.

Barry, A., Osborne, T. and Rose, N. (1996). *Foucault and Political Reason: Liberalism, Neo-liberalism, and Rationalities of Government*. Chicago: University of Chicago Press.

Basch, L. G., Schiller, N. G. and Szanton Blanc, C. (1994). *Nations Unbound: Transnational Projects, Postcolonial Predicaments and Deterritorialized Nation-states*. Reading: Gordon & Breach.

Bashford, A. (2006). 'Global Biopolitics and the History of World Health'. *History of the Human Sciences*, *19*(1), 67–88.

Bataille, G. (1986). *Erotism: Death and Sensuality*. San Francisco: City Lights Books.

Bauman, Z. (1993). *Postmodern Ethics*. Oxford: Blackwell.

Bayertz, K. (1995). 'Eine kurze Geschichte der Herkunft der Verantwortung'. In K. Bayertz (ed.), *Verantwortung: Prinzip oder Problem?* (pp. 3–71). Darmstadt: Wissenschaftliche Buchgesellschaft.

Beck, U. (1992). *Risk Society: Towards a New Modernity*. London: Sage.

Beck, U. (2000). *The Brave New World of Work*. Malden, Mass.: Polity Press.

Beck, U. (2002). 'The Terrorist Threat: World Risk Society Revisited'. *Theory, Culture and Society*, *19*(4), 39–56.

Beck, U. and Grande, E. (2004). *Das kosmopolitische Europa: Gesellschaft und Politik in der zweiten Moderne*. Frankfurt am Main: Suhrkamp.

Bell, N. and Berg, S. (2002). 'Der bittere Geschmack von unserem Obst und Gemüse'. *Forum Wissenschaft*, *4*, 23–7.

Benjamin, W. (1996a). 'Critique of Violence'. In W. Benjamin (ed.), *Selected Writings, Vol. 1: 1913–1926* (pp. 236–52). Cambridge, Mass.: Harvard University Press.

Benjamin, W. (1996b). 'On Language as Such and on the Language of Man'. In W. Benjamin (ed.), *Selected Writings, Vol. 1: 1913–1926* (pp. 62–74). Cambridge, Mass.: Harvard University Press.

Benjamin, W. (1996c). 'On the Programme of the Coming Philosophy'. In W. Benjamin (ed.), *Selected Writings, Vol. 1: 1913–1926* (pp. 100–10). Cambridge, Mass.: Harvard University Press.

Benjamin, W. (1999). *The Arcades Project*. Cambridge, Mass.: Belknap Press.

Bennett, J. (2001). *The Enchantment of Modern Life: Attachments, Crossings and Ethics*. Princeton and Oxford: Princeton University Press.

Bennett, J. (2003). 'Tenebrae After September 11'. In J. Bennett and R. Kennedy (eds), *World Memory: Personal Trajectories in a Global Time* (pp. 177–94). London: Palgrave.

Berlant, L. G. (2007). 'Nearly Utopian, Nearly Normal: Post-Fordist Affect in La Promesse and Rosetta'. *Public Culture*, *19*(2), 273–301.

Berlin, I. S. (1958). *Two Concepts of Liberty*. Oxford: Clarendon Press.

Bersani, L. (1987). 'Is the Rectum a Grave?' *October*, *43*, 197–222.

Beynon, H. (2002). *Managing Employment Change: The New Realities of Work*. Oxford: Oxford University Press.

Bhabha, H. K. (1990). *Nation and Narration*. London: Routledge.

Bhabha, H. K. (1994). *The Location of Culture*. London: Routledge.

Bigo, D. and Guild, E. (2003). 'Le visa Schengen: expression d'une stratégie de "police" à distance'. *Culture and Conflicts*, *49–50*, 19–33.

Black, J. (1997). *Maps and Politics*. London: Reaktion.

Blackman, L. and Cromby, J. (2007). 'Affect and Feeling (Editorial)'. *International Journal of Critical Psychology, 21*, 5–22.

Bloch, E. (1986). *The Principle of Hope*. Cambridge, Mass.: MIT Press.

Bohrer, K. H. (1994). *Suddenness: On the Moment of Aesthetic Appearance*. New York: Columbia University Press.

Bojadzijev, M., Karakayali, S. and Tsianos, V. (2004). 'Le mystère de l'arrivée. Des camps et des spectres'. *Multitudes, 19*, 41–52.

Bologna, S. (2006). *Die Zerstörung der Mittelschichten: Thesen zur Neuen Selbstständigkeit*. Graz: Nausner & Nausner.

Boltanski, L. and Chiapello, E. (1999). *Le nouvel esprit du capitalisme*. Paris: Gallimard.

Bordo, S. (1993). *Unbearable Weight: Feminism, Western Culture, and the Body*. Berkeley: University of California Press.

Boscagli, M. (1996). *Eye on the Flesh. Fashions of Masculinity in the Early Twentieth Century*. Boulder, Colo.: Westview Press.

Boudry, P., Kuster, B. and Lorenz, R. (eds). (2000). *Reproduktionskonten fälschen! Heterosexualität, Arbeit und Zuhause*. Berlin: b_books.

Bourdieu, P. (1987). *Sozialer Sinn: Kritik der theoretischen Vernunft*. Frankfurt am Main: Suhrkamp.

Bourdieu, P. (1990). *The Logic of Practice*. Cambridge: Polity Press.

Bowker, G. C. and Star, S. L. (1999). *Sorting Things Out: Classification and Its Consequences*. Cambridge, Mass.: MIT Press.

Bowring, F. (2002). 'Post-Fordism and the End of Work'. *Futures, 34*, 159–72.

Braidotti, R. (1993). 'Embodiment, Sexual Difference, and the Nomadic Subject'. *Hypatia, 8*(1) 1–13.

Braidotti, R. (2006). *Transpositions: On Nomadic Ethics*. Cambridge: Polity Press.

Braveman, P. and Tarimbo, E. (2002). 'Social Inequalities in Health Within Countries: Not Only an Issue for Affluent Nations'. *Social Science and Medicine, 54*, 1621–35.

Brekke, J. K. (2008). 'Organising in the Dark: Interviews about Migrants' Struggles. (Jaya Klara Brekke talks to four UK based groups working to improve conditions for migrants)'. *Mute magazine – Culture and politics after the net*, http://www.metamute.org/en/Organising-in-the-Dark-Interviews-about-Migrants-Struggles, last accessed 20 January 2008.

Breman, J. (1989). *Taming the Coolie Beast: Plantation Society and the Colonial Order in Southeast Asia*. Delhi: Oxford University Press.

Brenner, N. (2004). *New State Spaces: Urban Governance and the Rescaling of Statehood*. Oxford and New York: Oxford University Press.

Brinkmann, U., Dörre, K., Röbenack, S., Kraemer, K. and Speidel, F. (2006). *Prekäre Arbeit: Ursachen, Ausmaß, soziale Folgen und subjektive Verarbeitungsformen unsicherer Beschäftigungsverhältnisse*. Bonn: Friedrich-Ebert-Stiftung.

Brooks, R. A. (2002). *Flesh and Machines: How Robots Will Change Us*. New York: Pantheon Books.

Brown, W. (1995). *States of Injury: Power and Freedom in Late Modernity*. Princeton, N.J.: Princeton University Press.

Buchanan, J. M. (1986). *Liberty, Market, and State: Political Economy in the 1980s*. Brighton: Harvester Wheatsheaf.

Buchanan, J. M. (1998). 'Has Economics Lost Its Way? Reflections on the Economists' Enterprise at Century's End'. In J. M. Buchanan and B. Monissen (eds), *The Economists' Vision: Essays in Modern Economic Perspectives*. Frankfurt am Main: Campus.

Buchanan, J. M. and Tullock, G. (1962). *The Calculus of Consent: Logical Foundations of Constitutional Democracy*. Ann Arbor: University of Michigan Press.

Bunton, R. (2001). 'Knowledge, Embodiment and Neo-liberal Drug Policy'. *Contemporary Drug Problems, 28*(2), 221.

Burchell, G. (1996). 'Liberal Government and Techniques of the Self'. In A. Barry, T. Osborne and N. Rose (eds), *Foucault and Political Reason. Liberalism, Neo-liberalism and Rationalities of Goverment* (pp. 19–36). London: University College London Press.

Burchell, G., Gordon, C. and Miller, P. (1991). *The Foucault Effect: Studies in Governmentality*. Chicago: University of Chicago Press.

Burt, R. (1998). *Alien Bodies: Representations of Modernity, 'Race' and Nation in Early Modern Dance*. London: Routledge.

Buse, P., Hirschkop, K., McCracken, S. and Taithe, B. (1999). *Benjamin's Arcades: An Unguided Tour*. Manchester: Manchester University Press.

Butler, J. (1990). *Gender Trouble: Feminism and the Subversion of Identity*. New York: Routledge.

Butler, J., Laclau, E. and Žižek, S. (2000). *Contingency, Hegemony, Universality: Contemporary Dialogues on the Left*. London: Verso.

Caldwell, L. (1986). 'Reproducers of the Nation: Women and the Family in Fascist Italy'. In D. Forgacs (ed.), *Rethinking Italian Fascism: Capitalism, Populism and Culture* (pp. 110–41). London: Lawrence & Wishart.

Callinicos, A. (1994). *Marxism and the New Imperialism*. London: Bookmarks.

Campbell, I. and Burgess, J. (2001). 'Casual Employment in Australia and Temporary Work in Europe: Developing a Cross-national Comparison'. *Work, Employment and Society, 15*(1), 171–84.

Carrigan, T. (1995). 'Eric Michaels and the Stakes of History'. *Critical InQueeries, 1*(1), 103–12.

Casas-Cortes, M. and Cobarrubias, S. (2007). 'Drawing Escape Tunnels Through Borders'. In L. Mogel and A. Bhagat (eds), *An Atlas of Radical Cartography* (pp. 51–66). Los Angeles, Calif.: Journal of Aesthetics and Protest Press.

Castel, R. (2003). *From Manual Workers to Wage Laborers: Transformation of the Social Question*. New Brunswick, N.J.: Transaction Publishers.

Castells, M. (1996). *The Rise of the Network Society*. Oxford: Blackwell.

Castells, M. (1997). *The Power of Identity*. Malden, Mass.: Blackwell.

Caygill, H. (1998). *Walter Benjamin: The Colour of Experience*. London: Routledge.

Chakrabarty, D. (2000). *Provincializing Europe: Postcolonial Thought and Historical Difference*. Princeton, N.J.: Princeton University Press.

Chambers, R. (1998). *Facing It: AIDS Diaries and the Death of the Author*. Ann Arbor: University of Michigan Press.

Chan, C. K. and Wildt, G. de (2007). *Developing Countries, Donor Leverage and Access to Bird Flu Vaccines*. New York: United Nations, Department of Economic and Social Affairs.

Chang, D. (2006). 'Globalising the Factory and Informalising Labour: Overview of the Informalisation of Labour in Asia'. *Asian Labour Update, 58–9*.

Chapman, T. (2003). *Gender and Domestic Life: Changing Practices in Families and Household*. Basingstoke: Palgrave Macmillan.

Charlesworth, S. J. (2000). *A Phenomenology of Working Class Experience*. Cambridge: Cambridge University Press.

Chatterjee, P. (2004). *Politics of the Governed: Reflections on Popular Politics in Most of the World*. New York: Columbia University Press.

Chesters, G. and Welsh, I. (2006). *Complexity and Social Movements: Multitudes at the Edge of Chaos*. London: Routledge.

Chevalier, L. (2000). *Laboring Classes and Dangerous Classes in Paris During the First Half of the Nineteenth Century*. New York: Howard Fertig.

Cholewinski, R. (2000). 'The EU Acquis on Irregular Migration: Reinforcing Security at the Expense of Rights'. *European Journal of Migration and Law, 2*(3/4), 361–405.

Chretien, J.-P. (2006a). 'Epidemiologic Applications of Emerging Infectious Disease Modeling to Support US Military Readiness and National Security (Conference Summary)'. Emerging Infectious Diseases (electronic journal), *12*(1). Available from http://www.cdc.gov/ncidod/EID/vol12no01/05-1214.htm.

Chretien, J.-P. (2006b). 'Department of Defense Global Emerging Infections Surveillance and Response System Indian Ocean Tsunami Response'. *Military Medicine, 171*(1), S12–S14, October 2006,

Chretien, J.-P. (2007). 'Evaluating Pandemic Influenza Surveillance and Response Systems in Developing Countries: Framework and Pilot Application'. *Advances in Disease Surveillance, 2*, 146.

Christopher, E., Pybus, C. and Rediker, M. B. (eds). (2007). *Many Middle Passages: Forced Migration and the Making of the Modern World*. Berkeley: University of California Press.

Clark, A. (1997). *Being There: Putting Brain, Body, and World Together Again*. Cambridge, Mass.: MIT Press.

Clifford, J. (1986). 'Partial Truths'. In J. Clifford and G. E. Marcus (eds), *Writing Culture: The Poetics and Politics of Ethnography* (pp. 1–27). Berkeley: University of California Press.

Clough, P. T. (2007). 'Introduction'. In P. T. Clough and J. O. M. Halley (eds), *The Affective Turn: Theorizing the Social* (pp. 1–33). Durham, N.C.: Duke University Press.

Colectivo Precarias a la Deriva. (2004). *A la deriva, por los circuitos de la precariedad femenina*. Madrid: Traficantes de Sueños.

Collier, S. J. and Lakoff, A. (2006). 'Vital Systems Security'. ARC Working Paper No. 2, 2 February 2006: Anthropology of the Contemporary Research Collaboratory.

Commission of the European Communities. (2001). *European Governance: White Paper. COM(2001) 428 final*. http://europa.eu.int/comm/governance/white_paper/index_en.htm.

Connery, C. (1999). 'Actually Existing Left Conservatism'. *boundary 2, 26*(3), 3–11.

Connery, C. (2005). 'The World Sixties'. In R. Wilson and C. Connery (eds), *Worldings: World Literature, Field Imaginaries, Future Practices. Doing Cultural Studies Inside the U.S. War-machine.* Santa Cruz: New Pacific Press.

Cooper, M. (2006). 'Pre-empting Emergence: The Biological Turn in the War on Terror'. *Theory, Culture and Society, 23,* 113–36.

Corsani, A. (2004). 'Wissen und Arbeit im kognitiven Kapitalismus. Die Sackgassen der politischen Ökonomie'. In T. Atzert and J. Müller (eds), *Immaterielle Arbeit und imperiale Souveränität. Analysen und Diskussionen zu Empire* (pp. 156–74). Münster: Westfälisches Dampfboot.

Crawford, J., Kippax, S., Onyx, J., Gault, U. and Benton, P. (1992). *Emotion and Gender: Constructing Meaning from Memory.* London, California and New Delhi: Sage.

Crimp, D. (1988). 'How to Have Promiscuity in an Epidemic'. In D. Crimp and L. Bersani (eds), *AIDS: Cultural Analysis, Cultural Activism* (pp. 237–71). Cambridge, Mass.: MIT Press.

Cromby, J. (2007). 'Integrating Social Science with Neuroscience: Potentials and Problems'. *BioSocieties, 2,* 149–69.

Cruikshank, B. (1993). 'Revolutions Within: Self-government and Self-esteem'. *Economy and Society, 22,* 327–44.

Csordas, T. J. (1994). 'Introduction: The Body as Representation and Being-in-the-world'. In T. J. Csordas (ed.), *Embodiment and Experience: The Existential Ground of Culture and Self* (pp. 1–24). Cambridge and New York: Cambridge University Press.

Curtis, M. (1959). *Three Against the Third Republic: Sorel, Barrès, and Maurras.* Princeton, N.J.: Princeton University Press.

Cyrus, N. (2001). 'Den Einwanderungskontrollen entgangen'. In B. Danckwortt and C. Lepp (eds), *Von Grenzen und Ausgrenzung* (pp. 35–56). Marburg: Schueren Presseverlag.

Damasio, A. R. (1999). *The Feeling of What Happens: Body and Emotion in the Making of Consciousness.* New York: Harcourt Brace.

De Genova, N. (2005). *Working the Boundaries: Race, Space, and 'Illegality' in Mexican Chicago.* Durham, N.C.: Duke University Press.

De Grand, A. (2000). *Italian Fascism. Its Origins and Development.* Lincoln: University of Nebraska Press.

De Landa, M. (2002). *Intensive Science and Virtual Philosophy.* New York: Continuum.

De Lauretis, T. (1987). *Technologies of Gender: Essays on Theory, Film, and Fiction.* Bloomington: Indiana University Press.

Dean, M. (1995). 'Governing the Unemployed Self in an Active Society'. *Economy and Society, 24*(4), 559–83.

Dean, M. (1999). *Governmentality: Power and Rule in Modern Society.* London: Sage.

Debord, G. (1981). 'Perspectives for Conscious Alterations in Everyday Life'. In K. Knabb (ed.), *Situationist International Anthology* (pp. 68–75). Berkeley: Bureau of Public Secrets.

Debord, G. (1994). *The Society of the Spectacle.* New York: Zone Books.

Declaration of Alma-Ata (1978). Declaration made at the International Conference on Primary Health Care, Alma-Ata, Soviet Union, 6–12 September.

Deleuze, G. (1991). 'A Philosophical Concept ...' In E. Cadava, P. Connor and J.-L. Nancy (eds), *Who Comes After the Subject?* (pp. 94–5). London: Routledge.

Deleuze, G. (1992). 'Postscript on the Societies of Control'. *October, 59,* 3–7.

Deleuze, G. and Guattari, F. (1987). *A Thousand Plateaus: Capitalism and Schizophrenia.* Minneapolis: University of Minnesota Press.

Diminescou, D. (2003). 'Das System D gegen das System D. Reisende, Navigierende, Schleuser und Gefangene virtueller Grenzen'. In M. von Osten (ed.), *Moneynations: Constructing the border – constructing East-West* (pp. 22–7). Wien: edition selene.

Dobb, M. and Becker, F. (1972). *Entwicklung des Kapitalismus: vom Spätfeudalismus bis zur Gegenwart.* Köln: Kiepenheuer & Witsch.

Doezema, J. (2005). 'Now You See Her, Now You Don't: Sex Workers at the UN Trafficking Protocol Negotiations'. *Social and Legal Studies, 14,* 61–90.

Donzelot, J. (1984). 'Die Förderung des Sozialen'. In J. Donzelot, D. Meuret, P. Miller and N. Rose (eds), *Zur Genealogie der Regulation. Anschlüsse an Michel Foucault* (pp. 109–60). Mainz: Decaton.

Douglas, M. (1992). *Risk and Blame: Essays in Cultural Theory.* London: Routledge.

Dowling, E., Nunes, R. and Trott, B. (2007). 'Immaterial and Affective Labour: Explored'. *ephemera, 7*(1), 1–7.

Düvell, F. (2002). *Die Globalisierung des Migrationsregimes. Zur neuen Einwanderungspolitik in Europa.* Berlin: Assoziation A.

Dyer-Witheford, N. (1999). *Cyber-Marx: Cycles and Circuits of Struggle in High-technology Capitalism.* Urbana: University of Illinois Press.

Dyer-Witheford, N. (2001). 'Empire, Immaterial Labour, the New Combination, and the Global Worker'. *Rethinking Marxism, 13*(3–4), 70–81.

Eaton, A. E. (1995). 'New Production Techniques, Employee Involvement and Unions'. *Labor Studies Journal, 20*(3), 19–41.

Ehrenstein, A. (2006a). 'Elusive Aspects of Precarity: The Question of Subversion in Affective Labour'. Paper presented at the 6th International Crossroads in Cultural Studies conference at Istanbul, 20–23 July 2006.

Ehrenstein, A. (2006b). *Social Relationality and Affective Experience in Precarious Labour Conditions: A Study of Young Immaterial Workers in the Arts Industries in Cardiff* (unpublished dissertation). School of Social Sciences, Cardiff University, Cardiff.

Eichorn, C. (2004). 'Gelschlechtliche Teilung der Arbeit. Eine feministische Kritik'. In T. Atzert and J. Müller (eds), *Immaterielle Arbeit und imperiale Souveränität: Analysen und Diskussionen zu Empire* (pp. 189–203). Münster: Westfälisches Dampfboot.

Elias, N. (1978). *What Is Sociology?* London: Hutchinson.

Elias, N. (1981). 'Zivilisation und Gewalt. Über das Staatsmonopol der körperlichen Gewalt und seine Durchbrechungen'. In J. Matthes (ed.), *Lebenswelt und soziale Probleme. Verhandlungen des 20. Deutschen Soziologentages zu Bremen 1980* (pp. 98–122). Frankfurt am Main: Campus.

Elias, N. (1994). *The Civilizing Process: Sociogenetic and Psychogenetic Investigations.* Oxford: Blackwell.

Emmer, P. C. (1986). *Colonialism and Migration: Indentured Labour Before and After Slavery.* Dordrecht, Netherlands and Lancaster: Nijhoff.

Erickson, C. (1984). 'Why Did Contract Labor Not Work in the Nineteenth Century United States?' In S. Marks and P. Richardson (eds), *International Labour Migration: Historical Perspectives* (pp. 34–56). Hounslow: Temple Smith.

Ewald, F. (1986). *L'Etat providence.* Paris: B. Grasset.

Ewald, F. (1991). 'Insurance and Risk'. In G. Burchell, C. Gordon and P. Miller (eds), *The Foucault Effect* (pp. 197–210). Sydney: Harvester Wheatsheaf.

Faist, T. (2000). *The Volume and Dynamics of International Migration and Transnational Social Spaces.* Oxford: Clarendon.

Fakiolas, R. (2003). 'Regularising Undocumented Immigrants in Greece: Procedures and Effects'. *Journal of Ethnic and Migration Studies, 29*(3), 535–62.

Falasca-Zamponi, S. (1997). *Fascist Spectacle: The Aesthetics of Power in Mussolini's Italy.* Berkeley: University of California Press.

Fantone, L. (2007). 'Precarious Changes: Gender and Generational Politics in Contemporary Italy'. *Feminist Review, 87,* 5–20.

Fearnley, L. (2006). *Pathogens and the Strategy of Preparedness: Disease Surveillance in Civil Defense Planning.* ARC Working Paper No. 3, 23 March 2006: Anthropology of the Contemporary Research Collaboratory.

Federici, S. (2004). *Caliban and the Witch.* New York: Autonomedia.

Ferrari Bravo, L. (2001). *Dal fordismo alla globalizzazione. Cristalli di tempo politico.* Roma: Manifestolibri.

Florida, R. L. (2004). *The Rise of the Creative Class: And How It's Transforming Work, Leisure, Community and Everyday Life.* New York: Basic Books.

Foucault, M. (1977). *Discipline and Punish: The Birth of the Prison.* London: Penguin.

Foucault, M. (1978). *The History of Sexuality, Vol. 1: An Introduction.* London: Penguin.

Foucault, M. (1987). *The History of Sexuality, Vol. 2: The Use of Pleasure.* London: Penguin.

Foucault, M. (1990). *The History of Sexuality, Vol. 3: The Care of the Self.* London: Penguin.

Foucault, M. (1991). 'Governmentality'. In G. Burchell, C. Gordon and P. Miller (eds), *The Foucault Effect: Studies in Governmentality* (pp. 87–104). Chicago: University of Chicago Press.

Foucault, M. (2001). *The Order of Things: An Archaeology of the Human Sciences.* London: Routledge.

Foucault, M. (2004a). *Geschichte der Gouvernementalität I: Sicherheit, Territorium, Bevölkerung. Vorlesungen am Collège de France 1977–1978.* Frankfurt am Main: Suhrkamp.

Foucault, M. (2004b). *Geschichte der Gouvernementalität II: Geburt der Biopolitik. Vorlesungen am Collège de France 1978–1979.* Frankfurt am Main: Suhrkamp.

Foucault, M. (2005). *Die Heterotopien. Zwei Radiovorträge (7. und 21. Dezember 1966).* Frankfurt am Main: Suhrkamp.

Frangenberg, F., Cologne Kunstverein and Projekt Migration (2005). *Projekt Migration.* Köln: DuMont.

Frank, A. (1995). *The Wounded Storyteller: Body, Illness, and Ethics.* Chicago: Chicago University Press.

Franklin, B. (1840/1794). 'Information to Those Who Would Remove to America'. In J. Sparks (ed.), *The Works of Benjamin Franklin, Vol. 2* (pp. 467–77). Boston, Mass.: Hilliard, Gray & Company.

Franklin, S. (2000). 'Life Itself: Global Nature and the Genetic Imaginary'. In S. Franklin, C. Lury and J. Stacey (eds), *Global Nature, Global Culture* (pp. 188–227). London: Sage.

Fraser, M., Kember, S. and Lury, C. (2005). 'Inventive Life: Approaches to the New Vitalism'. *Theory Culture and Society, 22*(1), 1–14.

Friedman, M. (1962). *Capitalism and Freedom.* Chicago: University of Chicago Press.

Fumagalli, A. and Lucarelli, S. (2006). *Basic Income Sustainability and Productivity Growth.* Paper presented at the Association for Social Economics Meeting, 6–8 January 2006, Boston, Mass.

Fungueiriño-Lorenzo, R. (2002). *Visa-, Asyl- und Einwanderungspolitik vor und nach dem Amsterdamer Vertrag: Entwicklung der gemeinschaftlichen Kompetenzen in Visa-, Asyl- und Einwanderungspolitik.* Frankfurt am Main: Lang.

Gallie, D. and Paugam, S. (2003). *Social Precarity and Social Integration: Report for the European Commission, Directorate-General for Employment, Industrial Relations and Social Affairs.* Luxembourg: Office for Official Publications of the European Communities.

Gallop, J. (1988). *Thinking Through the Body.* New York: Columbia University Press.

Gare, A. (1999). 'Speculative Metaphysics and the Future of Philosophy: The Contemporary Relevance of Whitehead's Defence of Speculative Metaphysics'. *Australasian Journal of Philosophy, 77*(2), 127–45.

Garrett, L. (1994). *The Coming Plague: Newly Emerging Diseases in a World Out of Balance.* New York: Farra, Straus & Giroux.

Garrett, L. (1996). 'The Return of Infectious Diseases'. *Foreign Affairs, 75*(1), 66–79.

Garrett, L. (2005). 'The Next Pandemic?' *Foreign Affairs, 84*(4), 3–23.

Garrett, L. (2007). 'The Challenge of Global Health'. *Foreign Affairs, 86*(1), 14–38.

Gatens, M. (1996). *Imaginary Bodies: Ethics, Power, and Corporeality.* London: Routledge.

Geddes, A. C. (2002). *The Politics of Migration and Immigration in Europe.* London: Sage.

Geremek, B. (1994). *Poverty: A History.* Oxford: Blackwell.

Gill, R. (2002). 'Cool, Creative and Egalitarian? Exploring Gender in Project-based New Media Work in Europe'. *Information Communication and Society, 5*, 70–89.

Gill, R. (2006). *Gender and the Media.* Cambridge: Polity Press.

Giroux, H. A. (2002). 'Global Capitalism and the Return of the Garrison State'. *Arena Journal,* (19), 141–60.

Glaeser, E., Weiskopf, F. C. and Kurella, A. (1931). *Der Staat ohne Arbeitslose: drei Jahre 'Fünfjahresplan'.* Berlin: Kiepenheuer.

Glucksmann, M. (2000). *Cottons and Casuals: The Gendered Organisation of Labour in Time and Space.* Durham, UK: Sociologypress.

Gorz, A. (1999). *Reclaiming Work: Beyond the Wage-based Society.* Cambridge: Polity Press.

Gorz, A. (2004). *Wissen, Wert und Kapital: zur Kritik der Wissensökonomie.* Zürich: Rotpunktverlag.

Gottlieb, G. (1992). *Individual Development and Evolution: The Genesis of Novel Behavior.* New York: Oxford University Press.

Gramsci, A. (1991). *Gefängnishefte. Bd. 1: 1. Heft.* Hamburg: Argument.

Greco, M. (2005). 'On the Vitality of Vitalism'. *Theory Culture and Society,* 22(1), 15–28.

Greven, M. and Pauly, L. W. (2000). *Democracy Beyond the State? The European Dilemma and the Emerging Global Order.* Lanham, Md.: Rowman & Littlefield.

Griffin, D. R. (1998). *Unsnarling the World-knot: Consciousness, Freedom, and the Mind–Body Problem.* Berkeley: University of California Press.

Griffin, R. (1995). *Fascism.* Oxford: Oxford University Press.

Groenendijk, C. A., Guild, E. and Minderhoud, P. E. (eds). (2003). *In Search of Europe's Borders.* The Hague: Kluwer Law International.

Grosz, E. (1986). 'On Irigaray and Sexual Difference'. *Australian Feminist Studies,* 2, 63–74.

Grosz, E. (1989a). 'Sexual Difference Feminism and the Problem of Essentialism'. In J. Clifford and V. Dhareshwa (eds), *Inscriptions, Vol. 5: Traveling Theories: Traveling Theorists* (pp. 86–101). Santa Cruz, Calif.: Center for Cultural Studies.

Grosz, E. (1989b). *Sexual Subversions: Three French Feminists.* Sydney: Allen & Unwin.

Grosz, E. (1993). 'A Thousand Tiny Sexes: Feminism and Rhizomatics'. In C. V. Boundas and D. Olkowski (eds), *Gilles Deleuze and the Theater of Philosophy* (pp. 187–210). London: Routledge.

Grosz, E. (1994). *Volatile Bodies: Towards a Corporeal Feminism.* Sydney: Allen & Unwin.

Gunsteren, H. van (1998). *A Theory of Citizenship: Organizing Plurality in Contemporary Democracies.* Boulder, Colo.: Westview Press.

Guttsman, W. L. (1990). *Worker's Culture in Weimar Germany: Between Tradition and Commitment.* New York: Berg.

Habermas, J. (2001). *The Postnational Constellation: Political Essays.* Cambridge, Mass.: MIT Press.

Hage, G. (1998). *White Nation: Fantasies of White Supremacy in a Multicultural Society.* Annandale, NSW: Pluto Press.

Hage, G. (2003). *Against Paranoid Nationalism: Searching for Hope in a Shrinking Society.* London: Merlin.

Hall, S. (1985). 'Realignment – for What?' *Marxism Today,* December 1985, 12–17.

Hall, S. (1994). 'Cultural Identity and Diaspora'. In P. Williams and L. Chrisman (eds), *Colonial Discourse and Post-Colonial Theory: A Reader* (pp. 392–403). New York: Columbia University Press.

Hall, S. and Jefferson, T. (1976). *Resistance Through Rituals: Youth Subcultures in Post-war Britain.* London: Hutchinson.

Haraway, D. J. (1991a). 'The Biopolitics of Postmodern Bodies: Constitutions of Self in Immune System Discourse'. In *Simians, Cyborgs, and Women: The Reinvention of Nature* (pp. 203–30). New York: Routledge.

Haraway, D. J. (1991b). *Simians, Cyborgs, and Women: The Reinvention of Nature*. New York: Routledge.

Haraway, D. J. (1991c). 'Situated Knowledges: The Science Question in Feminism and the Privilege of Partial Perspective'. In *Simians, Cyborgs, and Women: The Reinvention of Nature* (pp. 183–201). New York: Routledge.

Haraway, D. J. (1992). 'The Promises of Monsters: A Regenerative Politics for Inappropriate/d Others'. In L. Grossberg, C. Nelson and P. A. Treichler (eds), *Cultural Studies* (pp. 295–337). London: Routledge.

Haraway, D. J. (1997). *Modest_Witness@Second_Millennium. FemaleMan©_ Meets_OncoMouse™: Feminism and Technoscience*. New York: Routledge.

Haraway, D. J. (2003). *The Companion Species Manifesto: Dogs, People, and Significant Otherness*. Chicago: Prickly Paradigm Press.

Haraway, D. J. (2004). 'Ecce Homo, Ain't (Ar'n't) I a Woman, and Inappropriate/ d Others: The Human in a Post-humanist Landscape'. In D. J. Haraway (ed.), *The Haraway Reader* (pp. 47–61). New York: Routledge.

Haraway, D. J. (2007). *When Species Meet*. Minneapolis: University of Minnesota Press.

Hardt, M. and Negri, A. (2000). *Empire*. Cambridge, Mass.: Harvard University Press.

Harvey, D. (2003). *The New Imperialism*. Oxford: Oxford University Press.

Harvey, D. (2005). *A Brief History of Neoliberalism*. Oxford: Oxford University Press.

Haug, F. (1987). *Female Sexualization: A Collective Work of Memory* (translated by E. Carter). London and New York: Verso.

Haug, F. (1992). *Beyond Female Masochism: Memory-work and Politics*. London/ New York: Verso.

Hayek, F. A. von (1973). *Law, Legislation and Liberty: A New Statement of the Liberal Principles of Justice and Political Economy, Vol. 1: Rules and Order*. London: Routledge & Kegan Paul.

Hayek, F. A. von (1976). *Law, Legislation and Liberty: A New Statement of the Liberal Principles of Justice and Political Economy, Vol. 2: The Mirage of Social Justice*. London: Routledge & Kegan Paul.

Heery, E. (2005). 'Sources of Change in Trade Unions'. *Work Employment and Society*, *19*(1), 91–106.

Heery, E. and Salmon, J. (eds). (2000). *The Insecure Workforce*. London: Routledge.

Held, D. (1995). *Democracy and the Global Order: From the Modern State to Cosmopolitan Governance*. Cambridge: Polity Press.

Henry, N. and Massey, D. (1995). 'Competitive Time–Space in High Technology'. *Geoforum*, *26*(1), 49–64.

Hermand, J. and Trommler, F. (1988). *Die Kultur der Weimarer Republik*. Frankfurt am Main: Fischer-Taschenbuch-Verlag.

Hess, D. J. (1995). *Science and Technology in a Multicultural World: The Cultural Politics of Facts and Artifacts*. New York: Columbia University Press.

Hess, S. (2005). *Globalisierte Hausarbeit: Au-pair als Migrationsstrategie von Frauen aus Osteuropa*. Wiesbaden: Verlag für Sozialwissenschaften.

Hess, S. and Karakayali, S. (2007). 'New Governance oder die imperiale Kunst des Regierens. Asyldiskurs und Menschenrechtsdispositiv im neuen EU-Migrationsmanagement'. In T. M. Forschungsgruppe (ed.), *Turbulente*

Ränder. Neue Perspektiven auf Migration an den Grenzen Europas (pp. 41–58). Bielefeld: Transcript.

Hess, S. and Lenz, R. (eds). (2001). *Geschlecht und Globalisierung: ein kultur-wissenschaftlicher Streifzug durch transnationale Räume*. Königstein/Taunus: Helmer.

Hess, S. and Tsianos, V. (2007). 'Europeanizing Transnationalism! Provincializing Europe! – Konturen eines neuen Grenzregimes'. In T. M. Forschungsgruppe (ed.), *Turbulente Ränder. Neue Perspektiven auf Migration an den Grenzen Europas* (pp. 23–40). Bielefeld: Transcript.

Hewitt, A. (1993). *Fascist Modernism: Aesthetics, Politics, and the Avant-garde*. Stanford, Calif.: Stanford University Press.

Hindess, B. (1996). 'Liberalism, Socialism and Democracy: Variations on a Governmental Theme'. In A. Barry, T. Osborne and N. Rose (eds), *Foucault and Political Reason: Liberalism, Neo-liberalism and Rationalities of Goverment* (pp. 65–80). London: University College London Press.

Hitz, H., Keil, R., Lehrer, U., Ronneberger, K., Schmid, C. and Wolff, R. (eds). (1995). *Capitales fatales. Urbanisierung und Politik in den Finanzmetropolen Frankfurt und Zürich*. Zürich: Rotpunktverlag.

Hobbes, T. (1994). *Leviathan*. Indianapolis: Hackett Publishing Company.

Hobsbawm, E. J. (1990). *Nations and Nationalism Since 1780: Programme, Myth, Reality*. Cambridge: Cambridge University Press.

Hochschild, A. R. (1983). *The Managed Heart: Commercialization of Human Feeling*. Berkeley: University of California Press.

Hochschild, A. R. (1997). *The Time Bind: When Work Becomes Home and Home Becomes Work*. New York: Metropolitan Books.

Hochschild, A. R. and Ehrenreich, B. (eds). (2002). *Global Woman: Nannies, Maids and Sexworkers in the New Economy*. New York: Metropolitan Books.

Hoerder, D. (2002). *Cultures in Contact: World Migrations in the Second Millennium*. Durham, N.C.: Duke University Press.

Holzberger, M. (2003). 'Polizeiliche Verbindungsbeamte: Vorverlagerte Migrationskontrolle'. *Bürgerrechte und Polizei-Cilip*, 75(2), 57–66.

Honig, B. (2001). *Democracy and the Foreigner*. Princeton, N.J. and Oxford: Princeton University Press.

Hoy, D. C. (2004). *Critical Resistance: From Poststructuralism to Post-critique*. Cambridge, Mass.: MIT Press.

Hulten, P. (1986). *Futurism and Futurisms*. New York: Abbeville Press.

Huws, U. (2003). *The Making of a Cybertariat: Virtual Work in a Real World*. New York: Monthly Review Press.

Icduygu, A. and Toktas, S. (2002). 'How do Smuggling and Trafficking Operate via Irregular Border Crossings in the Middle East? Evidence from Fieldwork in Turkey'. *International Migration*, 40(6), 25–54.

Ignatieff, M. (1978). *A Just Measure of Pain: The Penitentiary in the Industrial Revolution, 1750–1850*. New York: Columbia University Press.

Imperato, J. (2005). 'The Growing Challenge of Avian Influenza'. *Journal of Community Health: The Publication for Health Promotion and Disease Prevention*, 30(5), 327–30.

Institute of Medicine (1992). *Emerging Infections: Microbial Threats to Health in the United States* Washington, D.C.: National Academy Press.

Irigaray, L. (1977). 'Women's Exile'. *Ideology and Consciousness*, 1, 62–76.

Irigaray, L. (1981). 'This Sex Which Is Not One'. In E. Marks and I. de Courtivron (eds), *New French Feminisms* (pp. 99–106). New York: Shocken Books.

Irigaray, L. (1985a). *Speculum of the Other Woman*. Ithaca, N.Y.: Cornell University Press.

Irigaray, L. (1985b). *This Sex Which Is Not One*. Ithaca, N.Y.: Cornell University Press.

Isin, E. F. (2002). *Being Political: Genealogies of Citizenship*. Minneapolis: University of Minnesota Press.

Jachtenfuchs, M. and Kohler-Koch, B. (1996). *Europäische Integration*. Opladen: Leske + Budrich.

Jain, S. L. (2007). 'Cancer Butch'. *Cultural Anthropology*, 22(4), 502–38.

Jameson, F. (1991). *Postmodernism, or the Cultural Logic of Late Capitalism*. Durham, N.C.: Duke University Press.

Jessop, B. (1990). *State Theory: Putting the Capitalist State in Its Place*. Cambridge: Polity.

Jessop, B. (1994). 'The Transition to Post-Fordism and the Schumpeterian Workfare State'. In R. Burrows and B. Loader (eds), *Towards a Post-Fordist Welfare State?* (pp. 13–37). London: Routledge.

Jessop, B. (2001). *Regulation Theory and the Crisis of Capitalism*. Cheltenham, UK: Edward Elgar.

Jessop, B. and Sum, N.-L. (2006). *Beyond the Regulation Approach: Putting Capitalist Economies in Their Place*. Cheltenham: Edward Elgar.

Jordan, B. and Düvell, F. (2002). *Irregular Migration: The Dilemmas of Transnational Mobility*. Cheltenham: Edward Elgar.

Kaiser, G. (1971a). *Five Plays*. London: Calder & Boyars.

Kaiser, G. (1971b). *Werke*. Frankfurt am Main: Propyläen.

Karakayali, S. (2008). *Zwei, drei, viele Wege... Zur Genealogie illegaler Migration in der Bundesrepublik Deutschland* (unpublished PhD dissertation). Fachbereich Gesellschaftswissenschaften, Johann-Wolfgang-Goethe-Universität, Frankfurt am Main.

Kasimis, C. and Papadopoulos, A. G. (2005). 'The Multifunctional Role of Migrants in the Greek Countryside: Implications for the Rural Economy and Society'. *Journal of Ethnic and Migration Studies*, 31, 99–128.

Katschnig-Fasch, E. (2003). *Das ganz alltägliche Elend: Begegnungen im Schatten des Neoliberalismus*. Wien: Löcker.

Kaufmann, F.-X. (2003). *Varianten des Wohlfahrtsstaats. Der deutsche Sozialstaat im internationalen Vergleich*. Frankfurt am Main: Suhrkamp.

Kautsky, K. (1915). *Nationalstaat, imperialistischer Staat und Staatenbund*. Nürnberg: Fränkische Verlagsanstalt.

Kelly, P. (2006). 'The Entrepreneurial Self and Youth at-Risk: Exploring the Horizons of Identity in the Twenty-first Century'. *Journal of Youth Studies*, 9(1), 17–32.

Kenworthy, B. J. (1957). *Georg Kaiser*. Oxford: Blackwell.

Kenworthy, B. J. (1980). 'Georg Kaiser: The Ambiguity of the Expressionist New Man'. In H. A. Pausch and E. Reinhold (eds), *Georg Kaiser* (pp. 95–111). Darmstadt: Agora Verlag.

Kern, S. (2000). *The Culture of Time and Space 1880–1918*. Cambridge, Mass.: Harvard University Press.

Kessler-Harris, A. (1981). *Women Have Always Worked: A Historical Overview*. Old Westbury, N.Y.: Feminist Press.

Khor, M. (2007). *Health: WHO Admits Patents Taken on Avian Flu Virus*: Third World Network, http://www.twnside.org.sg/title2/health.info/twninfohealth090.htm.

Kilani, L. (2002) (dir.). *Tanger, le rêve des brûleurs* (film). Morocco/France.

King, N. (2002). 'Security, Disease, Commerce: Ideologies of Postcolonial Global Health'. *Social Studies of Science, 32*(5–6), 763–89.

King, R., Lazaridis, G. and Tsardanides, C. (2000). *Eldorado or Fortress? Migration in Southern Europe*. Basingstoke: Palgrave Macmillan.

Kippax, S. and Race, K. (2003). 'Sustaining Safe Practice: Twenty Years On'. *Social Science and Medicine, 57*, 1–12.

Klages, L. (1964). *Sämtliche Werke*. Bonn: Bouvier.

Kolb, E. (1988). *The Weimar Republic*. London: Unwin Hyman.

Koschorke, A. (2007). *Der fiktive Staat: Konstruktionen des politischen Körpers in der Geschichte Europas*. Frankfurt am Main: Fischer.

Kozloff, M. (1973). *Cubism/Futurism*. New York: Harper & Row.

Krahl, H.-J. (1984). *Vom Ende der abstrakten Arbeit. Die Aufhebung der sinnlosen Arbeit ist in der Transzendentalität des Kapitals angelegt und in der Verweltlichung der Philosophie begründet*. Frankfurt am Main: Materialis Verlag.

Krannhals, P. (1928). *Das organische Weltbild: Grundlagen einer neuentstehenden deutschen Kultur*. München: Bruckmann.

Kuster, B. (2006a). 'Die Grenze filmen. In Transit Migration Forschungsgruppe' (ed.), *Turbulente Ränder. Neue Perspektiven auf Migration an den Grenzen Europas*. Bielefeld: Transcript.

Kuster, B. (2006b). 'Forms of Cooperation in Documentary Videofilms on Migration'. Paper presented at the 6th International Crossroads in Cultural Studies conference, Istanbul, July, 20–23, 2006.

Kuster, B. and Tsianos, V. (2005). '... und sie verlassen das Bild'. Paper presented at the Transnational Europe II Symposium: Germany, Europe, and global migration movements, Cologne, 10–13 November, 2005.

Kuster, B. and Tsianos, V. (2007). 'Experience without me, oder das verstörende Grinsen der Prekarität'. In G. Raunig and U. Wuggenig (eds), *Kritik der Kreativität* (pp. 137–44). Wien: Verlag Turia + Kant.

Lachmann, R. (1997). *Memory and Literature: Intertextuality in Russian Modernism*. Minneapolis: University of Minnesota Press.

Laclau, E. (1996). *Emancipation(s)*. London: Verso.

Laclau, E. and Mouffe, C. (1985). *Hegemony and Socialist Strategy: Towards a Radical Democratic Politics*. London: Verso.

Lafazani, O. (2006). *Migration and Borders: The Transit of Evros* (unpublished masters dissertation). National Metsobio Polytechnicum, Athens.

Lahav, G. (1998). 'Immigration and the State: The Devolution and Privatisation of Immigration Control in the EU'. *Journal of Ethnic and Migration Studies, 24*(4), 675–94.

Lahav, G. and Guiraudon, V. (2000). 'Comparative Perspectives on Border Control: Away from the Border and Outside the State'. In P. Andreas and T. Snyder (eds), *The Wall Around the West: State Borders and Immigration Controls in North America and Europe* (pp. 55–80). Lanham: Rowman & Littlefield.

Lancet (2007). 'Global Solidarity Needed in Preparing for Pandemic Influenza' (editorial). *The Lancet, 369*(9561), 532.

Lango, J. W. (2004). 'Alfred North Whitehead, 1861–1947'. In A. Marsoobian and J. Ryder (eds), *The Blackwell Guide to American Philosophy* (pp. 210–25). Malden, Mass.: Blackwell Publishers.

Larner, W. and Walters, W. (2004). *Global Governmentality: Governing International Spaces*. New York: Routledge.

Latour, B. (1987). *Science in Action: How to Follow Scientists and Engineers Through Society*. Cambridge, Mass.: Harvard University Press.

Latour, B. (2005). 'What is Given in Experience? A Review of Isabelle Stengers "Penser avec Whitehead"'. *Boundary 2, 2*(1), 222–37.

Lawrence, N. M. (1956). *Whitehead's Philosophical Development: A Critical History of the Background of Process and Reality*. Berkeley: University of California Press.

Lazzarato, M. (1996). 'Immaterial Labor'. In P. Virno and M. Hardt (eds), *Radical Thought in Italy: A Potential Politics* (pp. 133–146). Minneapolis: University of Minnesota Press.

Lazzarato, M. (2004). 'From Capital–Labour to Capital–Life'. *ephemera, 4*(3), 187–208.

Lederberg, J. (1996). 'Infection Emergent'. *Journal of the American Medical Association, 275*, 243–5.

Lefebvre, H. (1991). *Critique of Everyday Life, Vol.1: Introduction*. London: Verso.

Lefort, C. (1986). *The Political Forms of Modern Society: Bureaucracy, Democracy, Totalitarianism*. Cambridge: Polity Press.

Leigh Star, S. (1991). 'Power, Technologies and the Phenomenology of Conventions: On Being Allergic to Onions'. In J. Law (ed.), *A Sociology of Monsters: Essays on Power, Technology and Domination* (pp. 26–56). London: Routledge.

Lemke, T. (1997). *Eine Kritik der politischen Vernunft: Foucaults Analyse der modernen Gouvernementalität*. Berlin: Argument-Verlag.

Lenin, V. I. (1902). 'What Is To Be Done? Burning Questions of our Movement'. In V. I. Lenin (ed.), *Collected Works, Vol. 5* (pp. 347–530). Moscow: Foreign Languages Publishing House.

Lenin, V. I. (1917). 'The State and Revolution: The Marxist Theory of the State and the Tasks of the Proletariat in the Revolution'. In V. I. Lenin (ed.), *Collected Works, Vol. 25* (pp. 381–492). Moscow: Foreign Languages Publishing House.

Lessard, B. and Baldwin, S. (2003). *Netslaves 2.0: Tales of 'Surviving' the Great Tech Gold Rush*. New York: Allworth Press.

Leuthardt, B. (1999). *An den Rändern Europas: Berichte von den Grenzen*. Zürich: Rotpunktverlag.

Linebaugh, P. (2003). *The London Hanged: Crime and Civil Society in the Eighteenth Century*. London: Verso.

Linebaugh, P. and Rediker, M. (2000). *The Many-headed Hydra: Sailors, Slaves, Commoners, and the Hidden History of the Revolutionary Atlantic*. London: Verso.

Lipietz, A. (1992). *Towards a New Economic Order: Postfordism, Ecology, and Democracy*. New York: Oxford University Press.

Lipietz, A. (1998). *Nach dem Ende des 'Goldenen Zeitalters'. Regulation und Transformation kapitalistischer Gesellschaften*. Berlin: Argument Verlag.

Lohr, K. and Nickel, H. (2005). *Subjektivierung von Arbeit – riskante Chancen*. Münster: Westfälisches Dampfboot.

Lorenz, R. and Kuster, B. (eds). (2007). *Sexuell arbeiten. Eine queere Perspektive auf Arbeit und prekäres Leben*. Berlin: b_books.

Lorey, I. (2006). 'Als das Leben in die Politik eintrat'. In M. Pieper, T. Atzert, S. Karakayali and V. Tsianos (eds), *Empire und die biopolitische Wende*. Frankfurt am Main: Campus.

Lovink, G. (2002). *Uncanny Networks: Dialogues with the Virtual Intelligentsia*. Cambridge, Mass.: MIT Press.

Lowe, L. (1996). *Immigrant Acts: On Asian American Cultural Politics*. Durham, N.C.: Duke University Press.

Lucassen, J. and Lucassen, L. (1997). *Migration, Migration History, History: Old Paradigms and New Perspectives*. Bern: International Institute of Social History.

Luhmann, N. (1985). 'Die Autopoiesis des Bewusstseins'. *Soziale Welt, 36*, 402–46.

Luhmann, N. (1995). *Social Systems*. Stanford, Calif.: Stanford University Press.

Luibheid, E. (2002). *Entry Denied: Controlling Sexuality at the Border*. Minneapolis: University of Minnesota Press.

Lyttelton, A. (1973). *Italian Fascisms: From Pareto to Gentile*. New York: Harper & Row.

Lyttelton, A. (1991). 'Italian Fascism'. In W. Laqueur (ed.), *Fascism: A Reader's Guide: Analyses, Interpretations, Bibliography* (pp. 125–50). Aldershot: Scolar Press.

Macciocchi, M. A. (1973). *Letters from Inside the Italian Communist Party to Louis Althusser*. London: New Left Books.

Mak, G. (2005). *Der Mord an Theo van Gogh: Geschichte einer moralischen Panik*. Frankfurt am Main: Suhrkamp.

Mann, G. (1958). *Deutsche Geschichte des 19. und 20. Jahrhunderts*. Frankfurt am Main: Fischer.

Manning, E. (2007a). *Grace*. Paper presented at the New Mobilities academic workshop, Sydney, 6–8 December, 2007.

Manning, E. (2007b). 'Sensing Beyond Security'. In A. Hickey-Moody and P. Malins (eds), *Deleuzian Encounters: Studies in Contemporary Social Issues* (pp. 111–21). Basingstoke: Palgrave Macmillan.

Manning, S. A. (1993). *Ecstasy and the Demon. Feminism and Nationalism in the Dances of Mary Wigman*. Berkeley: University of California Press.

Marazzi, C. (1998). *Der Stammplatz der Socken. Die linguistische Wende der Ökonomie und ihre Auswirkungen in der Politik*. Zürich: Seismo Verlag.

Marinetti, F. T. (1971). *Selected Writings*. New York: Farrar, Straus & Giroux.

Martin, E. (1990). 'Towards an Anthropology of Immunology: The Body as Nation State'. *Medical Anthropology Quarterly, 4*, 410–26.

Martin, E. (1994). *Flexible Bodies: Tracking Immunity in American Culture from the Days of Polio to the Age of AIDS*. Boston, Mass.: Beacon Press.

Marvakis, A. (2005). 'The Utopian Surplus in Human Agency: Ernst Bloch's Relevance for an Emancipatory Psychology'. Paper presented at the

International Society for Theoretical Psychology conference, Cape Town, 20–24 June 2005.

Marx, K. (1988). *Capital, Vol. I*. In K. Marx and F. Engels (eds), *Collected Works, Vol. 35*. London: Lawrence & Wishart.

Massumi, B. (1993). 'Everywhere you Want To Be: Introduction to Fear'. In B. Massumi (ed.), *The Politics of Everyday Fear* (pp. 3–38). Minneapolis: University of Minnesota Press.

Mauss, M. (1978). 'Der Begriff der Technik des Körpers'. In M. Mauss (ed.), *Soziologie und Anthropologie. Band II: Gabentausch, Todesvorstellung, Körpertechniken*. Frankfurt am Main: Ullstein.

Mayer, H. E. (1988). *The Crusades*. Oxford: Oxford University Press.

Mayer-Ahuja, N. (2004). 'Three Worlds of Cleaning: Women's Experiences of Precarious Labor in the Public Sector, Cleaning Companies and Private Households of West Germany, 1973–1998'. *Journal of Women's History*, 16(2), 116–41.

McDowell, L., Batnitzky, A. and Dyer, S. (2007). 'Division, Segmentation, and Interpellation: The Embodied Labors of Migrant Workers in a Greater London Hotel'. *Economic Geography*, *83*, 1–26.

McKibbon, W. (2006). *Global Macroeconomic Consequences of Pandemic Influenza*. Sydney: Lowy Institute for International Policy.

McRobbie, A. (2004). 'Everyone is Creative: Artists as Pioneers of the New Economy?' In E. B. Silva and T. Bennett (eds), *Contemporary Culture and Everyday Life* (pp. 184–210). Durham: Sociology Press.

Mehran, A. and Donkin, A. (2004). *The Terminal Man*. London: Corgi Books.

Meisel, J. H. (1951). *The Genesis of Georges Sorel: An Account of His Formative Period Followed by a Study of His Influence*. Ann Arbor: George Wahr Publishing Company.

Mezzadra, S. (2001). *Diritto di fuga. Migrazioni, cittadinanza, globalizzazione*. Verona: Ombre Corte.

Mezzadra, S. (2005). *Citizen and Subject: A Postcolonial Constitution for the European Union?* Paper presented at the Conflicts, Law, and Constitutionalism conference, Paris, 16–18 February 2005.

Mezzadra, S. (2006). 'Kapitalismus, Migration, Soziale Kämpfe. Vorbemerkungen zu einer Theorie der Autonomie der Migration'. In M. Pieper, T. Atzert, S. Karakayali and V. Tsianos (eds), *Empire und die biopolitische Wende* (pp. 171–86). Frankfurt am Main: Campus.

Mezzadra, S. and Neilson, B. (2003). 'Né qui, né altrove – Migration, Detention, Desertion: A Dialogue'. *borderlands*, *2*(1).

Michaels, E. (1990). *Unbecoming: An AIDS Diary*. Rose Bay, NSW: Empress Publishing.

Middleton, D. and Brown, S. (2005). *The Social Psychology of Experience: Studies in Remembering and Forgetting*. London: Sage.

Milkman, R. (2000). *Organizing Immigrants: The Challenge for Unions in Contemporary California*. Ithaca, N.Y.: Cornell University Press.

Mills, C. (2008). *The Philosophy of Agamben*. Chesham: Acumen Press.

Mirchandani, K. (2003). 'Challenging Racial Silences in Studies of Emotion Work: Contributions from Anti-racist Feminist Theory'. *Organization Studies*, *24*(5), 721–42.

Mogel, L. and Bhagat, A. (eds). (2007). *An Atlas of Radical Cartography*. Los Angeles, Calif.: Journal of Aesthetics and Protest Press.

Moi, T. (1985). *Sexual/Textual Politics: Feminist Literary Theory*. London: Methuen.

Mol, A. (2002). *The Body Multiple: Ontology in Medical Practice*. Durham, N.C.: Duke University Press.

Moldaschl, M. and Voss, G. G. (eds). (2003). *Subjektivierung von Arbeit*. München: Hampp.

Mollat, M. (1986). *The Poor in the Middle Ages: An Essay in Social History*. New Haven: Yale University Press.

Monsell Prado, P., de Soto Suárez, P., Escofet Planas, J., Pérez de Lama, J., Paz Naveiro, M., Lama Jiménez, M., et al. (eds). (2006). *Fadaiat: Libertad de Movimiento – Libertad de Conocimiento*. Málaga: Imagraf Impresores.

Morini, C. (2007). 'The Feminization of Labour in Cognitive Capitalism'. *Feminist Review, 87*, 40–59.

Morokvasic, M., Erel, U. and Shinozaki, K. (eds). (2003). *Crossing Borders and Shifting Boundaries*. Opladen: Leske + Budrich.

Mosse, G. L. (1980). 'Faschismus und Avantgarde'. In G. Reinhold and J. Hermand (eds), *Faschismus und Avantgarde* (pp. 133–49). Königstein im Taunus: Athenäum-Verlag.

Mottek, H. (1974). *Wirtschaftsgeschichte Deutschlands, Vol 1. Von den Anfängen bis zur Zeit der Französischen Revolution*. Berlin: Deutscher Verlag der Wissenschaften.

Mouffe, C. (2000). *The Democratic Paradox*. London: Verso.

Moulier Boutang, Y. (1997). 'Papiere für alle. Frankreich, die Europäische Union und die Migration'. *Die Beute, 13*, 50–63.

Moulier Boutang, Y. (1998). *De l'esclavage au salariat. Economie historique du salariat bridé*. Paris: Presses Universitaires de France.

Moulier Boutang, Y. (2001a). 'The Art of Flight: Stany Grelet's Interview with Yann Moulier Boutang'. *Rethinking Marxism: A Journal of economics, culture, and society, 13*(3–4), 227–35.

Moulier Boutang, Y. (2001b). 'Marx in Kalifornien: Der dritte Kapitalismus und die alte politische Ökonomie'. *Aus Politik und Zeitgeschichte, B 52–3*, 29–37.

NATO. (2005). *Policy Implications of the Risk Society, Draft Report 171 ESC 05 E*: NATO Parliamentary Assembly, http://www.nato-pa.int/Default.asp?CAT 2=1159&CAT1=16&CAT0=576&shortcut=798, last accessed 20 December 2007.

Navarro, V. and Shi, L. (2001). 'The Political Context of Social Inequalities and Health'. *Social Science and Medicine, 52*, 481–91.

Nead, L. (1992). *The Female Nude: Art, Obscenity, and Sexuality*. London: Routledge.

Negri, A. (1991). *The Savage Anomaly: The Power of Spinoza's Metaphysics and Politics*. Minneapolis: University of Minnesota Press.

Negri, A. (1999). *Insurgencies: Constituent Power and the Modern State*. Minneapolis: University of Minnesota Press.

Negri, A. (2003). 'The Constitution of Time'. In A. Negri (ed.), *Time for Revolution* (pp. 19–135). New York: Continuum.

Negri, A. (2006). 'Zur gesellschaftlichen Ontologie: materielle Arbeit, immaterialle Arbeit, Biopolitik'. In M. Pieper, T. Atzert, S. Karakayali and

V. Tsianos (eds), *Empire. Die biopolitische Wende* (pp. 17–32). Frankfurt am Main: Campus.

Negt, O. and Kluge, A. (2001). *Geschichte und Eigensinn: Geschichtliche Organisation der Arbeitsvermögen, Deutschland als Produktionsöffentlichkeit, Gewalt des Zusammenhangs.* Frankfurt am Main: Suhrkamp.

Neilson, B. (2005). 'Provincialising the Italian effect'. *Cultural Studies Review, 11*(2), 11–24.

Neilson, B. and Rossiter, N. (2005). 'From Precarity to Precariousness and Back Again: Labour, Life and Unstable Networks'. *Fibreculture*, 5, http://journal. fibreculture.org/issue5/neilson_rossiter.html.

Nerlich, B. and Halliday, C. (2007). 'Avian Flu: The Creation of Expectations in the Interplay Between Science and the Media'. *Sociology of Health and Illness, 29*(1), 46–65.

Neroth, P. (2004). 'Protecting Profits'. *The Lancet, 364*(9441), 1207–8.

Nickel, H. M., Frey, M. and Hüning, H. (2003). 'Wandel von Arbeit – Chancen für Frauen?' *Berliner Journal für Soziologie, 4*, 531–43.

Nicolaïdis, K. and Howse, R. (2001). *The Federal Vision: Legitimacy and Levels of Governance in the United States and the European Union.* Oxford: Oxford University Press.

Niessen, J. (2002). 'Zwischen Harmonisierung und kleinstem gemeinsamen Nenner'. In K. J. Bade and R. Münz (eds), *Migrationsreport 2002. Fakten, Analysen, Perspektiven* (pp. 207–30). Frankfurt am Main: Campus.

Nietzsche, F. (1999). *Die Geburt der Tragödie. Unzeitgemässe Betrachtungen I-IV. Nachgelassene Schriften 1870 – 1873.* München: Dt. Taschenbuch-Verlag.

O'Doherty, D. and Willmott, H. (2001). 'Debating Labour Process Theory: The Issue of Subjectivity and the Relevance of Poststructuralism'. *Sociology, 35*(2), 457–76.

Öncü, A. and Karamustafa, G. (1999). 'Kofferökonomie'. In J. Hoffmann and M. von Osten (eds), *Das Phantom sucht seinen Mörder. Ein Reader zur Kulturalisierung der Ökonomie* (pp. 203–10). Berlin: b_books.

Ong, A. (1999). *Flexible Citizenship: The Cultural Logics of Transnationality.* Durham, N.C.: Duke University Press.

Ong, A. (2005). 'Ecologies of Expertise: Assembling Flows, Managing Citizenship'. In A. Ong and S. J. Collier (eds), *Global Assemblages: Technology, Politics, and Ethics as Anthropological Problems* (pp. 337–53). Malden, Mass.: Blackwell Publishing.

Orr, J. (2006). *Panic Diaries: A Genealogy of Panic Disorder.* Durham, N.C.: Duke University Press.

Osten, M. von (2006). 'Irene ist Viele! oder was die Produktivkräfte genannt wird'. In M. Pieper, T. Atzert, S. Karakayali and V. Tsianos (eds), *Empire und die biopolitische Wende* (pp. 109–24). Frankfurt am Main: Campus.

Osten, M. von (ed.). (2003). *Norm der Abweichung.* Zürich: Institut für Theorie und Gestaltung und Kunst/Edition Voldemeer Zürich.

Oswald, A. von (2002). 'Volkswagen, Wolfsburg und die italienischen "Gastarbeiter"'. *Archiv für Sozialgeschichte, 42*, 55–79.

Panagiotidis, E. and Tsianos, V. (2007) 'Denaturalizing Camps: Überwachen und Entschleunigen in der schengener Ägäis-Zone'. In T. M. Forschungsgruppe (ed.), *Turbulente Ränder. Neue Perspektiven auf Migration an den Grenzen Europas* (pp. 59–86). Bielefeld: Transcript.

Panitch, L. and Gindin, S. (2003). 'Globaler Kapitalismus und amerikanisches Imperium'. In J. Bischoff (ed.), *Klassen und soziale Bewegungen: Strukturen im modernen Kapitalismus* (pp. 194–218). Hamburg: VSA-Verlag.

Papadopoulos, D. (2002). 'Dialectics of Subjectivity: North-Atlantic Certainties, Neo-liberal Rationality, and Liberation Promises'. *International Journal of Critical Psychology, 6*, 99–122.

Papadopoulos, D. (2003). 'The Ordinary Superstition of Subjectivity: Liberalism and Technostructural Violence'. *Theory and Psychology, 13*(1), 73–93.

Papadopoulos, D. (2004). 'Psychology and the Political (Editorial)'. *International Journal for Critical Psychology, 12*, 5–13.

Papadopoulos, D. (2005). 'For a New Materialist Understanding of Social Science: Decomposing the Fact–Value Debate'. In A. H. A. Gülerce, I. Staeuble, G. Saunders and J. Kay (eds), *Contemporary Theorizing in Psychology: Global Perspectives* (pp. 39–47). Concord, Ontario: Captus Press.

Papadopoulos, D. (2006). 'World 2: On the Significance and Impossibility of Articulation'. *Culture, Theory and Critique, 47*(2), 165–79.

Papadopoulos, D. (2008). 'In the Ruins of Representation: Identity, Individuality, Subjectification'. *British Journal of Social Psychology, 47*(1), 139–65.

Papadopoulos, D. and Sharma, S. (2008). 'Race/Matter: Materialism and the Politics of Racialization (guest edited special issue)', *Darkmatter Journal, 2*, http://www.darkmatter101.org/site/category/issues/race-matter/, accessed 15 March 2008.

Papastergiadis, N. (2005). 'Hybridity and Ambivalence: Places and Flows in Contemporary Art and Culture'. *Theory, Culture and Society, 22*, 39–64.

Parreñas, R. S. (2001). *Servants of Globalization: Women, Migration and Domestic Work*. Stanford, Calif.: Stanford University Press.

Patton, P. (2000). *Deleuze and the Political*. London: Routledge.

People's Health Movement (2000). 'People's Charter for Health', http://www.phmovement.org/charter/pch-english.html.

Peukert, D. (1987). *Die Weimarer Republik. Krisenjahre der klassischen Moderne*. Frankfurt am Main: Suhrkamp.

Pieper, M. (2006). 'Biopolitik: Die Umwendung eines Machtparadigmas'. In M. Pieper, T. Atzert, S. Karakayali and V. Tsianos (eds), *Empire und die biopolitische Wende* (pp. 217–46). Frankfurt am Main: Campus.

Pieper, M. and Gutiérrez Rodríguez, E. (eds). (2003). *Gouvernementalität. Ein sozialwissenschaftliches Konzept in Anschluss an Foucault*. Frankfurt am Main and New York: Campus.

Pieper, M., Panagiotidis E., and Tsianos V. (2008). 'Performing the context – crossing the orders' *Darkmatter Journal, 2*, http://www.darkmatter101.org/site/2008/02/23/performing-the-context-crossing-the-orders', last accessed 25 May 2008.

Pink, D. H. (2001). *Free Agent Nation: How America's New Independent Workers Are Transforming the Way We Live*. New York: Warner Books.

Polanyi, K. (2001). *The Great Transformation: The Political and Economic Origins of Our Time*. Boston, Mass.: Beacon Press.

Portes, A., Castells, M. and Benton, L. A. (1989). *The Informal Economy: Studies in Advanced and Less Developed Countries*. Baltimore, Mass. and London: Johns Hopkins University Press.

Potts, L. (1990). *The World Labour Market: A History of Migration*. London: Zed Books.

Poulantzas, N. (1974). *Fascism and Dictatorship: The Third International and the Problem of Fascism*. London: New Left Books.

Poulantzas, N. (1978). *State, Power, Socialism*. London: New Left Books.

Preciado, B. (2003). *Kontrasexuelles Manifest*. Berlin: b_books.

Priddat, B. P. (2002). 'Das Verschwinden der langen Verträge'. In D. Baecker (ed.), *Archäologie der Arbeit* (pp. 65–86). Berlin: Kulturverlag Kadmos.

Puig de la Bellacasa, M. (2008a). *Penser nous devons. Savoirs, politiques et 'care'*. Paris: Les Empêcheurs de Penser en Rond.

Puig de la Bellacasa, M. (2008b). 'Thinking-with-care'. In G. Tabrizi (ed.), *Thinking with Donna Haraway*. Cambridge, Mass.: MIT Press.

Rabinow, P. (1996). *Essays on the Anthropology of Reason*. Princeton, N.J.: Princeton University Press.

Race, K. (2001). 'The Undetectable Crisis: Changing Technologies of Risk'. *Sexualities*, 4(2), 167–89.

Rambach, A. and Rambach, M. (2001). *Les intellos précaires*. Paris: Fayard.

Rancière, J. (1998). *Disagreement: Politics and Philosophy*. Minneapolis: University of Minnesota Press.

Rancière, J. (2000). 'Dissenting Words: A Conversation with Jacques Rancière'. *Diacritics*, 30, 113–26.

Rasch, W. (1967). *Zur deutschen Literatur seit der Jahrhundertwende: gesammelte Aufsätze*. Stuttgart: Metzler.

Raunig, G. and Wuggenig, U. (eds). (2007). *Kritik der Kreativität*. Wien: Verlag Turia + Kant.

Redlener, I. (2006). *Americans at Risk: Why We Are Not Prepared for Megadisasters and What We Can Do Now*. New York: Alfred A. Knopf.

Retort collective (Boal, I., Clark, T. J., Matthews, J. and Watts, M.) (2005). *Afflicted Powers: Capital in a New Age of War*. London: Verso.

Revel, J. (2006). 'Biopolitik'. In M. Pieper, T. Atzert, S. Karakayali and V. Tsianos (eds), *Empire und die biopolitische Wende* (pp. 247–54). Frankfurt am Main: Campus.

Revelli, M. (1999). *Die gesellschaftliche Linke: jenseits der Zivilisation der Arbeit*. Münster: Westfälisches Dampfboot.

Revista Contrapoder (ed.). (2006). *Fronteras interiores y exteriores*. Madrid: Traficantes de sueños.

Rigo, E. (2005). 'Citizenship at Europe's Borders: Some Reflections on the Post-colonial Condition of Europe in the Context of EU Enlargement'. *Citizenship Studies*, 9(1), 3–22.

Rigo, E. (2007). *Europa di confine. Trasformazioni della cittadinanza nell'Unione allargata*. Roma: Meltemi.

Robbins, R. (2005). *Subjectivity*. Basingstoke: Palgrave Macmillan.

Roberts, C., Kippax, S., Spongberg, M. and Crawford, J. (1996). '"Going Down": Oral Sex, Imaginary Bodies and HIV'. *Body and Society*, 2, 107–24.

Rodgers, G. and Rodgers, J. (eds). (1989). *Precarious Jobs in Labour Market Regulation: The Growth of Atypical Employment in Western Europe*. Geneva: International Institute for Labour Studies.

Rosaldo, R. (1993). *Culture and Truth: The Remaking of Social Analysis*. Boston, Mass.: Beacon Press.

Rose, G. (1996). *Mourning Becomes the Law: Philosophy and Representation.* Cambridge: Cambridge University Press.

Rose, G. (1997). *Love's Work.* London: Vintage.

Rose, H. (1994). *Love, Power and Knowledge.* Cambridge: Polity Press.

Rose, J. (2001). *The Intellectual Life of the British Working Classes.* New Haven, Conn.: Yale University Press.

Rose, N. (1996a). 'Identity, Genealogy, History'. In S. Hall and P. du Gay (eds), *Questions of Cultural Identity* (pp. 128–50). London: Sage.

Rose, N. (1996b). *Inventing our Selves: Psychology, Power and Personhood.* Cambridge: Cambridge University Press.

Rose, N. (1999). *Powers of Freedom: Reframing Political Thought.* Cambridge: Cambridge University Press.

Rose, N. (2001). 'The Politics of Life Itself'. *Theory, Culture and Society, 18*(6), 1–30.

Rose, S. (1998). *Lifelines: Biology Beyond Determinism.* Oxford and New York: Oxford University Press.

Rosenau, J. N. and Czempiel, E. O. (1992). *Governance Without Government: Order and Change in World Politics.* Cambridge: Cambridge University Press.

Rosengarten, M. (2004). 'Consumer Activism in the Pharmacology of HIV'. *Body and Society, 10*(1), 91–107.

Rousseau, J.-J. (1997). *The Social Contract and Other Later Political Writings.* Cambridge: Cambridge University Press.

Rubin, G. S. (1984). 'Thinking Sex: Notes for a Radical Theory of the Politics of Sexuality'. In C. Vance (ed.), *Pleasure and Danger* (pp. 267–319). London: Routledge & Kegan Paul.

Sachße, C. and Tennstedt, F. (1986). *Soziale Sicherheit und soziale Disziplinierung: Beiträge zu einer histor. Theorie der Sozialpolitik.* Frankfurt am Main: Suhrkamp.

Sachße, C. and Tennstedt, F. (1998). *Bettler, Gauner und Proleten: Armut und Armenfürsorge in der deutschen Geschichte.* Frankfurt am Main: Fachhochschulverlag.

Saldanha, A. (2006). 'Reontologising Race: The Machinic Geography of Phenotype'. *Environment and Planning, 24,* 9–24.

Salih, R. (2003). *Gender in Transnationalism: Home, Longing and Belonging Among Moroccan Migrant Women.* New York: Routledge.

Sandbothe, M. (1998). *Die Verzeitlichung der Zeit: Grundtendenzen der modernen Zeitdebatte in Philosophie und Wissenschaft.* Darmstadt: Wissenschaftliche Buchgesellschaft.

Santos, B. de S. (2001). 'Nuestra America: Reinventing a Subaltern Paradigm of Recognition and Redistribution'. *Theory, Culture and Society, 18*(2/3), 185–218.

Santos, B. de S. (2003). 'Towards a Counter-hegemonic Globalisation'. Paper presented at the 24th International Congress of the Latin American Studies Association, Dallas, 27–29 March 2003.

Sassen, S. (2000). 'Spatialities and Temporalities of the Global: Elements for Theorization'. *Public Culture, 12*(1), 215–32.

Sassen, S. (2004). 'The Repositioning of Citizenship: Emergent Subjects and Spaces for Politics'. In P. A. Passavant and J. Dean (eds), *Empire's New Clothes: Reading Hardt and Negri* (pp. 175–98). New York: Routledge.

Sassen, S. (2006). *Territory, Authority, Rights: From Medieval to Global Assemblages.* Princeton, N.J.: Princeton University Press.

Satcher, D. (1995). 'Emerging Infections: Getting Ahead of the Curve'. *Emerging Infectious Diseases, 1*(1), 1–7.

Scarry, E. (1985). *The Body in Pain: The Making and Unmaking of the World.* New York: Oxford University Press.

Schenck, C. (2008). *De la crise de l'Homme moderne à la construction de l'Homme nouveau dans les arts du spectacle (théâtre et danse) français et allemands des années 1880–1940* (unpublished PhD dissertation). Ecole normale supérieure, Paris.

Schmitt, C. (1963). *Der Begriff des Politischen: Text von 1932 mit einem Vorwort und drei Corollarien.* Berlin: Duncker & Humblot.

Schmitt, C. (1997). *Der Nomos der Erde im Völkerrecht des Jus Publicum Europaeum* (4. ed.). Berlin: Duncker & Humblot.

Schnapp, J. T. (2000). *A Primer of Italian Fascism.* Lincoln: University of Nebraska Press.

Schönberger, K. and Springer, S. (eds). (2003). *Subjektivierte Arbeit: Mensch, Organisation und Technik in einer entgrenzten Arbeitswelt.* Frankfurt am Main: Campus.

Schraube, E. (1998). *Auf den Spuren der Dinge: Psychologie in einer Welt der Technik.* Berlin: Argument-Verlag.

Schraube, E. (2003). 'Der Blick vom Turm. Günther Anders und das Problem der Versprachlichung technologischer Praxis'. *Handlung, Kultur, Interpretation, 12*(2), 215–29.

Schraube, E. (2005). 'Torturing Things Until They Confess. Günther Anders's Critique of Technology'. *Science as Culture, 14*(1), 77–85.

Sciortino, G. (2004). 'Between Phantoms and Necessary Evils. Some Critical Points in the Study of Irregular Migrations to Western Europe'. *IMIS – Beiträge, 24,* 17–44.

Sedgwick, E. K. (1990). *Epistemology of the Closet.* Berkeley: University of California Press.

Sedgwick, E. K. (1992). 'Epidemics of the Will'. In J. Crary and S. Kwinter (eds), *Incorporations* (pp. 582–95). New York: Zone.

Segel, H. B. (1998). *Body Ascendant: Modernism and the Physical Imperative.* Baltimore, Mass.: Johns Hopkins University Press.

Sennett, R. (1994). *Flesh and Stone: The Body and the City in Western Civilization.* London: Faber.

Sennett, R. (1998). *The Corrosion of Character: The Personal Consequences of Work in the New Capitalism.* New York: Norton.

Sharma, S. and Sharma, A. (2003). 'White Paranoia: Orientalism in the Age of Empire'. *Fashion Theory, 7*(3/4), 301–18.

Shome, R. (2006). 'Thinking Through the Diaspora: Call Centers, India, and a New Politics of Hybridity'. *International Journal of Cultural Studies, 9*(1), 105–24.

Simmel, G. (1968). *The Conflict in Modern Culture and Other Essays.* New York: Teachers College Press.

Simons, P. (1998). 'Metaphysical Systematics: A Lesson from Whitehead'. *Erkenntnis, 48*, 377–93.

Skeggs, B. (1997). *Formations of Class and Gender: Becoming Respectable*. London: Sage.

Smith, D. E. (1987). *The Everyday World as Problematic: A Feminist Sociology*. Boston, Mass.: Northeastern University Press.

Smith, M. P. and Guarnizo, L. (eds). (1998). *Transnationalism from Below*. New Brunswick, N.J.: Transaction Publishers.

Soper, K. (1996). 'Love's Work'. *New Left Review, 218*, 155–60.

Sorel, G. (1915). *Reflections on Violence*. London: Allen & Unwin.

Spengler, O. (1928). *The Decline of the West, Vol. 1: Form and Actuality; Vol. 2: Perspectives of World-history*. London: Allen & Unwin.

Spillmann, P. (2007). 'Strategien des Mappings'. In T. M. Forschungsgruppe (ed.), *Turbulente Ränder. Neue Perspektiven auf Migration an den Grenzen Europas* (pp. 155–68). Bielefeld: Transcript.

Spivak, G. C. (1999). *A Critique of Postcolonial Reason: Toward a History of the Vanishing Present*. Cambridge, Mass.: Harvard University Press.

Spongberg, M. (1997). *Feminizing Venereal Disease: The Body of the Prostitute in Nineteenth-century Medical Discourse*. New York: New York University Press.

Stanley, J. L. (1976). 'Editor's Introduction'. In G. Sorel, *From Georges Sorel: Essays in Socialism and Philosophy* (pp. 1–61). New York: Oxford University Press.

Steinem, G. (1992). *Revolution from Within: A Book of Self Esteem*. Boston, Mass.: Little, Brown and Company.

Steinfeld, R. J. (2001). *Coercion, Contract, and Free Labor in the Nineteenth Century*. Cambridge: Cambridge University Press.

Stengers, I. (2008). 'Experimenting with Refrains: Subjectivity and the Challenge of Escaping Modern Dualism'. *Subjectivity, 22*, 38–59.

Stenner, P. (2008). 'A.N. Whitehead and Subjectivity'. *Subjectivity, 22*, 90–109.

Stephenson, N. and Papadopoulos, D. (2006). *Analysing Everyday Experience: Social Research and Political Change*. Basingstoke: Palgrave Macmillan.

Sternhell, Z. (1986). *Neither Right nor Left: Fascist Ideology in France*. Berkeley: University of California Press.

Sternhell, Z. (1991). 'Fascist Ideology'. In W. Laqueur (ed.), *Fascism: A Reader's Guide. Analyses, Interpretations, Bibliography* (pp. 315–76). Aldershot: Scolar Press.

Sternhell, Z., Sznajder, M. and Asheri, M. (1994). *The Birth of Fascist Ideology: from Cultural Rebellion to Political Revolution*. Princeton, N.J.: Princeton University Press.

Strathern, M. (1992). *After Nature: English Kinship in the Late Twentieth Century*. Cambridge and New York: Cambridge University Press.

Suchman, L. A. (2007). *Human–Machine Reconfigurations: Plans and Situated Actions* (2nd edn.). Cambridge: Cambridge University Press.

Sunder Rajan, K. (2006). *Biocapital: The Constitution of Postgenomic Life*. Durham, N.C.: Duke University Press.

Swaan, A. de (1994). *Social Policy Beyond Borders: The Social Question in Transnational Perspective*. Amsterdam: Amsterdam University Press.

Tálos, E. (1999). *Atypische Beschäftigung: internationale Trends und sozialstaatliche Regelungen, Europa, USA*. Wien: Manz.

Tangcharoensathien, V. (2007). *Developing Countries Perspective: Increasing the Access of Developing Countries to H5N1 and Other Potentially Pandemic Vaccines, WHO*. Geneva: World Health Organisation.

Tarantola, D. (2005a). 'Global Health and National Governance'. *American Journal of Public Health, 95*(1), 8.

Tarantola, D. (2005b). *The Tensions and Interface between International Health, Global Health and Human Rights*. Paper presented at the inaugural John Hirshman lecture, 24 October, University of New South Wales.

Taylor, M. C. (2001). *The Moment of Complexity: Emerging Network Culture*. Chicago and London: University of Chicago Press.

Thatcher, M. (1987). 'Douglas Keay's interview with Margaret Thatcher'. *Woman's Own*, 31 October.

Theunissen, M. (1991). *Negative Theologie der Zeit*. Frankfurt am Main: Suhrkamp.

Theweleit, K. (1987). *Male Fantasies*. Cambridge: Polity Press.

Thoburn, N. (2003). *Deleuze, Marx, and Politics*. London: Routledge.

Tickell, A. and Peck, J. (2003). 'Making Global Rules: Globalization or Neoliberalization?' In J. Peck and H. Wai-chung Yeung (eds), *Remaking the Global Economy* (pp. 163–81). London: Sage.

Tocqueville, A. de (1963). *Democracy in America, Volume II*. New York: Alfred A. Knopf.

Todorov, T. (1984). *The Conquest of America: The Question of the Other*. New York: Harper & Row.

Toepfer, K. (1997). *Empire of Ecstasy: Nudity and Movement in German Body Culture, 1910–1935*. Berkeley: University of California Press.

Tomei, V. (1997). *Europäische Migrationspolitik zwischen Kooperationszwang und Souveränitätsansprüchen*. Bonn: Europa-Union-Verlag.

Transit Migration Forschungsgruppe (ed.). (2006). *Turbulente Ränder. Neue Perspektiven auf Migration an den Grenzen Europas*. Bielefeld: Transcript.

Treichler, P. A. (1988). 'AIDS, an Epidemic of Signification'. In D. Crimp (ed.), *AIDS: Cultural Analysis, Cultural Activism* (pp. 31–70). Cambridge, Mass.: MIT Press.

Trinh T. Minh-ha. (1987). 'She, the Inappropriate/d Other'. *Discourse, 8*, 1–37.

Tronti, M. (1966). 'The Strategy of the Refusal'. In *Operai e Capitale* (pp. 234–52). Turin: Einaudi.

TWN Info Service (2007). 'WHO: Meet discusses proposals to reform WHO's influenza surveillance system'. TWN Info Service on WTO and Trade Issues, 30 November 2007. http://www.twnside.org.sg/title2/wto.info/ twninfo110726.htm.

Tyson, P. K. (1984). *The Reception of Georg Kaiser (1915–45): Text and Analysis*. New York: Peter Lang.

Urbinati, N. (2003). 'Can Cosmopolitical Democracy Be Democratic?' In D. Archibugi (ed.), *Debating Cosmopolitics* (pp. 67–85). London: Verso.

Varela, F. J., Thompson, E. and Rosch, E. (1991). *The Embodied Mind: Cognitive Science and Human Experience*. Cambridge, Mass.: MIT Press.

Veenkamp, T., Bentley, T. and Buonfino, A. (2003). *People Flow: Managing Migration in a New European Commonwealth*. London: Demos.

Virilio, P. (1986). *Speed and Politics: An Essay on Dromology*. New York: Semiotext(e).

Virno, P. (2003). *A Grammar of the Multitude: For an Analysis of Contemporary Forms of Life*. Cambridge: Semiotext(e).

Virno, P. (2005). 'About Exodus'. *Grey Room*, *21*, 17–20.

Vishmidt, M. and Gilligan, M. (eds). (2003). *Immaterial Labour: Work, Research and Art*. London: Black Dog Publishing.

Wade, P. (2005). 'Hybridity Theory and Kinship Thinking'. *Cultural Studies*, *19*(5), 602–21.

Waldby, C. (1996). *AIDS and the Body Politic: Biomedicine and Sexual Difference*. London: Routledge.

Waldby, C. and Cooper, M. (2008). 'The Biopolitics of Reproduction: Post-Fordist Biotechnology and Women's Clinical Labour'. *Australian Feminist Studies 23*(55), 57–73.

Waldby, C. and Mitchell, R. (2006). *Tissue Economies: Blood, Organs, and Cell Lines in Late Capitalism*. Durham, N.C.: Duke University Press.

Waldby, C., Kippax, S. and Crawford, J. (1993). 'Cordon Sanitaire: Clean and Unclean Women in the AIDS Discourse of Young Heterosexual Men'. In P. Aggleton, G. Hart, and P. Davies (eds), *AIDS: The Second Decade* (pp. 29–39). Sussex: Falmer Press.

Walkerdine, V. (1990). *Schoolgirl Fictions*. London and New York: Verso.

Walkerdine, V., Lucey, H. and Melody, J. (2001). *Growing up Girl: Psychosocial Explorations of Gender and Class*. New York: New York University Press.

Wallerstein, I. M. (1976). *The Modern World System*. New York: Academic Press.

Wallerstein, I. M. (1983). *Historical Capitalism*. London: Verso.

Wallerstein, I. M. (1995). *After Liberalism*. New York: New Press.

Wallerstein, I. M. (1998). *Utopistics, or, Historical Choices of the Twenty-first Century*. New York: The New Press.

Wallerstein, I. M. (2003). *The Decline of American Power: The U.S. in a Chaotic World*. New York: New Press.

Walters, W. (2002). 'Mapping Schengenland: Denaturalizing the Border'. *Environment and Planning*, *20*(5), 1–38.

Walters, W. (2004). 'Secure Borders, Safe Haven, Domopolitics'. *Citizenship Studies*, *8*(3), 237–60.

Walters, W. (2006). 'Border/Control'. *European Journal of Social Theory*, *9*, 187–204.

Warner, M. (1999a). 'Liberalism and the Cultural Studies Imagination: A Comment on John Frow'. *The Yale Journal of Criticism*, *12*(2), 431–3.

Warner, M. (1999b). *The Trouble with Normal: Sex, Politics, and the Ethics of Queer Life*. New York: Free Press.

Weeks, J. (1995). *Invented Moralities: Sexual Values in the Age of Uncertainty*. Cambridge: Polity Press.

Weidt, J. (1968). *Der rote Tänzer: ein Lebensbericht*. Berlin: Henschel.

Weizman, E. (2006). 'Walking Through Walls'. *Radical Philosophy*, *136* (March/April), 8–22.

Werbner, P. and Modood, T. E. (1997). 'Debating Cultural Hybridity: Multicultural Identities and the Politics of Anti-racism'.

Whitehead, A. N. (1933). *Adventures of Ideas*. New York: Free Press, 1967.

Whitehead, A. N. (1979). *Process and Reality. An Essay in Cosmology* (corrected edition edited by D. R. Griffin and D. W. Sherburne). New York: Free Press.

Whitford, M. (1988). 'Luce Irigaray's Critique of Rationality'. In M. Griffiths and M. Whitford (eds), *Feminist Perspectives in Philosophy* (pp. 109–30). Bloomington: Indiana University Press.

WHO (1998). *The World Health Report 1998: Life in the Twenty-first Century*. Geneva: World Health Organisation.

WHO (2007a) 'International Health Regulations' (2005). Geneva: World Health Organisation.

WHO (2007b). *Indonesia to Resume Sharing H5N1 Avian Influenza Virus Samples Following a WHO Meeting in Jakarta*. Geneva: World Health Organisation. 27 March.

WHO (2007c). *Global Stockpile of H5N1 Vaccine 'Feasible', Meeting at WHO Agrees Stockpile a Realistic Expectation*. Geneva: World Health Organisation. 26 April.

Widuch, W. (2005). *Produktive Subjektivität und prekäre Lebenssituationen: Auswirkungen und Widersprüche postindustrieller Arbeit* (unpublished MSc dissertation). Department of Education and Psychology, Free University of Berlin, Berlin.

Willeke, A. B. (1995). *Georg Kaiser and the Critics: A Profile of Expressionism's Leading Playwright*. Columbia: Camden House.

Willenbücher, M. (2007). *Das Scharnier der Macht: Der Illegalisierte als homo sacer des Postfordismus*. Berlin: b_books.

Willett, J. (1978). *The New Sobriety. 1917–1933: Art and Politics in the Weimar Period*. London: Thames & Hudson.

Williams, C. C. and Windebank, J. (1998). *Informal Employment in the Advanced Economies: Implications for Work and Welfare*. London: Routledge.

Winner, L. (1986). *The Whale and the Reactor: A Search for Limits in an Age of High Technology*. Chicago: University of Chicago Press.

Wittel, A. (2001). 'Toward a Network Sociality'. *Theory, Culture and Society*, *18*(6), 51–76.

Wolfe, K. (2006). 'From Aesthetics to Politics: Rancière, Kant and Deleuze'. *Contemporary Aesthetics*, (electronic journal) http://www.contempaesthetics. org/newvolume/pages/article.php?articleID=2382, date last accessed 19 July 2006.

Wolkowitz, C. (2006). *Bodies at Work*. London: Sage.

World Health Assembly (2007). 'Resolution 60.28: Pandemic Influenza Preparedness: Sharing of Influenza Viruses and Access to Vaccines and Other Benefits'. Geneva: World Health Organisation.

Young, R. (1995). *Colonial Desire: Hybridity in Theory, Culture, and Race*. London: Routledge.

Žižek, S. (2005a). 'The Constitution is Dead: Long Live Proper Politics'. *The Guardian*, 4 June 2005.

Žižek, S. (2005b). *Die politische Suspension des Ethischen*. Frankfurt am Main: Suhrkamp.

INDEX

Compiled by Sue Carlton

logocentrism 97
Luhmann, Niklas 19, 20

machines 104, 106, 107, 248
majoritarian subject-form 57, 58, 61, 69
Manning, Erin 145, 154
manufacture 47
maps
    asubjective 213–14
    grid 9–10, 25, 137
    Map of the Estrecho de Gibraltar
        213–14
    MigMap ix, 167
    psycho geographical 20–1
Mardi Gras 149
Marinetti, Filippo 91, 99, 104, 105, 107
market ideology 114
maroons 54–5
    see also vagabonds
Martin, Emily 110, 111, 112
Marx, Karl 50, 58, 59, 239, 258
Marxism 13, 100, 257
masculinity 107, 110
mass gymnastics 93
Massumi, Brian 81, 131
material presencing 142, 156–7
Material Transfer Agreements 123–4
materialisation 70, 156, 157
materialism 155, 239
materiality 25, 64–5, 87, 92–3, 98,
    102–4, 106, 147, 156–7, 216, 224
Medicaid 109
Mehran, Sir Alfred 210–11
mendicant orders see charitable
    institutions
messianism 90, 221
Mezzadra, Sandro 196, 203, 206, 207
Michaels, Eric 147–52, 155, 156, 160
MigMap 167
migrants
    cyber-deportability 176–8, 197
    illegal 202
    repatriations 191–2
    and rights 253–4
    victimisation of 203
migration 14, 16–17
    Aegean transit xvii–xviii, 183–202
    arrival 182, 189, 199, 202, 210–11,
        212, 215, 217
        enigma of 210, 215, 217
    autonomy of xviii, 202–21
    becoming and 216–17, 219, 220
    becoming animal and 211–13, 215–16
    brûleurs (burners) 215–16, 219
    clandestine 163, 178, 198, 219, 256
    and continuous experience 221

    and cunning 219–20
    de-individualised 212, 215
    dislocation 211
    and documentation 210–11, 215,
        229, 243, 256
    Europeanisation of migration control
        162–3, 164–6, 169–70, 171–3, 194
    excessive movements 187–91
    Gastarbeit 217
    illegal 79–80, 169, 178, 179–80, 192–3
    as individual strategy 211
    informal networks of 197, 209, 212,
        217, 218, 253, 256
    legalisation 200–1
    mapping 167–9, 213–14
    people trafficking 178, 179, 185–7,
        191, 211–13
    reception centres 179, 189
    transnational 163, 172–3
    visa requirements 215
    and visibility 217–19
    see also borders; camps; mobility
misrecognition 68
mobility xv
    and capitalism 206–8
    control of flows 177–8
    control of passages 79
    decelerated circulation 197–9
    liminal porocratic institutions
        173–202, 203–21, 225, 232
        see also camps
    management of pores 175, 196, 209
    and postliberal sovereignty 209–10
    productionist reading of 196, 208,
        221
    Schengen Information System (SIS)
        174, 192
    transit spaces 167, 175, 179, 197–9,
        209, 217
        see also camps
    transnational 164–6
    virtualisation of borders 178–82
    see also borders; camps; migration;
        regimes, of mobility control
modernism 96–7
morality 8, 81
    see also ethics
Moulier Boutang, Yann 61, 203–5, 206,
    207
multiculturalism 30, 71
multiplicity 63, 81, 217

name (naming) xii, xiii, 66, 69, 70, 215
narratives xii, 86, 108, 182, 255
    illness narratives 136, 144–5, 146,
        147